SOURCES FOR *WORLD IN THE MAKING*

SOURCES FOR
WORLD IN THE MAKING

A Global History

VOLUME II SINCE 1300

BONNIE G. SMITH

RUTGERS UNIVERSITY

MARC VAN DE MIEROOP

COLUMBIA UNIVERSITY

RICHARD VON GLAHN

UNIVERSITY OF CALIFORNIA, LOS ANGELES

KRIS LANE

TULANE UNIVERSITY

NEW YORK   OXFORD
OXFORD UNIVERSITY PRESS

Oxford University Press is a department of the University of Oxford.
It furthers the University's objective of excellence in research, scholarship,
and education by publishing worldwide. Oxford is a registered trade mark of
Oxford University Press in the UK and certain other countries.

Published in the United States of America by Oxford University Press
198 Madison Avenue, New York, NY 10016, United States of America.

For titles covered by Section 112 of the US Higher Education Opportunity
Act, please visit www.oup.com/us/he for the latest information about pricing
and alternate formats.

Library of Congress Cataloging-in-Publication Data
Names: Smith, Bonnie G., 1940- author. | Smith, Bonnie G., 1940- World in the
  making.
Title: Sources for world in the making : a global history / Bonnie G. Smith,
  Rutgers University, Marc Van de Mieroop, Columbia University, Richard von
  Glahn, University of California, Los Angeles, Kris Lane, Tulane University.
Description: New York : Oxford University Press, [2019] |
  Includes bibliographical references.
Identifiers: LCCN 2018013216 (print) | LCCN 2018015988 (ebook) | ISBN
  9780190849351 (Volume 1 Ebook) | ISBN 9780190849368 (Volume 2 Ebook) |
  ISBN 9780190849337 (volume 1 print) | ISBN 9780190849344 (volume 2 print)
Subjects: LCSH: World history—Sources.
Classification: LCC D21 (ebook) | LCC D21 .S625 2019 (print) | DDC 909—dc23
LC record available at https://lccn.loc.gov/2018013216

9 8 7 6 5 4 3 2 1
Printed by Sheridan Books, Inc., United States of America

CONTENTS

PREFACE

Designed to accompany *World in the Making: A Global History*, *Sources for World in the Making* reflects the textbook's integrated and multidimensional approach to the global past. We, the authors of *World in the Making*, have carefully selected sources that complement the topics and themes in each chapter of the textbook and that will spark students' interest. The documents in this collection buttress our belief that world history can best be taught by emphasizing the crossroads of human interaction. For example, the *Florentine Codex* and *Codex Mendoza* (Documents 15.1 and 15.2) were produced at a crossroads at which learned local people in New Spain and priests from Spain itself came together to create documents recording everyday life and religious observances of the Aztec people. Persian manuscript illuminations (Document 14.4) reflect the influence of Chinese paintings that circulated throughout Asia during the Mongol era. Other crossroads appear as political exchanges and disputes, such as letters concerning diplomatic marriages among Babylonian and Egyptian royalty (Document 2.3) and Cold War confrontations in Chapter 27. These documents reinforce our theme of exchange, contestation, encounters, and other points of cross-cultural and transnational contact. We present these themes in conjunction with political, social, cultural, and economic aspects of past experience so that students will understand what it means to live in global history.

We have selected sources representing not only the pivotal moments and world-changing actors of the global past but also the lives and thoughts of ordinary people—another major theme of *World in the Making*. We "people" this documents reader with the songs, diaries, and expressions of outrage and support in politics from across social classes and from across the globe. Document 22.1, for example, presents Enlightenment values from the perspective of a glassworker, and Chapter 24 provides diary excerpts written by an Indian soldier—himself a colonial subject—serving in the British army during the Boxer Rebellion. We set these in a world historical context to show the ways in which people have contributed to the global past despite appearing to some as being outside world history. Indeed, we integrate ordinary folks with major actors because world history only comes alive in the stories of people who experienced the global past.

Documents come in all forms, and we have attempted to give students a sense of their variety by including letters, epics, memoirs, religious and political texts, travel accounts, ethnographic evidence, and much more. To underscore the importance of images in historical analysis, we provide a range of visual documents throughout, from an Indus Valley clay tablet to Cold War–era advertisements. These sources engage students' visual proclivities, while the accompanying pedagogy helps guide their analysis of visual details and prompts reflection on their historical significance. To give students access to periods and peoples for which there are few, if any, written records, we have occasionally included alternative documents. For example, Chapter 1 includes later sources on evolution to supplement the textbook's discussion of human origins. Such sources will help generate discussion of what a document is, how evidence is constituted through the development of new knowledge and techniques, and what nonhistorians can teach us about the past.

PEDAGOGICAL FEATURES

Contextualization, evaluation, and synthesis are fundamental skills needed by all students of history, and we aimed to make this documents reader a place where students can find tools for historical thinking and where the instructor will have access to an array of devices to help develop the analytical skills of students. Each chapter therefore opens with an introductory paragraph that provides a broad overview of the chapter's themes, and then individual document headnotes set each source within a more specific historical context. At the end of each document or set of documents are questions to guide students in examining the evidence, probing students to review their understanding of a document's content, and encouraging analysis of deeper issues. Finally, we want students to be able to assess the significance of the documents within the context of larger global developments. A set of Making Connections questions at the end of each chapter invites students to trace similarities and differences among documents as they set them in the context of the chapter's overall themes. We have also defined unfamiliar terms and concepts throughout the collection to aid students' comprehension of the sources.

Again, emphasizing the individual voices of people—grand and humble—the Contrasting Views feature (five are included in this volume) presents differing perspectives on a development, issue, or event and encourages students' synthesis of multiple sources. In Chapter 4, students encounter contrasting opinions about the value of democracy in ancient Greece, and in Chapter 21 the pros and cons of Spanish activity in the Americas in the sixteenth and seventeenth centuries—discussions that we still have today and that students love to participate in. Chapter 23 presents differing viewpoints on the Industrial Revolution from people living at the time, many of them participants in the developments of that period. Certainly we hope that the Contrasting Views section in Chapter 27 on Cold War diplomatic debates will not only provide students with opinions for the development of lasting analytical skills but that consideration of this timely topic will also spark their interest and enliven your classroom.

Given the demands of reading primary sources from distant times and places, we have done our best to select documents that speak to a range of students with a variety of skill levels, even as we aim for balanced coverage within the chapters. Overall, our goal is to build into the classroom experience both familiarity with the methods of historians and student proficiency in the historical method. Through grouping documents as the basis of their own narrative, students learn how historians synthesize their findings into a coherent account. Thus, we believe that these selections can serve as the foundation for students to act as historians in small-group activities, writing assignments, and classroom debates. We recognize that this is a tall order in the face of the enormity of world history, but we fervently hope that the selections and teaching aids in *Sources for World in the Making* benefit you and your students.

ACKNOWLEDGMENTS

In compiling *Sources for World in the Making*, the author team has tapped the extensive expertise of the editors and staff at Oxford University Press who helped us every step of the way. Our editor, Charles Cavaliere, kept us on task and disciplined our efforts. Editorial assistant Katie Tunkavige prepared the manuscript and oversaw clearing permissions. Our sincere thanks are offered to them as well as to Phil Scott, who oversaw production. We are grateful for this stellar team. Bonnie Smith also thanks Molly Giblin, Courtney Doucette, and Donald R. Kelley for their contributions, large and small.

INTRODUCTION FOR STUDENTS

WHY STUDY PRIMARY SOURCES?

If events of the past are to be understood simply as matters of fact, why do historians disagree about them? Can't they just give us the facts and let us interpret them? Can't they just tell us the objective truth about what happened? Many believe that the historian, like the archaeologist digging up a broken pot, simply has to recover the pieces and put them back together. History in this view is the piecing together of an uncontested, objective past, a reconstruction composed of facts and dates.

Yet, as any archaeologist or historian knows, a reassembled pot is not a story, much less a history, and telling one—explaining the pot's historical significance—requires careful attention to context as well as asking many questions. Where was the pot buried? How was it broken? What did it contain? Who might have made it? Who might have owned it? How old is it? The questions may go on and on, but the point is that the pot, even when reconstructed, does not explain itself. Properly telling its story, its *history*, is not a simple and straightforward task. Historians, like archaeologists, try to answer as many questions as they can about their evidence. Historians use the term *primary sources* to refer to evidence produced as close to the events in question as possible. At best, primary sources are firsthand descriptions or eyewitness accounts.

Imagine that someone studying the pot in question came across a text in an archive or a library that described the use of pots in the same area from which the pot had been excavated. Suppose that several hundred years ago a traveler wrote an account of a visit to the region and remarked that women there made special pots for the drinking of a beverage considered sacred, and that these pots were customarily smashed following royal weddings. Does this eyewitness account then explain the broken pot that the archaeologist found and pieced together? It is a tantalizing clue, to be sure, but many questions remain. Does the archaeologist's pot match those in the written description, or is the travel narrative too vague to make such a determination? Does the pot contain any residue that might link it to the sacred beverage mentioned by the traveler? Was it found in the right location for such a ritual smashing, or was it discovered in a household trash dump?

In this case, a written primary source, the usual raw material of historians, would seem to provide the smoking gun, or definitive explanation, for the archaeologist. But as helpful as it may be, the text, like the pot, is not self-explanatory; it must be thoroughly examined before any conclusions can be drawn. First, the document is itself a physical object, an artifact like the archaeologist's pot. Historians first evaluate the document's age and the context of its production. What is its form? Is this a copy, a translation, or an original manuscript? Or is it a forgery? Inadequate evaluation of primary sources as artifacts, that is, testing their veracity at the most basic or "forensic" level, can lead to wildly inaccurate historical claims.

Second, the primary source text is often a narrative: an attempt to record an event or experience based on an individual's perception and memory, which are often colored by his or her own biases and beliefs. The traveler's account, though clearly valuable in some way, is limited by these and other constraints, including the traveler's abilities to convey lived experience in written form, that is to say, the writer's ability as a writer. The more we examine this seemingly objective, firsthand description, the more subjective, or specific to this individual, it appears.

The contents of the traveler's account are as subject to doubt, or at least close scrutiny, as testimony provided by an eyewitness in a criminal trial. Even when an objective sequence of events such as in an armed robbery occurs, not everyone sees, much less remembers—or *narrates*—the same thing. This is not to say that the traveler's account cannot be trusted at all simply because it is subjective, or fallible, but rather that its claims must be analyzed carefully before we deploy them in our historical narrative, our legalistic "case" about the smashed pot. We must evaluate the source to determine how plausible the traveler's account is. Evaluating the account's plausibility—and therefore its utility and limitations as evidence in our quest for the historical significance of the pot—requires formulating and answering questions similar to those raised by the archaeologist. Who was the writer of the account? Who was the intended audience? Are there other accounts that might be consulted to verify the writer's claims in this instance? Are other works by this writer known to be trustworthy? Does the date of the narrative roughly match the date assigned to the pot in question, or was it written so much later—or so much earlier—that it could not possibly relate to the same thing?

What about our traveler's perspective on a foreign culture, seeing it and reporting on it as an outsider? Is the traveler's account biased or distorted by personal opinion or prejudice? Or is it simply mistaken, prone to error or poor observation? The traveler may have witnessed an event such as the breaking of a pot, but how is the historian to know if the pot was broken for ritual purposes, as the traveler claimed? Did this breaking take place after a royal wedding, as the traveler "testified," or had the preceding ritual actually been a reenactment of some other union, perhaps between two deities? The fact of the broken pot seems indisputable, inasmuch as it is mentioned in the account and was discovered by the archaeologist, but the reason for its breaking remains uncertain. Perhaps the archaeologist's pot simply collapsed under the weight of the earth that covered it.

Imagine that the historian then happened on a book by an ethnographer who lived among the descendants of the group studied by the archaeologist, and in it there was a description of ritual pot breaking following royal wedding ceremonies. Would this ethnographic evidence at last provide the necessary proof to close the case? Perhaps, but the historian would still have to ask more questions. In essence, can recent ethnographic sources be considered primary when used as evidence for much earlier practices or beliefs? This remains a vexing question for many world historians seeking to explain the actions of past cultures that lack a written tradition.

This may seem a tiresome exercise with only a small payoff, but by combining the variety of evidence and approaches, we have come closer to understanding some small part of this past foreign culture that may have otherwise escaped our notice. We can do this only by rigorously interrogating all kinds of sources. Even the most explicit texts cannot entirely speak for themselves.

INTERPRETING PRIMARY SOURCES

Primary sources express a point of view, or perspective, and are therefore always subject to interpretation. Beyond verification and classification, then, the historian must examine primary sources with a detective's eye for telling details or turns of phrase, searching for clues as to the author's purpose. Is the author making an argument, or is the author simply relaying information with nothing at stake? Is he or she writing to impress some authority or to defame a rival? Interpreting texts written by individuals who openly display their opinions or biases may seem straightforward, and sometimes it is, but what can we make of primary sources whose biases or assumptions are concealed, or were created at times and places so different from our own that they are difficult to identify?

A classic example is the law code, such as "The Placard of the People's Instructions" (Document 14.3), which was composed in late-medieval China. Such codes, especially when read by foreigners like us, far removed from those who wrote them in space and time, often reveal the differences between their cultural assumptions and ours. Again, asking the right questions brings us to a closer understanding of the context in which the document was created. In this case, what constituted a crime and what was considered a just punishment? Was the placard issued by those in power in response to a credible threat, or did it reflect some wider consensus? Ultimately, historians must "unpack" the source for clues into what it can reveal about the people and period in question. When possible, historians try to assemble as broad a range of sources as possible, including those that contradict each other. When interpreted in light of many other sources from the period, the Chinese placard may make a great deal more sense. Like the reassembled pot, it may not remain such a mystery.

History, then, is not the recovery of a single, uncontested narrative of the past. It is instead an ongoing conversation about the past, a conversation constantly enriched—and occasionally revolutionized—by new evidence and new perspectives. As students of history, we must continue to challenge or improve on accepted or "master" narratives of the past by searching for new evidence and examining it with rigor. To put it another way, we should make a habit of questioning authority, not for the sake of defiance, but rather with the intention of improving our knowledge.

The good historian, like the good detective, follows every promising lead, knowing many will be dead ends. When a historian or detective is trying to solve a thorny problem, or answer a tough question, one good lead trumps a thousand bad ones. The good historian must also be willing to confront and reveal his or her own biases, assumptions, and tastes.

What is your personal point of view, and how have you arrived at it? What aspects of the human past and what kinds of primary sources do you find most compelling, and why? The great conversation that is history has plenty of space for you to enter in and make an original contribution. Your perspective counts.

SOURCES IN WORLD HISTORY

As the example of the broken pot suggests, world history presents special challenges, especially in cases in which written sources are rare, but it also presents many opportunities. The study of world history, like that of large regions such as East Asia, western Europe, or Latin America, remains largely reliant on written sources, but by its very global nature it demands incorporation of other types of evidence. This includes material objects, archaeological findings, ethnographic fieldwork, oral interviews, linguistic studies, photographs, video recordings, DNA analysis, and much else. It may even be useful to think in terms of an all-encompassing global archive that includes everything touched by or relevant to humans.

This is casting an awfully wide net, so it should be kept in mind that the broader academic discipline of history has traditionally focused on evaluating and interpreting written primary sources, be they inscriptions, law codes, letters, memoirs, censuses, or chronicles. Anything written is fair game for historians. As we have seen, what makes a written source useful depends in large part on what questions we ask of it. We must interrogate not only its contents but also the context of its production and the aims of its writer or writers.

When sources have been produced by outsiders, as in the case of our traveler's account mentioned earlier, we must work hard to assess what is valuable for our purposes and what is the product of the writer's prejudices, ignorance, or emotional state. In world history, it is especially important not to discard such obviously biased sources simply because we find them offensive. Instead we must ask what led the writer to think in such a way. Is the source's overall validity completely compromised by prejudice, or might it still contain useful observations? Or might it be useful only in the study of prejudiced outsiders and their views on the culture at hand? As mentioned earlier, other sources in world history may be puzzling to us because they derive from a radically foreign perspective or worldview. Insiders, then, can be as difficult to understand as outsiders. Harder, but of key importance, is asking how such worldviews fit into our larger model of world history. What does this one source about a single group of people mean in the larger scheme of things?

Some of the questions generated by world history are small and regionally specific. For example, we may want to know when the Dutch conquered Southeast Asia's Banda Islands and took over the global trade in nutmeg. A variety of published primary sources can be readily consulted and compared, and a quite specific answer given. But world history also lends itself to much larger questions, most of them not easily answered in such a definitive, *Jeopardy!*-style way. For example: How does the early modern transatlantic slave trade compare with other slave trades in world history? Addressing such a big question requires quantifying the various slave trades we know about and can document with some assurance, then comparing them and answering various subsidiary questions. Such big and often comparative questions are what most compel world historians writing today, and they are what make world history such a vibrant and exciting field.

Although no collection of documents can encompass the vast global archive, *Sources for World in the Making* aims to present global history on a more human scale, giving pride of place to individual voices—to people telling their stories. You will encounter traditional documents such as law codes, chronicles, court histories, and literary works, as well as less familiar ones such as textiles and oracle bone fragments. You will also be exposed to a rich variety of perspectives, from influential figures to lesser known local and personal voices that nonetheless shed light on larger, global concerns.

Think of these documents as your chance to "overhear" the ideas and expressions of people who lived in the past. By examining a document, you are now in closer touch with the reality of a past that is indeed in many ways a foreign country and filled with total strangers. Because of this strangeness, you, the apprentice–historian, need to have knowledge not only of these sources but also of the conditions in which the original speakers and authors lived and acted. The chapter introductions and document headnotes in this sourcebook, along with the *World in the Making* textbook, provide this context. Some of these sources will strike a chord with you and others will not. The master narrative you create in reading them in tandem with the *World in the Making* textbook will be your own, the product of your conversation with the global past.

SOURCES FOR *WORLD IN THE MAKING*

CHAPTER 14

Collapse and Revival in Afro-Eurasia, 1300–1450

The Black Death pandemic disrupted the social order of Latin Christendom, as we see in Buonaiuti's account of the plague in Florence. The widespread, devastating disease exposed deep social fissures that erupted into violent conflicts such as the English Peasant Revolt of 1381. As Sanudo's praise of Venice shows, however, by the fifteenth century the Italian city-states had regained their former prosperity. The devastation wrought by the Black Death lingered much longer in the central Islamic lands. Despite the plague's effects, the Islamic world continued to expand, sometimes through conquest—notably in the Ottoman conquest of the Byzantine Empire—but more commonly through conversion, for example, in Mali in West Africa. With the passing of the Mongol empires, commercial and cultural traffic across Central Asia ebbed. The founder of the Ming dynasty, Emperor Hongwu, was determined to eradicate all Mongol influences from Chinese culture and society. However, in the European and Muslim imagination, China remained the fabled land of majesty and mystery evoked in the popular Persian tale of Prince Humay.

Marchionne di Coppo Buonaiuti, *Florentine Chronicle* (c. 1370–1380)

Marchionne di Coppo Buonaiuti (1336–1385) was born into a wealthy patrician family, probably bankers, in Florence. He was active in Florentine politics in the 1360s and 1370s, when he became a member of the city's executive council and frequently represented Florence on diplomatic missions. His *Florentine Chronicle*, written after his retirement from politics, glorifies the history and accomplishments of his native city. Buonaiuti's account of the effects of the Black Death on Florence was written three decades after the event. His description of the devastation caused by the pandemic draws perhaps on his own eyewitness observations—he was twelve at the time. It also draws on the inherited memory of the Black Death shared by his contemporaries and on literary accounts such as Boccaccio's *Decameron*, completed in 1351.

Concerning the deadly outbreak of disease which happened in the city of Florence, where many people died

In the year of our lord 1348 there occurred in the city and *contado* [county] of Florence a great pestilence, and such was its fury and violence that in whatever household it took hold, whosoever took care of the sick, all the caregivers died of the same illness, and almost nobody survived beyond the fourth day, neither doctors nor medicine proving of any avail, and there appeared to be no remedy, either because those illnesses were not yet recognized, or because doctors had never previously had cause to study them properly. Such was the fear that nobody knew what to do: when it caught hold in a household, it often happened that not a single person escaped death. And it wasn't just men and women: even sentient [capable of feeling] animals such as dogs and cats, hens, oxen, donkeys and sheep, died from that same disease and with those symptoms, and almost none who displayed those symptoms, or very few indeed, effected a recovery. Those symptoms were as follows: either between the thigh and the body, in the groin region, or under the armpit, there appeared a lump, and a sudden fever, and when the victim spat, he spat blood mixed with saliva, and none of those who spat blood survived. Such was the terror this caused that seeing it take hold in a household, as soon as it started, nobody remained: everybody abandoned the dwelling in fear, and fled to another; some fled into the city and others into the countryside. No doctors were to be found, because they were dying like everybody else; those who could be found wanted exorbitant fees cash-in-hand before entering the house, and having entered, they took the patient's pulse with their heads turned away, and assayed the urine samples from afar, with aromatic herbs held to their noses. Sons abandoned fathers, husbands wives, one brother the other, one sister the other. The city was reduced to bearing the dead to burial; many died who at their passing had neither confession nor last sacraments, and many died unseen, and many died of hunger, for when somebody took ill to his bed, the other occupants in panic told him: "I'm going for the doctor"; and quietly locked the door from the outside and didn't come back. The victim, abandoned by both people and nourishment, yet kept constant company by fever, wasted away. Many were those who begged their families not to abandon them; when evening came, the relatives said to the patient: "So that you don't have to wake up the people looking after you at night, asking for things, because this is going on day and night, you yourself can reach for cakes and wine or water, here they are on the shelf above your bed, you can get the stuff you want." And when the patient fell asleep, they went away and did not return. If,

Jonathan Usher, trans., *Florentine Chronicle of Marchionne di Coppo di Stefano Buonaiuti (1216–1385)*, http://www.brown.edu/Departments/Italian_Studies/dweb/plague/perspectives/marchionne.php.

through good fortune the victim had been strengthened by that food, the next morning alive and still strong enough to get to the window, he would have to wait half an hour before anybody came past, if this was not a busy thoroughfare, and even when the odd person passed by, and the patient had enough voice to be heard a little, if he shouted, sometimes he would be answered and sometimes not, and even if he were to be answered, there was no help to be had. For not only none or very few wished to enter a house where there were any sick people, but they didn't even want to have contact with those who issued healthy from a sick person's house, saying "He's jinxed, don't speak to him," saying: "He's got it because there's the '*gavocciolo*' in his house"; and "*gavocciolo*" was the name they gave to these swellings. Many died without being seen, remaining on their beds till they stank. And the neighbors, if any were left, having smelled the stench, did a whip round and sent him for burial. Houses remained open, nobody dared to touch anything, for it seemed that things remained poisoned, and whoever had anything to do with them caught the disease.

At every church, or at most of them, pits were dug, down to the water-table, as wide and deep as the parish was populous; and therein, whosoever was not very rich, having died during the night, would be shouldered by those whose duty it was, and would either be thrown into this pit, or they would pay big money for somebody else to do it for them. The next morning there would be very many in the pit. Earth would be taken and thrown down on them; and then others would come on top of them, and then earth on top again, in layers, with very little earth, like garnishing lasagna with cheese. The gravediggers who carried out these functions were so handsomely paid that many became rich and many died, some already rich and others having earned little, despite the high fees. The female and male sick-bay attendants demanded from one to three florins a day, plus sumptuous expenses. The foodstuffs suitable for the sick, cakes and sugar, reached outrageous prices. A pound of sugar was sold at between three and eight florins, and the same went for other confectionery. Chickens and other poultry were unbelievably expensive, and eggs were between 12 and 24 *denari* each: you were lucky to find three in a day, even searching through the whole city. Wax

was unbelievable: a pound of wax rose to more than a florin, nevertheless an age-old arrogance of the Florentines was curbed, in that an order was given not to parade more than two large candles. The churches only had one bier apiece, as was the custom, and this was insufficient. Pharmacists and grave-diggers had obtained biers, hangings and laying-out pillows at great price. The shroud-cloth apparel which used to cost, for a woman, in terms of petticoat, outer garment, cloak and veils, three florins, rose in price to thirty florins, and would have risen to one hundred florins, except that they stopped using shroud-cloth, and whoever was rich was dressed with plain cloth, and those who weren't rich were sewn up in a sheet. The benches placed for the dead cost a ludicrous amount, and there weren't enough of them even if there had been a hundred times more. The priests couldn't get enough of ringing the bells: so an order was passed, what with the panic caused by the bells ringing and the sale of benches and the curbing of spending, that nobody should be allowed the death-knell, nor should benches be placed, nor should there be a public announcement by the crier, because the sick could hear them, and the healthy took fright as well as the sick. The priests and friars thronged to the rich, and were paid such great sums that they all enriched themselves. And so an ordinance was passed that only one rule [of religious houses] and the local church could be had, and from that rule a maximum of six friars. All harmful fruit, such as unripe plums, unripe almonds, fresh beans, figs and all other inessential unhealthy fruit, was forbidden from entering the city.

Many processions and relics and the painting of Santa Maria Impruneta were paraded around the city, to cries of "Mercy," and with prayers, coming to a halt at the rostrum of the Priori.[1] There peace was made settling great disputes and questions of woundings and killings. Such was the panic this plague provoked that people met for meals as a *brigata* [assembly] to cheer themselves up; one person would offer a dinner to ten friends, and the next evening it would be the turn of one of the others to offer

---

[1] **the Priori:** The nine members of Florence's chief governing body—also known as the Signoria—chosen from the city's chief merchant guilds.

the dinner, and sometimes they thought they were going to dine with him, and he had no dinner ready, because he was ill, and sometimes the dinner had been prepared for ten and two or three less turned up. Some fled to the country, and some to provincial towns, to get a change of air; where there was no plague they brought it, and where it already existed they added to it. No industry was busy in Florence; all the workshops were locked up, all the inns were closed, only chemists and churches were open. Wherever you went, you could find almost nobody; many rich good men were borne from their house to church in their coffin with just four undertakers and a lowly cleric carrying the cross, and even then they demanded a florin apiece. Those who especially profited from the plague were the chemists, the doctors, the poulterers, the undertakers, and the women who sold mallow, nettles, mercury plant and other poultice herbs for drawing abscesses. And those who made the most were these herb sellers. Woolen merchants and retailers when they came across cloth could sell it for whatever price they asked. Once the plague had finished, anybody who could get hold of whatsoever kind of cloth, or found the raw materials to make it, became rich; but many ended up moth-eaten, spoilt and useless for the looms, and thread and raw wool lost in the city and the *contado*. This plague began in March as has been said, and finished in September 1348. And people began

to return to their homes and belongings. And such was the number of houses full of goods that had no owner, that it was amazing. Then the heirs to this wealth began to turn up. And someone who had previously had nothing suddenly found himself rich, and couldn't believe it was all his, and even felt himself it wasn't quite right. And both men and women began to show off with clothes and horses.

The quantity of people who died during the plague outbreak of the year of our lord 1348

The bishop and the Signoria in Florence having ordered a careful count of how many were dying of plague in the city of Florence, and seeing finally at the beginning of October that nobody was dying of that pestilence any more, it was discovered that putting together men and women, children and adults, from March to October, ninety-six thousand had died.

Examining the Evidence

1. Many Christians attributed the Black Death to divine wrath and punishment. Does Buonaiuti seem to share this view?
2. According to Buonaiuti's account, what were the economic consequences of the plague in Florence?
3. In what ways did the extensive mortality resulting from the Black Death affect the social order in Florence?

14.2 THE ENGLISH PEASANT REVOLT

Jean Froissart, *Chronicles of England, France, Spain, and the Adjoining Countries* (1400)

Jean Froissart (c. 1337–c. 1410) was born in Valenciennes, in the duchy of Hainault in Flanders, on the eve of the outbreak of the Hundred Years' War (1339–1453) between England and France. Froissart enjoyed a long career as a poet and court historian. He began to compile his *Chronicles*, which cover the years from 1326 to 1400,

after arriving in England in 1361, during a truce declared by the English and French monarchs. In England, he gained the patronage of Queen Philippa, who, like Froissart, was a native of Hainault. In 1369, after the war resumed and his benefactress died, Froissart returned to the Continent but continued to work on his voluminous history. The following passages from Froissart's *Chronicles* describe the Peasant Revolt of 1381, which was triggered by a new head tax that King Richard II (r. 1377–1399) had imposed on his subjects.

Jean Froissart, *Chronicles of England, France, Spain, and the Adjoining Countries* (London: William Smith, 1839), 652–653, 657–662, 664.

It is customary in England, as well as in several other countries, for the nobility to have great privileges over the commonalty, whom they keep in bondage; that is to say, they are bound by law and custom to plough the lands of gentlemen, to harvest the grain, to carry it home to the barn, to thrash and winnow it; they are also bound to harvest the hay and bring it home. All these sources they are obliged to perform for their lords, and many more in England than in other countries. The prelates and gentlemen are thus served. In the counties of Kent, Essex, Sussex, and Bedford these services are more oppressive than in all the rest of the kingdom.

The evil-disposed in these districts began to rise, saying, they were too severely oppressed; that at the beginning of the world there were no slaves, and that no one ought to be treated as such, unless he had committed treason against his lord, as Lucifer had done against God; but they had done no such thing, for they were neither angels nor spirits, but men formed after the same likeness with their lords, who treated them as beasts. This they would no longer bear, but had determined to be free, and if they labored or did any other works for the lords, they would be paid for it.

A crazy priest in the county of Kent, called John Ball, who, for his absurd preaching, had been thrice confined in the prison of the archbishop of Canterbury, was greatly instrumental in inflaming them with those ideas. He was accustomed, every Sunday after mass, as the people were coming out of the church, to preach to them in the marketplace and assemble a crowd around him; to whom he would say: "My good friends, things cannot go on well in England, nor ever will until every thing shall be in common; when there shall neither be vassal nor lord, and all distinctions leveled; when the lords shall be no more masters than ourselves. How ill have they used us! And for what reasons do they thus hold us in bondage? Are we not all descended from the same parents, Adam and Eve? And what can they show, or what reasons give, why they should be more the masters than ourselves? Except, perhaps, in making us labor and work, for them to spend. They are clothed in velvets and rich stuffs, ornamented with ermine and other furs, while we are forced to wear poor cloth. They have wines, spices, and fine bread, when we have only rye and the refuse of the straw; and, if we drink, it must be water. . . . Let us go to the king, who is young, and remonstrate with him on our servitude, telling him we must have it otherwise, or that we shall find a remedy for it ourselves. . . ."

On Corpus Christi day King Richard heard mass in the Tower of London, with all his lords, and afterwards entered his barge, attended by the earls of Salisbury, Warwick, and Suffolk, with other knights. He rowed down the Thames toward Rotherhithe, a manor belonging to the crown, where were upwards of ten thousand men, who had come from Blackheath to see the king and to speak to him. When they perceived his barge approach, they set up such shouts and cries as if all the devils in hell had been in their company. . . .

When the king and his lords saw this crowd of people, and the wildness of their manner, there was not one among them so bold and determined, but felt alarmed: the king was advised by his barons not to land. . . ."What do ye wish for?" demanded the king, "I am come hither to hear what you have to say." Those near him cried out with one voice, "We wish thee to land, when we will remonstrate with thee, and tell thee more at our ease what our wants are." The Earl of Salisbury then replied for the king and said, "Gentlemen, you are not properly dressed, nor in a fit condition for the king to talk with you."

Nothing more was said, for the king desired to return to the Tower of London. When the people saw they could obtain nothing more, they were inflamed with passion, and went back to Blackheath, where the main body was, to relate the answer they had received, and how the king was returned to the Tower. They all then cried out, "Let us march instantly to London." They immediately set off, and in their road thither, they destroyed the houses of lawyers, courtiers, and monasteries. Advancing into the suburbs of London, which were very handsome and extensive, they pulled down many fine houses. In particular they demolished the prison of the king called the Marshalsea, and set at liberty all those confined within it. They did much damage to the suburbs, and menaced the Londoners at the entrance of the bridge for having shut the gates of it, saying, they would set fire to the suburbs, take the city by storm, and afterwards burn and destroy it.

With respect to the common people of London, numbers were of their opinions, and on assembling together said, "Why will you refuse admittance to these honest men? They are our friends, and what they are doing is for our good." It was then found necessary to open the gates, when crowds rushed in, and ran to those shops which seemed well stored with provision. If they sought for meat or drink, it was placed before them, and nothing refused, but all manner of good cheer offered, in hopes of appeasing them. . . .

On Friday morning those lodged in the square before St. Catherine's, near the Tower, began to make themselves ready; they shouted much, and said that if the king would not come out to them, they would attack the Tower, storm it, and slay all in it. The king was alarmed at these menaces, and resolved to speak with them; he therefore sent orders for them to retire to a handsome meadow at Mile-end, where, in the summertime, people go to amuse themselves, and that there the king would grant them their demands. . . .

On the king's arrival, attended by the barons, he found upwards of sixty thousand men assembled from different villages and counties of England; he instantly advanced into the midst of them, saying in a pleasant manner, "My good people, I am your king and your lord. What is it you want? And what do you wish to say to me?" Those who heard him answered, "We wish thou wouldst make us free forever: us, our heirs, and our lands, and that we should no longer be called slaves, nor held in bondage." The king replied, "I grant your wish; now, therefore, return to your homes and the places from whence you came, leaving behind two or three men from each village, to whom I will order letters to be given sealed with my seal. . . . " The people were thus quieted, and began to return towards London.

On the Saturday morning . . . all the rabble were again assembled, under the conduct of Wat Tyler, Jack Straw, and John Ball, to parley at a place called Smithfield. . . . These reprobates wanted to pillage the city this same day, their leaders saying, ". . . The pardons which the king has granted us will not be of much use to us. . . . If we now plunder the city of the wealth that is in it, we shall have been beforehand, and shall not have repent of so doing; but if we wait

for their arrival, they will wrest it from us." To this opinion all had agreed, when the king appeared in sight, attended by sixty horse. . . .

Wat Tyler, seeing the king, said to his men, "Here is the king. I will go and speak with him; do not stir from hence until I give you a signal." . . . On saying this he spurred the horse on which he rode and, leaving his men, galloped up to the king, and came so near that his horse's head touched the crupper of that of the king. The first words he said, when he addressed the king, were, "King, dost thou see all those men there?" "Yes," replied the king, "why dost thou ask?" "Because they are all under my command, and have sworn by their faith and loyalty to do whatever I shall order." "Very well," said the king, "I have no objections to it." Tyler, who was only desirous of a riot, answered, "And thinkest thou, king, that those people and as many more who are in the city, also under my command, ought to depart without having had thy letters? Oh no, we will carry them with us." "Why," replied the king, "so it has been ordered, and they will be delivered out one after the other. But friend, return to thy companions, and tell them to depart from London. Be peaceable and careful of yourselves, for it is our determination that you shall all of you have your letters by villages and towns, as it had been agreed upon."

As the king finished speaking, Wat Tyler, casting his eyes around him, spied a squire attached to the king's person bearing his sword. Tyler mortally hated this squire; formerly they had had words together, when the squire ill-treated him. . . . [Tyler demanded:] "Give me that sword." "I will not," replied the squire, "for it is the king's sword, and thou are not worthy to bear it, who art but a mechanic; and if only thou and I were together, thou wouldst not have dared to say what thou hast for as large a heap of gold as this church." "By my troth," answered Tyler, "I will not eat this day before I have thy head." At these words the mayor of London, with about twelve more, rode forward, armed under their robes. . . . "Truly," [said] the mayor, who found himself supported by the king, "does it become such a stinking rascal as thou art to use such speech in the presence of the king, my natural lord? I will not live a day, if thou pay not for it." Upon this, he drew a kind of scimitar he wore, and struck Tyler such a blow on the head as felled him to his horse's feet. When he was down, he was surrounded on all sides, so that his men could not see him; and one of the king's squires, called John Standwich, immediately leaped from his horse and, drawing a handsome sword which he bore, thrust it into his belly, and thus killed him. . . .

[The king's men quickly routed the insurgents.]

A proclamation was made through all the streets, that every person who was not an inhabitant of London, and who had not resided there for a whole year, should instantly depart. . . . After this proclamation had been heard, no one dared to infringe it; but all departed instantly to their homes, quite

discomfited. John Ball and Jack Straw were found hidden in an old ruin, thinking to steal away; but this they could not do, for they were betrayed by their own men. The king and the lords were well pleased with their seizure; their heads were cut off, as was that of Tyler, and fixed on London Bridge.

Examining the Evidence

1. How do the leaders of the rebellion justify their demands for social equality?
2. Does Froissart portray King Richard as a hero?
3. Do Froissart's sympathies lie with the rebels or the nobles? Why?

14.3 THE MING EMPEROR'S RULES FOR VILLAGE GOVERNMENT

Emperor Hongwu, *The Placard of the People's Instructions* (1398)

In 1368, Zhu Yuanzhang, a general of peasant birth who had taken up arms against the Mongol rulers of China, founded his new Ming (1368–1644) dynasty. During his reign as Emperor Hongwu (r. 1368–1398), China's new sovereign dedicated himself to reasserting Chinese culture by restoring Confucian values and traditions. But Hongwu also was deeply skeptical about the scholar–official elite who traditionally dominated Chinese government and society. Therefore, he created a system of village self-government that would protect ordinary people from abuses of power by imperial officials. Shortly before his death, Hongwu issued the "Placard of the People's Instructions" in forty-one articles to set down rules that he hoped would preserve his principles of civil governance—and his dynasty—for all time.

Since ancient times, rulers have represented Heaven in managing human affairs by setting up separate offices to order the various affairs and bring peace to the lives of the people. Worthies and

gentlemen of bygone times feared only that they would not be employed by their rulers. All who were employed exerted the utmost diligence to serve the rulers, thus bringing glory to their parents, wives and children, and to establish fine reputations in the world. How could there have been any lawbreaking conduct? Therefore, the officials were competent for their posts and the people were content in their livelihoods. Since the world was unified I have set up the cardinal principles, promulgated laws and established offices according to ancient rules: in the capital, the six ministries and the Censorate; in the provinces, the provincial administration commissions, the provincial surveillance commissions, prefectures, subprefectures, and districts. Although the titles are different from previous dynasties the system of government is the same.

That most of the appointed officials are from among the common people could not be helped. For some time it has been difficult to tell whether they were virtuous or wicked. Scholars are not real scholars and the officials are all cunning. They often take bribes and break the law, turn benevolence and

Edward L. Farmer, *Zhu Yuanzhang and Early Ming Legislation: The Reordering of Chinese Society Following the Era of Mongol Rule* (Leiden The Netherlands: Brill, 1995), 197–201, 204–206.

righteousness upside down, and injure the good people, so that the common people bring all of their complaints to the capital. So it has been for years without cease. Now this order is promulgated to declare to the people of the realm that all minor matters concerning households and marriage, land, and disputes involving assault and battery shall be judged by the elders and the community headmen. Serious matters involving sexual crime, robbery, fraud, or homicide shall be reported to the officials. After this order is promulgated, any officials or functionaries who dare to confound it shall be sentenced to the death penalty. For those commoners who dare to confound it, their entire families shall be banished to the frontiers. . . .

1. In all minor matters involving household and marriage, land, assault and battery, and disputes among the people, it is not permitted to bring lawsuits directly to government offices. These matters must go through the local community headmen and elders for judgment. Those who do not go to the community headmen and elders, regardless of the merits of the cases, shall be sentenced to beating with sixty strokes of the heavy stick and the cases sent back to the community headmen and elders for judgment.

2. The elders and community headmen live close to and have fields side by side with the common people of the village . . . so that matters of right and wrong, good and evil, are all known to them. Whenever there is an accusation from the people, a meeting shall be held immediately and the case judged fairly. The bamboo or thorn stick may be used for appropriate torture. If the case cannot be settled, causing the people to go bother the government offices, the community headmen and elders shall each be sentenced to sixty strokes of the heavy stick. Those who are over seventy years of age shall not be beaten, but redeem the punishment according to the [statutes of the *Ming Law*] *Code*. They shall still make an appropriate judgment in the case. If they act wrongly out of personal consideration and confound right and wrong, the community headmen and elders shall be punished for the crimes of judges implicating the innocent and exonerating the guilty.

The litigations which shall be judged by the elders and community headmen are as follows: household and marriage, land, assault and battery, suits over ownership, fires, theft, abusive language, money lending, gambling, eating fruits of gardens and orchards without permission, illegal killing of plowing oxen, discarding or destroying utensils or crops, animals biting and killing people, unauthorized use of property by junior or younger members of the family, dishonoring the spirits, son or grandson violating instructions, witchcraft and heterodoxy, domestic animals trampling or eating crops, equally dividing irrigation water. . . .

12. After a case among the common people has been settled by the elders and community headmen, if crafty persons disagree with the judgment and repeatedly appeal to the officials by fabricating evidence and making false accusations, they shall be sentenced to capital punishment and their families banished to the frontier. If the officials fail to check the reasons for accepting appeals, thereby taking bribes and practicing fraud, they shall all be punished.

13. Elders and community headmen, when judging suits, shall not establish a jail. Regardless of [what crimes] men or women commit, they shall not be imprisoned. The interrogation takes place during the day and the accused shall be released at night. If the case is not settled they shall return the next day for questioning. . . .

17. The elders of each [village] shall send reports of the facts of good conduct of filial sons, obedient grandsons, virtuous husbands, chaste widows, or even persons having only a single praiseworthy virtue to the Imperial Court, and to the officials who shall then forward them to the Court. . . .

25. Villagers are not equal in wealth. No family is without the happy and sad events of marriages and funerals. From now on, the households of the community shall help one another whenever these events occur. For example, in case the marriage of the child of a certain poor family cannot be managed temporarily, if every household of the community contributes one *guan* of paper currency and there are a hundred households, there will be

one hundred *guan*; if every household contributes five *guan*, there will be five hundred *guan*. With help like this, could it not be accomplished? From now on when a family has a marriage this rule shall be used to take turns giving help. If the father or the mother of a family dies and has to be buried, each family shall contribute some amount of money or some rice to help the family with the inner and outer coffins, or rites performed by Buddhist or Daoist priests to secure a good destiny for the deceased. . . .

27. The purpose of the community wine drinking ceremony is to rank the elder and younger and distinguish the worthy from the unworthy. This is a good way to improve customs. The people have already been ordered to carry it out. Now it is declared again: it must be carried out in accordance with the regulations previously issued; elder and younger are to be seated in ranked order, the worthy and unworthy are to be seated separately. When this is done for a long time, will not the people pursue good and avoid evil? The customs will be pure and honest and every individual will become a good subject. . . .

29. Now the realm is at peace. Except for paying taxes and performing corvée [compulsory] labor service, the people do not have other obligations. Everyone shall be attentive to his livelihood so as to have sufficient clothing and food. It is essential that every household follow the regulations in planting mulberries, dates, persimmons, and cotton. Every year silkworms shall be reared. The production of silk and cotton will be sufficient to provide clothing. The dates and persimmons during the prosperous years can be exchanged for money, and during the lean years they can be used for food. Such activity is beneficial to you people. The community headmen and the elders shall oversee and inspect as usual. If any dare to disobey, their families shall be banished to the frontier. . . .

31. From the ancient times, the purpose of the people's paying taxes and performing corvée service is essentially to secure peace. In recent years, those in office are incompetent, officials and functionaries are unable to teach people to do good and are bent solely on taking bribes. When the time comes for tax collection and corvée service, they always receive money in return for extending the time limit, exempting the duties of the rich and sending the poor to perform them instead. This causes the ignorant people to follow their example: to refuse to pay their allocated taxes punctually, to claim to have sold grain which they actually still have, to refuse to perform their share of corvée service. From now on, when paying taxes and performing corvée service, the people shall not bribe the officials. The allocated taxes shall be paid punctually, and their corvée service shall be performed on time. If taxes have already been paid and the corvée service performed but the officials, functionaries, tax captains, and community headmen collect them again the suffering families may gather a number of people to tie up the offenders and send them to the capital for severe punishment. . . .

33. The favor which our parents bestow in giving us birth is extremely great. Their toilsome labors of nurture are recorded in detail in the *Grand Pronouncements*. Now it is declared again that among the people those who have living agnatic [related through male kin] grandparents and parents shall unstintingly support them in accordance with their families' means. Those whose agnatic grandparents and parents are dead shall sacrifice to them at the appointed times to show their filial respects. Parents shall instruct their children; children shall be filial to their agnatic uncles; wives shall encourage their husbands to do good. In this way the clans will become harmonious, no one will break the law, and parents, wives, and children will care for one another day and night. Will this not lead naturally to the enjoyment of peace?

Examining the Evidence

1. What are the chief responsibilities that the emperor delegated to village leaders, and what powers did he reserve for government officials?
2. In what ways was the emperor's conception of village self-government modeled on the family institution?
3. What seem to have been the most common sources of dispute and social conflict in Chinese villages? Why might this have been the case?

RELIGIOUS ALLEGORY IN PERSIAN MANUSCRIPT ILLUMINATIONS

Prince Humay Meets the Lady Humayun in Her Garden by Moonlight (Early Fifteenth Century)

"Persian miniature painting" is a conventional term for manuscript illuminations that embellished Persian-language books composed throughout the eastern half of the Islamic world, from Istanbul to Delhi. Persian miniature painting reached its height of accomplishment during the heyday of the Ottoman, Safavid, and Mughal empires in the fifteenth and sixteenth centuries. In addition to its eclectic blend of Islamic motifs, Persian miniature painting also reflects the influence of Chinese paintings that circulated throughout Asia during the Mongol era.

One of the major inspirations for Persian miniature painting was "The Romance of Humay and Humayun," an allegorical tale of the quest of the human soul to achieve mystical union with God. The poem was written in Persian by Khwaju Kirmani (1290–1353), who dedicated it to the Ilkhan ruler Abu Said (r. 1316–1335). It describes the pilgrimage undertaken by Humay, a Syrian prince, after a dream in which he is transported to an enchanted castle where he sees an image of the Chinese princess Humayun. The vision arouses the prince's desire, and upon awakening he sets out for China. His journey and his eventual meeting with the Chinese princess, conveyed in romantic and at times erotic imagery, was intended to symbolize the mystical pursuit and apprehension of the divine associated with the Sufi tradition of Islam. The prince's journey from Syria (the Persian word for Syria also means "dusk" or "misfortune") to China (the dawning east) also signifies the spiritual awakening of the soul aroused by contemplation of divine beauty.

The illustration shown here [*See next page*] was composed by an unknown artist in Iran in the early fifteenth century. In this scene Humay in his dream sees Humayun in her fairyland garden. Enchanted by the beauty of the Chinese princess, Humay calls out to her in the verses from Khwaju's poem that appear in the upper right-hand corner:

> Your waist is fine and finer than a single hair,
> From grief I waste and thinner wax
> Than a single hair in a ringlet twisted
> Upon a pyre:
> Like a Hindu prince casting himself into my sati's[1]
>   flame
> Before the ringlet
> Of Your sun-like Face, I fall into my flame
> And never saw an icon like unto your Face—
> No! Not a trace! What icon here?
> Nor ever did I hear the like of You!

Examining the Evidence

1. How does the painter portray the Chinese setting through motifs that would seem exotic to a Muslim audience?

2. In what ways do the painting and Khwaju's poem reflect the cultural synthesis that emerged in Islamic Central Asia in the aftermath of Mongol conquests?

3. Why would Muslims deem feminine beauty and romantic courtship appropriate metaphors for a spiritual quest? Why might some Muslims object?

---

[1] **Sati:** The Hindu practice whereby a widow casts herself onto the burning pyre of her deceased husband to accompany him in death.

Poem translation, Michael Barry, *Figurative Art in Medieval Islam and the Riddle of Bihzad of Herat (1465–1535)* (Paris: Flammarion, 2004), 130.

The Persian Price Humay Meeting the Chinese Princess Humayun in a Garden, c. 1450 (gouache on paper) by Islamic School (fifteenth century). Musée des Arts Decoratifs, Paris, France/ Giraudon/Bridgeman Images.

14.5 THE FALL OF CONSTANTINOPLE TO THE OTTOMAN TURKS

Nestor-Iskander, *Tale of the Capture of Constantinople* (c. 1500)

Nestor-Iskander's "Tale of the Capture of Constantino-ple" purportedly is an eyewitness account of the Otto-man Turks' conquest of the Byzantine capital in 1453. The author, who wrote in Russian, claimed to have been taken captive by the Turks as a boy and forced to fight on their side. However, his version of events contains several glar-ing inaccuracies. Most likely, this account was compiled from various Greek and Russian sources by an educated person, probably an Orthodox monk. At the conclusion of his narrative Nestor-Iskander cites an old Byzantine prophecy, predicting that the "red-haired" people (*rhu-sios*) would become masters of Constantinople. In Nestor-Iskander's telling, however, *rhusios* is rendered as "the Rus," that is, the Russians. He takes this prophecy to mean that Moscow would succeed Constantinople as "the Third Rome," and that Moscow's metropolitan would replace Constantinople's patriarch as the head of the Orthodox Christian Church.

The godless Sultan Mohammed [Mehmed II, r. 1451–1481], son of Murad [Murad II, r. 1421–1451], who at that time ruled the Turks, took note of all the problems that plagued Constantinople. And, although he professed peace, he wanted to put an end to Emperor Constantine XI [r. 1449–1453]. To-wards that end he assembled a large army and, by land and by sea, suddenly appeared with that large force before the city and laid siege to it. The Emperor, his nobles, and the rest of the population did not know what to do. . . . The Emperor . . . sent his envoys to Sultan Mehmed in order to discuss peace and past relations. But Mehmed did not trust them, and as soon as the envoys departed, he ordered can-nons and guns to fire at the city. Others were com-manded to make ready wall-scaling equipment and build assault structures. Such city inhabitants as Greeks, Venetians, and Genoese left because they did not want to fight the Turks. . . .

When the Emperor saw this exodus, he ordered his nobles and high officials to assign the remain-ing soldiers to each sector of the city's wall, to main gates, and to windows. The entire popula-tion was mobilized and alarm bells were hoisted throughout the city. Each person was informed of his assignment and each was told to defend his country. . . . Meanwhile, day and night, the Turks bombarded all parts of the city without stopping, and gave its defenders no time to rest. They also made preparations for the final assault. This activity went on for thirteen days.

On the fourteenth day, after they had said their heathen prayers, the Turks sounded trumpets, beat their drums, and played on all other of their musical instruments. Then they brought many cannons and guns closer to the walls and began to bombard the city. They also fired their muskets and thousands of arrows. Because of continued heavy shooting, city defenders could not stand safely on the wall. Some crouched down awaiting the attack; others fired their cannons and guns as much as they could, killing many Turks. The Patriarch, bishops, and all clergy prayed constantly, pleading for God's mercy and for His help in saving the city.

When the Turks surmised that they had killed all the defenders on the wall, they ordered their forces to give a loud shout. Some soldiers carried incendiary devices, others ladders, still others wall-destroying equipment, and the rest many other instruments of destruction. They were ordered to attack and capture the city. City defenders, too, cried out and shouted back and engaged them in fierce battle. The Emperor toured the city, encouraging his people, promising them God's help and ordering the ringing of church

A. Stender-Petersen, ed., *Anthology of Old Russian Literature* (New York: Columbia University Press, 1954), 214–220.

bells so as to summon all the inhabitants to defend their city. When the Turks heard the ringing of church bells, they ordered their trumpets, flutes, and thousands of other musical instruments to sound out. And there was a great and terrible slaughter! . . .

Deploying all of these forces the Turks concentrated their assault on the Poloe Mesto. When city defenders retreated from the Poloe Mesto, Turkish foot soldiers hurriedly cleared the way for other units to advance. Turkish units broke through and their light cavalry units overwhelmed city defenders. All city inhabitants came to the rescue of city commanders, dignitaries, and the regular forces, and they engaged the Turks. The Emperor joined the battle with all of his nobles, his special cavalry units, and his foot soldiers. They attacked the Turks inside the city, engaged them in fierce hand-to-hand combat, and drove them away from the Poloe Mesto. . . .

When Mehmed learned about the death of his eastern military commander, he wept profusely because he admired the commander's bravery and wisdom. He also became very angry and led all of his forces to the Sublime Porte. He ordered that the Emperor's positions be bombarded with cannons and guns, being concerned that the Emperor's forces might attack him. Then, the godless Mehmed appeared opposite the Poloe Mesto and ordered his forces to fire cannons and guns at defenders in order to induce them to retreat. He also instructed the Turkish admiral Balta-Oghlu, in charge of many regiments and a select force of 3,000, to capture the Emperor dead or alive.

When they noticed the determination of the godless Mehmed, the Byzantine military commanders, officials, and nobles joined the battle and implored the Emperor to leave in order to escape death. He wept bitterly and told them, "Remember the words I said earlier! Do not try to protect me! I want to die with you!" And they replied, "All of us will die for God's church and for you!" . . .

The impious Mehmed then ordered all of his forces to occupy all city streets and gates in order to capture the Emperor. In his camp he retained only the Janissaries,[1] who readied their cannons and guns in fear of a sudden attack by the emperor. Sensing God's command, the Emperor went to the Great Church [Hagia Sophia], where he fell to the ground pleading for God's mercy and forgiveness for his sins. Then he bade farewell to the Patriarch, the clergy, and the Empress, bowed to those who were present and left the church. Then all the clergy, indeed the entire people, countless women and children, cried and moaned, hoping that their plea would reach heaven. As he left the church the Emperor said, "If you want to suffer for God's church and the Orthodox faith, then follow me!"

Then he mounted his horse and went to the Golden Gate, hoping to encounter there the godless. He was able to attract some 3,000 soldiers. Near the Gate they met a multitude of Turks whom they defeated. The Emperor wanted to reach the Gate but could not on account of many corpses. Then he encountered another large Turkish force and they fought till darkness. In this manner the Orthodox Emperor Constantine suffered for God's churches and for the Orthodox faith. On May 29, according to eyewitnesses, he killed more than 600 Turks with his own hand. And the saying was fulfilled: "It started with Constantine, and it ended with Constantine." . . .

[After the capture of the city, the sultan, accompanied by his high officials,] went from the Sublime Porte to the Gate of St. Romanus to a church where the Patriarch, his clergy, and a multitude of people, including women and children, were assembled. He came to the square before the church, dismounted his horse, prostrated himself on the ground, put a handful of dust on his head, and thanked God. And, as he admired the wonderful structure, he said, "Truly no one can transcend the people who are here and who were here before!"

Then he went inside the church. The holy place resembled a wasteland. He stopped at a place reserved for the highest dignitaries. The Patriarch, his clergy, and all who were present there cried, sobbed, and knelt before him. With his hands he motioned for them to rise and then said, "Athanasius! I am telling you, your suite and all of your people: From now on, do not fear my anger. Henceforth neither killing nor enslavement will be permitted!" . . .

---

[1] **Janissaries:** An elite corps of slave–soldiers who served as the Ottoman sultan's household troops and bodyguards.

Then [the sultan] went to the imperial palace. There he met a certain Serb who handed him the Emperor's [Constantine's] head. Mehmed was pleased with it and called Byzantine nobles and military commanders and asked them to verify whether or not the head was really the Emperor's. Because they were afraid, they all said, "It is the Emperor's head!" He examined it and said, "It is clear that God is the creator of all, including emperors. Why then does everyone have to die?"

Then he sent the head to the Patriarch, instructing him to inlay it with gold and silver and to preserve it the best he knew how. The Patriarch placed it in a silver chest, gilded it, and hid it under the altar of the great church. I have heard from others that the survivors of the battle at the Golden Gate where the Emperor was killed took the Emperor's corpse that night and buried it in Galati. . . .

[2] **Methodius of Patera** . . . **Leo the Wise:** Methodius was a third-century church father and martyr; Leo the Wise (Leo VI), emperor of Byzantium from 886 to 912, was said to have been the author of several prophetic books.

All of this happened as a consequence of our sins, that the godless Mehmed ascended the imperial throne. . . . Yet, those who know history also know that all of this was prophesied by Methodius of Patera and by Leo the Wise[2] concerning the destiny of this city. Its past has been fulfilled and so will be its future. For it is written: "A nation of Rus, as has been prophesied in the vision of St. Daniel, will triumph. And they will inherit the traditions of the seven hills [Rome], as well as its laws, and will disseminate them among five or six nations that comprise Rus, and they will implant seeds among them and will harvest many benefits."

Examining the Evidence

1. In Nestor-Iskander's account, how and why did the Turks succeed in capturing Constantinople?

2. In what ways does the author depict Emperor Constantine as a hero?

3. Does Nestor-Iskander portray the Ottoman conquest of Constantinople as a catastrophe for the Christian religion? Why or why not?

14.6 THE SULTAN OF MALI

Ibn Battuta, *Rihla* (1356)

A native of Morocco, Ibn Battuta (1304–1368) set out on a pilgrimage to Mecca in 1325 that extended into a series of journeys lasting nearly thirty years, taking him to every corner of the Muslim world. He made his final journey, an expedition across the Sahara Desert to the sultanate of Mali in West Africa—known among Arabs as the Sudan, "the country of the blacks"—in 1352–1353. Upon his return to Morocco, Ibn Battuta composed a *rihla*, or travel diary. As a literary genre, *rihla* flowered among North African Muslims during this time. Most were written by pilgrims to Mecca who surveyed the places, people, and customs they visited. Ibn Battuta's more ambitious work drew both on his personal experiences

and on other writings and legendary lore. His account of Mali seems to have been based on his personal experiences.

The Sultan of Mali

He is the sultan Mansa Sulayman. *Mansa* means "sultan" and Sulayman is his name. He is a miserly king from whom no great donation is to be expected. It happened that I remained for this period without seeing him on account of my illness. Then he gave a memorial feast for our lord Abu'l-Hasan [sultan of Morocco, r. 1331–1348] (may God be content with him) and invited the emirs and *faqihs* [jurists] and the *qadi* [chief judge] and the

Nehemia Levtzion and Jay Spaulding, eds., *Medieval West Africa: Views from Arab Scholars and Merchants* (Princeton, NJ: Markus Wiener, 2003), 72–73, 75, 78–83.

khatib [prayer leader], and I went with them. They brought copies of the Qur'an and the Qur'an was recited in full. . . .

Their trivial reception gift and their respect for it

When I departed the reception a gift was sent to me and dispatched to the qadi's house. The qadi sent it with his men to the house of Ibn al-Faqih. Ibn al-Faqih hastened out of his house barefooted and came in to me saying, "Come! The cloth and gift of the sultan have come to you!" I got up, thinking that it would be robes of honor and money, but behold! It was three loaves of bread and a piece of beef fried in gharti and a gourd containing yogurt. When I saw it I laughed, and was long astonished at their feeble intellect and their respect for mean things.

My speaking to the Sultan after this and his kindness toward me

After this reception gift I remained for two months during which the sultan sent nothing to me and the month of Ramadan came in. Meanwhile I frequented the mashwar [council-place] and used to greet him and sit with the qadi and khatib. I spoke with Dugha the interpreter, who said, "Speak with him, and I will express what you want to say in the proper fashion." So when he held a session at the beginning of Ramadan I stood before him and said, "I have journeyed to the countries of the world and met their kings. I have been four months in your country without your giving me a reception gift or anything else. What shall I say of you in the presence of other sultans?" He replied, "I have not seen you or known about you." The qadi and Ibn al-Faqih rose and replied to him saying, "He greeted you and you sent to him some food." Thereupon he ordered that a house be provided for me to stay in and an allowance be allotted to me. Then, on the night of 27 Ramadan, he distributed among the qadi and the khatib and the faqihs a sum of money that they call zakah and gave

to me 33-1/3 mithqals [of gold].[1] When I departed he bestowed on me 100 mithqals of gold. . . .

The self-debasement of the Sudan before their king

The Sudan are the humblest of people before their king and the most submissive towards him. They swear by his name, saying "Mansa Sulayman ki." When he calls to one of them at his sessions in the pavilion, the person called takes off his clothes and puts on ragged clothes, and removes his turban and puts on a dirty shashiyya [cap], and goes in holding up his garments and trousers half-way up his leg, and advances with submissiveness and humility. He then beats the ground vigorously with his two elbows, and stands like one performing a rak'a [prayer cycle] to listen to his words.

If one of them addresses the sultan and the latter replies, he uncovers the clothes from his back and sprinkles dust on his head and back, like one washing with water. I used to marvel how their eyes did not become blinded.

An amusing story about the poets' reciting to the sultan

On the feast day, when Dugha has finished his performance, the poets come. They are called jula, of which the singular is jali. Each of them has enclosed himself within an effigy made of feathers, resembling a bird called shaqshaq, on which is fixed a head made of wood with a red beak as though it were the head of the shaqshaq. They stand in front of the sultan in this comical shape and recite their poems. I was told that their poetry was a kind of exhortation in which they say to the sultan, "This banbi [dais] on which you are sitting was sat upon by such-and-such a king and among his good deeds were so-and-so; and such-and-such a king, and among his good deeds were so-and-so, so you too do good deeds which will be remembered after you." Then the chief of the poets mounts the steps of the banbi and places his head in the lap of the sultan. Then he mounts to the top of the banbi and places his head on the sultan's right shoulder, then upon his left shoulder, talking in their language. Then he descends. I was

---

[1] *mithqal:* A unit of measurement (4.25 grams) mostly used to weigh precious metals.

informed that this act was already old before Islam, and they had continued with it. . . .

Anecdote

It happened during my sojourn at Mali that the sultan was displeased with his chief wife, the daughter of his maternal uncle, called Qasa. The meaning of *qasa* with them is "queen." She was his partner in rule according to the custom of the Sudan, and her name was mentioned with his from the pulpit. He imprisoned her in the house of one of the *farariyya* [chiefs] and appointed in her place his other wife Banju, who was not of royal blood. People talked much about this and disapproved of his act. His female cousins went in to congratulate Banju on her queenship. They put ashes on their forearms and did not scatter dust on their heads. Then the sultan released Qasa from her confinement. His cousins went in to congratulate her on her release and scattered dust over themselves according to the custom. Banju complained about this to the sultan and he was angry with his cousins. They were afraid of him and sought sanctuary in the mosque. He pardoned them and summoned them into his presence. The women's custom when they go into the sultan's presence is that they divest themselves of their clothes and enter naked. This they did and he was pleased with them. They proceeded to come to the door of the sultan morning and evening for a period of seven days, this being the practice of anyone whom the sultan has pardoned.

Qasa began to ride every day with her slave girls and men with dust on their heads and to stand by the council face veiled, her face being invisible. The emirs talked much about her affair, so the sultan gathered them at the council place and said to them through Dugha: "You have been talking a great deal about the affair of Qasa. She has committed a great crime." Then one of her slave girls was brought forth bound and shackled and he said to her, "Say what you have to say!" She informed them that Qasa had sent her to Jatil, the sultan's cousin who was in flight from him at Kanburni, and invited him to depose the sultan from his kingship, saying, "I and all the army are at your service!" When the emirs heard that they said, "Indeed, that is a great crime and for it she deserves to be killed!" Qasa was fearful at

this and sought refuge at the house of the *khatib*. It is their custom there that they seek sanctuary in the mosque, or if that is not possible then in the house of the *khatib*.

The Sudan disliked Mansa Sulayman on account of his avarice. Before him was the king Mansa Magha, and before Mansa Magha, Mansa Musa. Mansa Musa was generous and virtuous. He liked white men and treated them kindly. It was he who gave to Abu Ishaq al-Sahili in a single day 4,000 *mithqals*. Reliable persons have informed me that he gave to Mudrik b. Faqqus 3,000 *mithqals* in a single day. His grandfather Sariq Jata embraced Islam at the hands of the grandfather of this Mudrik. . . .

What I approved of and what I disapproved of among the acts of the Sudan

One of their good features is their lack of oppression. They are the farthest removed of people from it and their sultan does not permit anyone to practice it. Another is the security embracing the whole country, so that neither the traveler there nor dweller has anything to fear from thief or usurper. Another is that they do not interfere with the wealth of any white man who dies among them. They simply leave it in the hands of a trustworthy white man until the one to whom it is due takes it. Another is their assiduity [diligence] in prayer and their persistence in performing it in congregation and beating their children to make them perform it. If it is Friday and a man does not go early to the mosque he will not find anywhere to pray because of the press of people. It is their habit that every man sends his servant with his prayer-mat to spread it for him in a place that he thereby has a right to until he goes to the mosque. Their prayer-carpets are made from the fronds of a tree resembling the palm that has no fruit. Another of their good features is their dressing in fine white clothes on Friday. If any one of them possesses nothing but a ragged shirt he washes it and cleanses it and attends the Friday prayer in it. Another is their eagerness to memorize the great Qur'an. . . .

One of their disapproved acts is that their female servants and slave girls and little girls appear before men naked, with their privy parts uncovered.

During Ramadan I saw many of them in this state, for it is the custom of the *farariyya* to break their fast in the house of the sultan, and each one brings his food carried by twenty or more of his slave girls, they all being naked. Another is that their women go into the sultan's presence naked and uncovered, and that his daughters go naked. . . . Another is their sprinkling dust and ashes on their their heads out of good manners. . . . Another is that many of them eat carrion, and dogs, and donkeys.

Examining the Evidence

1. What is Ibn Battuta's initial opinion of the Mali sultan Sulayman? Does his assessment of the sultan's character change over the course of his stay in Mali?

2. What features of West African society does Ibn Battuta approve of, and what features does he find offensive?

3. What does Ibn Battuta's account reveal about the place of women in Mali society?

14.7 GLORIOUS VENICE

Marin Sanudo, *In Praise of the City of Venice* (1493)

In the fifteenth century, Venice reached its height as the dominant mercantile empire of the Mediterranean. Venice's commercial success, however, stemmed more from its military power and economic strength than from the entrepreneurial savvy of its seagoing traders. Thus, the well-being of the Venetian state became the chief priority of government and citizens alike. "In Praise of the City of Venice" was written in 1493 by a humanist scholar, Marin Sanudo (1466–1536), in homage to the wealth and power of his native city. Sanudo traced the founding of Venice in the fifth century to mainlanders who fled to this island refuge to escape the Huns and other barbarian invaders. However, he insisted that from its beginning Venice was blessed by liberty, wealth, and, above all, Christian piety.

This city of Venice is a free city, a common home to all men, and it has never been subjugated to anyone, as have been all other cities. It was built by Christians, not voluntarily but out of fear, not by deliberate decision but from necessity. Moreover it was founded not by shepherds as Rome was, but by powerful and rich people, such as have ever been since that time, with their faith in Christ, an obstacle to barbarians and attackers. . . .

David Chambers and Brian Pullan, eds., *Venice: A Documentary History, 1450–1630* (Oxford: Blackwell, 1992), 4–7, 11–13, 16–17, 20–21.

This city, amidst the billowing waves of the sea, stands on the crest of the main, almost like a queen restraining its force. It is situated in salt water and built there, because before there were just lagoons, and then, wanting to expand, firm ground was needed for the building of palaces and houses. These are being constructed all the time; they are built above the water by a very ingenious method of driving piles, so that the foundations are in water. Every day the tide rises and falls, but the city remains dry. At times of very low tides, it is difficult to go by boat to wherever one wants. The city is about 7 miles in circumference; it has no surrounding walls, no gates which are locked at night, no sentry keeping watch as other cities have for fear of enemies; it is so very safe at present, that no one can attack or frighten it. As another writer has said, its name has achieved such dignity and renown that it is fair to say Venice merits the title "Pillar of Italy"; "deservedly it may be called the bosom of Christendom." For it takes pride of place before all others, if I may say so, in prudence, fortitude, magnificence, benignity, and clemency; everyone throughout the world testifies to this. To conclude, this city was built more by divine than human will. . . .

The population of the city, according to a census which was made, is about 150,000 souls. There are three classes of inhabitants: gentlemen [nobles] who govern the state and republic, whose families will be mentioned below; citizens; and artisans or the lower class. The gentlemen are not distinguished from the citizens by their clothes, because they all dress in much the same way, except for the senatorial office-holders, who during their term of office have to wear the colored robes laid down by law. . . . The majority are merchants and all go to do business on Rialto. . . .

Venice is divided into six *sestieri* [districts]. . . . In [the sestier of San Polo] is the island of Rialto, which I would venture to call the richest place in the whole world. First of all, overlooking the [Grand] Canal, is the grain warehouse, large and well stocked, with two doorways and many booths; there are two lords appointed to supervise it, as I shall relate below. Then you come to Riva del Ferro, so called because iron is sold there; where it ends at the Rialto Bridge is the public weighhouse, where all the merchandise for sale has to be weighed, and the reckonings are made of customs and excise duty. Here is the Rialto itself, which is a piazzetta, not very large at all, where everyone goes both morning and afternoon. Here business deals are made with a single word "yes" or "no." There are a large number of brokers, who are trustworthy; if not they are reprimanded. There are four banks: the Pisani and Lippomani, both patricians, and the Garzoni and Augustini, citizens. They hold very great amounts of money, issue credits under different names, and are called authorized bankers; their decisions are binding. They have charge of the moneys of the Camerlenghi [Treasurers of the Republic]. Furthermore, throughout the said island of Rialto there are storehouses, both on ground level and above, filled with goods of very great value; it would be a marvelous thing were it possible to see everything at once, in spite of the fact that much is being sold all the time. Every year goods come in from both east and west, where galleys are sent on commission from the Signoria [Venice's chief governing body]; they are put in the charge of whoever wants this [responsibility], provided he is a patrician, by public auction. It should be noted that the Venetians, just as they were merchants in the beginning, continue to trade every year; they send galleys to Flanders, the Barbary Coast, Beirut, Alexandria, the Greek lands, and Aigues-Mortes. All the [galley] fleets have a captain elected by the great Council, and the Signoria appoints the galley patrons by auction at Rialto, i.e., according to whoever bids highest for the galleys. . . .

On the island of Rialto, these stores and warehouses, of which there are such a great number, pay rent for the most part to [the Procurators of] St. Mark's [the public treasury]; a high rent is paid for every small piece of space on Rialto, not only for these properties, but for those belonging to various private persons who rent out shops. Such a shop at Rialto may cost about 100 ducats in rent and be scarcely two paces wide or long. Property here is very expensive. Our own family, the Sanudi, can bear witness to this, having an inn called the Bell at the New Fishmarket. The ground floor is all let out as shops; it is a small place, but from this one building we get about 800 ducats a year in rent, which is a marvelous thing and a huge rent. This is because it is on such a good site; the inn itself brings in 250 ducats, more than the foremost palace in the city; I daresay it is the best property of its sort in Venice. On Rialto, moreover, there are all the skilled crafts; they have their separate streets, as I shall write below.

Here, on the Canal, there are embankments where on one side there are barges for timber, and on the other side for wine; they are rented as though they were shops. There is a very large butchery, which is full every day of good meat, and there is another one at St. Mark's. The Fishmarket overlooks the Grand Canal; here are the most beautiful fish, high in price and of good quality. The fish are caught in the Adriatic Sea by fishermen, for there is a neighborhood in Venice called San Niccolo where only fishermen live, and they speak an ancient Venetian dialect called *nicoloto*. . . . In this city nothing grows, yet whatever you want can be found in abundance. And this is because of the great turnover in merchandise; everything comes here, especially things to eat, from every city and every part of the world, and money is made quickly. . . . And on Rialto the prices of some things are controlled so that those who buy are not cheated. Mutton, sold at the butchery, cannot be sold for more than 3 *soldi* a pound, and if short weight is given the butchers are penalized by the lords in charge of them, because there are officials who weigh the meat which has been sold. . . . Oil is fixed at 4 *soldi* to the pound weight, candles at 4 *soldi* a pound; a barber's charge for hairdressing is the standard 3 *soldi*; a cartload of wood at all times cannot be more than 28 *soldi*, and there are loading-officials of the commune so that justice is done fairly to everyone. And for other goods the saying is "right weight and high price." Other comestibles are sold as they want, but the Guistizia Vecchia, who are lords with special responsibility, are free to fix a just price on things to eat. Thus the city is governed as well as any city in the world has ever been; everything is well ordered, and this is why the city has survived and grown. . . .

It only remains to mention the Ducal Palace, where our most serene Prince resides. It is at St. Mark's and is a most beautiful and worthy building. . . . The outside walls are all worked over and inlaid with white marble and with stones from all over the world. Inside, the walls on the ground floor are gilded and inlaid with paneling so that it is a very beautiful sight. There are four gilded chambers—I never saw any more beautiful—which took a very great time and elaborate workmanship apart from the gold and the labor. Excellent rooms are the Hall of Public Audience and the Hall of the Senate, which they are working on at present and will be very worthy. One can therefore compare the Venetians to the Romans . . . on account of the buildings, both private and public, being erected at the present

time. Indeed it can be said, as another writer has done, that our republic has followed the Romans in being as powerful in military strength as in virtue and learning. . . .

To conclude about the site of Venice: it is a marvelous thing, which must be seen to be believed; its greatness has grown up only through trade, based on navigation to different parts of the world. It is governed by its own statutes and laws, and is not subject to the legal authority of the [Holy Roman] Empire as everywhere else is. . . . And the order with which this holy Republic is governed is a wonder to behold; there is no sedition from the non-nobles [*populo*], no discord among the patricians, but all work together to [the Republic's] increase.

Examining the Evidence

1. According to Sanudo, in what ways did Venice surpass the achievements of ancient Rome? What seems to impress Sanudo the most about Venice?

2. How does Sanudo define the social hierarchy in Venice? Was the Venetian Republic a democracy?

3. What role did the state play in the city's economic life? Would you say that free enterprise prevailed in Venice?

MAKING CONNECTIONS

1. Compare the social turmoil caused by the Black Death in Florence—which experienced its own popular insurrection, the Ciompi revolt, in 1378—with the conflict between the upper and lower classes in England described by Froissart. Why was it unlikely that an uprising like the English Peasant Revolt would occur in the immediate aftermath of the Black Death?

2. Compare and contrast the vision of social order expressed by the Ming emperor Hongwu with Marin Sanudo's depiction of a harmonious society in Venice. Do they share any common principles?

3. Based on his assessment of Islamic practices in West Africa, would Ibn Battuta be likely to approve of the religious sentiments expressed in the painting "Prince Humay Meets the Lady Humayun in Her Garden by Moonlight"?

4. Compare the images of the Byzantine king and the Ottoman sultan in Nestor-Iskander's account of the capture of Constantinople with Ibn Battuta's depiction of the king of Mali. Do they share similar conceptions of the ideal king? Why or why not?

PART 3

The Early Modern World, 1450–1750

CHAPTER 15

Empires and Alternatives in the Americas, 1430–1530

The native peoples of the Americas adapted to diverse environments over the course of thousands of years, and in Mesoamerica (roughly Mexico and part of Central America) and the Andes (the western spine of South America), they developed complex empires that flourished in early modern times. Because only the Maya developed a decipherable writing system, however, most documents relating to the era before the arrival of the Europeans and Africans were composed soon after contact and conquest in the sixteenth and seventeenth centuries. The following selections offer glimpses of key concerns in religious, political, and everyday life from the Aztec, Inca, and Eastern Woodlands regions.

15.1   AZTEC SACRIFICE

Florentine Codex (c. 1540–1560)

One of the most comprehensive sources on Aztec life and history is known as the *Florentine Codex*. Now housed in a museum in Florence, Italy, it is a series of manuscripts compiled by the Spanish Franciscan priest Bernardino de Sahagún several decades after the Spanish Conquest. Despite Sahagún's oversight role, the codex was largely composed and entirely illustrated by a team of Aztecs and former Aztec subjects. Beginning in the 1520s, Aztec boys were trained by Franciscan missionaries to adapt Spanish phonetics and the Latin alphabet to Nahuatl, making it a true written language for the first time. The following selection, translated directly from courtly Nahuatl, describes the sacrificial feast of Toxcatl, in which a captive warrior impersonated the god Tezcatlipoca for an entire year.

In the time of Toxcatl there was Tezcatlipoca's great festival. At that time he was given human form; at that time he was set up. Wherefore died his impersonator, who for one year had lived [as Tezcatlipoca].

And at that time was appointed his [new] impersonator, who would again live [as Tezcatlipoca] for a year.

For many impersonators were living, whom stewards in various places guarded; whom they maintained. About ten [so] lived. These were indeed selected captives; they were selected when captives were taken. There one was chosen if he was seen to be suitable, if he was fair of body. Then he was taken. They entrusted these to stewards. But one destined to be a slave, him the captor slew.

Indeed he who was thus chosen was of fair countenance, of good understanding, quick, of clean body, slender, reed-like, long and thin, like a stout cane, like a stone column all over, not of overfed body, not corpulent, nor very small, nor exceedingly tall. . . .

For him who was thus, who had no flaw, who had no [bodily] defects, who had no blemish, who had no mark, who had on him no wart, [no such] small tumor, there was taken the greatest care that he be taught to blow the flute, that he be able to play his whistle; and that at the same time he hold all his flowers and his smoking tube. At the same time he would go playing the flute, he would go sucking [the smoking tube], he would go smelling [the flowers].

So [his flute], his flowers, his smoking tube went together when he followed the road.

And while yet he lived, while yet he was being trained in the home of the steward, before he appeared [in the presence of the people], very great care was taken that he should be very circumspect in his discourse, that he talk graciously, that he greet people agreeably on the road if he met anyone.

For he was indeed much honored when he appeared, when already he was an impersonator. Since he impersonated Titlacauan, he was indeed regarded as our lord. There was the assigning of lordship; he was importuned; he was sighed for; there was bowing before him; the commoners performed the earth-eating ceremony before him.

And if they saw that already his body fattened a little, they made him take brine; with it they thinned him; they thinned him with salt. Thus he became thin; he became firm; his body became hard.

And for one year he [thus] lived; at the time of Toxcatl he appeared [before the people], and at that time died the man who had been impersonator for one year, who had been led along the road, who had waited for one year, who had [thus] passed one year. Just then he went being substituted; one was set in his place [from among] all whom the various stewards were guarding, were maintaining, at the time that [the first impersonator] appeared [before the people].

Thereupon he began his office. He went about playing the flute. By day and by night he followed whatever way he wished.

Fray Bernardino de Sahagún, *The Florentine Codex*, 2d ed., vol. 2, ed. and trans. Arthur Anderson and Charles Dibble (Santa Fe: School of American Research and University of Utah, 1981), 66–71.

His eight servitors went following him. Four [of them] had fasted for a year. Their hair was shorn as if they were one's pages; their hair was cut; their hair was clipped; they were not clipped smooth like a gourd; they were not clipped bald like a gourd; their heads were not smooth like pots; they did not stick [hair] to the head.

And also there were four constables, masters of youths. They cut their hair similarly; their hair arrangement was similar. It was arranged upright for them on their foreheads.

At this time Moctezuma adorned [the impersonator]; he repeatedly adorned him; he gave him gifts; he arrayed him; he arrayed him with great pomp. He had all costly things placed on him, for verily he took him to be his beloved god. [The impersonator] fasted; hence it was said: "He fasteth in black," [for] he went with his face smoke-black. His head was pasted with feathers, with eagle down. They only covered his hair for him; it fell to his loins.

And when he was attired, he went about with popcorn flowers laid upon his head; they were his crown of flowers. And he was dressed in these same on both sides; they drew them out to his armpits. This was called "the flowery stole."

And from his ears on both sides went hanging curved golden shell pendants. And they fitted [his ears with] ear plugs made of turquoise, turquoise mosaic. And a shell necklace was his necklace. Moreover, his breast ornament was of white seashells.

And then his lip pendant, his slender lip pendant, was of snail shell. And down his back went hanging what was like a cord bag called *icpatoxin*.

Then on both sides, on his upper arms, he placed golden bracelets, and on both sides, on his wrists, he went placing turquoise bracelets taking up almost all his forearms. And he went putting on only his net cape like a fish net of wide mesh with a fringe of brown cotton thread. And his costly breechclout reached to the calves of his legs.

And then he went placing his bells on both sides, on his legs. All gold were the bells, called *oyoalli*. These [he wore] because they went jingling, because they went ringing; so did they resound. And his obsidian sandals had ocelot skin ears. Thus was arrayed he who died after one year.

When [the feast of] Toxcatl went drawing near, when it approached him, when already it went reaching him, first he married; he looked upon a woman; he was married at the time of Uey toçoztli.

And he shed, he put in various places, he abandoned what had been his ornaments in which he had walked about fasting in black. His hair was shorn; he was provided a tuft of hair upon his forehead, like that of a seasoned warrior. They bound it; they wound it round and round. They bound it with [brown cotton thread] called *tochyacatl*; it was tied with a slipknot. And his forked heron feather ornament with a quetzal feather spray they bound to his warrior's hairdressing.

It was for only twenty days that he lived lying with the women, that he lived married to them. The four women in whose company he lived had also lived for a year guarded in the steward's establishment.

The name of the first one was Xochiquetzal; the second was Xilonen; the third was Atlatonan; the fourth was Uixtociuatl.

And when it was already the eve of [the feast of] Toxcatl, still five [days] from it, on the fifth day [from it], five days before the feast of Toxcatl would pass, they began each to sing [and dance].

At this time, in all these days, one knew nothing more of Moctezuma. They who yet had been his companions provided people with food, provided people with favors.

On the first day they sang [and danced] at a place called Tecanman. On the second day it was in the place where was guarded the image of Titlacauan, in the home of him who was the steward who guarded it. On the third day it was at Tepetzinco, in the middle of the lagoon. The fourth time it was at Tepepulco, which is also quite near Tepetzinco.

When they had sung [and danced], thereupon he embarked in a boat. The women went, going with him. They went consoling him; they went encouraging him. The boat proceeded to a place called Acaquilpan or Caualtepec; there it proceeded to the shore; there it landed them.

For here they were left, rather near Tlapitzauhcan. The women then returned. And only they who for the time had become [and] were his servitors went following him while yet he lived.

Thus was it said: when he arrived where [the impersonators of Titlacauan] used to die, [where] a small temple called Tlacochcalco stood, he ascended by himself, he went up of his own free will, to where he was to die. As he was taken up a step, as he passed one [step], there he broke, he shattered his flute, his whistle, etc.

And when he had mounted all the steps, when he had risen to the summit, then the offering priests seized him. They threw him upon his back on the sacrificial stone; then [one of them] cut open his breast; he took his heart from him; he also raised it in dedication to the sun.

For in this manner were all [these] captives slain. But his body they did not roll down; rather, they lowered it. Four men carried it.

And his severed head they strung on the skull rack. Thus he was brought to an end in the adornment in which he died. Thus his life there ended; there they terminated his life when he went to die there at Tlapitzauayan.

And this betokened our life on earth. For he who rejoiced, who possessed riches, who sought, who esteemed our lord's sweetness, his fragrance — richness, prosperity — thus ended in great misery. Indeed it was said: "No one on earth went exhausting happiness, riches, wealth."

Examining the Evidence

1. According to the *Florentine Codex*, what characteristics were required of this sacrificial war captive?
2. What was life like for the captive during the long preparation for the Aztec sacrifice?
3. How might this deity impersonation and sacrifice be explained?

15.2 AZTEC CHILD REARING

Codex Mendoza (c. 1540)

The painted manuscript known as the *Codex Mendoza* was produced by former Aztec scribes around 1540, approximately two decades after the Spanish Conquest of Mexico (1519–1521). Even though it is a post–Conquest document, the codex was clearly informed by prominent elders who lived before the arrival of Hernando Cortés and other conquistadors. Aztec pictographic symbols, somewhat like modern computer icons, are explained with Spanish and Nahuatl text, translated into English below. In the following selection, stages of Aztec child rearing, from birth to marriage, are described in terms of ideal types.

After the mother gave birth, they placed the infant in its cradle. . . . And at the end of four days after the infant's birth, the midwife carried the infant, naked, and took it to the courtyard of the house of the one who has given birth. And in the courtyard they had placed a small earthen tub of water on rushes or reeds [as a mat] called *tule*, where the said midwife bathed the said infant. And after the bath three boys, who are seated next to the said rushes eating toasted maize rolled up with cooked beans, the food they called *yxicue*, purposefully put the food in the little earthen jug so they might eat it. And after the said bath, the said midwife ordered the said boys to call out loudly the new name of the infant who had been bathed. And the name they gave it was that which the midwife wished. And at the beginning, when the infant was taken to be bathed, if it was a boy, they carried him with his symbol in his hand; and the symbol was the tool used by the infant's father, whether of the military or professions like metalworker, woodcarver, or

The Codex Mendoza, Volume 4, edited by Frances F. Berdan and Patricia Rieff Anawalt, 118–127. © 1992 by the Regents of the University of California. Published by the University of California Press. Used by permission of the publisher.

whatever other profession. And after having done this, the midwife handed the infant to its mother. And if the infant was a girl, the symbol they gave her for bathing was a distaff with its spindle and its basket, and a broom, which were the things she would use when she grew up. And they offered the male infant's umbilical cord, along with the little shield and arrows symbol used in bathing, in the place where they warred with their enemies, where they buried it under the ground. And likewise for the girl, they buried her umbilical cord under the *metate*, a stone for grinding tortillas.

And after that, at the end of twenty days, the infant's parents took the infant to the temple or *mezquita* [literally, "mosque," from the Spanish], called *calmecac*. And, with offerings of cloaks, loincloths, and some food, they presented the infant to the priests. And after the infant had been reared by its parents and had reached [a proper] age, they delivered him to the head priest of the said temple to be trained there for priesthood.

And if the infant's parents decided that, upon coming of age, he would serve in the military, then they offered the infant to the master, promising him [to service]. The master of boys and youths was called *teachcauh* or *telpuchtlato*. They made the offering with presents of food and other things for the dedication. And when the infant was of age, they delivered him to the said master.

[This explains] . . . the time and means . . . [they] used in instructing their children in how they should live. . . . Parents corrected their children when they were three years old, by giving good advice. And the ration they gave them at each meal was a half a tortilla.

. . . Parents . . . likewise instructed their children when they were four years old. And they began to teach them to serve in minor and light tasks. The ration they gave them at each meal was one tortilla.

. . . The parents of five-year-old children . . . engaged them in personal services, like toting light loads of firewood and carrying light bundles to the *tiangues*, or marketplace. And they taught the girls of this age how they had to hold the spindle and distaff in order to spin. Ration: one tortilla.

. . . The parents of six-year-old children . . . instructed and engaged them in personal services,

from which the parents benefited, like, for the boys, [collecting] maize that has been spilled in the marketplace, and beans and other miserable things that traders left scattered. And they taught the girls to spin and [to do] other advantageous services. This was so that, by way of the said services and activities, they did not spend their time in idleness, and to avoid the bad vices that idleness tends to bring. The ration they gave the children at each meal was one and a half tortillas.

[For older children, the *Codex Mendoza*] deals with the time and means of the Mexican *naturales* used in instructing and correcting their children, to avoid all idleness, ensure that they pursue and engage in advantageous activities. . . .

. . . The parents of seven-year-old children [are to give] the boys nets for fishing, and the mothers taught their daughters to spin; and they gave them good advice so they would always apply themselves and spend their time in something to avoid all idleness. The ration they gave their children at each meal was one and a half tortillas.

. . . [As for] the parents of eight-year-old children: They punished them by putting before them the fear and terror of maguey thorns, so that being negligent and disobedient to their parents would be punished with the said thorns. And also the children wept from fear. . . . The ration per meal that they gave them was set at one and a half tortillas.

. . . [As for] the parents of nine-year-old children: For being incorrigible and rebellious toward them, the parents punished their children with the said maguey thorns, tying the stark-naked boy hand and foot and sticking the said thorns in his shoulders and body. And they pricked the girls' hands with the thorns. . . . The ration per meal they gave them was one and a half tortillas.

. . . [Then for] the parents of ten-year-old children: Likewise they punished them for being rebellious, beating them with sticks and offering other threats. . . . The set rate and ration per meal that they gave them was one and a half tortillas.

. . . They punished the eleven-year-old boy or girl who disregarded verbal correction by making them inhale chili smoke, which was a serious and even cruel torment; and they would chastise them so they not go about in vice and idleness but that they employ their time in gainful activities. They gave the children of that age the bread that is tortillas at the rate of only one and a half tortillas at each meal to teach them not to be gluttons.

. . . If a twelve-year-old boy or girl ignored their parents' corrections and advice, his father took the boy and tied him hand and foot and laid him stark naked on the damp ground, where he stayed an entire day, so that with his punishment he would be chastised and fearful. And for the girl of the same age, her mother made her [rise] before dawn to sweep the house and street, and always be occupied in personal services. Likewise the parents gave them to eat a set amount of one and a half tortillas at every meal.

. . . For the thirteen-year-old boy or girl, the parents engaged [the boys] in carrying firewood from the hills and in transporting sedges and other grasses for household services. And the girls would grind [maize] and make *tortillas* and other cooked foods for their parents. They gave the children a set rate of two tortillas to eat at each meal, etc.

. . . For the fourteen-year-old boy or girl, the parents occupied and engaged the boy in fishing with a canoe in the lakes, and they instructed the girl in weaving cloth. They gave them a set rate of two tortillas to eat, etc.

. . . The father having boys of a youthful age, took them to [one of] two houses . . . , either to the house of the master who taught and instructed youths or to the temple, according to how the youth was inclined. And he delivered him to the chief priest or the master of boys so the youths might be taught from the age of fifteen years.

. . . [The following are] the means and custom they had in making legitimate marriages. The ceremony began when the bride, just after dark, was carried on the back of an *amanteca*, who is a physician. They were accompanied by four other women carrying ignited pine torches, who went lighting their way. And when they arrived at the groom's house, the groom's parents led her to the patio of the house to receive her, and they put her in a room or house where the groom was waiting. And the bride and bridegroom sat on a mat with its seats, next to a burning hearth, and they tied their clothes together, and offered copal incense to their gods. And then two old women and two old men who were present as witnesses gave food to the bride and bridegroom, and then the elders ate. And when the old men and old women finished eating, each one individually addressed the bride and bridegroom, offering them good advice on how they ought to behave and live, and on how they ought to perform the responsibility and position they had acquired, in order to live in peace.

Examining the Evidence

1. As described in the *Codex Mendoza*, what rituals accompanied Aztec childbirth?
2. How were Aztec girls and boys raised differently?
3. According to the *Codex Mendoza*, what were the various steps in an Aztec marriage ceremony?

15.3 THE INCA HUAYNA CAPAC'S FINAL DAYS

Juan de Betanzos, *Narrative of the Incas* (1557)

Juan de Betanzos was a Spanish conquistador who married an Inca princess from Cuzco. Betanzos learned the courtly Quechua language spoken by the nobles of the imperial capital and wrote a bilingual conversion manual for Spanish priests. He also collected spoken histories of past rulers from his wife's mother-in-law and other elder women. Betanzos translated these oral testimonies into Spanish in hopes of publishing a book he called *Narrative of the Incas*. The manuscript was sent to Spain but was

Juan de Betanzos, *Narrative of the Incas*, ed. and trans. Roland Hamilton and Dana Buchanan (Austin: University of Texas Press, 1996), 182–185.

subsequently lost until the 1980s, when Spanish scholars discovered it in an archive on the Mediterranean island of Mallorca. The following passage relates the last deeds of the Inca Huayna Capac, the uncle of Betanzos's wife. Huayna Capac died in Quito, the northern Inca capital, around 1527 from what many scholars suspect was small-pox. The disease apparently spread into the Andes from the coastal regions where Spaniards had been recon-noitering for several years.

Since Huayna Capac had already decided to go to the province of Quito, he put his plan into action and, leaving the instructions he felt necessary to protect and preserve his city, he left it, taking with him fifty thousand warriors. He also took with him his son Atawalpa, who was at that time thirteen years old. When Huayna Capac left Cuzco to make this journey, he was sixty years old and he left his son Huascar in Cuzco with the rest of his sons and daughters. He took with him Huascar's mother, who was pregnant and gave birth on the road to a daughter whom they called Chuquihuipa.

Huayna Capac went through his provinces doing much good for all those he met. He was accustomed to doing this for the poor, the widows, and orphans. Even today they love him for the great familiarity that he displayed to all. They say that his solemn demeanor was the same with everyone, the most important and the least important. He answered all who brought him questions and pleased them. No one who came before him left unhappy.

Traveling through his provinces in the above-described way, he reached Tomebamba [modern Cuenca, Ecuador], the province of the Cañares, where Huayna Capac himself had been born. He spent a month there resting and then left for Quito, where he marshaled his forces.

After having rested for some time in the city of Quito and leaving it well guarded, he left in search of the province and the lake that they call Yaguar-cocha, sending his son Atawalpa ahead with twenty thousand warriors.

When the men of Yaguarcocha learned that war-riors were coming against them, they came out on the road to resist their enemies. When they met the men that Atawalpa was bringing ahead of the others, they offered battle. The men of Yaguarcocha defeated him and Atawalpa returned in flight.

When Huayna Capac learned that his son was re-treating, he hurried his warriors, which at that point numbered more than one hundred thousand men. When he saw the soldiers that his son had taken fleeing, he tore his clothes, ripping them in front. He rebuked them, calling them cowards and saying that women were worth more than they. He asked from what they were fleeing; was it from unseen animals, since those from whom they fled were not men like they; why did they flee?

Saying these things to them, he forced them to return and ordered Atawalpa to go at their head with Huayna Capac himself. The men he had with him attacked their enemies with great energy. Since the enemies were spread out in pursuit of Atawalpa, Huayna Capac met them with great strength. He vanquished and captured them.

Pressing his victory, Huayna Capac himself en-tered a town which contained the house of that leader who was his enemy. He entered these houses intending to capture him. When he entered he found a pile of many blankets one on top of another. Think-ing that the enemy leader he was chasing was hiding under them, he began with his hands to remove the blankets. He took down the mound of them and found a very small Indian dwarf underneath.

When Huayna Capac uncovered him, the dwarf said: "Who has uncovered me? I wanted to sleep!" When Huayna Capac heard these words and saw the height of the dwarf, he was so amused that finding the dwarf pleased him as much as the victory that they had achieved over their enemies.

Later he told all his men that since he had cap-tured that dwarf in that battle all should regard him as his eldest son. Thus from that point on they all called the dwarf the eldest son of the Inca. And the dwarf called the children of the Inca brothers and sisters.

After having conquered and subjected these Indi-ans of the province of Yaguarcocha, Huayna Capac returned to Quito with his victory. According to their custom, he entered the city triumphantly be-cause of the victory he had achieved. He remained for six years in the city of Quito, resting and amusing himself as he had in Cuzco.

At the end of those six years in Quito, he fell ill and the illness took his reason and understanding and gave him a skin irritation like leprosy that greatly weakened him. When the nobles saw him so far gone they came to him; it seemed to them that he had come a little to his senses, and they asked him to name a lord since he was at the end of his days.

To them he replied that he named as lord his son Ninancuyochi, who was barely a month old and was in the province of the Cañares. Seeing that he had named such a baby, they understood that he was not in his right mind and they left him and went out. They sent for the baby Ninancuyochi, whom he had named as lord.

The next day they returned and entered and asked him again whom he named and left as ruler. He answered that he named as lord Atawalpa his son, not remembering that the day before he had named the above-mentioned baby. The nobles went immediately to the lodgings of Atawalpa, whom they told was now lord, and they gave him their respects as such. He told them that he had no wish to be the ruler even though his father had named him. The next day the nobles returned to Huayna Capac and in view of the fact that Atawalpa did not wish to be ruler, without telling him anything of what happened the day before, they asked him to name a lord and he told them it would be Huascar his son.

The nobles immediately placed Ragua Ocllo, the mother of Huascar, and her daughter Chuquihuipa in a room so that they might fast according to their usage and custom when some noble was named and the woman who was to be his principal wife.

Two nobles of Cuzco who were brothers of this Ragua Ocllo, called Xauxigualpa and Amurimachi, learned that Huascar had been named Inca and that Atawalpa did not wish to be. They sent the news to the nobles who were in Cuzco and to Huascar via the post service [i.e., running messengers using the Inca roads].

Huascar retired for a period of fasting after he heard the news in Cuzco. Here we will leave him and return to Huayna Capac, who was in his final days. After having named Huascar as ruler in the way we have described, he died in four days. After he died, the messengers who had gone for the baby who had been named as ruler by Huayna Capac returned. The baby had died the same day they arrived of the same leprous disease as his father.

A short time after these messengers arrived, others sent by the leaders of Tumbes arrived to see Huayna Capac. These messengers gave news of how some white and bearded men had arrived at the port of Tumbes. They came in a *ganbo*, which means a ship. It was like a building, so large that no one would get sick on it. They themselves had entered it and found them to be men who did no evil to anyone. They gave them those things that the messengers brought. These were *chaquira* [beads], diamonds [cut glass], combs, knives, and things from bartering, all of which the leaders sent to Huayna Capac. They found that he was dead and had died at that moment. . . .

When he died, the nobles who were with him had him opened and took out all his entrails, preparing him so that no damage would be done to him and without breaking any bone. They prepared and dried him in the Sun and air. After he was dried and cured, they dressed him in costly clothes and placed him on an ornate litter well adorned with feathers and gold.

When the body was prepared, they sent it to Cuzco. All the rest of the nobles who were there went with it, including the mother of Huascar and her daughter. Atawalpa remained in Quito with 100 nobles from the city of Cuzco, all kinsmen of his.

Examining the Evidence

1. In de Betanzos's account, what kind of ruler was the Inca Huayna Capac in his last days?
2. How does this passage treat the problem of Inca succession?
3. According to de Betanzos, what is made of the arrival of Europeans on Pacific shores at the time of Huayna Capac's death?

15.4 ANDEAN RELIGION

Huarochirí Manuscript (c. 1600)

Unlike Mexico and Guatemala, where many native-language writings have survived from the pre-Columbian and colonial periods, Andean documents in languages other than Spanish are rare. A remarkable exception is the *Huarochirí Manuscript*, composed in Quechua some time around 1600 by a native speaker trained by a Spanish priest to render the language phonetically. The manuscript was composed during a search for alleged idolaters in and around the village of Huarochirí, high in the Andes Mountains east of Lima and thus demonstrates a clear interest in locating shrines and other sacred places and objects. Although some post–Conquest elements such as Roman Catholic notions of sin and guilt creep into the narrative from time to time, the following passage relates the adventures of the deity Huayta Curi in a way that probably would not have differed much from precolonial oral narratives. In treating shamanism and relations between the sexes in a humorous and frank manner, for example, it is clearly Andean in tone and content.

These people, the ones who lived in that era, used to spend their lives warring on each other and conquering each other. For their leaders, they recognized only the strong and the rich. We speak of them as the Purum Runa, "people of desolation."

It was at this time that the one called Paria Caca was born in the form of five eggs on Condor Coto mountain.

A certain man, and a poor friendless one at that, was the first to see and know the fact of his birth; he was called Huayta Curi, but was also known as Paria Caca's son.

Now we'll speak of this discovery of his, and of the many wonders he performed.

They say that fellow called Huayta Curi subsisted at the time just by baking potatoes in earth pits, eating the way a poor man does, and people named him "Baked Potato Gleaner."

At that time there was another man named Tamta Ñamca, a very rich and powerful lord.

Both his own house and all his other [wives' and servants'] houses looked like *cassa* and *cancho* feather weavings, for they were thatched with wings of birds. His llamas were yellow llamas, red and blue llamas; he owned llamas of every hue.

Seeing that this man lived so well, people who came from all the villages paid him homage and worshiped him.

For his part, he pretended to be very wise and spent his life deceiving a whole lot of people with the little that he really knew.

Then this man called Tamta Ñamca, who pretended to be so wise, even to be a god, contracted a really horrible disease.

His illness went on for many years, and in time people talked. "How can a man who knows so much, who's so powerful, be so sick?" they said.

Just like the Spaniards who, on such occasions, summon experts and doctors, Tamta Ñamca, hoping to recover, summoned all sorts of shamans and wise men. But no one at all could diagnose that disease of his.

Just then Huayta Curi was coming from the vicinity of Ura Cocha, and he went to sleep on the mountain by which we descend to Sieneguilla. . . .

While he was sleeping, a fox who'd come up from down below and one who'd come from up above met face to face there. One fox asked the other, "Brother, how are things in Upper Villca?"

"What's good is good. But a lord in Anchi Cocha, a *villca* [literally "priest"] as a matter of fact, one who claims to know a whole lot, to be a god himself, is terribly ill. All the wise men who found their way to him are wondering, "Why's he so ill?" No one can identify his sickness. But his disease is this: while

Frank Salomon and George Urioste, eds. and trans., *The Huarochirí Manuscript: A Testament of Ancient and Colonial Andean Religion* (Austin: University of Texas Press, 1991), 54–57.

his wife was toasting maize, a grain of *muro* [speck-led] maize popped from the griddle and got into her private part.

"She picked it out and served it to a man to eat. Because of having served it, she became a sinner in relation to the man who ate it." . . .

"As a result of this fault," he told the fox who'd come from down below, "a snake has made its dwelling on top of that magnificent house and is eating them up. What's more, a toad, a two-headed one, lives under their grinding stone. And nobody is aware of these devouring animals."

And then he asked, "And how are people doing in Lower Villca, brother?"

The other fox answered similarly, saying, "There's a woman, the offspring of a great lord and a *villca*, who almost died because of a penis." . . .

As the foxes were telling each other these tidings, the man called Huayta Curi heard that the great lord who pretended to be a god was ill.

This great man had two daughters. He had joined the elder daughter to a fellow *ayllu* [community] member who was very rich. He married her.

The poor man called Huayta Curi came to the lord while he was still ill. When he arrived, he went around asking surreptitiously, "Isn't someone sick in this town?"

"It's my father who's sick," replied the younger daughter.

Huayta Curi answered, "Let's get together. For your sake I'll cure your father." . . .

The young woman didn't agree right away.

She told her father, "Father, there's a poor man here. He came and said to me, 'I'll cure your father.'"

All the wise men who were sitting there burst into laughter when they heard these words, and said, "If we ourselves can't cure him, how can this nobody make him well?"

But that lord wanted a cure so badly that he called for Huayta Curi. "Let him come, never mind what sort of man he is," he said.

When the great lord summoned him, Huayta Curi entered and said, "Father, if you want to get well, I'll make you well. But you'll have to give me your daughter."

Overjoyed, Tamta Ñamca replied, "Very well then!"

But when his older daughter's husband heard this proposition he flew into a rage. "How dare he join her, the sister-in-law of such a powerful man as me, to a nobody like that?" . . .

Huayta Curi began his cure by saying, "Father, your wife is an adulteress. Because she's an adulteress, a sinner, she's made you ill. As for what's eating you, it's the two snakes that dwell on top of this magnificent house of yours. And there's a toad, a two-headed one, that lives under your grinding stone."

"Now we'll kill them all. Then you'll get well. After you recover, you must worship my father [Paria Caca] above all things. He'll be born tomorrow or the day after. And as for you, you're not such a powerful man. If you were really powerful, you wouldn't be sick."

The rich man was astonished when Huayta Curi said this.

And when Huayta Curi said, "Now I'll take apart this gorgeous house of his," he became distraught. And his wife said, "This nobody, this crook, is slandering me! I'm no adulteress!"

Nonetheless the sick man wanted his health back very badly, and he let his house be dismantled. Then Huayta Curi removed the two snakes and killed them. Next he clearly explained the facts to the rich man's wife: just how a grain of *muro* maize had popped out and gotten in her private part, and how she, after picking it out, had served it to a man.

After that, the woman confessed everything. "It's all true," she said.

Next he had the grinding stone lifted. A toad, a two-headed one, came out from under it and fled to Anchi Cocha ravine.

It exists as a spring there to this day.

When the people come to that spring, it either makes them disappear or else drives them crazy.

Once Huayta Curi finished all these deeds the ailing man got well.

After Tamta Ñamca's recovery, on the day that had been foretold, Huayta Curi went for the first time to Condor Coto mountain.

It was there that the one called Paria Caca dwelled in the form of five eggs. All around him a wind rose up and began to blow.

In earlier times no wind had been observed.

Just before he went there on the appointed day, the man who'd recovered his health gave him his unmarried daughter.

While the two of them were traveling in the vicinity of that mountain they sinned together.

Examining the Evidence

1. Who are the main characters in this folk tale, and what is the central problem?
2. How is disease explained in this story from the *Huarochirí Manuscript*?
3. What is the resolution of this tale, and what does it tell us about Andean religious beliefs in the time of the Incas?

15.5 JESUIT VIEWS ON HURON SOCIETY

Jesuit Relations (1632–1637)

The native peoples of North America's Eastern Woodlands lacked a written language, but like most cultures worldwide, they possessed rich oral traditions and respected the men and women who memorized and recited mythical and historical narratives. As with most of the Mesoamerican and Andean sources included in this chapter, the earliest written sources date to the early post–Conquest era rather than pre-Columbian times and often were recorded by highly opinionated foreign soldiers or missionaries. In the case of the Huron of eastern Canada, it was French Jesuit missionaries who proved interested enough in their Native American cultural tradition to collect and translate what today would be regarded as ethnographic research. As can be seen in the selections in this document on shamanism and youthful sexuality, the Jesuits were unable to withhold moral judgments derived from their own Roman Catholic upbringing and training.

Variety of Huron Shamans

[The Hurons] say that the Sorcerers [i.e., shamans] ruin them; for if anyone has succeeded in an enterprise, if his trading or hunting is successful, immediately these wicked men bewitch him, or some member of his family, so that they have to spend it all in Doctors and Medicines. Hence, to cure these

and other diseases, there are a large number of Doctors whom they call *Arendiouane*. These persons, in my opinion, are true Sorcerers, who have access to the Devil. Some only judge of the evil, and that in diverse ways, namely, by Pyromancy, by Hydromancy, Necromancy, by feasts, dances, and songs; the others endeavor to cure the disease by blowing, by potions, and by other ridiculous tricks, which have neither any virtue nor natural efficacy. But neither class does anything without generous presents and good pay.

There are some Soothsayers [conjurers], whom they call also *Arendiouane* and who undertake to cause the rain to fall or to cease, and to predict future events. The Devil reveals to them some secrets, but with so much obscurity that one is unable to accuse them of falsehood; witness one of the village of *Scanonaenrat* . . . who, a little while before the [accidental] burning of the villages before mentioned, had seen in a dream three flames falling from the Sky on those villages. But the Devil had not declared to him the meaning of this enigma; for, having obtained from the village a white dog, to make a feast with it and to seek information by it, he remained as ignorant afterward as before.

Lastly, when I was in the house of [Amantacha, a Huron convert], an old woman, a sorceress, or female soothsayer of that village, said she had seen those who had gone to the war, and that they were

James Axtell, ed., *The Indian Peoples of Eastern America: A Documentary History of the Sexes* (New York: Oxford University Press, 1981), 73–75, 190.

bringing back a prisoner. We shall see if she has spoken the truth. Her method is by pyromancy. She draws for you in her hut the lake of the Iroquois; then on one side she makes as many fires as there are persons who have gone on the expedition, and on the other as many fires as they have enemies to fight. Then, if her spell succeeds, she lets it be understood that the fires from this side have run over, and that signifies that the warriors have already crossed the lake. One fire extinguishing another marks an enemy defeated; but if it attracts it to itself without extinguishing it, that is a prisoner taken at mercy.

It Takes a Village

We read that Caesar praised the Germans highly for having in their ancient savage life such continence as to consider it a very vile thing for a young man to have the company of a woman or girl before he was twenty years old. It is the reverse with the boys and young men of Canada, and especially with those of the Huron country, who are at liberty to give themselves over to this wickedness as soon as they can, and the young girls to prostitute themselves as soon as they are capable of doing so. Nay even the parents are often procurers of their own daughters; although I can truthfully say that I have never seen a single kiss given, or any immodest gesture or look, and for this reason I venture to assert that they are less prone to this vice than people here [in France]. This may be attributed partly to their lack of clothing, especially about the head, partly to the absence of spices and wine, and partly to their habitual use of tobacco, the smoke of which deadens the senses and ascends to the brain.

Many young men, instead of marrying, often keep and possess girls on terms of supplying food and fire, and they call them not wives, *Aténonha*, because the ceremony of marriage has not been performed, but *Asqua*, that is to say, companion, or rather concubine; and they live together for as long as it suits them, without that hindering the young man or the girl from going freely at times to see their other friends, male or female, and without fear of reproach or blame, such being the custom of the country.

But their preliminary marriage ceremony is this: when a young man wishes to have a girl in marriage he must ask her parents for her, without whose consent the girl cannot be his (although most frequently the girl does not accept their consent and advice, only the best and most sensible doing so). The lover who would make love to his mistress and obtain her good graces will paint his face and wear the finest adornments he can get, so as to appear more handsome; then he will make a present to the girl of some necklace, bracelet, or earring made of wampum [shell]. If the girl likes this suitor she accepts the present, whereupon the lover will come and sleep with her for three or four nights, and so far there is still no complete marriage nor promise of one made, because after they have slept together it happens quite often that the kindness is not maintained, and that the girl, who in obedience to her father has allowed this unauthorized favor, has in spite of it no affection for this suitor, and he must then withdraw without further steps. This happened in our time to a savage in regard to the second daughter of the great chief of Quieunonascaran, as the father of the girl himself complained to us, in view of the girl's obstinacy in not wishing to go on to the last marriage ceremony, because she did not like the suitor.

When the parties are agreed and the consent of the parents given, they proceed to the second marriage ceremony in the following manner. A feast is served of dog, bear, moose, fish, or other meat prepared for them, to which all the relations and friends of the espoused couple are invited. When all are assembled and seated, each according to his rank, all round the lodge, the father of the girl, or the master of ceremonies deputed to the office, announces before the whole gathering, pronouncing his words aloud and clearly, that such and such are being married and that it is for that reason the company is assembled and this feast of bear, dog, fish, etc., prepared for the enjoyment of all and to complete so worthy a proceeding. All meeting with approval, and the kettle cleaned out, everyone withdraws. Then all the women and girls bring the newly married wife a load of wood for her store, if she is married at the season when she cannot do it easily herself. . . .

If in course of time husband and wife like to separate for any reason whatever, or have no children, they are free to part, it being sufficient for the husband to say to the wife's relations and to herself that she is no good and may provide elsewhere for herself, and after that she lives in common with the rest until some other man seeks her out; and not only the men procure this divorce when their wives have given them some cause for doing so, but the wives also leave their husbands with ease when the latter do not please them. Hence it often happens that some woman spends her youth in this fashion, having had more than a dozen or fifteen husbands, all of whom nevertheless are not the only men to enjoy the woman, however much married they be; for after nightfall the young women and girls run about from one lodge to another, as do the young men for their part on the same quest, possessing them wherever it seems good to them, yet without any violence, leaving all to the wishes of the woman. The husband will do the like to his neighbor's wife and the wife to her neighbor, no jealousy intervening on that account, and no shame, disgrace, or dishonor being incurred.

But when they have children begotten from the marriage they rarely separate and leave one another except for some important reason, and when that does happen they are not long without being married again to someone else, notwithstanding their children, as to the possession of whom they come to an agreement.

Examining the Evidence

1. In the descriptions provided by the Jesuit observer in these selections, in what activities did male and female Huron shamans participate?
2. According to the Jesuit's observations, how did the Huron decide on mates and marriage partners, and how did they separate?
3. Given the opinions of the Jesuit author, how accurately do these passages reflect Huron life in the early modern period?

MAKING CONNECTIONS

1. What do these selections reveal about warfare and captive taking in the Americas?
2. How do these documents portray childhood and mating or marriage practices?
3. What insights do these readings offer on Native American humor and imagination?

CHAPTER 16

The Rise of an Atlantic World, 1450–1600

One of the great watersheds of world history was the connecting of Europe and Africa to the Americas following Columbus's famous 1492 voyage across the Atlantic. This linking of previously separate continents was often violent, marked by ongoing captive taking, conquest, and plunder. However, sometimes it also entailed peaceful endeavors such as trade or barter and proselytization, or the spread of religious ideas by missionaries. Columbus's voyage was preceded by many Portuguese endeavors in West and West Central Africa, which laid the groundwork for the transatlantic slave trade that would follow in Columbus's wake. They also shaped the eventual interactions of the Portuguese with native Brazilians. Although this was a time of European global expansion, Africans and Native Americans did not sit idly by or simply fall victim to European aggression. This selection of documents balances European and non-European reactions to contact and conquest. It also highlights some contrasting views, as a reminder that the creation of this new, "Atlantic" world was always being debated, reframed, and adjusted as different groups jostled for power, influence, wealth, and spiritual or temporal gratification.

16.1 "HOW THEY SAILED TO THE LAND OF THE BLACKS"

Gomes Eannes de Azurara, *During the Conquest of Guinea* (1453)

The Portuguese chronicler Gomes Eannes de Azurara (or "Zurara," c. 1410–1474) is one of very few authors to describe the first European voyages to West Africa. Most of Eannes de Azurara's accounts celebrate the deeds of Portuguese knights, navigators, and merchants in the service of Prince Henry, the famed sponsor of overseas endeavors. Much of what Eannes de Azurara wrote chronicled the conquest of Islamic enclaves in North Africa, such as Ceuta. The following passage relates a series of unprovoked Portuguese attacks on African settlers living near the mouth of the Senegal River in the early 1440s. The captives taken, including children, were among the very first victims of what we now call the transatlantic slave trade.

And now, perceiving that they could win no further profit in that land [Morocco] by reason of the news that the Moors had already received, the captains began to consult with the chief men of their ships concerning the manner of the action they should take.

"We," said some, "are not able, nor ought we to wait longer in this land, since we know that our stay brings no profit with it, but rather manifest loss, for we are wasting our provisions and wearying our bodies without hope of success. Wherefore it would be a counsel profitable for us, since God hath given us enough, that we should turn back to our country, contenting ourselves with the booty we have taken, the which is not so small that it will not be of value sufficient to compensate for our toils, and to save us from shame in the presence of our neighbors."

"Of a surety," replied others, "such a return would be shameful for such men as we are, for if we were to turn back in this way it would be indeed an abatement of our honor; but let us go to the land of the blacks, where Dinis Dias with only one ship went last year to make his capture [i.e., slave raid]; and even if we do nothing more than see the land, and afterwards give a relation thereof to the lord Infante [Prince Henry], this would be to our honor. Let us reach it, then, since we are so near, and though we accomplish but little, a great profit will be ours." All agreed that it was very well that they should go to that land, for it might be that God would give them a greater success than they expected.

And so they hoisted their sails forthwith and pursued their voyage, and sailing on their course a space of 80 leagues they came near the coast of Guinea, where they made them ready with their boats to land, but when the black men caught sight of them they ran down to the shore with their shields and assegais, as men who sought to make themselves ready for battle; but although they showed so fierce a countenance, yet our men would have gone on shore if the roughness of the sea had consented thereto; and, far as they were from the shore, our men did yet perceive that it was a land very green, peopled by human folk and tame cattle, which the inhabitants of the land had with them for their use. And they would have gone further on still, but the storm increased upon them with much disturbance of the weather, so that they were forced to turn back without remedy. . . .

[And later, a fleet under Gomes Pires returned on order of Prince Henry.] Now these caravels having passed by the land of Sahara, as hath been said, came in sight of the two palm trees that Dinis Dias had met with before, by which they understood that they were at the beginning of the land of the blacks. And at this sight they were glad indeed, and would have landed at once, but they found the sea so rough upon that coast that by no manner or means could they accomplish their purpose. And some of those who were present said afterwards that it was clear

Gomes Eannes de Azurara, *Chronicle of the Notable Deeds That Took Place During the Conquest of Guinea at the Behest of Prince Henry* (1453) (London: Hakluyt Society, 1899), 135–136, 176–183.

from the smell that came off the land how good must be the fruits of that country, for it was so delicious that from the point they reached, though they were on the sea, it seemed to them that they stood in some gracious fruit garden ordained for the sole end of their delight. And if our men showed on their side a great desire of gaining the land, no less did the natives of it show their eagerness to receive them into it; but of the reception they offered I do not care to speak, for according to the signs they made to our men from the first, they did not intend to abandon the beach without very great loss to one side or the other. Now the people of this green land are wholly black, and hence this is called the land of the blacks, or Land of Guinea. Wherefore also the men and women thereof are called "Guineas," as if one were to say "Black Men." . . .

[Eight men from the caravel of Vicente Dias then went ashore in a small boat near the mouth of the Senegal River.] And as all the eight were going in the boat, one of them, looking out towards the mouth of the river, espied the door of a hut, and said to his companions: "I know not how the huts of this land are built, but judging by the fashion of those I have seen before, that should be a hut that I see before me, and I presume it belongs to fishing folk who have come to fish in this stream. And if you think well, it seemeth to me that we ought to go and land beyond that point, in such wise that we may not be discovered from the door of the hut; and let some land, and approach from behind those sandbanks, and if any natives are lying in the hut, it may be that they will be taken before they are perceived." Now it appeared to the others that this was good advice, and so they began to put it into execution. And as soon as they reached the land, Estevão Afonso leapt out, and five others with him, and they proceeded in the manner that the other had suggested. And while they were going thus concealed even until they neared the hut, they saw come out of it a black boy, stark naked, with a spear in his hand. Him they seized at once, and coming up close to the hut, they lighted upon a girl, his sister, who was about eight years old. This boy the Infante [Prince Henry] afterwards caused to be taught to read and write, with all other knowledge that a Christian should have. . . .

And when they had captured those young prisoners and other booty [the spear and an elephant-skin shield], they took them forthwith to the boat. "Well were it," said "Estevão Afonso to the others, "if we were to go through this country near here, to see if we can find the father and mother of these children, for, judging by their age and disposition, it cannot be that the parents would leave them and go far off." The others said that he should go, with good luck, wherever he pleased, for there was nothing to prevent them from following him. And after they had journeyed a short way, Estevão Afonso began to hear the blows of an axe, or of some other iron instrument, with which someone was carpentering upon a piece of timber, and he stopped to assure himself of what he had heard, and put the others into the same attention. And then they all recognized that they were near what they sought. "Now," said he, "you come behind and allow me to go in front, because, if we all move forward in company, however softly we walk, we shall be discovered without fail, so that if we come at him, whosoever he be, if alone, he must run off and put himself in safety; but if I go softly and crouching down, I shall be able to capture him by a sudden surprise without his perceiving me; but do not be so slow of pace that you will come late to my aid, where perhaps I may be in such danger as to need you."

And they agreeing to this, Estevão Afonso began to move forward; and what with the careful guard that he kept in stepping quietly, and the intentness with which the Guinea labored at his work, he never perceived the approach of this enemy till the latter leapt upon him. And I say leapt, since Estevão Afonso was of small frame and slender, while the Guinea was of quite different build; and so he seized him lustily by the hair, so that when the Guinea raised himself erect, Estevão Afonso remained hanging in the air with his feet off the ground. The Guinea was a brave and powerful man, and he thought it a reproach that he should thus be subjected by such a small thing. Also he wondered within himself what this thing could be; but though he struggled very hard, he was never able to free himself, and so strongly had his enemy entwined himself in his hair, that the efforts of those two men could be compared to nothing else than a rash and fearless hound who has fixed on the ear of some mighty bull. And, to speak the truth, the help that the rest of the company were to render to Estevão Afonso seemed to be rather tardy, so that I believe that he was quite sorry at heart for having started this. And if at this point there had been room for a bargain, I know he would have deemed it profitable to leave his gain to secure himself from loss. But while those two were in their struggle, Afonso's companions came upon them, and seized the Guinea by his arms and neck in order to bind him. And Estevão Afonso, thinking that he was now taken into custody and in the hands of others, let go of his hair; whereupon, the Guinea, seeing that his head was free, shook off the others from his arms, flinging them away on either side, and began to flee. And it was of little avail to the others to pursue him, for his agility gave him a great advantage over his pursuers in running, and in his course he took refuge in a wood full of thick undergrowth; and while the others thought they had him, and sought to find him, he was already in his hut, with the intention of saving his children and taking his arms, which he had left with them. But all his former toil was nothing in comparison to the great grief which came upon him at the absence of his children, whom he found gone — but as there yet remained for him a ray of hope, and he thought that perchance they were hidden somewhere, he began to look towards every side to see if he could catch any glimpse of them. And at this appeared Vicente Dias, that trader who was the chief captain of the caravel to which the boat belonged wherein the others had come on land. And it seems that he, thinking he was only out to go for a walk along the shore, as he tended to do back in Lagos town [in southern Portugal], had not bothered to bring with him any arms except a boat hook. But the Guinea, as soon as he caught sight of him, burning with rage as you may well imagine, made for him with right good will.

And although Vicente Dias saw him coming on with such fury, and understood that for his own defense he should have had better arms, yet thinking that running would be of no use, but rather would do him harm in many ways, he awaited his enemy without showing him any sign of fear. And the Guinea rushing boldly upon him, gave him right off a wound in the face with his assegai [a kind of sword], with which he cut open the whole of one of his jaws; in return for this the Guinea received another wound, though not as serious as the one he had just bestowed. And because their weapons were not sufficient for such a struggle, they threw them aside and wrestled; and so for a short space they were rolling one over the other, each one striving for victory. And while this was proceeding, Vicente Dias saw another Guinea, one who was passing from youth to manhood; and he came to aid his countryman; and although the first Guinea was so strenuous and brave and inclined to fight with such good will as we have described, he could not have escaped being made prisoner if the second man had not come up: and for fear of him [the second man] he [Dias] now had to loose his hold of the first. And at this moment came up the other Portuguese, but the Guinea, being now once again free from his enemy's hands, began to put himself in safety with his companion, like men accustomed to running, little fearing the enemy who attempted to pursue them. And at last our men turned back to their caravels, with the small booty they had already stored in their boats.

Examining the Evidence

1. According to Eannes de Azurara's account, what seems to have motivated these early Portuguese slave raiders?
2. How did the Portuguese acquire slaves, and how did local inhabitants of Guinea respond?
3. How might such kidnapping raids in Guinea have set a tone for future relations?

16.2 FEARING CARIB CANNIBALS

Michele da Cuneo, *News of the Islands of the Hesperian Ocean* (1495)

Little is known of Michele da Cuneo (1450–?) except that he was a friend of Columbus born in the Italian town of Savona, near Genoa, and that he accompanied Columbus on his second voyage to the Caribbean. Da Cuneo's "self-incriminating" candor in the following letter from 1495 suggests he did not intend to seek favors from the king and queen of Spain. Cuneo appears to have been an experienced sailor, and Columbus named an island off Hispaniola's southeastern tip "Saona" in honor of his friend.

On 25 September 1493 we departed from Cádiz [in southern Spain] with seventeen vessels in excellent order with regard to every thing, that is, fifteen square-rigged and two lateen vessels, and on 2 October we reached Grand Canary. The following night we set sail and on the fifth of the same month we reached Gomera, one of the Canary Islands. If I were to tell you all we did there, what with the parading and bombard shots and fireworks, it would be too long to tell. This was done because of the lady of the place with whom our lord admiral had once been in love. There we supplied ourselves with what we needed. On 10 October we set sail on our direct course, but due to contrary weather we remained three days longer in the vicinity of the Canary Islands. On the morning of 13 October, a Sunday, we left behind the island of Hierro, the last of the Canary Islands and our course was west by south. On 26 October, the eve of Saints Simon and Jude, at about 4 p.m. a sea storm hit us in such a way that you would never have believed it. We thought our days had come to an end. It lasted all night until dawn in such a way that one ship lost sight of the other. Finally, as pleased God, we regrouped and on

3 November, a Sunday, we sighted land, that is, five unknown islands. Our lord admiral named the first Dominica for the day, Sunday, on which it was discovered; the second Mariagalante for love of the ship in which he sailed, which was called *María la Galante*. The two islands were not very large; nevertheless the lord admiral charted them. If I remember well, from the island Hierro to the island Mariagalante it took us twenty-two days, but I believe with a good wind one could cross over easily in sixteen days.

We obtained water and firewood at that island of Mariagalante, which was uninhabited though it is filled with trees and level. We sailed from there that same day and reached a big island populated by Cannibals, who, upon sighting us, immediately fled to the woods. We landed on that island and stayed there about six days, and the reason was that eleven of our men joined a raiding party and went five or six miles into the wilderness, so that when they wished to turn back, they were unable to find their way, even though they were all sailors and observed the sun, which they could not see well because of the thick and dense bush. In this situation, the lord admiral, observing that those men did not return and could not be found, sent 200 men divided into four squads, with trumpets, horns, and lanterns; and still with all this, they could not be found, and there was a moment when we feared more for the 200 than for the initial eleven. But the 200 returned (as pleased God) exhausted and very hungry. We believed the eleven had been eaten by those Cannibals, who are accustomed to doing that.

Nevertheless, at the end of five or six days, those eleven, as pleased God, although they had almost lost hope of ever finding us, made a fire above a cape. Sighting the fire we believed it was them, and we sent the boat to them, and by this means they were rescued. If it had not been for an old woman

Geoffrey Symcox and Blair Sullivan, *Christopher Columbus and the Enterprise of the Indies: A Brief History with Documents* (Boston: Bedford/St. Martin's, 2005), 87–90.

who showed them by signs the way, they were done for, because we intended to continue on our voyage the following day. On that island we seized twelve beautiful and very fat females, aged between fifteen and sixteen, with two boys of the same age whose genital members had been cut away clean to the belly. We figured that they had done it to keep them from mixing with their women or perhaps to fatten them up and eat them later. These boys and girls had been captured by the Cannibals; we sent them to Spain as an exhibit for the king. The lord admiral named that island Santa María de Guadalupe [now French Guadeloupe].

On 10 November we set sail from Guadalupe, which is occupied by the Cannibals, and on the fourteenth of that month we reached another beautiful and lush Cannibal island and made our way to a fine harbor. As soon as the Cannibals sighted us they fled toward the woods, just as they had done on the other island; they abandoned their houses, which we proceeded to and took whatever we wished. In those few days we discovered many islands where we did not land, but sometimes stood at anchor, that is, at night, and when we did not stand at anchor the ship hove-to, in order to avoid drifting and running into those islands, which, as they were so many and so close together, the lord admiral called them the 11,000 Virgin Islands [from the legend of St. Ursula], and he named the island mentioned before Santa Cruz.

One of those days while standing at anchor we saw a canoe (that is, a boat, for that is what they call it in their language) approaching from around a cape, with such a beating of oars as to look like a well-manned brigantine. There were three or four Cannibal men with two Cannibal women aboard, and two captured Indian slaves (as the Cannibals call their neighbors from the other islands) whose genital members they had also cut away clean to the belly so that they were still ailing. Since we were ashore with the captain's boat, as soon as we saw that canoe coming, we promptly jumped into the boat and gave chase to the canoe. As we were getting close to it, the Cannibals shot at us fiercely with their bows, so that had it not been for our shields they would have wounded half our number. You must know that one of the seamen who held a shield in his hand was struck by an arrow which passed through the shield and entered three fingers deep into his chest, so that he died in a few days. We captured that canoe as well as all those men, and one of the Cannibals was wounded by a lance in such a way that we thought he was dead; after leaving him for dead in the sea, we saw him suddenly start swimming. At this we seized him with the grapple and pulled him over the ship's edge where we cut off his head with a hatchet. We later sent the other Cannibals, together with their slaves, to Spain. While I was in the boat I laid my hands on a gorgeous Cannibal woman whom the lord admiral granted me; when I had her in my quarters, naked, as is their custom, I felt a craving to sport with her. When I tried to satisfy my craving, she, wanting none of it, gave me such a treatment with her nails that at that point I wished I had never started. At this, to tell you how it all ended, I got hold of a rope and thrashed her so thoroughly that she raised unheard-of cries that you would never believe. Finally we were of such accord that, in the act, I can tell you, she seemed to have been trained in a school of harlots. The lord admiral gave that cape the name Cabo de la Flecha because of the man who died there from the arrow. . . .

Examining the Evidence

1. What do you learn about the length and difficulty of the transatlantic voyage in da Cuneo's account of the second crossing?

2. How did Columbus's men interact with native peoples of the Caribbean? Does da Cuneo's labeling the natives "Cannibals" seem justified?

3. Is da Cuneo's account a narrative of discovery or something else?

NATIVE PEOPLES AND CONQUISTADORS NARRATE THE CONQUEST OF MEXICO

16.3   NAHUA ELDERS OF TLATELOLCO, *ACCOUNT OF THE CONQUEST OF MEXICO* (C. 1540S)

As seen in the previous chapter (Document 15.1), a main source of indigenous views of pre– and post–Conquest Mexican life comes from the so-called *Florentine Codex*, a vast collection of Nahuatl documents and drawings collated and edited by the Franciscan priest Bernardino de Sahagún. Contrary to his wishes, they were not published, and they drew serious scholarly attention only in the twentieth century. In the following selection, translated directly from the Nahuatl in the 1960s, elders from Tlatelolco recall the march of Cortés and his Tlaxcalan allies on Tenochtitlan, and the subsequent capture of their emperor, Moctezuma.

The Tlaxcalans guided, accompanied, and led them until they brought them to their palaces and housed them there. They showed them great honors, they gave them what they needed and attended to them, and then they gave them their daughters.

Then [the Spaniards] asked them, "Where is Mexico? What kind of place is it? Is it still far?"

They answered them, "It's not far now. Perhaps one can get there in three days. It is a very favored place, and the Mexica are very strong, great warriors, conquerors, who go about conquering everywhere."

Now before this there had been friction between the Tlaxcalans and the Cholulans. They viewed each other with anger, fury, hatred, and disgust; they could come together on nothing. Because of this they [the Tlaxcalans] persuaded the Spaniards to kill them treacherously.

They said to them, "The Cholulans are very evil; they are our enemies. They are as strong as the Mexica, and they are the Mexica's allies."

When the Spaniards heard this, they went to Cholula. The Tlaxcalans and Cempoalans went with them, outfitted for war. When they arrived, there was a general summons and cry that all the noblemen, rulers, subordinate leaders, warriors, and commoners should come, and everyone assembled in the temple courtyard. When they all came together, [the Spaniards and their allies] blocked the entrances, all of the places where one entered. Then people were stabbed, struck, and killed. No such thing was on the mind of the Cholulans; they did not meet the Spaniards with weapons of war. It just seemed that they were stealthily and treacherously killed, because the Tlaxcalans persuaded the Spaniards to do it.

And a report of everything that was happening was given and relayed to Moteuczoma. Some of the messengers arrived as others were leaving; they just turned around and ran back. There was no time when they were not listening, when reports were not being given. And all the common people went about in a state of excitement; there were frequent disturbances, as if the earth moved, as if everything were spinning before one's eyes. People were frightened.

And after the dying in Cholula, the Spaniards set off on their way to Mexico, coming gathered and bunched, raising dust. Their iron lances and halberds [lances fitted with axe heads] seemed to sparkle, and their iron swords were curved like a stream of water. Their cuirasses [breastplates] and iron helmets seemed to make a clattering sound. Some of them came wearing iron all over, turned into iron beings, gleaming, so that they aroused great fear and were generally seen with great fear and dread. Their dogs came in front, coming ahead of them, keeping to the front, panting, with their spittle hanging down. . . .

Thereupon Moteuczoma named and sent the noblemen and a great many other agents of his, with Tzihuacpopocatzin as their leader, to meet Cortés between [the volcanoes] Popocatepetl and Iztactepetl, at Quauhtechcac. They gave the Spaniards golden banners, banners of precious feathers, and golden necklaces.

Matthew Restall, Lisa Sousa, and Kevin Terraciano, eds., *Mesoamerican Voices: Native-Language Writings from Colonial Mexico, Oaxaca, Yucatan, and Guatemala* (New York: Cambridge University Press, 2005), 28–33.

And when they had given the things to them, they seemed to smile, to rejoice and be very happy. Like monkeys they grabbed the gold. It was as though their hearts were put to rest, brightened, renewed. For gold was what they thirsted for; they were gluttonous for it, starved for it, they piggishly wanted it. They came lifting up the golden banners, waving them from side to side, showing them to each other. They seemed to babble; they spoke to each other in a babbling tongue.

And when they saw Tzihuacpopocatzin, they said, "Is this one then Moteuzcoma?" They said it to the Tlaxcalans and Cempoalans, their lookouts, who came among them, questioning them secretly. They said, "It is not that one, our lords. This is Tzihuacpopocatzin, who is representing Moteuczoma."

The Spaniards said to him, . . . "Get out of here! Why do you lie to us? What do you take us for? You can't lie to us, you can't fool us, turn our heads, flatter us, make faces at us, trick us, blur our vision, distort things for us, put muddy hands on our faces. It is not you. Moteuczoma lives; he will not be able to hide from us, he will not be able to find refuge. Where will he go? Is he a bird? Will he fly? Or will he take an underground route? Will he go somewhere into a mountain that is hollow inside? We will see him, we will not fail to see his face and hear his words from his lips."

Thus they scorned and disregarded him, and so another of their meetings and greetings came to naught. They then went straight back, directly to Mexico. . . .

And when the Spaniards had come as far as Xoloco, when they had stopped there, Moteuczoma dressed and prepared himself for a meeting, along with other great rulers and high nobles, his rulers and nobles. . . . On gourd bases they set out different precious flowers; in the midst of the shield flowers and heart flowers stood popcorn flowers, yellow tobacco flowers, cacao flowers, made into wreaths for the head, wreaths to be girded around. And they carried golden necklaces, necklaces with pendants, wide necklaces.

And when Moteuczoma went out to meet them at Huitzillan, he gave various things to the war leader [Cortés], the commander of the warriors; he gave him flowers, he put necklaces on him, he put flower necklaces on him, he adorned him with flowers, he put flower wreaths on his head. Then he laid before him the golden necklaces, all the different things for greeting people. He ended by putting some necklaces on him.

Then Cortés said in reply to Moteuczoma, "Is it not you? Is it not you, then? Moteuczoma?"

Moteuczoma said, "Yes, it is me." Then he stood up straight, he stood up with their faces meeting. He bowed down deeply to him. He stretched as far as he could, standing stiffly. Addressing him, he said to him,

"O our lord, be doubly welcomed on your arrival in this land; you have come to satisfy your curiosity about your altepetl [city-state] of Mexico, you have come to sit on your seat of authority, which I have kept a while for you, where I have been in charge for you, for your agents the rulers Itzcoatzin, the elder Moteuczoma, Axayacatl, Tizoçic, and Ahuitzotl have gone, who for a very short time came to be in charge for you, to govern the altepetl of Mexico. It is after them that your poor commoner [myself] came. Will they come back to the place of their absence? If only one of them could see and behold what has now happened in my time, what I now see after our lords are gone! For I am not just dreaming, not just sleepwalking, not just seeing it in my sleep. I am not just dreaming that I have seen you, have looked upon your face. For a time I have been concerned, looking toward the mysterious place from which you have come, among clouds and mist. It is so, that the rulers on departing said that you would come in order to acquaint yourself with your altepetl and sit upon your seat of authority. And now it has come true, you have come. Be doubly welcomed, enter the land, go to enjoy your palace; rest your body. May our lords arrive in the land."

And when the speech that Moteuczoma directed to the marquis [Cortés] had concluded, Malintzin reported it to him, translating it for him. And when the marquis had heard what Moteuczoma had said, he spoke to Marina [Malintzin] in return, babbling back to them, replying in his babbling tongue, "Let Moteuczoma be at ease, let him be not afraid, for we greatly esteem him. Now we are truly satisfied to see him in person and hear him, for until now we have greatly desired to see him, to look upon his face. Well, now we have seen him, we have come to his homeland of Mexico. Little by little he will hear what we have to say."

Then the Spaniards took Moteuczoma by the hand. They came along with him, stroking his hair to show their good feeling. And the Spaniards looked at him, each of them giving him a close look. They would start along walking, then mount, then dismount again in order to see him.

(continued)

And as to each of the rulers who went with him, they were: first, Cacamatzin, ruler of Texcoco; second, Tetlepanquetzatzin, ruler of Tlacopan; third, the Tlacochcalcatl Itzquauhtzin, ruler of Tlatelolco; fourth, Topantemoctzin, Moteuczoma's storekeeper in Tlatelolco. These were the ones who went. And the other Tenochca [i.e., Aztec] noblemen were Atlixcatzin, the Tlacateccatl; Tepehuatzin, the Tlacochcalcatl; Quetzalaztatzin, the Ticocyahuacatl; Totomotzin; Ecatenpatiltzin; and Quappiaztzin. When Moteuczoma was taken prisoner, they not only hid themselves and took refuge, they abandoned him in anger. . . .

And when they had reached the palace and gone in, immediately they [the Spanish] seized Moteuczoma and kept close watch over him, not letting him out of their sight, and Itzquauhtzin (ruler of Tlatelolco) along with him. But the others were just allowed to come back out.

And when this happened, the various guns were fired. It seemed that everything became confused; people went this way and that, scattering and running about. It was as though everyone's tongue were out, everyone were preoccupied, everyone had been eating [hallucinogenic] mushrooms, as though who knows what had been shown to everyone. Fear reigned, as though everyone had swallowed his heart. It was still that way at night; everyone was terrified, taken aback, thunderstruck, stunned.

16.4 | HERNANDO CORTÉS, *A LETTER TO HOLY ROMAN EMPEROR CHARLES V (CHARLES I OF SPAIN)* (1519)

Hernando Cortés (1485–1547), like his distant cousin, Francisco Pizarro (who led the conquest of the Incas), was a native of the province of Extremadura in southwestern Spain. After serving in the conquest of Cuba, Cortés led a reconnaissance expedition to Mexico's Gulf Coast in 1519, sponsored by Cuba's governor, Diego de Velázquez. En route, Cortés acquired a young indigenous woman, known as Malintzin or La Malinche, to serve as interpreter. Once it became clear that he and his well-armed party might be able to reach the Aztec capital of Tenochtitlan, high in the mountainous interior, Cortés persuaded his followers to break ties with Governor Velázquez to share spoils among themselves should they achieve any conquests. As a breakaway leader trying to redeem himself and seek reward for his maverick efforts, Cortés wrote several formal letters directly to Charles I, king of Spain (also Charles V of the Holy Roman Empire). The following is a selection from Cortés's second letter.

The people of Tascalteca [the Tlaxcalans] . . . warned me many times not to trust Moctezuma's vassals [the Cholulans], for they were traitors and everything they did was done with treachery and cunning; and that in this manner they had subjugated the whole land. They warned me of all this as true friends, and inasmuch as they were people who were well acquainted with their behavior. When I saw the discord and animosity between these two peoples I was not a little pleased, for it seemed to further my purpose considerably; consequently I might have the opportunity of subduing them more quickly, for, as the saying goes, "divided they fall." And I remember that one of the Gospels says, "*Omne regnum in seipsum divisum desolabitur*" ["Every kingdom divided against itself is brought to desolation." Matthew 12:25]. So I maneuvered one against the other and

thanked each side for their warnings and told each that I held his friendship to be of more worth than the other's. . . .

. . . During the three days I remained in that city [Cholula] they fed us worse each day, and the lords and principal persons of the city came only rarely to see and speak with me. And being somewhat disturbed by this, my interpreter, who is an Indian woman [Malinche, or Malintzin] from Putunchan, which is the great river of which I spoke to Your Majesty in the first letter, was told by another Indian woman and a native of this city that very close by many of Moctezuma's men were gathered, and that the people of the city had sent away their children and all their belongings, and were about to fall on us and kill us all; and that if she wished to escape she should go with her and she would shelter her. All this she

Hernán Cortés, *Letters from Mexico*, ed. and trans. Anthony R. Pagden (New York: Orion Press, 1971), 69–88.

told to Gerónimo de Aguilar, an interpreter whom I acquired in Yucatan, of whom I have also written to Your Highness; and he informed me. I then seized one of the natives of this city who was passing by and took him aside secretly and questioned him; and he confirmed what the woman and the natives of Tascalteca [the Tlaxcalans] had told me. Because of this and because of the signs I had observed, I decided to forestall an attack, and I sent for some of the chiefs of the city, saying that I wished to speak with them. I put them in a room and meanwhile warned our men to be prepared, when a harquebus [musket-like gun] was fired, to fall on the many Indians who were outside our quarters and on those who were inside. And so it was done, that after I had put the chiefs in the room, I left them bound up and rode away and had the harquebus fired, and we fought so hard that in two hours more than three thousand men were killed. So that Your Majesty should realize how well prepared they were, even before I left my quarters they had occupied all the streets and had placed all their people at the ready, although, as we took them by surprise, they were easy to disperse, especially because I had imprisoned their leaders. I ordered some towers and fortified houses from which they were attacking us to be set on fire. And so I proceeded through the city fighting for five hours or more, leaving our quarters, which were in a strong position, secure. Finally all the people were driven out of the city in many directions, for some five thousand Indians from Tascalteca [Tlaxcalans] and another four hundred from Cempoala [near the Gulf Coast] were assisting me. . . .

At daybreak I departed for a town . . . called Amecameca. . . . In the aforementioned town we were quartered in some very good houses belonging to the lord of the place. And many persons who seemed to be of high rank came to speak with me, saying that Moctezuma, their lord, had sent them to wait for me there and to provide me with all that I might need. The chief of this province and town gave me as many as forty slave girls and three thousand *castellanos* [about 14 kg of gold], and, in the two days that we were there, he provided us very adequately with all the food we needed. On the following day, traveling with those messengers of Moctezuma who said that they had come to wait for me, I left and put up for the night four leagues from there in a small town which is by a great lake [Lake Texcoco]. . . .

On the following day I left this city and after traveling for half a league came to a causeway which runs through the middle of the lake for two leagues until it reaches the great city of Tenochtitlan, which is built in the middle of the lake. The causeway is as wide as two lances, and well built, so that eight horsemen can ride abreast. . . .

Thus I continued along this causeway, and half a league before the main body of the city of Tenochtitlan, at the entrance to another causeway which meets this one from the shore, there is a very strong fortification with two towers ringed by a wall of four yards wide with merloned [chimney-like] battlements all around commanding both causeways. There are only two gates, one for entering and one for leaving. Here as many as a thousand men came out to see and speak with me, important persons from that city, all dressed very richly after their own fashion. When they reached me, each one performed a ceremony which they practice among themselves; each placed his hand on the ground and kissed it. And so I stood there for nearly an hour until everyone had performed his ceremony. Close to this city there is a wooden bridge ten paces wide across a breach in the causeway to allow the water to flow, as it rises and falls. The bridge is also for the defense of the city, because whenever they so wish they can remove some very long broad beams of which this bridge is made. There are many such bridges throughout the city as later Your Majesty will see in the account I give of it.

After we had crossed this bridge, Moctezuma came to greet us and with him some two hundred lords, all barefoot and dressed in different costume, but also very rich in their way and more so than the others. They came in two columns, pressed very close to the walls of the street, which is very wide and beautiful and so straight that you can see from one end to the other. It is two-thirds of a league long and has on both sides very good and big houses, both dwellings and temples.

Moctezuma came down the middle of this street with two chiefs, one on his right hand and the other on his left. One of these was that great chief who had come on a litter to speak with me [earlier], and the other was Moctezuma's brother, chief of the city of Yztapalapa, which I had left that day. And they were all dressed alike except that Moctezuma wore sandals whereas the others went barefoot; and they held his arm on either side. When we met I dismounted and stepped forward to embrace him, but the two lords who were with him stopped me with their hands so that I should not touch him; and they likewise all performed the ceremony of kissing the earth. When this was over Moctezuma requested his brother to remain with me and to take me by the arm

(continued)

while he went a little way ahead with the other; and after he had spoken to me all the others in the two columns came and spoke with me, one after another, and then each returned to his column.

When at last I came to speak with Moctezuma himself I took off a necklace of pearls and cut glass that I was wearing and placed it round his neck; after we had walked a little way up the street a servant of his came with two necklaces, wrapped in a cloth, made from red snails' shells, which they hold in great esteem; and from each necklace hung eight shrimps of refined gold almost a span in length. When they had been brought he turned to me and placed them around my neck, and then continued up the street in the manner already described until we reached a very large and beautiful house which had been very well prepared to accommodate us. There he took me by the hand and led me to a great room facing the courtyard through which we entered. And he bade me sit on a very rich throne, which he had had built for him and then left saying that I should wait for him. After a short while, when all those of my company had been quartered, he returned with many and various treasures of gold and silver and featherwork, and as many as five or six thousand cotton garments, all very rich and woven and embroidered in various ways. And after he had given me these things he sat on another throne which they placed there next to the one on which I was sitting, and addressed me in the following way:

"For a long time we have known from the writings of our ancestors that neither I, nor any of those who dwell in this land, are natives of it, but foreigners who came from very distant parts; and likewise we know that a chieftain, of whom they were all vassals, brought our people to this region. And he returned to his native land and after many years came again, by which time all those who had remained were married to native women and had built villages and raised children. And when he wished to lead them away again they would not go nor even admit him as their chief; and so he departed. And we have always held that those who descended from him would come and conquer this land and take us as their vassals. So because of the place from which you claim to come, namely, from where the sun rises, and the things you tell us of the great lord or king who sent you here, we believe and are certain that he is our natural lord, especially as you say that he has known of us for some time. So be assured that we shall obey you and hold you as our lord in place of that great

sovereign of whom you speak; and in this there shall be no offense or betrayal whatsoever. And in all the land that lies in my domain, you may command as you will, for you shall be obeyed; and all that we own is for you to dispose of as you choose. Thus, as you are in your own country and your own house, rest now from the hardships of your journey and the battles which you have fought, for I know full well of all that has happened to you from Puntunchan [Tabasco] to here, and I know how those of Cempoala and Tlaxcala have told you much evil of me; believe only what you see with your eyes, for those are my enemies, and some were my vassals, and have rebelled against me at your coming and said those things to gain favor with you. I also know that they have told you the walls of my houses are made of gold, and that the floor mats in my rooms and many other things in my household are likewise of gold, and that I was, and claimed to be, a god; and many other things besides. The houses as you see are of stone and lime and clay."

Then he raised his clothes and showed me his body, saying, as he grasped his arms and trunk with his hands, "See that I am of flesh and blood like you and all other men, and I am mortal and substantial. See how they have lied to you? It is true that I have some pieces of gold left to me by my ancestors; anything I might have shall be given to you whenever you ask. Now I shall go to other houses where I live, but here you shall be provided with all that you and your people require, and you shall receive no hurt, for you are in your own land and your own house." . . .

Most Invincible Lord [Charles V], six days having passed since we first entered this great city of Tenochtitlan, during which time I had seen something of it, though little compared with how much there is to see and record, I decided from what I had seen that it would benefit Your Royal service and our safety if Moctezuma were in my power and not in complete liberty, in order that he should not retreat from the willingness he showed to serve Your Majesty; but chiefly because we Spaniards are rather obstinate and persistent, and should we annoy him he might, as he is so powerful, obliterate all memory of us. Furthermore, by having him with me, all those other lands which were subject to him would come more swiftly to the recognition and service of Your Majesty, as later happened. I resolved, therefore, to take him and keep him in the quarters where I was, which were very strong.

<table>
<tr><td>**16.5**</td><td>**BERNAL DÍAZ DEL CASTILLO, *A FOOT SOLDIER RECALLS THE MARCH TO TENOCHTITLAN* (C. 1560)**</td></tr>
</table>

Although he was never mentioned by Cortés (who rarely referred to anyone other than his lieutenants by name in his letters to Charles V), Bernal Díaz del Castillo (c. 1492–1584) served as a foot soldier in the conquest of Mexico. Late in life, as an *encomienda* holder living in Guatemala, Díaz read a published account of the Conquest written by a non-eyewitness. He was so annoyed by its inaccuracies that he composed what he called the "True History of the Conquest of New Spain." He sent the manuscript off to Spain to be published in the 1570s, not long before his death in 1584, but it was not printed until 1632.

One morning we started on our march to the city of Cholula and that day we went on to sleep at a river which runs within a short league of the city, and there they put up for us some huts and ranchos. This same night the caciques [headmen] of Cholula sent some chieftains to bid us welcome to their country, and they brought supplies of poultry and maize bread, and said that in the morning all the caciques and priests would come out to receive us, and they asked us to forgive their not having come sooner. Cortés thanked them both for the food they had brought and for the good will which they showed us.

At dawn we began to march and the caciques and priests and many other Indians came out to receive us; most of them were clothed in cotton garments made like tunics. They came in a most peaceful manner and willingly, and the priests carried braziers containing incense with which they fumigated our Captain [Cortés] and us soldiers who were standing near him. When these priests and chiefs saw the Tlaxcalan Indians who came with us, they asked Doña Marina [Malintzin] to tell the General [Cortés] that it was not right that their enemies with arms in their hands should enter their city in that manner. When our Captain understood this, he ordered the soldiers and baggage to halt, and, when he saw us all together and that no one was moving, he said: "It seems to me, Sirs, that before we enter Cholula these caciques and chiefs should be put to the proof with a friendly speech, so that we can see what their wishes may be; for they come complaining of our friends the Tlaxcalans and they have much cause for what they say, and I want to make them understand in fair words the reason why we come to their city, and as you gentlemen already know, the Tlaxcalans have told us that the Cholulans are a turbulent people, and, as it would be a good thing that by fair means they should render their obedience to His Majesty [Charles V], this appears to me to be the proper thing to do."

Then he told Doña Marina to call up the caciques and priests to where he was stationed on horseback with all of us around him, and three chieftains and two priests came at once, and they said: "Malinche [the name used by this time for Cortés in combination with Malintzin], forgive us for not coming to Tlaxcala to see you and bring food, it was not for want of good will but because [the Tlaxcalans] are our enemies, and have said many evil things of us and of the Great Moctezuma our Prince, and as though what they said were not enough, they now have the boldness, under your protection, to come armed into our city, and we beg you as a favor to order them to return to their country, or at least stay outside in the fields and not to enter our city in such a manner." But as for us they said that we were very welcome.

As our Captain saw that what they said was reasonable, he at once sent Pedro de Alvarado and Cristóbal de Olid to ask the Tlaxcalans to put up their huts and ranchos there in the fields, and not to enter the city with us, excepting those who were carrying the cannon, and our friends from Cempoala, and he told them to explain to the Tlaxcalans that the reason why he asked them to do so was that all the caciques and priests were afraid of them, and that when we left Cholula on our way to Mexico [Tenochtitlan] we would send to summon them, and that they were not to be annoyed at what he was doing. When the people of Cholula knew what Cortés had done, they appeared to be much more at ease.

Then Cortés began to make a speech to them, saying that our Lord and King had sent us to these countries to give them warning and command them not to worship idols, nor sacrifice human beings, or eat their flesh, and as the road to Mexico [Tenochtitlan], whither we were going to speak with the Great Moctezuma, passed by there and there was no other shorter road, we had come to visit their city and to treat them as brothers. As other great caciques had given their obedience to His Majesty, it would be well that they should give theirs as the others had done.

Bernal Díaz del Castillo, *The Discovery and Conquest of Mexico*, ed. Irving Leonard, trans. Alfred P. Maudslay (New York: Farrar, Straus, and Cudahy, 1956), 169–227.

(continued)

They replied that we had hardly entered into their country, yet we already ordered them to give up their Teules [gods], and that they could not do it. As to giving their obedience to our King, they were content to do so. And thus they pledged their word, but it was not done before a notary. When this was over we at once began our march towards the city, and so great was the number of people who came out to see us that both the streets and the house tops were crowded, and I do not wonder at this for they had never seen men such as we are, nor had they ever seen horses.

They lodged us in some large rooms where we were all together with our friends from Cempoala and the Tlaxcalans who carried the baggage, and they fed us on that day and the next very well and abundantly.

After the people of Cholula had received us in the festive manner already described, and most certainly with a show of good will, it presently appeared that Moctezuma sent orders to his ambassadors, who were still in our company, to negotiate with the Cholulans that an army of 20,000 men which Moctezuma had sent and equipped should, on entering the city, join with them in attacking us by night or by day, get us into a hopeless plight and bring all of us that they could capture bound to Mexico [Tenochtitlan]. And he sent many presents of jewels and cloths, also a golden drum, and he also sent word to the priests of the city that they were to retain twenty of us to sacrifice to their idols. . . .

Then Cortés told them that the royal laws decreed that such treasons as those should not remain unpunished and that for their crime they must die. Then he ordered a musket to be fired, which was the signal that we had agreed upon for that purpose, and a blow was given to them which they will remember forever, for we killed many of them, so that they gained nothing from the promises of their false idols.

Not two hours passed before our allies, the Tlaxcalans, arrived, and they had fought very fiercely where the Cholulans had posted other companies to defend the streets and prevent their being entered, but these were soon defeated. The Tlaxcalans went about the city, plundering and making prisoners and we could not stop them, and the next day more companies from the Tlaxcalan towns arrived, and did great damage, for they were very hostile to the people of Cholula, and when we saw this, both Cortés and the captains and the soldiers, on account of

the compassion that we had felt, restrained the Tlaxcalans from doing further damage. . . .

Just as we were starting our march to Mexico there came before Cortés four Mexican [Aztec] chiefs sent by Moctezuma who brought a present of gold and cloths. After they had made obeisance according to their custom, they said: "Malinche, our lord the Great Moctezuma sends you this present and says that he is greatly concerned for the hardships you have endured in coming from such a distant land in order to see him, and that he has already sent to tell you that he will give you much gold and silver and chalchihuites [greenstones] as tribute for your Emperor and for yourself and the other Teules [gods] in your company, provided you do not come to Mexico, and now again he begs as a favor, that you will not advance any further but return whence you have come." . . .

During the morning we arrived at a broad causeway and continued our march toward Iztapalapa, and when we saw so many cities and villages built in the water and other great towns on dry land and that straight and level causeway going towards Mexico [Tenochtitlan], we were amazed and said that it was like the enchantments they tell of in the legend of Amadis [of Gaul], on account of the great towers and *cues* [temple-pyramids] and buildings rising from the water, and all built of masonry. And some of our soldiers even asked whether the things that we saw were not a dream. It is not to be wondered at that I here write it down in this manner, for there is so much to think over that I do not know how to describe it, seeing things as we did that had never been heard of or seen before, not even dreamed about. . . .

. . . When we arrived near to Mexico, where there were some other small towers, the Great Moctezuma got down from his litter, and those great caciques supported him with their arms beneath a marvelously rich canopy of green colored feathers with much gold and silver embroidery and with pearls and [greenstones] suspended from a sort of bordering, which was wonderful to look at. The Great Moctezuma was richly attired according to his usage, and he was shod with sandals, the soles were of gold and the upper part adorned with precious stones. The four chieftains who supported him were also richly adorned according to their usage, in garments which were apparently held ready for them on the road to enable them to accompany their prince, for they did not appear in such attire when they came to receive us [earlier]. Besides these four chieftains, there were four other great caciques who supported the canopy over their heads, and many other lords who walked before the Great Moctezuma, sweeping the ground where he would tread and spreading cloths on it, so that he should not tread on the earth. Not one of these chieftains dared even to think of looking him in the face, but kept their eyes lowered with great reverence, except those four relations, his nephews, who supported him with their arms.

When Cortés was told that the Great Moctezuma was approaching, and he saw him coming, he dismounted from his horse, and when he was near Moctezuma, they simultaneously paid great reverence to one another. Moctezuma bade him welcome and our Cortés replied through Doña Marina [Malintzin] wishing him very good health. And it seems to me that Cortés, through Doña Marina, offered him his right hand, and Moctezuma did not wish to take it, but he did give his hand to Cortés and then Cortés brought out a necklace which he had ready at hand, made of glass stones, which I have already said are called Margaritas [seed-pearls], which have within them many patterns of diverse colors, these were strung on a cord of gold and with musk so that it should have a sweet scent, and he placed it round the neck of the Great Moctezuma and when he had so placed it he was going to embrace him, and those great princes who accompanied Moctezuma held back Cortés by the arm so that he should not embrace him, for they considered it an indignity.

Then Cortés through the mouth of Doña Marina told him that now his heart rejoiced at having seen such a great prince, and that he took it as a great honor that he had come in person to meet him and had frequently shown him such favor.

Then Moctezuma spoke other words of politeness to him, and told two of his nephews who supported his arms, the lord of Texcoco and the lord of Coyoacán, to go with us and show us to our quarters, and Moctezuma with his other two relations, the lord of Cuitlahuac and the lord of Tacuba who accompanied him, returned to the city, and all those grand companies of caciques and chieftains who had come with him returned in his train. As they turned back after their prince we stood watching them and observed how they all marched with their eyes fixed on the ground without looking at him, keeping close to the wall, following him with great reverence. Thus space was made for us to enter the streets of Mexico, without being so much crowded. But who could now count the multitude of men and women and boys who were in the streets and on the azoteas [roof terraces], and in canoes on the canals, who had come out to see us. It was indeed wonderful, and, now that I am writing about it, it all comes before my eyes as though it had happened but yesterday. . . .

. . . [Days later] four of our captains took Cortés aside in the [makeshift] church, with a dozen soldiers in whom he trusted and confided, and I was one of them, and we asked him to look at the net and trap in which we found ourselves, and to consider the great strength of that city, and observe the causeways and bridges, and to think over the words of warning that we had been given in all the towns we had passed through, that Moctezuma had been advised by his Huitzilopochtli to allow us to enter into the city, and when we were there, to kill us. That he [Cortés] should remember that the hearts of men are very changeable, especially those of Indians, and that he should not repose trust in the good will and affection that Moctezuma was showing us, for at some time or other, when the wish occurred to him, he would order us to be attacked, and by the stoppage of our supplies of food or water, or by the raising of any of the bridges, we should be rendered helpless. Then, considering the great multitude of Indian warriors that Moctezuma had as his guard, what should we be able to do either in offense or defense? And as all the houses were built in the water, how could our friends the Tlaxcalans enter and come to our aid? He should think over all this that we had said, and if we wished to safeguard our lives, that we should at once, without further delay, seize Moctezuma and should not wait until the next day to do it.

COMPARING THE EVIDENCE

1. How do these different writers characterize regional rivalries among the Aztecs, Tlaxcalans, Cholulans, and other native peoples in highland Mexico at the time of the Spanish arrival in 1519?

2. How was the Spanish attack on the Cholulans justified, according to the authors of these documents?

3. How do the writers describe the Spanish and their allies' entrance to Tenochtitlan and the first encounter between Moctezuma and Cortés? Why is Moctezuma seized?

4. What role does the interpreter Malintzin ("La Malinche") play in each account?

16.6 NATIVE ALLIES WITH A GRIEVANCE

Nahua Nobles of Xochimilco, *Letter to the King of Spain* (1563)

The following letter from Nahuatl-speaking nobles from the city-state, or altepetl, of Xochimilco [show-chee-MEAL-coh] is one of many from the early post–Conquest era written by indigenous allies of the Spanish conquistadors asking to be recognized for their service, either as porters, fighters, or suppliers of food, shelter, and critical information. Most of these groups were chagrined to find themselves treated like conquered subjects soon after being recruited as "co-conquistadors." In hopes of getting the king's ear, the nobles wrote this letter in Spanish rather than Nahuatl.

Sacred Catholic Royal Majesty

We the caciques (lords) and Indians who are natives of the city of Xochimilco, which is a part of the royal crown and is five leagues from Mexico City in New Spain, humbly implore your majesty and your royal council of the Indies to be informed that we did not make war against nor resist the Marquis of Valle [Cortés] and the Christian army. Rather we aided and favored them then and in the time since in whatever has presented itself. So that the said Marquis could take Mexico City, we gave him 2,000 canoes in the lake, loaded with provisions, with 12,000 fighting men, with which they were aided and with whom they won Mexico City. As for the Tlaxcalans, since they came from a distant land, fatigued and without supplies, they were aided also. And the true help, after God's, was what Xochimilco gave.

In addition to this, we served your majesty in the conquest of Honduras and Guatemala with Adelantado [Pedro de] Alvarado, our *encomendero*. We gave him 2,500 fighting men for the voyage and all the provisions and other things necessary. As a result those jurisdictions were won and put under the royal crown, because the Spaniards were few and poorly supplied and were going through lands where they would not

have known the way if we had not shown them; a thousand times we saved them from death.

In addition, when the said Marquis and the said Adelantado Alvarado went to conquer the province of Pánuco, where there were as many men as leaves of grass, we helped them with many provisions and munitions and with 500 fighting men who went with them. Along with those who went to Honduras and Guatemala, none returned, because all died of the cruel, hard labor.

Likewise, we served your majesty in the conquest of Jalisco with Nuño de Guzmán, and we gave him 600 fighting men with many supplies and munitions, and they served the Spaniards, your majesty's soldiers; with this aid the said kingdom was won, and not an Indian returned home. And since we have done your majesty so many services and we are poor and have been dispossessed of many lands and jurisdictions that the Marquis and other judges who have governed took away from us, confident that we know little of litigation and cannot defend ourselves . . . , and aside from the prejudice and loss suffered by the said city, the damage pertains to the royal crown whose vassals we are. For all of these reasons we implore — without long lawsuits but immediately on the establishment of the truth — that restitution be made, since all of it is almost at the walls of Mexico City, from where the Spanish citizens are sustained and supplied. And since your majesty gave great boons and privileges to Tlaxcala, it is only fair that your majesty should show the same favors to us, who have served no less.

Examining the Evidence

1. What do the Xochimilco elders claim to have done when Cortés arrived in the Aztec capital?
2. How did the Nahua continue to serve the Spanish following the conquest of the Aztecs?
3. Why might the Nahua elders make such claims to the king of Spain more than forty years after the conquest?

Matthew Restall, Lisa Sousa, and Kevin Terraciano, eds., *Mesoamerican Voices: Native-Language Writings from Colonial Mexico, Oaxaca, Yucatan, and Guatemala* (New York: Cambridge University Press, 2005), 66–67.

16.7 A CAPTIVE IN BRAZIL

Hans Staden, *True History* (1557)

While on a Spanish vessel bound for Río de la Plata in the summer of 1549, Hans Staden (c. 1525–1579), a young German gunner, became shipwrecked in Brazil. Because of his expertise with cannons, he was quickly employed by the Portuguese in a small coastal fort near São Vicente, southwest of Rio de Janeiro. In 1550, Staden was captured by Tupinamba warriors allied with the French, who were then competing with the Portuguese for control of the lucrative trade in Brazilian dyewood, pepper, and exotic animals. Sugar production for export was also under way. Originally expecting to be executed and possibly eaten, Staden survived thanks to a variety of chance circumstances and was rescued by French traders after nine months' captivity. He lived to write down his extraordinary tale, which he presented as a divine test of his Catholic faith, soon after returning to Germany. His *True History* was published in German in Marburg and Frankfurt in 1557.

I had a savage man from a group called Carijós. He was my slave. He caught game for me, and I sometimes went along with him, into the forest.

However, after some time it so happened that a Spaniard from São Vicente came to me in the fort where I lived, on the island of São Maro that lies 5 miles away. A German called Heliodorus Hesse, son of the late Eobanus Hesse, also came along with him. He had been stationed on the island of São Vicente in an *engenho* [mill] where they make sugar. This *engenho* belonged to a Genoese named Giuseppe Adorno. He was the clerk and manager of the merchants who belonged to the *engenho*. (The houses where sugar is made are called engenho.)

I had had dealings with this Heliodorus before. When I was shipwrecked with the Spaniards, I met him on the island of São Vicente, and he had been friendly to me. He came to see how I was doing, for he had probably heard that I was rumored to be ill. The day before, I had sent my slave into the forest to hunt for game. I wanted to follow the next day to fetch the catch, so we might have something to eat, for in that country there is little to be had, except what comes out of the wilderness.

As I was walking through the forest, loud screaming—such as that made by savages—sounded both sides of the path. People came running towards me. Then I recognized them. They had surrounded me on all sides and were pointing their bows and arrows at me and shot at me. Then I cried out: May God now have mercy on my soul. I had scarcely uttered these words, when they beat me to the ground, and shot and stabbed at me. God be praised that they only wounded me in the leg. They tore the clothes from my body: one the jerkin [tight jacket], the other the hat, a third the shirt, and so forth. Then they began to quarrel over me. One said that he had gotten to me first, another protested that it was he who captured me. In the meanwhile, the rest hit me with their bows. Finally, two of them seized me and lifted me up from the ground, naked as I was. One of them grabbed one of my arms, another took the other one; several stayed behind me, while others were in front. Thus they carried me swiftly through the forest towards the sea, where they had their canoes. As they brought me to the sea, I saw the canoes about a stone's throw away. They had dragged them out of the water and hidden them behind the bushes. A great crowd was gathered next to them. As soon as they saw how I was being led there, they all rushed towards me. They were all decorated with feathers according to their custom, and they bit their arms, threatening me that they wanted to eat me in this way. A king walked in front of me, carrying the club with which they kill their captives. He preached and told them how they had captured me, their slave, the Perot (that is how they name the Portuguese). They would now avenge the deaths of their friends on me. And as they brought me to the canoes, several among them beat me with their fists. . . .

Hans Staden, *Hans Staden's True History: An Account of Cannibal Captivity in Brazil*, ed. and trans. Neil L. Whitehead and Michael Harbsmeier (Durham, NC: Duke University Press, 2008), 47–49, 54–56, 82–83, 97–99.

When we came close to their dwellings, it turned out to be a small village with seven huts, called Ubatuba. We landed on a beach by the sea. Close by, their women had a field with the root vegetables, which they call manioc. Many of their women were walking in the field, tearing up roots. I had to shout to them in their language: *A Junesche been ermi vramme*, which means: I, your food, am coming.

As we now landed, all of them, both young and old, came running out of the huts, which were built on a hill, to look at me. The men went to their huts with their bows and arrows, and left me to their women. They led me along, some in front and some behind, dancing and singing a song—the song which they usually sing to their own people, when they want to eat them. . . .

The women led me away, some by the arms, some by the rope around my neck, pulling it so hard that I could hardly breathe. While they were dragging me with them, I was unsure about what they wanted to do with me. I began to think about the suffering our Savior Jesus Christ suffered innocently at the hands of the mean Jews. In this way, I comforted myself and was all the more patient. They then brought me to the hut of their king who was called Guaratinga-açú; in German this means the Great White Bird. There was a small heap of fresh earth in front of this hut. They brought me to it and placed me there, and several held me fast. I was certain that they would slay me there at once. They answered: not yet. Then a woman from the crowd approached me. She had a sliver made out of crystal fastened to a thing that looked like a bent branch, and she scraped off my eyebrows with this crystal. She also wanted to scrape off the beard around my mouth, but I would not suffer this and said that she should kill me with my beard. Then they answered that they did not want to kill me yet and left me my beard. But a few days later, they cut it off with a pair of scissors, which the Frenchmen had given to them. . . .

[Staden then endured six months in captivity, during which he made several failed escape attempts.] Some eight days before the savages planned to set out for war, a French ship had arrived in a harbor, which the Portuguese call Rio de Janeiro and which is called Niterói in the language of the savages.

There, the French usually load brazil wood. Thus, they now also arrived with their boat at the village where I was kept, and bargained with the savages for pepper, long-tailed monkeys, and parrots. One of the crew came ashore in the boat. He was called Jacob and knew the language of the savages. While he was trading with them, I begged him to bring me along to his ship. However, my master said that no, they would not send me there like that. Rather they wanted to have many goods [as a ransom] for me. Then I told them to bring me to the ship themselves; my friends would give them plenty of goods. They said no, these are not your real friends.

For those who have arrived with the boat would surely have given you a shirt, since you walk around naked; but they do not care about you at all (which was true). Yet, I told them that they would clothe me when I reached the big ship. They said that the ship would not depart right away; they first had to go to war, but when they returned, they would take me there. Now the boat [with the French traders] then wanted to travel on, because it had already anchored for one night at the village.

Now when I saw that they wanted to sail off again with the boat, I thought: O merciful God, if the ship now also sails away without taking me along, I am surely going to die among them [the savages], for this is a people one cannot trust.

With these thoughts [in mind], I left the hut, going towards the water, but the savages saw me and came after me. I ran in front of them, and they wanted to catch me. The first man that caught up with me, I struck him down. The whole village was running after me, but I escaped them and swam to the boat. When I tried to climb into the boat, the Frenchmen pushed me away, for they thought that if they took me along without the consent of the savages, these might rise against them and become their enemies. Depressed, I swam back to the shore and thought: now I see that it is God's will that I should remain in misery for some time. If I had not tried to escape, then I should have blamed myself afterwards.

As I now returned to shore, they rejoiced and said: Look at that, he is coming back. Then I got angry with them and said: Do you think that I wanted to run away from you like that? I went to the boat to tell my people that they should prepare themselves. Thus, they will have gathered a lot of goods to give you when you return from war and bring me here [to the ships again]. This pleased them and they were once again content. . . .

[Some weeks later] news was brought to me by the savages that two men had arrived from . . . [a different French] ship. I was happy and went to them and greeted them in the savage language. As they now saw me walking about so miserably, they were filled with pity and gave me some of their clothes. I asked them why they had come. They said that it was because of me; they had been given orders to take me to the ship, using whatever means necessary. Then my heart rejoiced at the mercy of God. I told one of them, who was called Perot and knew the savage tongue, that in order for the savages to take me to the ship, he had to pretend he was my brother, who had brought me several chests full of merchandise, which they [the savages] would then want to collect. He was also to tell the savages that I would then remain with them to gather pepper and other goods until the ship returned again, next year. Everyone aboard the ship had pity on me and showed me great kindness. After we had been some five days on the ship, the savage king Abatí-poçanga, to whom I had been given, asked me for the chests [of goods]. He said that I should have them give these to me, so that we might return home in time. I reported his intent to the commander of the ship. He ordered me to put him [King Abatí-poçanga] off until his ship had taken a full cargo, so that they would not become angry and plan some mischief or plot some treachery when they saw that they were going to keep me on the ship; for they were a people that you could not trust. However, my master had set his mind on taking me home. Yet, I put him off with empty words for some time, telling him not to be in such a hurry: he ought to know that when good friends get together, they cannot part at once. However, once they [the Frenchmen] wanted to sail away with the ship, we would then also be on our way back to his hut. Thus I stalled him.

At last the ship was ready to set sail and the Frenchmen all gathered on the ship. I stood next to them and the king, my master, was also there together with those [savages] he had taken along. Then the ship's captain spoke to the savages through his interpreter: he was very pleased that they had not killed me after they had captured me among their enemies. He also told them (in order to get me away from them with more decency) that he had ordered me to be brought from land to the ship so that he might give them something in return for having taken such good care of me. He also wanted to give me goods and leave me, who was familiar with them, to collect pepper and other useful goods, until he returned again. We had arranged between us that some ten crewmen, who more or less resembled me, should now gather together and pretend to be my brothers, who wanted to take me home. This resolve was presented to them: these brothers of mine would on no account allow me to return on land with the savages. They wanted me to return home, for my father longed to see me once more before he died. Then the captain let them [the savages] know that he was the commander of the ship and wanted me to return to shore with them. However, he was only one man, he said, and my brothers were many, so he could not oppose them. All this was done to enable them to part from the savages on friendly terms. I told the king, my master, that I very much wanted to return with him, but that, as he could see, my brothers would not allow me to do so. Then he began to shout all over the ship, saying that if they really wanted to take me away, I then had to return with the first ship, for he looked upon me as his son and was very angry with those from Ubatuba [where he had first been taken], who had wanted to eat me.

And one of his wives who was with him on the ship lamented over me, according to their custom, and I also cried as they usually do. After all of this, the captain gave them a number of goods; some five ducats' worth of knives, axes, mirrors, and combs. Then they went ashore toward their dwellings.

Thus the Almighty Lord, the God of Abraham, Isaac, and Jacob, saved me from the hands of these tyrants. Praise, glory, and honor be to Him through Jesus Christ, His Son, our Redeemer. Amen.

Examining the Evidence

1. How does Staden end up in Brazil, and what does he describe as the circumstances of his capture?

2. What does Staden believe will happen to him as a captive of the Tupinamba?

3. What does Staden's passage suggest about early relations between native Brazilians and Europeans?

MAKING CONNECTIONS

1. What do the Eannes de Azurara and Staden selections say about captive taking in the early modern Atlantic world?

2. How do Native American documents from the period compare with European documents?

3. How might one determine non-European feelings about first contact or conquest in cases in which only European descriptions of such actions survive?

CHAPTER 17

Western Africa in the Era of the Atlantic Slave Trade, 1450–1800

Africa is a vast continent, but the extensive, mostly tropical region whose rivers drain into the Atlantic constitute what we have called western Africa. It was this ecologically complex and often densely populated region that supplied the Atlantic world with the greatest number of enslaved captive laborers until the nineteenth century, when the slave trade was abolished. Western Africa was also a region of lasting, autonomous cultures and empires, including those of Mali and Songhai, and it is important to acknowledge the diversity of its peoples and their independence as well as their interactions with Europeans searching for gold, pepper, ivory, and captives. The main story here was not one of conquest but of trade. Even in its early years, as described by the Spanish priest Tomás de Mercado (Document 17.4), the commerce in African captives was marked by considerable violence and deception, and the so-called Middle Passage across the Atlantic was deadly. Not everyone participated in the slave trade or was victimized by it, but by the end of early modern times few western African societies were unaffected by its reverberations.

17.1   THE POWERFUL MALI DYNASTY

Al-Sa'di, *Mali and Its Provinces* (c. 1655)

The historian known as Al-Sa'di (1594–c. 1656) was an imam, or Islamic religious scholar, descended from the Moroccan Sa'dis who invaded and then toppled the Songhai Empire on the middle Niger River in 1591 (see Document 17.2). He lived in the cities of Timbuktu and Jenne, and appears to have learned most of what he knew about the region's past from a mix of written sources in Arabic and local oral historians who spoke the Songhai language. The following is translated from Al-Sa'di's Arabic history of the middle Niger from medieval times to his own.

Observation. Mali is a very large and extensive region in the far west, extending toward the Atlantic Ocean. The first ruler to establish a state there was Qayamagha, the seat of his sovereignty being Ghana, a large city in the land of Baghana. It is said that the state [sultanate] was founded before the Prophet Muhammad's mission, and that twenty-two kings ruled before that event, and twenty-two after, making a total of forty-four in all. They were all *bidan* [literally "whites," i.e., Arabs or Berbers] in origin—though we do not know from whom they were originally descended—and their vassals were Soninke. When their dynasty came to an end they were succeeded by the Malians, who belong to the *sudan* [i.e., "blacks"]. Their state grew very large, and they ruled a territory, including Kala, Bendugu, and Sibiridugu, up to the borders of the land of Jenne. Each of these three territories had twelve sultans. . . .

The ruler of Mali brought Songhay, Timbuktu, Diakha, Mema, and Baghana, and their neighboring territories under his sway to as far as the salt sea. The Malians enjoyed tremendous power and extraordinary might. Their ruler had two principal commanders: one in charge of the south, who had the title Sanqara-zum'a, and one in charge of the north

called Faran-Sura. Each had a number of officers and troops under his command. This led to tyranny, high-handedness, and violation of people's rights in the latter days of their rule, so God Most High punished them by destroying them. One day in the early morning an army of God Most High in the form of human children appeared before them in the sultan's palace. These children attacked them with swords, killing almost all of them, and then disappeared in the space of a single hour, by the power of the Mighty and Powerful One. No one knew where they came from or where they went to, but from that time onwards the Malians became weak and enfeebled. Later on, the emir al-mu'minin Askiya al-hajj Muhammad [of Songhai] made continuous expeditions against them, as did his sons who succeeded him, until there was no one left among the Malians who could hold up his head. They split up into three groups, each under a leader ruling a particular area with his supporters and claiming to be the sultan. The two principal commanders opposed these claimants, and each declared its independence in his own territory.

At the height of their power the Malians sought to subject the people of Jenne, but the latter refused to submit. The Malians made numerous expeditions against them, and many terrible, hard-fought encounters took place—a total of some ninety-nine, in each of which the people of Jenne were victorious. Some say that there must needs be a hundredth battle at the end of time, and that the people of Jenne will be victorious in this one as well.

Examining the Evidence

1. How does Al-Sa'di describe the origins of the Malian dynasty?
2. According to Al-Sa'di's account, how and why did the Malian dynasty fall?
3. To what extent is this history of Mali mythical?

John O. Hunwick, ed., *Timbuktu and the Songhay Empire: Al-Sadi's Tarikh al-sudan Down to 1613 and Other Contemporary Documents* (Leiden, The Netherlands: Brill, 1999), 13–21.

17.2 THE KEBBI KINGDOM

Mulay Ahmad al-Mansur of Morocco, *Letter to Kanta Dawud of Kebbi* (c. 1591)

The following letter was written by the Moroccan sultan Mulay Ahmad al-Mansur (1549–1603) to the ruler of one of Songhai's tributaries, the Kebbi kingdom of the Middle Niger. Songhai had just fallen to the sultan's forces, and some of the empire's warriors were said to be hiding in Kebbi. Kebbi was famously home to the Sorko boatmen whose access to trees and centuries of craftsmanship allowed them to control the transport of commodities and people (including soldiers) on the Niger River. As such, they were critically important tributaries and allies of anyone hoping to dominate this region of sub-Saharan Africa.

To the ruler of the Kebbi kingdom within the borders of our Sudanese dominions, Dawud Kantah—may God inspire you with right guidance and lead you by the forelock to that which you will find praiseworthy today, tomorrow, and yesterday. Peace be upon you and the mercy of God and His blessings.

And now, after praise to God who made clear through this prophetic mission the paths of guidance to all who desire, and set aright by our victorious swords the course of whomsoever deviates and swerves from the Truth; and blessing and peace be upon our lord and master Muhammad, whom He sent with the Truth to mankind, and to which he bore witness with the Communication [the Qur'an]; and (may His) good pleasure be upon his Family [the Prophet's descendants], who extirpated with the blades of their swords every insurgent and rebel, and upon his Companions, by the spittle of whose swords unbelief was choked without finding a means of being swallowed; and [I offer] prayer for the victory of this exalted and mighty endeavor [i.e., the conquest of Songhai]—victory through whose swords shall the chains of dominion be forged

and fashioned in truth, and upon whose shining blades shall glisten the stains of the enemy's blood, through the might and protection of God.

This letter of ours comes to you from our Marrakesh residence—may God protect it; and our responsibility for the Community obliges us, by God's might, to establish [our] allies under the shade of security and well-being, and to dispatch upon [our] wretched enemies clouds of distress and adversity, through the might and power of God.

You are aware that your neighbor Sukya, who has been cut down by our sharp swords, though we previously had no desire for his lands, and, as regards him, existed as our swords were sleeping in their scabbards, until we wrote to him concerning one of the important utilities of the Muslims. Then we obliged him with obedience to us, which God has made incumbent upon the [Islamic] Community (*al-umma*). When he neither responded in regard to the utility about which we wrote him, nor in regard to the [oath of] obedience with which we charged him, the mightiest flood of our soldiers, victorious through God, poured upon him. And you are aware of what came to pass in this affair from our vanguard, which ground him to dust, and from our swords which mowed him down, so that no trace or sign remained of him, and God despoiled him at our hands, effaced his tracks, and caused our swords—through God's benevolence—to possess his land and his dwellings.

We observe that you have been negligent over this matter, and have undertaken acts which will lead to what is most calamitous and bitter. This is on account of your ignoring the [oath of] obedience which God has made binding upon you, and by your giving asylum to the remnants of the Songhai which [our swords] spared, and of which—through God's might—nothing shall remain standing until the Hour of Judgment. Information has reached us that

John O. Hunwick, ed., *Timbuktu and the Songhay Empire: Al-Sadi's Tarikh al-sudan Down to 1613 and Other Contemporary Documents* (Leiden, The Netherlands: Brill, 1999), 302–305.

you are giving them protection, aiding them, and reinforcing them with cavalry, seeking to oppose what God has predestined for those whom He has despoiled, and for whom he has decreed perdition and woe. Furthermore, you are closing the path to those who come from kingdoms which lie beyond you, such as the people of Kano and Katsina, and those around them who desire to enter into obedience to us, so that they may take their place in the victorious party of God, repulsing them and blocking their way from the path which brings success.

Although God Most High, through His aid, has given us power over present punishment of all who deviate from the path of guidance, and do not pursue a path of upright conduct, we must of necessity run the course of fair warning, in accordance with the paths of the Sunna, and in accordance with the word of Him who is Exalted, "Summon to the path of your Lord with wisdom and goodly exhortation." And we summon you first of all to obedience, and to enter into the bond of the Community (*al-jamaa*), although if you are holding fast to the tenets of Islam, you will not be unaware of the obligation of obedience to our prophetic imamate, which God has imposed upon you, and upon the petty states of the Sudan (*tawa'if al-sudan*), in accordance with the Qur'an and the Sunna, and the consensus of the learned imams.

Next we command you to cut off the rebellious Songhai band by arresting those of them who are in your territory, and by enabling the commanders of our kingdom to have power over them at your hand; then closing the door of acceptance in the face of any of them who come to you, and banishing such persons utterly, so that none takes refuge with you, nor does help reach them through you. Then to hand over [to us] the whole annual quota of boats, which you used to give to Askiya [Songhai's ruler], and to continue to perform their necessary duties, for you did not disdain to give them to Askiya who is so much your equal and peer that he has no superiority over you in any respect, except through conquest; how then should you not give them to the Imam, obedience to whom God has imposed upon you, and upon those Sudanese kingdoms which lie beyond you north, south, east, and west—that Imam whom God has molded from the metal of

prophethood which has superiority and perfect nobility over one and all.

To sum up: if you respond to [the oath of] obedience, and its conditions—to hand over to the governors of our Sudanese dominions those Songhai who are with you; to expel into the wilderness all those of them who come to your country; to continue providing the boats that you used to give to Askiya; to allow free passage to all people of the kingdoms lying beyond you, who come to enter into obedience to us—which is an obligatory duty both for them and for you—then you and your subjects and your lands are safe and secure, guarded by our sovereignty, which shall protect you from all sides, so that you shall not experience from our Exalted Abode anything that might harm you or alarm you, to the end of time, if God wills. Nay, you shall sleep safe and secure in your place of rest, and you shall have the support of our divinely victorious armies against your enemies and opponents.

But, if you refuse to respond, and your bad judgment causes you to deviate from the path of success, then receive tidings of our conquering armies aided by God, and our extensive military forces made victorious by God, which shall pour over your land from here—if God wills—and from Tigurarin and Tuwat, and from the forces which are there facing you, like torrential flood-water or a raging sea. You will imagine it to be a downpour flowing with ignominy [humiliation] and destruction, until—by God's might—they shall reduce your land to a barren wilderness, and bring you to the same plight as Askiya, whom they made to taste death, and whom, together with his kingdom, they swallowed up, since he had disobeyed our Exalted Command. We have given you fair warning and notice, so choose for yourself and pursue the path which your better judgment commends. Peace.

Examining the Evidence

1. How does the sultan justify his conquest of Songhai?
2. What is al-Mansur asking the ruler of Kebbi to do, and what does he say will happen if he does not comply?
3. What is the role of religion in this passage?

17.3 THE SPLENDOR OF BENIN

Pieter de Marees, *Description of the Situation and Character of the Great City of Benin* (1602)

Little is known of Pieter de Marees, but he appears to have been a Flemish merchant from Antwerp who sailed with the Dutch during early trade and reconnaissance voyages to western Africa. Dutch engagement with West Africa's Gold Coast, in particular, grew rapidly after 1590, and included not only peaceful trade and diplomatic overtures to monarchs such as the king of Benin, but also military attacks on Portuguese trading posts such as São Jorge da Mina. De Marees visited the Gold Coast between November 1600 and November 1601, and wrote his account immediately upon his return to Amsterdam where he published it, with illustrations done by a hired engraver, in 1602. He published a French edition in 1605. The following excerpts are from a translation of the first Dutch edition. In the first selection, de Marees offers a rare description of a sub-Saharan African city at the height of its splendor and power.

At first sight the city seems very big, and as soon as one enters it, one comes to a great, wide, unpaved street, which appears to be not less than 7 or 8 times as wide as Warmoes Street [the Warmoesstraat] in Amsterdam. It is straight, without any bends. The house where I lodged with [fellow trader] Matheus Corneliszen was a quarter of an hour from the gate, and even from there I could not see the end of the street; but I did see a great tall tree, which was as far as I could see, and I was told that the street was still much longer. I talked with a Dutchman there who said that he had been where that tree was, but that he could not see the end either, though he did see that the houses thereabouts began to become much smaller and that some of the houses there were dilapidated, so that it may be assumed that the end

must be thereabouts. This tree was situated more than half a mile from the house where I lodged, so that the street can be reckoned to be at least a mile long, without counting the suburb.

Next to the gate, which I entered on horseback, I saw a very tall bulwark, very thick, made of earth, with a very deep and wide moat, which is, however, dry and full of tall trees. I spoke to someone who had walked some distance along the moat, but he did not see any other moat than the one mentioned, nor did he know for certain whether it runs around the city or not. This aforesaid gate is a fair size, made in their fashion out of wood, so that it can be closed. One will always find a guard there. Outside this gate is a big suburb. When one is in the aforesaid great street, one also sees many side streets which are straight, but whose end one cannot see either, because of their great length. One could write more matters of interest about this city if only one were allowed to see more of it, as one is in the cities of Holland, but this is forbidden by the person who always accompanies you; for one is not allowed to go out alone there. Some people say that this person goes along with you in order that no mishap befalls you, but even then, you are not allowed to go any farther than he wants you to go.

About Their Livestock and Fruits

They have many excellent fruits and livestock on which they are able to live, such as yams, sweet potatoes, banana, and plantain, oranges and lemons. The palm wine here is excellent and very good to drink: there are two kinds of sour palm wine, namely, *vino de palma* and *vino de bordão*. They drink the *palma* wine in the morning, when they consider it very good for drinking, and the *bordão* in the evening, as they consider it better for drinking in the evening than in the morning.

Pieter de Marees, *Description and Historical Account of the Gold Kingdom of Guinea (1602)*, trans. and ed. Albert van Dantzig and Adam Jones (Oxford: Oxford University Press, 1987), 226–232.

They have another species of fruit, whose taste is close to that of garlic and which looks purplish red, the very same species as is found on the Gold Coast. If they want to make a promise or swear an oath, they say and promise that they will not eat any such garlic which breaks into so many [i.e., a certain inauspicious number of] pieces. Others swear to eat garlic which breaks into so many pieces, so that each has a different explanation with regard to this.

The Manner of Their Houses

The houses in this city are built in good order, one standing next to the other, and are linked to one another in the same way as the houses in Holland are. The houses in which people of quality live, whether they are nobles or not, have their entrance two or three steps up. They have a kind of [covered] porch in which one can sit down dry, and this porch is swept clean every morning by their slaves, who spread out a mat upon which one can sit. Their rooms form a square, with a sloping roof all around, leaving an opening in the middle, through which the rain, wind, and daylight can penetrate; and there they also sleep and eat. But they also have special cooking houses and other small apartments in a separate place.

The common houses are not like this. They are just straight blocks in which there is a wooden door; they do not know how to make windows, and the air they breathe in the house has to come through the roof. Their houses are altogether red and consist of smooth walls, built of the soil they dig up, which is generally sticky. Most of their earth is altogether red; they mix it with water, make it very much like clay in our country, and stick lumps of it on top of one another, after which they let it dry. They make their walls about two feet thick. Although they make their walls so thick, walls do here and there collapse from time to time when there is some heavy rain, and then they again have the work of rebuilding them.

About the King's Court

The king's court is very big and has inside it many large, square courtyards surrounded by galleries, in which one always finds guards. I have gone so far into that court that I passed through no less than four such large courtyards. Wherever I looked I saw other places through the gates, and thus I went farther than any Dutchman has been, which was into the stables of the best horses, passing through a long corridor, so that it seems that the king has many warriors, as I myself sometimes also saw at court.

The king also has very many noblemen. When a nobleman comes to court, he comes on horseback. They sit on their horses as the women do in our country, and on both sides they have a man to whom they hold on. They have as many servants walking behind them as befits their status. Some servants have great shields with which they protect the nobleman against the sun, and they go alongside the nobleman, apart from the two to whom he holds on. The others follow behind, making music: some play drums, others horns and flutes, and some have a hollow piece of iron [or gong] which they tap. The horse is led by one man and thus he rides to the court. They have little nets, of the kind which men in our country go to the fish-market, and this little net is filled with things which they tap with their hand, so that they rattle as if the little net were filled with big nuts. A nobleman has many servants who go behind him with such nets.

The king has very many male and female slaves, and one frequently sees female slaves carrying a lot of water, as well as yams and also palm oil. It is said that these are for the king's wives. One also sees many men carrying yams and palm oil and water which are for the king. One often sees people carrying grass, too, which is for the horses, and all the aforesaid goods are carried to court. The king often sends out presents (of food), which are carried in good order along the street. Likewise, when the aforementioned things are carried, the carriers always go in single file; and there are always one or two people who go along with a little white stick, so that everybody has to give way, even noblemen.

About the King's Wives and Annual Procession

The king has many wives and makes two processions every year, when he goes out of the palace and visits the city. On these occasions he shows all his might and means and all the finery he has and can muster. He is then also accompanied by all his wives, who are said to number more than six hundred, although they are not all his married wives. The noblemen too have many wives, and some have no less than eighty, ninety, or even more. There is not a gentleman, no matter how low his rank, who does not have at least ten or twelve wives. Thus one finds here more women than men.

About Their Markets

They also have specific places where they have their various markets: in one place they have their great market day . . . and in another their little market day. . . . It is to these places that they take all their things for sale, such as live dogs, which they often eat, roasted monkeys and small apes, rats, parrots, fowls, yams, malaguetta pepper in pods, dried lizards, palm oil, coconuts, large beans, various kinds of cakes, and various other herbs and beasts which can be eaten. They also bring a lot of firewood, as well as calabashes from which they eat and drink and other kinds of wooden dishes and cups serving that purpose; furthermore, much cotton yarn, from which they make many cloths to clothe themselves. Their dress is of the same fashion as that of the Gold Coast, though more refined and neat, but to discuss this here would take too long. Furthermore, many different kinds of ironware are taken there for sale, such as tools used in fishing, in tilling the soil, and in agriculture, and also many weapons, such as assegais and knives for use in war. This market and the trade are maintained in proper order, and each person who comes to the market with any such wares or merchandise knows his place and quarter of the market where he should offer his goods for sale. They sell their womenfolk, too, as they do on the Gold Coast.

About the Noblemen and Their Wives

It is with great reverence that the noblemen go to court, having with them various kinds of [musical] instruments to play, and they are accompanied by many other blacks, some having drums on which they play, and others [playing] their instruments. They place on [the back of] the horse a small wooden chair, and around the neck of the horse they hang a cowbell, which rings as the horse proceeds. Two people also walk alongside him [the nobleman], and he leans on them with his arms. In the morning these escorts or pages come to the nobleman's door and wait there till he comes, in order to accompany him. Their horses are very small, and not much bigger than calves in our country, which is why our horses are considered so valuable there. The king has many warriors who are subservient to him. These soldiers also have an officer under whose command they are, as [under] a captain. This captain has a number of soldiers under his command and will always go in the midst of his soldiers, surrounded by other people leaping, singing, and having lots of fun. But the captains in particular are very proud of their office; they always maintain a stately air and go around the streets in a haughty manner. Their rapier is rather broad and they hang it around their neck on a leather strap, below their armpit. They also use shields and assegais, as do the men of the Gold Coast.

About Their Clothing

They shave their hair in various ways, each after the finest manner and fashion possible. The same is true of their dress, and they have many strange fashions, not one of them like another. All their clothes are nicely made out of cotton, on top of which they generally wear Holland linen [first introduced by the Portuguese]. Girls and boys go about stark naked until they are married or the king gives them permission and license to cover themselves; and on that occasion they greatly rejoice on account of the friendship and honor which the king has shown them. They then make their bodies very pretty, daubing them with white earth, and sit in state with great magnificence; the others then come to congratulate them, as if they were brides.

They have themselves circumcised too, girls as well as boys, in which they follow the law of Mohammed. They make incisions in their body, from above their shoulders down to their waist, three big cuts on each side, each of them the width of a finger; they consider this to be a great virtue which serves toward their salvation.

They are also very fair and will do no injustice to one another. Nor will they take away the least thing from strangers, as it would be a cause for [suffering] the death penalty; for they are very quick to put to death a person who does any harm to a stranger. In this they practice a very strange form of justice: they bind the culprit's arms behind his back and blindfold him, whereupon one of the judges comes and lifts him up by his arms, so that his head sinks toward the ground; then the executioner comes and cuts his head off. He is then quartered, and the quarters are thrown to the birds, of which they have great fear. They have a great fear of these birds, and nobody would dare to do them any harm or thwart them in any way. They also have people who are specially appointed to take to these birds food, which they carry with great magnificence. Nobody (except those appointed thereto) is allowed to see them carry it or be present: everyone runs out of the way when these people come with food for these birds, and they have a specific place where the birds come to fetch it.

They show great respect for strangers, and when someone meets them on the road, they will show him the way and step out of the way. They will not be so bold as to pass unless one expressly orders them to do so, desiring that they continue on their way; no matter how heavy their load, they will not have the boldness to pass, for they would be punished. They are also very ambitious and keen to be rewarded for their friendship.

Examining the Evidence

1. What impresses Pieter de Marees most about the city of Benin?
2. How does de Marees describe the king's palace and retinue?
3. What does de Marees say about more common folk and about trade in Benin?

17.4 THOUGHTS ON THE SLAVE TRADE

Tomás de Mercado, *On the Trade in the Blacks of Cape Verde* (1569)

The Spanish Dominican priest Tomás de Mercado (c. 1525–1575) was born in Seville and was among the first students to attend the University of Mexico, founded in 1552. Back in Seville in the 1560s, he wrote a treatise for merchants inspired by the writings of his fellow Dominican and crusader for Native American rights, Bartolomé de las Casas. The manual, *Suma de Tratos y Contratos* (roughly, *Treatise on Trade and Contracts*), was intended to bring Spain's burgeoning overseas commerce and complex financial arrangements in line with Catholic doctrine, which treated lending money at interest, or usury, as a sin. In a brief chapter, Mercado offers his observations on the growing trade in enslaved sub-Saharan Africans, at the time monopolized by the Portuguese, and known to Spaniards rather incompletely as the "trade in the Blacks of Cape Verde."

As for the [trade in] blacks, I probably should not touch upon it or say anything, as it would be to enter a labyrinth, since the jurisdiction over [the blacks] in those parts [of Africa] pertains to the king of Portugal, as do the laws or decrees that establish and proclaim the means that must be followed in the trafficking and sale of them. Still, I may venture that it is as follows: he holds lordship, dominion, and authority, according to reason and justice, at least on the coasts. I may also venture that which in fact occurs, according to public opinion and renown, that in ransoming, removing, and carrying the blacks from their land to the Indies or here [to Spain] there are two thousand deceptions, and they commit a thousand robberies, and another thousand coercions. However, since this trade would take a long time to discuss and we must here be brief, all we can do is resolve with some clarity the right [the Portuguese claim] and pass on to the act [of slave

Translation by Kris Lane, based on Tomás de Mercado, *Suma de tratos y contratos*, ed. Nicolás Sánchez-Albornoz, vol. 1 (Madrid: Fábrica Nacional de Moneda y Timbre, 1977), 229–237.

trading], which is not only wrong, but also lamentable and miserable.

As for the first [i.e., legal rights], I say that to capture or sell blacks or any other group of people is a licit trade and *de jure gentium* [just according to the laws of nations] as the theologians say, like the repartition and division of [captured] things, and there are many reasons and causes under which one might be justly captured and sold.

The first is war, in which the vanquished belongs to the victor and cedes his liberty. And, even if among Christians it is not customary to ransom or barter [war captives], this is a special calling and pious ordination of the apostolic Church. Among all the other nations and peoples, however barbaric, rule-driven, or civilized they may be, at least among those whom up to now I have seen or read about, the general custom is that the captive becomes a slave, sold and transported as such. This title [or justification] is current and is practiced more in Guinea than in other regions, on account of the many petty kingdoms and lordships, which almost live in an old style, such that each town has its lord or king, not having above them a supreme prince whom all obey and respect, in which regard they differ from the Western Indians who, despite the fact that they had and still have in each place a native lord whom they call cacique, and many times two or three [of these], as a rule all these caciques held one up as emperor, which in New Spain was the King of Mexico, or of Michoacán, or of Tlaxcala, and in Peru, [the King] of Cuzco. But these blacks do not recognize such a lord and, if in certain provinces there is one, they are so barbarous that they are barely subject to him. And thus there always flare up continuous wars between towns, like in Italy, where there are so many secular duchies and leaders that a universal peace would only come about miraculously. And from such continual warfare and dissention there proceed many captives from one side or the other.

Another pretext or reason [for enslavement] is public crimes, for which they [sub-Saharan Africans] have just laws among themselves—and which the Indians had as well, keeping some even after they became Christians—such that he who commits such and such a crime loses his liberty. Our laws say: He who kills must die, or go to the gallows; he

who steals shall be exiled. Theirs say: [for either of these crimes] he shall be made a slave, and sold, and his value will pertain to the polity or the aggrieved party. And since they are vicious and barbarians, they commit grievous and detestable crimes, for which, according to their laws, they are licitly captured and sold.

There is yet another reason [for enslavement]: that parents in extreme necessity have the natural right to sell their children for their relief, because the child is a thing that very much pertains to the father and received from him its life and existence and it is just that he gives and loses liberty, which is less, when there is no other means to carry on living or to support the parents. Of this authority and license there is mention in the most ancient laws, although due to the harsh sound of it, it has never been followed, nor was it kept in ancient times, in any place. In Rome it was denounced by Numa Pompilius, second king of the Romans, and in Athens by Solon, according to Plutarch in his *Lives*. Nor generally, thanks be to God, among the faithful has this miserable practice been used, [people] being provided with charity in such dire need; no one up till now, as far as I know, has had to resort to offering their children for sale. But in Guinea this is done, and I have seen arrive many from there who, asked in the confession how they got here, respond that their parents sold them.

Supposing all this, the general conclusion is that all those who come as a result of one of these three reasons or pretexts can be sold and traded and carried off to whatever place, because any one of these [reasons] is sufficient to deprive a man of his liberty, if such is true. But the evil thing is that with these three licit and sufficient [reasons for enslavement] they mix an infinite number of pretended and unjust ones, such that they come deceived, violated, forced, and stolen.

As for the first pretext of just war it is so mixed that many, indeed almost all cases are unjust. Since they are barbarians they are not moved by reason, but rather passion, nor do they examine the legal right they might have. Beyond this, since the Portuguese and Spanish offer such and such for a black even when there is no war, they go out to hunt for one another as if they were deer, these same individual

Ethiopians [i.e., Africans] moved by personal interest; and they make war and treat as a business the hunting and taking of captives in the bush, where [ordinary people] hunt for game, an extremely common practice among them, or to cut firewood for their dwellings. In this way there come to us an infinite number of captives contrary to all justice.

Under pretext of punishing their vassals for demerits and crimes by depriving them of their liberty, those princes and judges mix things together, getting angry with some, or if one should displease the king, as among us one might be tossed out of the [royal] court and lose favor and privilege, there they manage to deprive him of his freedom, making him and all his family slaves, bartering them off with two thousand deceptions and false testimonies, for which there can always be found a pair of witnesses who will go along. Others they send along craggy trails, through forest and mountain, where their servants and guards are already placed, and where they cannot defend themselves they capture them and then dispatch the poor wretches from behind closed doors, so that by chance no one from their own house sees them. And no one is shocked to see people treated so badly, and selling one another, because they are a barbarous and savage and wild people, and it follows that when this barbarity, baseness, and rusticity is so great, that they treat each other like beasts, as some fables say, that the savages strike and beat one another. The Indians also had [this custom], going so far as eating those who were not even enemies.

As for the [third] pretext, whereby parents sell their children out of extreme necessity, it is just the same, given their bestial nature, selling them for no reason and many times out of anger or rage over some displeasure or show of disrespect to them. And as here [in Spain] in fury one falls into saying to them: "Get out of my house!" or just kicking them out, [there in Africa] they take the miserable youngsters and offer them to be sold in the plaza. And since the trade is so huge, in nearly every part there are Portuguese standing by—or even the blacks themselves—to trade them away. Indeed, among them [the blacks] there are already traders specializing in this beastly and brutal business who canvass the interior for natives just like them to take to sell at higher prices on the coast and islands. I have seen many arrive here [in Spain] by this means.

Aside from these injustices and thefts that they commit among themselves, there pass another thousand deceptions in those parts [i.e., on the African coast] done by Spaniards [or Portuguese?] who lure them and attract them, uncultured as they are, to the waterside with little caps, bells, beads, and trifles that they give them, and, through dissimulation enticing them to board their vessels, they weigh anchor and hoist sails and go out to sea with their prey. Now, it is true that this corrupt practice was far more common in the past. It is nowadays mostly remedied, in part because the blacks themselves, after suffering such great calamities, got wise and accustomed [to the Europeans], and no longer allow themselves to be so easily deceived. The king of Portugal also established legal penalties that have been enforced with rigor. Still, in the end, some of this still goes on. And I know a man who recently sailed to one of those islands and with less than 4,000 ducats' worth of merchandise took away 400 blacks without any license or registry, and since he was not able to personally benefit from his efforts in this theft, God desiring that someone else [i.e., other investors] gain from work they did not do, and he enjoying the hunt, has returned and is there now doing, if he can, the same thing; of these cases there have been not a few.

Now, those claims and unjust pretexts that I first mentioned grow and continue to expand at present more than ever due to the great interest and monies they give to the blacks [i.e., black slavers] themselves, so much so that it is and always has been common knowledge that of every two parts [i.e., slave shipments] that go out, half is deceived or tyrannically captured or forced.

Furthermore, although incidental, they treat them most cruelly along the way [to the coast from the interior] with regard to clothing, food, and drink. They think it a savings to bring them naked, killing them with thirst and hunger, and it is certain they would misrepresent them to prevent a loss. They are embarked on a vessel, often not even a carrack [i.e., a ship meant for numerous passengers], 400 or 500 of them, such that the smell alone is enough to kill the majority, and indeed many die, so many that it is a miracle if only twenty percent are lost. And so that no one may think I exaggerate, only four months ago two shipping merchants took away for New Spain from Cape Verde a vessel filled with 500 [captives] and after only one night they had 120 dead, because they had packed them in like pigs, and even worse, all of them covered [i.e., in the hold]; they were killed by their own respiration and stench, which was enough to corrupt a hundred airs and take all their lives, and it would have been a just punishment from God if right along with them had died those beastly men who took them as cargo; and they did not cease in this business, since before reaching Mexico almost 300 had died. To recount the treatment of those who survived would be an endless story. Here we are shocked by the cruelty with which the Turks use Christian captives, placing them in their dungeons at night, yet it is certain that these Christian merchants treat the blacks much worse. And these [i.e., the captives] are already among the faithful, having been baptized en masse along the shore with a sprinkler—which is yet another great barbarity.

This practice understood, I say, in that which relates to law, leads me to two conclusions: first, that the purchase and sale of blacks in Cape Verde is itself licit and just; and second, given the knowledge of how it operates, and more so the reality and truth of what happens, it is a mortal sin, and those shipping merchants who engage in the extraction of blacks from Cape Verde live in a state of evil and in great danger [for their souls]. The reason is that this trade is so infamous, and it is such common knowledge that many of them [i.e., captive Africans] are brought by force and violence. Therefore, those here [in Spain] are simply obligated not to involve themselves in it so as not to participate in such injustice. And one cannot get around it by saying, "This cost me good money," nor is cost in any way an excuse, for the sadness of the captive is not alleviated to know that he cost his master dearly, but rather it only adds pain and sorrow, knowing that making savings or ransoming himself is only more difficult. The second reason, which in substance is the same, is: when a person is known to be bringing something from abroad that is ill-gotten, then citizens are obliged

not to trade that thing, no matter if that same person also comes and goes with licit [merchandise] with good title; rather, that bad opinion, known to be well founded, not just vicious talk, is enough therefore to obligate them not to take anything from him, under penalty of losing it should its owner appear.

The Portuguese who trade in Cape Verde and carry off blacks from Santo Tomé de Biafara [Guinea Bissau], Zape [Sierra Leone], and Iolofe [Senegambia] and the same blacks who sell them are infamous, as we all know, as they often treat them [i.e., the captives] badly and by evil means. For this reason it is necessary that those here [in Spain], if they do not wish to spread the sin, must desist and separate themselves from this trade and traffic. And so much more in this species of commerce than that of dry goods is one capable of injury and violence, done to them [i.e., captives] most gravely and irrecoverably, such that they lose forever their liberty, which is invaluable and has no price. And even with any other type of goods, being incapable of injury since they are irrational, if one only knows that they were ill-gotten or illicit, no one can sell them but rather only return them to their owner; and for this we condemn the second-hand clothes sellers when they trade that which is probably stolen, and the jewelers who trade with known thieves. How much less agreeable then, to traffic in blacks whom one knows for certain that the better part or most of them were ill gotten, and carried even worse.

A general rule is that in order for a sale or purchase to be licit it is necessary that I [as buyer] be certain that what the merchant has and is selling is his, held with just title; at the very least he must not be suspected of the contrary, and if such is rumored, I am obliged not to receive anything from him. If there arrived in this port [of Seville] a fleet of Bretons and it was said that the greater part of their linens were stolen, no one could trade them, even though without a doubt they were also carrying some that were truly their own. Thus, saying it publicly, as they say, that the greater part of the blacks they take [out of Africa] come captured unjustly, no one may trade nor engage in such a negotiation under penalty of sin and restitution. And one could even say in truth that in a sense he who takes them away from their land sins more than he who inside it unjustly captures them, because the former negates the possibility of liberty by way of ransom [e.g., self-purchase or purchase by relatives] by exiling and transporting them away, for if they remained in their land, however unjustly captive, they would at least have the hope of some chance of freedom.

And it is a clear and certain doctrine, or even natural law, that although there are civil laws that permit or dissimulate certain abuses that only God can extirpate [eliminate], they do not dissimulate on this; rather, they mandate that once it is clear what violence or deception has been done to them, that they be restored to perfect freedom. And in Mexico there was once a merchant, now a priest of the Order of Preachers [i.e., Dominicans], selling a black who having become acculturated and knowledgeable in all this, filed a complaint with the royal *audiencia* [appeals court], and, with only the proof that when he was being embarked he cried out and pulled away, they declared him free, ordering that his owner be repaid [by the seller] the 150 ducats of his cost.

Many ask what means there might be to trade in them securely he who wishes to persist and not give up this business. My answer is that which Alcibiades gave to his uncle, Pericles, who, asking him how he might account for and explain a fort that had cost the republic of Athens a great sum; he responded: Well,

you cannot account for it or explain it, so perhaps you should see how you can keep them from asking and avoid trying. Thus I say to these men: that you should rather ask and search for ways not to trade or pursue a business that from the very start is illicit, given the circumstances above. And certainly, if those of this merchant guild [the Seville *consulado*] should follow my advice and agree—and it would be a good agreement—to content themselves with shipping for a few years only wine and dry goods, there is no reason why they could not bring about great effects: first, it would cost them nothing; second, the Portuguese would temper their avarice, lacking anyone to encourage it and keep it aflame; third, their most serene king would oversee it [the slave trade] with greater notice, study, and care.

Examining the Evidence

1. What does Mercado consider the main legal justifications for enslavement and slave trading?
2. What does Mercado make of the everyday practice of slave trading in western Africa (which he calls Guinea) versus its legal underpinnings?
3. How does Mercado characterize the Middle Passage, or crossing of the Atlantic, for the captured slaves?
4. What does Mercado finally conclude about the morality and legality of the slave trade?

17.5 OBSERVATIONS OF THE CONGO, LOANGO, AND ANGOLAN KINGDOMS

Pieter van den Broecke, *Journal of Voyages* (c. 1630)

Like Pieter de Marees (Document 17.3), Pieter van den Broecke (1585–1640) was a Flemish trader from Antwerp who kept a careful record of his visits to Africa. Van den Broecke's family had been engaged in the processing

and sale of sugar from Brazil and other Portuguese possessions prior to the Spanish attacks on Antwerp in the 1580s. After 1600, van den Broecke joined Dutch commercial ventures in Africa, mostly to trade for ivory, and prepared some of his journals for publication in 1630. They remained in manuscript form until 1950 and were translated into English only in 2000. In the following

J. D. La Fleur, trans. and ed., *Pieter van den Broecke's Journal of Voyages to Cape Verde, Guinea and Angol (1605–1612)*, vol. 5 (London: Hakluyt Society, 2000), 57–59, 94–97, 100–101.

selections, van den Broecke describes his arrival in the court of one of the counts of the Congo kingdom, living in the town of Mbanza Sonyo, near the mouth of the Congo, or Zaire River. Then he relates his visit to the king of Loango, located along the coast to the north.

August 1608, the eighth day. In the morning I sailed with the yacht [belonging] to the [ship] *Merminne* to the River Congo. I arrived, after many difficulties, only on the 24th at the ship the *Merman* of Jan Janssen Backer and chief factor Wemmer van Barchum. September first: The general Wemmer van Barchum sent me with Baltasaer Jacodt, his clerk, to the town of Sonyo, [and there] to the count with a letter of credentials to request permission from him [to trade]. This count keeps his residence in a town named Mbanza Sonyo, around seven miles upriver. When I came to him, he sat on a Spanish chair with a red velvet covering and covered with gold tacks. The stool stood on an expensive carpet. His clothing was a red damask robe with three wide gold trimmings, a black embroidered hat with gold and pearls, which his subjects had themselves made. On his neck hung a thick gold chain, wrapped three times around his neck. His subjects respect him greatly. The principal nobles stood by him with precious robes and hats in their hands. He knows how to maintain authority despite the fact that he is blind. They said that he was over 140 years old. His son read him the letter, which was written in Portuguese, in perfect form. This count is named Dom Miguel, count of Sonyo. He keeps very good law and order in his land. They are mostly Christians and go to mass every day, twice a day when it rains. They maintain five or six churches and have a Portuguese priest named Dom Gonsalves who teaches them everything. There are eight to ten schools here like those in Portugal, where all the children are instructed and taught in Portuguese. Everyone goes the whole day with a book in hand and a rosary. They are a friendly people, of sturdy body, courageous in battle. They handle weapons exceptionally well, and they are moreover clever in all of their business. The women do most of the work, like tilling the land, seeding, and weeding, so that they provide sufficiently for their husband.

The count adheres to a custom, which is very old, that if there is a pretty young maiden then he sleeps with her, and as soon as she is with child he gives her with her child to [one of] his most principal nobles, who are therefore very favored, for he usually gives many goods with her. . . .

Loango, June 5–18, 1612. . . . The king keeps his residence less than a mile inland in a town named Mbanza Loango, which lies on a very high hill and is an extremely pleasant location. The king's court covers almost half of the city and is surrounded by palm-wine trees. Inside the stockade stand three or four large houses and another 250 small ones, in which live the king's wives, who are said to total more than 1,500 in number. These aforementioned wives are distinguished by their ivory arm-rings, which they wear on their arms with much red paint. They are very closely guarded, and if any of them are found to be committing adultery, they are immediately put to a cruel death along with the adulterer.

This aforementioned king keeps his subjects under tight control and is terribly feared.

He has tremendous income, with houses full of elephant's tusks, some of them full of copper, and many of them with *lebongos*, which are common currency here and are made from grass and are woven by the natives.

This king has over 500 children by his concubines, but all these children are of little status. The sons are mostly thieves and the daughters, whores. Also, these children cannot come to the crown, but his sister's children can. They say that they know that the children from the sister's side are royalty and that the king's children are not.

When the king drinks, no one can watch him, or else forfeit his neck. When he wants to drink, a little bell is rung. Then everyone around him falls on their faces. After he has drunk, it is rung again. Then everyone rises once again.

During my time there, I saw that he continually spent his time with a young child who was his nephew, his own sister's son, and whom he kept with him and loved very much. This aforementioned child touched the king's arm by accident as he drank, and so he had this child immediately put to death, and had his blood brushed onto his idols and charms. When I asked him why he was so cruel to his own kin and to an innocent child, he answered that it was better the child than himself, because (as the Devil had suggested to him) if he had not immediately had him [the child] put to death, then he himself would have to die.

The king himself is a great magician and speaks often with the Devil. He knew long before my arrival that I was coming, and precisely on which day I would come to anchor in the bay, and also that I would bring him such and such goods, all of which was correct.

The father of this king is still alive and is said to be 160 years old. He has never been king. If he now outlives this king, then his sixth son will also become king, who is now more than thirty-six years old. This old man is named Manni Goy, is blind, and had so little strength that he could not lift the weight of a Dutch pound off of the table. The king has some holidays, on which he presents himself outside of his palace on a raised tomb which the natives decorated in a nice and curious manner. Around him sit his principal nobles, and on the other side stood a few music (as they know it) players who play very melodiously on curved horns made from large and small elephant's tusks; upon which [time] the majority of nobles, one from each state, present themselves very triumphantly, according to rank, with all of their slaves. After many strange leaps and bounds they end up lying on their bellies before the king, in submission until he orders them to rise.

The majority of their possessions is comprised of slaves, women, and children.

The people are pitch black all over, finely proportioned in body and limb with very well-shaped faces, good-natured, more loyal to our [Dutch] nation than to the Portuguese (who have frequented there for over forty years). They are not thievish, but instead hate very much those who are. They are most courteous and polite. When they meet each other, they clap their hands and call "sacarilla, sacarilla," which is to say "welcome."

The female population here is, on the average, lovelier than any other place in all of Africa. They are attentive in their dress, which are just *labongos* made of grass and are about a square ell [short yard] in size, which they wear on their right side and which just covers their nakedness, front and back.

They have their hair cut with a razor and smear their heads with oil from the coconut palm and smear their entire bodies with red paint made from stone-ground *taccola* [dye-wood]. These women always go with a mat under their arms on which to sit when they go somewhere for a chat. Many have a good number of beads, which they know how to make themselves from shells, and which are held in great esteem.

The men wear on their heads caps made of grass, very pretty and neatly stitched with a needle, some of which are decorated with feathers of different colors. Their clothes are also made of grass and bound like a skirt, which they tie around their middle with a quarter-ell of cloth, but more often with bark from trees, so that their bodies are usually covered from their hips down and above that they are naked. On top of that, decorative skins from exotic animals, such as leopards, monkeys, civet cats, and others, hang in front of their bellies. Also [they wear] many copper and silver armrings, and most of them have buffalo tails over their shoulders, to shoo away flies off their naked upper bodies as needed. . . .

Many elephants' tusks are found here. During my stay, more than 50,000 lb. were traded each year, of which I exchanged more than 30,000 lb. There is also much beautiful red copper, most of which comes from the kingdom of the Insiques [or Tio] (who are at war with Loango) in the form of large copper arm-rings weighing between 1½ and 14 lb., [and are] smuggled out of the country. Learned also that there lie silver, tin, and copper mines inland which are not being worked because the people are so lazy and are not accustomed to labor. Also found here in abundance are sugarcane and Benin pepper, and beautiful ginger, as well as other foods and victuals such as plantains, pineapples, sweet potatoes, bananas, yams, safu plums, Turkish [more likely American] beans, millet, large peas known as *ingobos* [peanuts], lemons, oranges, kola nuts, . . . [and] scores of palm trees which are very popular with the natives because of the wine, which is their principal drink. Furthermore the oil which comes from them is very medicinal, and they cook with it. With the leaves they cover their houses, which works very nicely.

Alonso de Sandoval, *On Restoring Ethiopian Salvation* (1627)

Alonso de Sandoval (1577–c. 1650) was a Jesuit priest born in Seville, Spain, and raised in Lima, Peru. He spent most of his adult life administering sacraments to enslaved Africans arriving at the Caribbean port city of Cartagena de Indias, in what is now Colombia. In 1627, he published a book, *On Restoring Ethiopian Salvation*, in which he discussed the transatlantic slave trade and its justifications. However, it mostly focused on cultural aspects of sub-Saharan African societies as he understood them, all with the aim of preaching to them more effectively. Most of what he learned of sub-Saharan Africa came from three sources: fellow Jesuits who wrote letters from the African missions, slave traders, and enslaved Africans themselves. In the following passage, Sandoval describes the West Central African coast between roughly the Equator and the island port of Luanda, Angola.

South of the Cape of Lope Gonsalves is a port called Mayumba, where instead of slaves a valuable red wood is traded. In this land it is called *tucula*; we call it sandalwood. Further south is a great kingdom called Loango, with an immense population and countless subject principalities. These people, their language, and their gentile rites and ceremonies are very different from the neighboring Congo and Angola. They are idolatrous, worshiping many different idols made of wood. One is not allowed to spit in front of the idols; the people become very angered when a Portuguese does this. Portuguese and Dutch live together in this kingdom's port and trade in ivory, cloth, parrot feathers, and elephant bristles. The bristles are used by black men and women to gird their heads and waists, and they are priceless in Angola. This nation buries its dead with a large part of their wealth, believing that they need their goods with them to navigate the road more securely and to be received in the afterworld by their idols and god.

To the south is a port called Cabinda, a freshwater stop for Spanish ships passing from São Tomé and other places. Further south is the Congo River, called Zaire by the blacks. It flows down from the Nile River [*sic*] to the sea, and it is one of the most powerful rivers in Africa, although the ancients knew nothing about it. It is ten leagues wide and so rapid that its freshwater extends twenty leagues into the sea. Often its currents carry islands with trees that seem like dry land. The Bamba and Barbela rivers also flow from the Nile. Other important rivers in this region are the Loanza, which runs on the border between the kingdoms of Congo and Angola, and the Lunda, where crocodiles and hippopotamuses live, as well as huge fish that can weigh five hundred pounds. The port of this river is called Pinda and is subject to the Congo king. One of his dukes lives there, called Manisonyo.

The Kingdom of Congo begins at the Cabo de las Vacas [near the city of Benguela], 13.5 degrees from the South Pole, and ends at Cape Catalina, at 2.5 degrees. It is about 600 miles wide and is divided into six provinces: Pomba [Mpemba Kasi]; the heart and center of the kingdom, Bata [Mbata]; Pango; Sunde [Nsundi], farthest to the south; Songo, beginning at the mouth of the Zaire River; and finally Bamba [Mbamba], the noblest and most important province.

The province of Bamba lies below Congo, 150 miles inland. The royal palace and court of this province are in a city called São Salvador [Mbanza Kongo], on the peak of a mountain. There are many great and noble men in this city. The king is given the title of Manicongo. He is a Christian, and a large part of his kingdom has also received the faith in the last 150 years. He is a friend to the Christians and does them many favors. The current king is called Pedro II [1622–1624, deposed by the Dutch]. He was previously the duke of Bamba. Even outside his kingdom, the world knows he is a wise Christian and Catholic king. He ordered all his subjects to immediately convert and receive Jesus Christ's law and faith, but everyone does not obey him, because they prefer to retain their numerous wives. Some have between 50 and 150 wives! The king venerates and reveres the Church. He encourages its growth

Alonso de Sandoval, *Treatise on Slavery: Selections from* De instauranda Aethiopum salute, ed. and trans. Nicole Von Germeten (Indianapolis, IN: Hackett, 2008), 38–43.

and attends Mass every day in the Holy Sacrament. Although kings in this country are forbidden to remove their golden silk cap, he takes his off and holds it in his hands before his Lord and God. This shocks and amazes his subjects and makes them realize the grandeur and majesty of that great Lord and King of Kings. Because he is so pious, he tries to find out if all the priests in the kingdom live well and guard their chastity. If he learns that they are careless, the king insults them publicly, saying that priests who hold the Holy Sacrament in their hands must live virtuously and chastely. Along with this concern for the priesthood, his good judgment and prudence make him want to encourage the young by having the Company of Jesus [the Jesuits] open a seminary college in his kingdom. The sons of the titled lords are nurtured with this healthy, saintly milk of the Catholic doctrine so that they will grow to govern for the benefit of the kingdom.

The monarchs of Portugal always show the Congo kings great love. They write them letters, which are read in public so that everyone knows of the honor and esteem bestowed upon them by the Portuguese. Some of the noblemen are allowed to join the Order of Christ. This friendship continues due to the excellence, grandeur, and Christianity of the current king, Pedro. His Holiness the pope also esteems the king: just in the last year, His holiness sent his ambassadors with a small but precious box full of relics and indulgences. This gift was received with great veneration, solemn processions, and great festivals.

The king and nobility dress in the Spanish manner, but they wear large capes made of fine cloth from London, or made of black velvet. These two fabrics are the best merchandise to bring to this kingdom. From the waist down, they wear rich silk and gold cloth made in their own kingdom. When the Spanish came there, the king received them seated on an ivory throne, wearing an intricately woven palm leaf bonnet in the manner of a diadem. He was nude to his waist, with a silk cloth covering his legs. On his right arm he had a golden bracelet, but his main jewelry took the form of a horsetail hanging from his shoulder, which only kings can wear. However, this style of dress is no more, because they have received the faith and Christian customs, so now the king and queen dress luxuriously in the Spanish style. The king adorns the palace with rich curtains and gifts from the Spanish of silk, silver, and gold. No black woman in the court covers her head or even has any hair. It is considered very stylish to keep the head very clean. The important women wear velvet slippers on their feet. These women also pride themselves on knowing how to read and go to Mass every day. Many Portuguese live in this city, mainly married to white women. There is a cathedral with a bishop and clerics, like all other churches. Among them there are many black men who are great Christians. Much of the clergy is this color, and they pride themselves on knowing how to play the organ.

[Luanda, Angola.] The freshwater Bengo passes by the island of Luanda, where many ships full of slaves leave Angola every year. The Portuguese live nearby on the navigable waters of this region, and from here more than 15,000 [enslaved] blacks leave annually for the Indies, including Brazil and other places.

The houses in this area are good, even though the royal palace is built of wood. The land of Luanda is enriched by religious orders and churches that sustain the faith of Our Lord. Among them is a college run by the fathers of our Company of Jesus. The Portuguese value this college and realize how necessary it is, so they have provided it with a liberal endowment [established in 1607 to create an African priesthood, but soon thereafter catered to local Portuguese]. The college is located in the middle of the central plaza, in the best, most sumptuous and pleasing building in the city. The Jesuit fathers who work there now show their customary charity, laboring in the Lord's vineyard, admired by the world, and gladdening heaven through the souls they convert. Besides the religious houses and the main church, there are other churches. One is called La Misericordia, and it has a large hospital that charitably takes in the sick and buries the poor. Another church is called San Anton. A church located on the beach is called San Telmo. This church serves as a hospital for the people who live near the sea. There is also an illustrious convent of the Franciscan Third Order.

All of the land of Angola and Luanda is very sterile, and thus the people of these lands import maize and millet from inland areas. They also import beans. The land is so dry because sometimes it does not rain for five or six years. They have a more abundant supply of goats and cattle. This kingdom also has minerals, including silver and copper, as well as red and brown sandalwood, the best possible kind, said to have marvelous medicinal value.

The Angolans currently wear clothing in our style, made from linen brought from eastern India. Women wear skirts in this style, with a huge number of pleats so that each skirt requires more than fifty varas [yards] of cloth, in the Flemish manner. In the past, sometimes even now, this style of dress was not possible in inland areas, and they only covered themselves with tree fronds. They eat the food we have already mentioned, eating off the floor, without any manners or cleanliness. They sleep on cane grills, without covering. Through their connections with the Spanish they now have cats and dogs, which make them very happy. They have naturally happy hearts and play little guitars called *banzas* [banjos], played by placing the head of the guitar on the breast in a very delicate and graceful way.

The Angolan king is very powerful and has numerous subject kings, who have enough armies to put 50,000 archers in the field. These archers are so skilled that they can let fly twenty arrows, one after the other, before the first one hits the ground. All of these people are very docile. It seems that we could easily teach them to become Christian because they do not worship idols. They believe in a god in the sky called Zambiampungo [Nzambi a Mpungu, "creator of the universe"]. All speak the same language, with some variation. The Mogiolos live in a land called Ocanga, north of Zaire. The Mogiolos are detested by everyone, but they are not as hated as the Jagas, a terribly cruel and cannibalistic people, greatly feared as warriors. Fifty Jagas can fight like 500 men from any other nation. They have very few women, because they kill anyone who cannot fight in war. They have no king and no laws but fight amongst themselves in a territory of 300 square leagues. South of Angola is Cape Negro, near a rugged, barren chain of mountains. From here, one navigates in search of the Cape of Good Hope.

Examining the Evidence

1. Compare van den Broecke's descriptions of Mbanza Sonyo and Loango.
2. How does van den Broecke interpret gender roles in these African societies?
3. Compare van den Broecke's and Sandoval's descriptions of polygamy and religious rituals.
4. What do these accounts by Europeans reveal about the extent of trade and consumer goods in these sub-Saharan societies?

MAKING CONNECTIONS

1. Based on the accounts provided in this chapter's documents, describe court life and kingship in early modern western Africa.
2. What do the accounts in this chapter reveal about slavery in western African societies?
3. Can we trust the accuracy of what the Moroccan and European observers tell us about these African societies? Why or why not?
4. What light do these documents shed on the Muslim and Christian conversions of many western Africans, and how does religion appear to have influenced these societies in early modern times?

CHAPTER 18

Trade and Empire in the Indian Ocean and South Asia, 1450–1750

Long before the Atlantic Ocean became integrated through trade and conquest, the Indian Ocean was a thriving crossroads of global trade. Monsoon winds enabled merchants and missionaries to circulate widely, from southeast Africa to the Arabian peninsula to Southeast Asia. In early modern times, change came on land and at sea with the arrival around 1500 of European weapons using gunpowder. These new weapons enabled the rise of vast empires such as that of the Mughals of the Indian subcontinent and also allowed small numbers of Europeans in ships to establish fortified trading posts from which they shipped huge quantities of spices, textiles, precious metals, war horses, and other luxury items, along with increasing amounts of more mundane goods such as lumber and iron. These selections highlight aspects of empire building as well as daily life in the greater Indian Ocean basin.

18.1   THE PORTUGUESE REACH SOFALA, MOZAMBIQUE

Martín Fernández de Figueroa, *A Spaniard in the Portuguese Indies* (1505)

Martín Fernández de Figueroa was one of several Spaniards who accompanied the Portuguese on their early voyages to the Indian Ocean. He traveled to East Africa, the Arabian peninsula, and India between 1505 and 1511. While in India, he took part in the 1510 conquest of Goa, which became Portugal's viceregal capital in all parts east. In this selection, Fernández de Figueroa describes the early Portuguese efforts to take over the trading city of Sofala, one of the most southerly outposts of the Swahili coast. His account was published in Salamanca, Spain, in 1512.

You can certainly believe that the men were happy to see that longed-for land on whose account they had suffered such tribulations at the mercy of a hateful sea. They arrived on the nineteenth of September, and the good knight Pedro de Añaya had the navigators take soundings to determine whether the ships could continue up the river to Sofala. Finding shallow water, they said no, but the smaller craft could; whereupon the good Captain ordered the men out of the large ships and into the smaller ones, which, as a welcome order, was immediately carried out, and three days later they entered Sofala. . . .

The good Captain Pedro de Añaya was delighted to find his men so anxious to go ashore, for this was why he was there. He had them make ready and arm themselves from their ample supply of weapons, and he sent an interpreter to the King of Sofala, saying: "He who is the King of Portugal's Captain Major for this coast wishes to meet and speak with you, if it please Your Highness." The king was delighted and answered: "Certainly, and immediately, if you

would like." Pedro de Añaya, prudent as well as brave, was pleased by this reply, knowing that it is far better to rule through love than fear. He ordered his well-prepared men into the longboats, leaving some behind to guard the ships, whence many rounds were fired in celebration. They say that everyone boarded the longboats in proper order, displaying their banners and standards. Pedro de Añaya went ashore with only ten men and would not allow the rest to leave the longboats. The reason he gave was that, should the King of Sofala not observe the agreement as he had said and have men in hiding to send against him, then ten men could more easily get back to the longboats than a thousand. From the ships they could then take advantage of their artillery or come ashore against the enemy, alert to the dangers. This was done just as he ordered. The number of blacks who came out to gaze at them was amazing. The King of Sofala welcomed Pedro de Añaya and bade him sit near him on a silken carpet, for there everyone sits on the ground. Pedro de Añaya ordered his [presumably Arabic or Swahili] interpreter to deliver his message in full, which he did. In it the King of Portugal requested land upon which to build a house to store his merchandise. The King of Sofala agreed to everything and provided a palm grove filled with houses where Pedro de Añaya's men could rest. The Christians encircled this with trenches, brought ashore a good deal of what they carried aboard ship, and installed themselves as the Captain Major directed.

The distance from Portugal to Sofala is 2500 leagues. It is a hot land that produces much rice and millet. There is no wheat. . . . From Sofala to the Strait of Mecca, 3000 leagues [*sic*] away, everyone is black. The inhabitants of Sofala are Kaffirs, who adore the sun and the stars. They wear colored cotton garments, and others cover only their shameful

Reprinted by permission of the publisher from *A Spaniard in the Portuguese Indies: The Narrative of Martín Fernández de Figueroa* by James B. McKenna, pp. 37, 39, 41, 43, 45, 47, 49, 51, 53, 55, 57. Cambridge, MA: Harvard University Press. Copyright © 1967 by the President and Fellows of Harvard College.

parts. There is no linen. The women wear nothing on their heads, and tin bracelets on their legs. They pierce their lips in six or seven places, which they consider very beautiful and elegant. There are white sandalwood, gold, amber, and other riches. . . . And one hundred leagues inland, in a Kaffir kingdom called Monomotapa [Zimbabwe], lies the gold in which they trade very copiously in those parts.

Since the King of Sofala had provided a parcel of land where they could build the King of Portugal's warehouse, quarter their men, and store their merchandise, as well as some empty houses in the field that the men of the good knight Pedro de Añaya encircled with trenches and wooden barriers as well and rapidly as they could, they came ashore to live there. They guarded it night and day, keeping the artillery ready, in the manner of men who anticipate war and make ready to fight it. Most of them began to fall sick with fever, and every day or so two or three would die. At this their souls trembled, and they began to waver in their convictions. They wanted to go and risk their lives in harsh ordeals rather than just wait for death in the land of the enemy. The determined Captain Major refused to consent to such a thing, for his life or death was their bond. . . .

At this juncture, two of Dom Francisco's [Francisco de Almeida's] Portuguese ships sailed in to exchange merchandise for gold, and when Pedro de Añaya learned of this, he was very pleased, as were they. Once the Captain Major had welcomed them he asked how they had taken Mozambique, Kilwa, and Mombasa, which there in Sofala they already knew had occurred. The captain of the ships replied that Dom Francisco had put in at Mozambique, which has a good port, and that from there he had set out against Kilwa, a principal city. On the eve of the Feast Day of St. James the Apostle he routed the defenders and took it, Thursday, the 25th of July, 1505. He had a fort built, and he acclaimed a wealthy Moorish merchant king of the city, for the former king, named Abraham, had run off. The second king's name was Mohammed Ankoni. . . . The Viceroy Dom Francisco then moved against the city of Mombasa, where he arrived on Wednesday, the 13th of August. They made ready for the attack, and on Friday, the Feast day of Our Lady, the Captain Major led his entire force ashore. The city and its people, who put up a fierce defense, were put to the torch and the sword. Carrying off all the city's wealth, Dom Francisco set sail for India.

The good knight Pedro de Añaya took great pleasure in hearing about Dom Francisco's victories. Bidding farewell to the ships, he continued on there with his men, who became so seriously ill that they were unable to stand but on three feet [*sic*], and there was no one to guard the fort or encampment. In order to keep this from the King of Sofala, Pedro de Añaya would send two or three little black boys to stand guard. On many occasions the captain himself would go up and ring a bell that was in the middle of the fort. He did so to hide the effects caused by the lack of health in his men and the sickness that was wearing them down. But since nothing can be kept secret for long, the King of Sofala learned about or assumed these conditions. He sent inland to a place in his kingdom called Nangabe for Kaffirs to come and seize the fort from Pedro de Añaya and kill all his men. A Moor who was a great friend of Pedro de Añaya informed him of all this. His name was Cidi Akoti, and he was hated by the Moors because he liked the Christians so much. They said he was a Christian [Abyssinian, or Ethiopian] and for this reason had sought to kill him. The King of Sofala and the Kaffirs came against the Christians, screaming and shouting, kicking up clouds of dust and sand, firing their arrows. On perceiving this, Pedro de Añaya quickly summoned his men to arms. Some came out in shirttails, although they were so weak that two with difficulty managed to wind up a crossbow. . . . The Christian gunners fired their mortars and artillery, and their shots killed a great many of the Kaffirs, who then retreated as far as they could. Oh, to be able to tell of the excellence, the grand spirit and composure of Pedro de Añaya, a fierce lion to his enemies, armed and ready, who, in the face of an infinite hail of Kaffir slings, arrows, darts, and spears, said: "Charge! Have at them, my friends and generous Christian brethren of Hispania!" . . . Thus the siege lasted three days, and, since [the attackers] could not conquer, but on the contrary their men were being killed, wounded, and beaten, the attackers fled from the encampment of Pedro de Añaya and his company, and the King of Sofala went back to where he had set out from.

The King of Sofala would very much have liked to have been able to make peace with Pedro de Añaya, to whom he sent two Moors. After listening to their proposal, the Captain Major replied that it was foolish to waste time negotiating something that would have no meaning. Because he knew they would not abide by any peace, he did not want to make one. Instead, he would allow the King of Sofala to continue to rule, for when the King of Portugal, who had stationed him there, sent out more Christians, he would then go looking for him and would cut off his head as punishment for him and an example for future generations. When this was reported, the king was reassured, thinking that Pedro de Añaya would do nothing more until more men arrived. But the latter had said these things in order to take the king unawares and when it pleased him, just as the king had done to him.

The Kaffirs, sorely afraid of the defensive weapons, abandoned their positions near the fort, and Pedro de Añaya was informed that the King of Sofala was all alone with his servants in the palace. He ordered fifty of those who felt healthiest and strongest to equip themselves very well. He assigned men to guard the fort carefully and ordered them not to sleep while he was away during the night. Then he boarded a brigantine and put part of his men in a longboat, giving strictest orders that under pain of death they must all stay together and no one wander off, and they did as directed. Up river, secretly and quietly, after midnight, they went ashore and set fire to some houses, causing as much damage as possible along the road to the King of Sofala's palace. There they killed many Moors who were sleeping at the entrance completely unawares. They knocked the door down, for they carried equipment for every eventuality. Pedro de Añaya, followed by six knights, led the way inside while the rest of the men remained outside killing Moors. The king jumped up from his bedchamber all excited and went running from chamber to chamber, terror-stricken by the sudden death he could feel hard upon him. Going from

room to room in search of him, Pedro de Añaya met up with him behind the door leading to the kitchen. The king with great fury hit Pedro de Añaya in the neck with a spear but only managed to break the skin. Nevertheless, Pedro de Añaya, knowing he had been wounded, called for his men to bring a light, if only to find out who had struck him. Arriving with a torch, they saw the Moorish King of Sofala standing there. They struck him blow upon blow, taking from him his kingdom and his life. Cutting off his head and placing it on a lance, they carried it back to the fort, where it remained in memory of their signal victory: that of having pillaged all the land and city where the King of Sofala had his palaces.

All great joys are but harbingers of imminent sorrow, for fickle fortune never permits a man to be either always sad or always happy. Thus, twenty days after the good knight Pedro de Añaya had so joyfully returned to his fort, since he was mortal and his lord the King of Portugal had not the power to guarantee him life, he fell sick with fever. By reason of this sickness it pleased Our Lord and Redeemer Jesus Christ to call him unto Himself. He died a Catholic Christian, gaining that glory to which we all, charting our course through this perilous and stormy sea of life, aspire. Although his death burdened his men with tears and sorrow, in equal measure did it leave them the glory of his fame as a valiant and dedicated Christian knight, a relentless foe of the Moorish enemies of our Faith. After saying their masses and exequies [funeral rites] as honorably as could be done out there, they buried him. In his place the Christians elected Manuel Fernandes, who had come out with them as factor [i.e., the king's merchant representative], and from then on he was considered their captain major.

Examining the Evidence

1. How does Fernández de Figueroa describe the Swahili coast of East Africa and its inhabitants?
2. How did the Portuguese gain entry into Sofala, and what did they do there?
3. What explains the Portuguese victory in Sofala given their trouble with disease?

18.2 A THRIVING KINGDOM IN SOUTH INDIA

Duarte Barbosa, *Description of Vijayanagara* (1518)

The following selections on the empire of Vijayanagara are from the 1518 account of Portuguese traveler Duarte Barbosa (d. 1521). Barbosa was one of very few outsiders to leave behind a written description of this last great Brahmanic kingdom of early modern southern India. Along with his father and uncle, Barbosa was among the first Portuguese to sail to and serve in India. He learned to speak the language of Malabar, on India's southwest pepper coast, and lived there in the cities of Cochin and Cannanore until 1517, when he returned to Portugal. Upon returning home, Barbosa almost immediately joined the Spanish-sponsored voyage of his brother-in-law Ferdinand Magellan. After an epic first crossing of both the Atlantic and Pacific oceans, Magellan and Barbosa were killed on the Philippine island of Sebu in 1521. Crusaders to the very end, they had unwisely provoked a local Muslim prince.

Forty leagues of this country farther inland there is a very great city called Vijayanagara [or Hampi, the capital of the Vijayanagar kingdom], wherein dwell folk without number; it is fenced about with strong ramparts and by a river as well, on the further side of a great chain of mountains. It stands on a very level plain. Here always dwells the king of Vijayanagara, who is a heathen and is called Rayen [Krishna Deva Raya], and here he has great and fair palaces, in which he always lodges, with many enclosed courts and great houses very well built, and within them are wide open spaces, with water tanks in great numbers, in which is reared abundance of fish. He also has gardens full of trees and sweet-scented herbs. In the city as well there are palaces after the same fashion, wherein dwell the great lords and governors thereof.

The other houses of the people are thatched, but none the less are very well built and arranged according to occupations, in long streets with many open places. And the folk here are ever in such numbers that the streets and places cannot contain them. There is great traffic and an endless number of merchants and wealthy men, as well among the natives of the city who abide therein as among those who come thither from outside, to whom the king allows such freedom that every man may come and go and live according to his own creed, without suffering any annoyance and without enquiry whether he is a Christian, Jew, Moor, or heathen. Great equity and justice is observed to all, not only by the rulers, but by people to one another. Here is a diamond mine as there is also in the kingdom of Daquem, whence are obtained many good diamonds; all other precious stones are brought hither for sale from Pegu [in Burma], Ceylon, and from Hormuz [in the Persian Gulf] they bring pearls and seed pearls. These precious stones circulate here more freely than elsewhere because of the great esteem in which they are held, for they deck their persons with them, for which reason they collect here in great quantities. Here also is used great store of the brocades of poorer quality brought from China, and much cloth dyed scarlet-in-grain and other colors and coral worked into paternosters [prayer beads] and in branches, also metals both wrought and unwrought, copper in abundance, quicksilver, vermillion, saffron, rosewater, great store of opium, sandalwood, aloe, camphor, musk (of which great quantity is consumed yearly, as they use to anoint themselves therewith), and scented materials. Likewise much pepper is used here and everywhere throughout the kingdom, which they bring hither from Malabar on asses and pack-cattle.

All this merchandise is bought and sold by *pardãos*. The gold coin which they call *pardão* is worth 300 *maravedis*, which are made in certain towns of this kingdom, and over the whole of India they make use of this coin, which is current in all these kingdoms. The gold is rather base. The coin is round

---

Mansel L. Dames, ed. and trans., *The Book of Duarte Barbosa* (London: Hakluyt Society, 1918), 200–212.

in form and is made with a die. Some of them have on one side Indian letters and on the other two figures, of a man and a woman, and others have only letters on one side. . . .

The king seldom goes forth from this city, he dwells therein with great luxury and without any trouble, for he passes on all the governance of the realm to his governors. The natives of this land are heathen like himself; they are tawny men, nearly white. Their hair is long, straight, and black. The men are of good height with [builds] like our own; the women go very trimly clad; their men wear certain clothes as a girdle below, wound very tightly in many folds, and short white shirts of cotton or silk or coarse brocade, which are gathered between the thighs but open in front; on their heads they carry small turbans, and some wear silk or brocade caps; they wear their rough shoes on their feet without stockings. They wear also other large garments thrown over their shoulders like capes, and are accompanied by pages walking behind them with their swords in their hands. The substances with which they are always anointed are these: white sandalwood, aloes, camphor, musk, and saffron, all ground fine and kneaded with rosewater. With these they anoint themselves after bathing, and so they are always very highly scented. They wear many rings set with precious stones and many earrings set with fine pearls in their ears. As well as the page armed with a sword, whom, as I have said, they take with them, they take also another who holds an umbrella to shade them and to keep off the rain, and of these some are made of finely worked silk with many golden tassels, and many precious stones and seed pearls. They are so made as to open and shut, and many cost three or four hundred *cruzados* [equivalent to a fine gold coin weighing 3.55g].

The women wear white garments of very thin cotton, or silk of bright colors, five yards long, one part of which is girt round them below, and the other part they throw over one shoulder and across their breasts in such a way that one arm and shoulder remains uncovered, as with a scarf. They wear leather shoes well embroidered in silk; their heads are uncovered and the hair is tightly gathered into a becoming knot on the top of the head, and in their hair they put many scented flowers. In the side of

one of the nostrils they make a small hole, through which they put a fine gold wire with a pearl, sapphire, or ruby pendant. They have their ears pierced as well, and in them they wear earrings set with many jewels; on their necks they wear necklaces of gold and jewels and very fine coral beads, and bracelets of gold and precious stones and many good coral beads are fitted to their arms. Thus the greater part of this people is very wealthy.

They teach their women from childhood to sing, play, and dance, and to turn about and take many light steps. These women are very beautiful and very bold. The king and the country-people marry almost in our way, and have a marriage law; yet they marry several wives, especially the rich who are able to maintain them. The king has in his palace many women of position, daughters of great lords of the realm, and others as well, some as concubines, some as handmaids. For this purpose the fairest and most healthy women are sought throughout the kingdom, that they may do him service with cleanliness and neatness, for all the service is carried out by women, and they do all the work inside the gates, and hold all the duties of the household. They are all gathered inside the palaces, where they have in plenty all that they require, and have many good lodgings. They sing and play and offer a thousand other pleasures as well to the king. They bathe daily in the many tanks, of which I spoke above, as kept for that purpose. The king goes to see them bathing, and she who pleases him most is sent for to come to his chamber. The firstborn son, whether of one woman or another, is heir to the kingdom. There is much envy and rivalry among these women with regard to the king's favor, that "some kill others" and some poison themselves. . . .

The King of Vijayanagara has always more than 900 elephants, which he purchases for 1500 or 2000 *cruzados* each; they are of great size and beauty, and he ever takes them with him for reasons of state as well as for war. He has also upwards of 20,000 horses, each of which costs him 400 to 600 *cruzados*; and some specially chosen for his own use he buys for 900 or 1000 *cruzados*. These horses are distributed among the great lords, to whom the king makes them over for maintenance, and they must continually give him accounts of them. In the same way he gives them to other noblemen. To the knights he gives one horse each for his own riding, a groom and a slave-girl for his service, and a monthly allowance of four or five *pardaos*, as the case may be; and daily supplies as well for the horse and groom, which they fetch from the great kitchens kept up by the king to feed his elephants and horses. These are in many large houses where [there] are very many great copper cauldrons, and in these are many officials who look after the preparation of the food and others who prepare it. The food is rice boiled with chick-peas and other pulse; and each man as I have said comes to draw the ration of his horse or elephant. And if they perceive that any horse or elephant thrives not when in charge of the man to whom it was entrusted they take it away from him and give him a worse. And in a similar way, you may well think, they act towards each man who keeps his horse or elephant in good condition. The great lords act in the same way to their vassals. Horses do not thrive well in this country, and live therein but a short time. Those that are here come from the kingdoms of Hormuz and Cambay, and bring high prices by reason of the great need for them here. Between both horse and foot the King of Vijayanagara has more than 100,000

men of war continually in his pay, and five or six thousand women whom he also pays to march in his train, and wheresoever he wishes to make war he distributes them according to the number of men whom he sends forth, and he says that war cannot be waged where there are no women. These are all unmarried, great musicians, dancers and acrobats, and very quick and nimble in their performances. The officials of war in choosing a man for the army strip him naked and look at him to find out how tall he is, what is his name, in what land he was born, the names of his father and mother, and in this way he is appointed without leave being given him to go to his country, and if he goes without leave and afterwards is captured he is very evilly entreated.

Examining the Evidence

1. What impresses Barbosa most about Vijayanagara?
2. According to Barbosa, what is courtly life like in Vijayanagara?
3. Who are the traders in Vijayanagara, and what do they trade?
4. Based on Barbosa's description, what role did elephants and horses play in Vijayanagara?

18.3 THE FOUNDER OF THE MUGHAL EMPIRE

Emperor Babur, *The Baburnama* (1499–1519)

Zahiruddin Muhammad Babur (1483–1530), founder of the Mughal Empire, kept a diary throughout much of his life. Known as *The Baburnama*, it contains an extraordinary range of observations about geography, natural history, politics, and courtly life. It is also a remarkably unguarded record of the emperor's personal feelings. In the first passage presented here, Babur briefly relates the story of his first marriage and then speaks at length about his infatuation with a boy in his camp (the italics represent a shift to

poetry in the original text). Like the samurai of Japan in this period, many Islamic warriors of the Central Asian tradition (Mughal, Safavid, and Ottoman) freely engaged in same-sex affairs of varying degrees of intimacy. The second passage relates the first use of matchlock firearms in Afghanistan by Babur's troops.

"Marriage and First Love"

Sultan-Ahmad Mirza's daughter Ayisha Sultan Begim, who had been affianced to me while my father and uncle were still alive, came to Khodzhent,

Wheeler M. Thackston, trans. and ed., *The Baburnama: Memoirs of Babur, Prince and Emperor* (New York: Smithsonian Institution/ Oxford University Press, 1996), 112–113, 269–271.

and we were married in the month of Sha'ban [March 1500]. In the early days after the wedding, although my affection for her was not lacking, since it was my first marriage and I was bashful, I went to her only once every ten, fifteen, or twenty days. Later on I lost my fondness for her altogether, and I was still shy. Once every month or forty days my mother the khanïm [empress] drove me to her with all the severity of a quartermaster.

During this time there was a boy from the camp market named Baburi. Even his name was amazingly appropriate [i.e., derived from the emperor's own].

I developed a strange inclination for him—
rather I made myself miserable over him.

Before this experience I had never felt desire for anyone, nor did I listen to talk of love and affection or speak of such things. At that time I used to compose single lines and couplets in Persian. I composed the following lines there:

May no one be so distraught and devastated
by love as I; May no beloved be so pitiless
and careless as you.

Occasionally Baburi came to me, but I was so bashful that I could not look him in the face, much less converse freely with him. In my excitement and agitation I could not thank him for coming, much less complain of his leaving. Who could bear to demand the ceremonies of fealty? One day, during this time of infatuation, a group was accompanying me down a lane, and all at once I found myself face to face with the boy. I was so ashamed I almost went to pieces. There was no possibility of looking straight at him or of speaking coherently. With a hundred embarrassments and difficulties I got past him. These lines by [the scribe and poet] Muhammad Salih came to my mind:

I am embarrassed every time I see my beloved.
My companions are looking at me, but my gaze
is elsewhere.

It is amazing how appropriate this verse was. In the throes of love, in the foment of youth and madness, I wandered bareheaded and barefoot around the lanes and streets and through the gardens and orchards, paying no attention to acquaintances or strangers, oblivious to self and others.

When I fell in love I became mad and crazed.
I knew not this to be part of loving beauties.

Sometimes I went out alone like a madman to the hills and wilderness, sometimes I roamed through the orchards and lanes of town, neither walking nor sitting within my own volition, restless in going and staying.

I have no strength to go, no power to stay. You
have snared us in this state, my heart.

"First Guns in Afghanistan" (1519)

On Monday the first of Muharram [January 3, 1519] a violent earthquake lasting nearly half an hour struck the foot of the Jandol glen.

The next morning, while marching from that camp to attack the Bajaur fortress, we dismounted our destination and sent an important man to Bajaur to the Dilazak Afghans to advise the sultan and people of Bajaur to pay homage to us and turn over the fortress. Those ignorant, wretched people refused to accept this advice and sent back ridiculous replies. The army was then ordered to make ready shields and ladders and implements of siege. To accomplish this, we stayed in camp for a day.

On Thursday the fourth of Muharram [January 6] the soldiers were ordered to arm themselves and get to horse. The left wing was commanded to charge forward, cross the river above the Bajaur fortress where the water entered, and stop on its northern side. The center was not to cross the river but was to stop on the rough, uneven ground to the northwest of the fortress. The right was to stop to the west of the lower gate. When the begs [commanders] of the right wing under Dost Beg's leadership forded the river and stopped, a hundred to 150 footsoldiers charged out of the fortress shooting arrows. The begs, brandishing swords, rushed in, pressed the footsoldiers back against the fortress, and got the bottom of the ramparts. Mulla Abdul-Malik of Khwast, acting like a madman, charged his horse up to the rampart. If the shields and ladders had been ready and it had not been late in the day, that very hour the fortress would have been taken. Mulla Turk Ali and Tengriberdi's liege man crossed swords with the enemy and brought back some heads. To each of them a reward was promised.

Although the Bajauris had never seen firearms, they showed no fear of the sound of matchlocks, and even made fun of the noise with obscene gestures when they heard it. Ustad Ali-Quli shot five men with his that day; Wali Khazin shot two men with his. Other men showed great prowess in firing their guns and performed well, shooting through shield, [chain-] mail, and gavsaru [body armor]. By evening, perhaps seven, eight, or ten Bajauris had been shot down. Thereafter it got so that no one could put his head up because there was so much matchlock fire. The order was given: "It is night. Let the army make ready its implements and swarm over the fortress at dawn."

At dawn on Friday the fifth of Muharram [January 7] it was ordered that the battle drums be beaten and every man should charge the fortress from his appointed place. The left wing and center advanced with their shields in place, fixed their ladders, and swarmed up the fortress. The entire left arm of the center, led by Khalifa, Shah-Hasan Arghun, and Ahmad Yusuf, was commanded to reinforce the left wing. Dost Beg's men went to the base of the northeastern tower of the fortress and began undermining and toppling it. Ustad Ali-Quli was there too. That day he fired his matchlock skillfully many times. Twice he fired his ballista [crossbow]. Wali Khazin also brought down a man with his matchlock. From the left arm of the center Malik Ali Qutbi was the first to climb the ladder, and he fought hard for a long time. From the post of the center Muhammad-Ali Jang-Jang and his brother Nawroz each went up a ladder and fought with spear and sword. Baba Yasavul scaled another one and got to work hacking through the roof with an ax. Most of the warriors performed well there, shooting volleys of arrows and preventing the enemy from putting their heads out. Some others, paying no attention to the enemy's battling and not regarding the arrows and stones in the slightest, busied themselves with determination to breach the fort. By breakfast time the northeastern tower, which Dost Beg's men had been undermining, was breached, and the men got up into the tower and drove the enemy out. At that same time the men of the center were the first to get up their ladders and into the fortress. Through God's grace and favor a strong and well-fortified fortress was conquered in two or three hours. Our valiant warriors distinguished themselves heroically and earned great name and fame.

Since the people of Bajaur were rebels, and infidel customs had spread among them, and the religion of Islam had been lost, they were put to massacre and their women and children were taken captive. As there had been no battle on the eastern side, a few men managed to escape from that direction but more than 3000 were put to death.

I entered the conquered fortress to make an inspection. On the walls and in the rooms, streets, and lanes lay corpses in untold numbers. Those who were coming and going had to step over the dead bodies. Upon returning from the investigation we sat in the sultans' house and gave the province of Bajaur to Khwaja Khan. Then, after assigning many great warriors as reinforcements, we returned to camp in the evening.

The next morning we marched out and stopped at the Baba Kara spring in the Bajaur glen. At Khwaja Kalan's intercession we pardoned all the remaining prisoners, rejoined them to their wives and children, and dismissed them. Some of the sultans and rebels who had been taken prisoner were executed. Their heads were sent to Kabul with news of the victory. Notices and heads were also sent to Badakhshan, Konduz, and Balkh.

Shah Mansur of the Yusufzai was there at the conquest and massacre. He was clad in a robe and given leave to depart after orders and threats were written for the Yusufzai.

Our minds at ease concerning the Bajaur fortress, we marched out on Tuesday the ninth of the month [January 11]. A league farther down the Bajaur glen, we stopped and ordered a tower of skulls erected on a rise.

On Wednesday the tenth of Muharram [January 12] we mounted for an excursion to the Bajaur fortress, and a drinking session was held in Khwaja Kalan's quarters. The Kafirs from the Bajaur vicinity brought a few jugs of wine. The wine and fruit of Bajaur all come from the neighboring regions of Kafiristan.

Examining the Evidence

1. How does Emperor Babur describe his first marriage and then his male love interest?
2. What role do guns play in the siege of Bajaur in Afghanistan?
3. According to his account in *The Barburnama*, how does Babur treat the conquered rebels?

18.4 "SCENES FROM MY LIFE"

Emperor Jahangir, *The Jahangirnama* (1612–1621)

Like his great-grandfather Babur, the fourth Mughal emperor of India, Jahangir (1569–1627) dictated a memoir that was then illustrated and bound as a kind of personal history of his reign. The resulting *Jahangirnama* is a treasure trove for historians interested in life in early modern India as viewed from the court. It is an often lofty and self-aggrandizing narrative, and it says little of what life as an ordinary Mughal subject might have been like. Even the many women of the court get short shrift. Nevertheless, Jahangir possessed a keen eye for telling detail. He loved to throw huge parties and go on long hunting expeditions, and his concern for justice as he imagined it was profound and far from despotic. Whereas his grandfather Babur had been a great warrior and his father Akbar a great student of world religions, Jahangir seems mostly to have been a lover of the good life—in short, he was an enlightened hedonist.

On the sixteenth of Farvardin [March 25, 1612] Muqarrab Khan, one of the most important and long-serving Jahangirid servants, who had been promoted to the rank of 3000/2000 [i.e., with a 3000-rupee salary and in charge of 2000 horsemen], arrived from the port of Cambay to pay homage. I had ordered him to go to the port of Goa on several items of business and see the [Portuguese] viceroy, the governor of Goa, and to purchase any rarities he could get hold of there for the royal treasury. As ordered, he went to Goa with all preparedness and stayed there a while. Without consideration for cost, he paid any price the Franks [i.e., Portuguese] asked for whatever rarities he could locate. When he returned from there to court, he presented the rarities he had brought for my inspection several times. He had every sort of thing and object. He had brought several very strange and unusual animals I had not

seen before. No one even knew what their names were. Although His Majesty Firdaws-Makani [Babur, Jahangir's predecessor] wrote in his memoirs of the shapes and forms of some animals, apparently he did not order the artists to depict them. Since these animals looked so extremely strange to me, I both wrote of them and ordered the artists to draw their likenesses in the *Jahangirnama* so that the astonishment one has at hearing of them would increase by seeing them.

One of the animals [an American turkey] was larger in body than a peahen and significantly smaller than a peacock. Sometimes when it displays itself during mating it spreads its tail and its other feathers like a peacock and dances. Its beak and legs are like a rooster's. Its head, neck, and wattle constantly change color. When it is mating they are as red as can be—you'd think it had all been set with coral. After a while these same places become white and look like cotton. Sometimes they look like turquoise. It keeps changing color like a chameleon. The piece of flesh it has on its head resembles a cock's comb. The strange part about it is that when it is mating, the piece of flesh hangs down a span from its head like an elephant's trunk, but then when it pulls it up it stands erect a distance of two fingers like a rhinoceros' horn. The area around its eyes is always turquoise colored and never changes. Its feathers appear to be of different colors, unlike a peacock's feathers.

He also brought a simian [probably a lemur from Madagascar] of a strange and curious shape. Its hands, feet, ears, and head are exactly like a monkey's, but its face resembles a fox's. The color of its eyes is like a hawk's, but its eyes are larger than a hawk's. It is an ordinary cubit [length from elbow to fingertips] from its head to the base of its tail, shorter than a monkey but longer than a fox. Its fur is like the wool of a sheep, and it is gray. From its earlobe to its chin is a wine-colored red. Its tail is longer than

Wheeler M. Thackston, trans. and ed., *The Jahangirnama: Memoirs of Jahangir, Emperor of India* (New York: Smithsonian Institution/ Oxford University Press, 1999), 133–134, 184–185, 368.

half a cubit and three fingers. Unlike other monkeys this one's tail hangs down like a cat's. Sometimes it makes a noise like the cry of an antelope fawn. All in all it was extremely strange.

"On Drinking" (1616)

On Friday the twenty-fifth [January 5, 1616], the [ritual] weighing of my son Khurram [the future Shah Jahan] was held. Until this year, when he is in his twenty-fourth year, is married, and has children, he had never defiled himself by drinking wine.

On this day, his weighing ceremony, I said, "Baba has children, and monarchs and princes have always drunk. Today, which is your weighing ceremony, I let you drink wine and give you permission to drink on festival days, on Nawroz, and on great occasions, but you must keep to the path of moderation because drinking wine to the point that you lose your reason is not allowed by the wise. There must be a profit and benefit in drinking. Avicenna, the greatest physician and doctor, has said this in poetry: 'Wine is an enemy to the drunk and a friend to the sober. A little is an antidote, but too much is venom. / In too much the harm is not insignificant; in a little there is much benefit.'" It took great persistence to get him to drink.

I myself did not drink until the age of eighteen, except during my infancy, when two or three times my mother and nurses asked my exalted father for liquor to treat infantile complaints and gave me a tola [c. 12 g] of it mixed with rose water and water as cough medicine. Then, when my exalted father's entourage was camped to deal with the Yusufzai Afghans in the Attock fortress on the banks of the Nilab River, one day I mounted to go hunting. Since I overdid it and got exhausted, a wonderful gunner named Ustad Shah-Quli, the chief of my uncle Mirza Muhammad-Hakim's gunners, said to me, "If you drink a beaker of wine, it will relieve the exhaustion." Since I was young and my nature was inclined to do these things, I ordered Mahmud the water-carrier to go to Hakim Ali's house and bring some alcoholic syrup. The physician sent a phial and a half of yellow-colored, sweet-tasting wine in a small bottle. I drank it and liked the feeling I got.

After that I started drinking wine, increasing it day by day until I no longer got a kick out of grape wine and started drinking liquor. Little by little, over nine years, it increased to twenty phials of double-distilled spirits, fourteen during the day and the rest at night. By weight that much is six Hindustani seers [of c. 1 kg each], which is equivalent to one and a half Iranian maunds. During those days my only food was the equivalent of one meal with bread and radishes. In this state no one had the power to stop me. Things got so bad that in my hangovers my hands shook and trembled so badly I couldn't drink myself but had to have others help me. Finally I summoned Hakim Humam, Hakim Abu'l-Fath's brother and one of my exalted father's confidants, and informed him of my condition. In perfect sincerity and compassion he said, with no beating around the bush, "Highness, the way you're drinking, in another six months—God forbid—things will be so bad it will be beyond remedy." Since his words were spoken in benevolence, and life is precious, it made a great impression on me.

From that date I began to decrease the amount and started taking philonium [an opium derivative], increasing it by the amount I decreased the wine. Then I ordered the spirits mixed with grape wine, two parts wine to one part spirits, and I kept decreasing the amount I drank every day. Over a period of seven years I got it down to six phials, the weight of a phial being seventeen and three-quarters mithcals [unit of c. 4.25 g]. I only drink at night, but not on Thursday, the day of my accession, or on Friday eve, a blessed night of the week. Out of these two considerations I drink at the end of the day because I don't like to let the night go by in negligence without rendering thanks to the True Benefactor. On Thursdays and Sundays I don't eat meat—Thursday because it is the day of my accession, and Sunday, my exalted father's birthday, because he venerated it greatly.

After a while I substituted opium for the philonium. Now that I am forty-six years and four months old by solar reckoning, or forty-seven years and nine months by lunar reckoning, I have eight surkhs [literally "cups," but probably "doses" of a smaller size] of opium after the elapse of five gharis [c. 2 hours] of the day and six surkhs after the first watch of the night.

"Nurjahan Begam: Wife, Nurse, and Empress" (1621)

[In my illness] there was nothing to do but abandon hope of [all the doctors], cease to rely on physical remedies, and entrust myself to the Absolute Physician. Since drinking wine gave me some relief, I began drinking during the day, contrary to established custom, and little by little I was overdoing it. At the same time the weather was growing hotter, and its effects could be felt too. My weakness and suffering were increasing.

Nurjahan Begam's remedies and experience were greater than any of the physicians', especially since she treated me with affection and sympathy. She made me drink less and applied remedies that were suitable and efficacious. Although the treatments the physicians had prescribed before were done with her approval, I now relied on her affection, gradually reduced my intake of wine, and avoided unsuitable things and disagreeable food. It is hoped that the True Physician will grant me a complete recovery from the other world.

On Monday the twenty-second of the month, corresponding to the twenty-fifth of Shawwal 1030 [September 2, 1621], the solar weighing ceremony was held under good auspices. Since I had been seriously ill during the past year and spent it in suffering and agony, I was thankful that such a year had ended well and in good health and that the new year promised recovery. Nurjahan Begam requested that her agents take charge of the ceremony. She really arranged a splendid celebration that astonished all who saw it. Although Nurjahan Begam has made suitable arrangements for every solar and lunar weighing ceremony since she entered into marriage with me—and she has considered it a pleasure to do so—she made this celebration even more ornate and took special pains to decorate the hall and arrange the banquet.

Examining the Evidence

1. What fascinates Jahangir about items brought from Goa?
2. How does he justify his use of alcohol, and how does he attempt to control it?
3. What role does the empress Nurjahan come to play as Jahangir's health fails?
4. What do these pieces of his memoir tell us about Jahangir's character and style of rule?

18.5 MAKASSAR'S KINGDOM OF TALLOQ: ISLAM, GUNS, AND A GOLDEN AGE

Talloq Chronicle (c. 1660)

The following selection is from the seventeenth-century *Talloq Chronicle*, one of the few surviving native-language texts relating the early modern history of the Makassarese kingdoms of Gowa and Talloq, which thrived on the Indonesian island of Sulawesi until they were destroyed by the Dutch and their local allies, the Bugis, in 1669. This selection, translated from original Makassarese manuscripts to English in 2007, relates the life of King, or "Karaeng," Matoaya, who ruled Talloq and conquered many neighboring principalities in the first third of the seventeenth century. He was the first king in the region to convert to Islam, and as such he was known as Sultan Abdullah.

At twenty years of age [Karaeng Matoaya] became ruler. At twelve he bore Sulengkaya. At age sixteen he became the guide of the people, the servants. At age eighteen [the previous ruler] Tunijalloq died. He became the speaker for the land. While Karaeng Tunijalloq still lived, he was honored with a royal sunshade.

William P. Cummings, ed. and trans., *A Chain of Kings: The Makassarese Chronicles of Gowa and Talloq* (Leiden, The Netherlands: KITLV Press, 2007), 87–91.

His personal name—may I not be cursed for bringing up, speaking about the ruling *karaeng*, those who recline on royal settles, those who rest on royal settles, the chain of kings, those who are of the purest gold—was I Mallingkang. His royal name was I Daeng Mannyonriq. His *karaeng* title before he became ruler was Karaeng Kanjilo. At the conquest of Segeri, he was given this too and was also called Karaeng Segeri. After becoming ruler he was called Karaeng ri Talloq. After the wars of Islamization he was called Karaeng Matoaya. At thirty-five years he entered Islam, on September twenty-second of the Christian year 1605, Islamic year 1015, on the ninth night of Jumadilawal, on Friday night. His Arabic name was Sultan Abdullah.

This *karaeng* Islamicized the people of Makassar until they became Islamic. Except for Luwuq, he Islamicized the Bugis throughout the Bugis lands, except only for the unbelievers.

It was he who conquered Bulukumba twice, marched on and battled in Meru the people of Boné, renewed the treaty with the Three Lands in Takaraq, conquered Bilusu, mastered Sidénréng and part of Bilawa, mastered lower Mario and Lamuru, mastered Pattojo, mastered the people of Soppéng and their vassals, the people of Wajoq and their vassals, conquered Boné. The people conquered entered Islam. These conquered people were taken as vassals and placed before him: part of Tempe, Buluq Cinrana, Wawonio, Bilokka, Lemo, Campaga, Pationgi, Pekang Lakbu.

Conquering the Bugis of the Tallambocco, he did not trample them and also did not take *saqbu katti*, did not take *raqba bate*. They were not taken. Then said Tumamenang ri Bontobiraeng, "Karaeng Matoaya said to me, 'At my conquest of the Tallumbocco, not a branch did I break. A sum of three hundred *katti* [c. 800 lb] of my own gold did I present, did I distribute.'"

This *karaeng* first swore oaths on the Qur'an, first swore oaths on Sudanga.

He was the *karaeng* who first armed [soldiers] with small firearms. He was the karaeng who first cast Makassarese cannons and also had people make gunpowder.

He was the *karaeng* who erected stone walls and irrigation works, strengthened the masts of cargo vessels, added sleeves to sailor's jackets, and first had people who built royal warships. It was he who first had masts of Makassarese ships attached with iron spikes and first had Makassarese who knew how to build galleys.

He was the *karaeng* who first conquered Bima twice, Dompu, Sumbawa twice, made a vassal of Sanggara, conquered Kekelu, conquered Papekang, conquered Buton, conquered the land of Pancana, Wawonio, conquered Tubungku, Banggea, Sula he did three times, conquered Taulaya, Bolotalowa, conquered Larompong, conquered Topeleqleng twice, mastered Tobong, conquered Maros, mastered I Daeng Marewa in Kaluku.

It was with this *karaeng* that those from Salaparang, Pasirika, Kutea came to us for protection.

It was this *karaeng* who expelled Karaeng Tunipasuluq, installing as ruler Tumamenang ri Gaukanna.

It was with this *karaeng* that the Portuguese came to dwell in Makassar, along with the English trading chief in Panyamang, and the Dutch, the Danes, and the French.

It was this *karaeng* who built stone walls in Talloq. All the workers alone [participated], not the servants, and the laborers, not the people. He built stone walls in Ujung Tana, fortified Ujung Pandang and Panakkukang. He also constructed an arched gate at Somba Opu.

It was he who first made gold coins, ordered tin coins made. It was this *karaeng* who first forged muskets and swivel guns, first armed soldiers with small firearms. It was with him that Makassarese became adept at forging swords.

This *karaeng* made rice and crops thrive. Fish were plentiful. Palm wine flowed. Cared for, people grew healthy.

[During his reign people] were adept at marking embroidery, adept at writing, adept at woodworking and embroidery, adept at striping ships, adept at surveying, adept at carving, adept at looking after [people and things], adept at making incense and mixing oil, adept at marking Javanese embroidery, Bugis embroidery. He was loved by merchants, by vassals, by *anaq karaeng*, by the *tumailalang*, by the *gallarrang*, by the household. [During his reign people] were adept at making gunpowder, firecrackers, fireworks, pyrotechnics in water. [During his reign people] were excellent at shooting, Maluku war dancing, constructing ships, building cargo ships and *palari* [passenger vessels], and ships were rowed rhythmically.

It was this *karaeng* who dreamed of drinking water from heaven called Sanjabila [from the Arabic *zandjabil*, water from a well in Paradise].

The *karaeng* was called an expert, a brave person, a renowned person, a wise person, an expert worker, adept at weaving, adept with his hands and knowledgeable about work for women and work for men, honest, good with people, a good host, cheerful, adept at grasping meanings, proficient in writing Arabic.

He often read holy books, never neglected [prayer] times once he became Muslim until his death, except when his foot swelled and he was given alcohol by an English physician. For eighteen nights he did not pray. He often performed [a variety of Islamic] prayers, such as *ratib, witr, wadduha, tasbih,* and *tahajjud.*

Said I Loqmoq ri Paotereka [one of his wives], "At the least he did two *rakaat* [units of Islamic prayer], at the most ten *rakaat.* On Friday nights he did the *tasbih* prayers. During Ramadan each night he gave out alms of gold." . . .

He ruled twenty-eight years, then left Talloq, going seawards to live in Bontoalaq and installing [a son by his main wife] Tumammaliang ri Timoroq as ruler. Twenty-three years after [a royal sunshade] was raised over him, he abdicated power on the first of October, the second night of Jumadilawal, on Wednesday. At eleven o'clock that day he left ruling behind. He was brought to Gowa for burial. On Thursday morning he was buried. He lived sixty-three years. He ruled thirty years, then removed himself and installed his child. For thirteen years he ruled together with his child, then died. As for his death, he died of disease.

He was praised by his equals, by his descendants. He was a good host, cheerful, friendly, adept at establishing fish ponds for new arrivals, adept at arousing the spirit of his warriors, adept at arousing the spirit of his household, adept at reciting to his fellow *karaeng,* adept at honoring people, adept at knowing the intent of the *anaq karaeng* and the *gallarang,* at commanding his subjects. He was loved and feared by the people. Christian year 1636, Islamic year 1026.

Examining the Evidence

1. How does this chronicle portray the history of Gowa and Talloq in the seventeenth century?
2. What roles do the introduction of Islam and gunpowder weapons appear to play in the story?
3. How is the ideal king, Karaeng Matoaya, described?

18.6 FROM LONDON WITH LOVE

English East India Company, *Letters to Princes in Sumatra and Borneo* (1734, 1740, 1744)

The following are copies of manuscript letters sent by the directors of the English East India Company to rajahs and sultans inhabiting the Indonesian islands of Sumatra and Borneo. As the letters indicate, company officials were eager to trade for black pepper, a tropical spice in high demand in Europe. By the time these letters were written, the English were engaged in fierce competition with the Dutch East India Company, or VOC, which had all but monopolized the Southeast Asian pepper trade. Unfortunately, we do not have the letters of the rajahs and sultans themselves and can only guess at their contents as described here.

East India Company Letter Books, E/3/106, ff. 184v–185v; E/3/108, ff. 98–98v; E/3/109, f. 89v, British Library, London.

To Sultan Gondam Shan,

Sir:

We the court of Directors of the United Company of Merchants of England Trading to the East Indies received from Capt. Jenkins your letter by the ship *Harrington* and we observe the contents; our trusty and beloved Governor, Mr. Everest, informed us last year of your princely qualities and attachment to our interest, and he was then ordered to pay our respects unto you by an annual present.

It is a great pleasure to us that the good Anak Soongey lies so near your heart, that the inhabitants, your subjects, have by your means improved the pepper plantations beyond any of their predecessors, no doubting but by your good example and wholesome advice they will go on to cultivate and plant every spot of ground in your kingdom which is capable of producing pepper, and thereby become the greatest people on the coast of Sumatra.

We have given orders that you and your people should be paid in cloth and money for the same according to custom, that our governor at Marlborough and our resident at Mocomoco should consult your welfare and happiness and upon all emergencies make your interest our own, what can we say more?

We wish you health, long life, and prosperity and are

your loving friends
[company seal]

* * *

East India House, London
20 December in the year
of our Lord and Saviour
Jesus Christ, 1734

To Pangaran Munco Rajah and Pangaran Soongey Etam,

Sirs:

We the court of Directors of the United Company of Merchants of England Trading to the East Indies received your joint letter by the ship *Harrington* and we observe the contents.

Our Governor Mr. Everest and his predecessors from time to time have informed us of your great pains to improve the country by exciting and stirring up your people to make large pepper plantations in which your wisdom is conspicuous by showing them their true interest.

Go on constantly to instill into their minds that to be an industrious [people] is the only way to be a happy people, and you may assure yourselves that you will feel the good effects of it in your government.

We have a great esteem for Mr. Everest and are persuaded that he will act for your good and for the good of the place; you may depend upon it that such and only such shall be our governors forever. You will do well therefore to confide in them and rest satisfied that their best advice and assistance to promote the happiness of you and your people will readily be afforded.

In answer to one part of your letter we must put you in mind that England is at a very great distance from Sumatra, so that the sending of ships so far and the expense of keeping a vast many servants both at home and abroad, hinder us from complying with your request in raising the custom or price of pepper, because we should thereby be losers by taking it off your hands, which we persuade ourselves from your just sentiments of things you will think highly unreasonable.

We are surprised you should ever entertain the thoughts of coming over to England and that for several reasons: our part of the world is not favored by God with such benign influences of the Sun as are your more happy climes, the passage hither is long and hazardous over the main ocean, our country does not produce rice, and the weather for half the year is piercing cold, to such a degree that it is scarce tolerable to those who are not used to it, and our manner of living is so widely different that you would run a great risk of your lives by such an undertaking, so that we advise you by all means entirely to lay aside the design of sending any of your brethren or children to Europe, in which advice we act the part of Friends and well wishers. We recommend you the divine protection and are

your loving friends
[company seal]

East India House
20 December
1734

* * *

To his highness Tamjeed Alha Sultan of the Kingdom of Benjar [Benjarmasin, on the southern shore of Borneo's Kalimantan Province],

May it Please your highness, We the United Company of Merchants of England Trading to the East Indies send greeting and embrace this first opportunity to acknowledge the receipt of your letter by Capt. Pelly, Mr. Liell, and Mr. Hodgson, who have fully acquainted us with your Highness's kind and courteous Treatment, for which we return you our most hearty thanks and from thence we persuade ourselves that our three ships *Marlborough*, *Walpole*, and *Duke* met with the like favorable reception.

We are most earnestly desirous of continuing a commerce with your Dominions and cultivating a strict, lasting friendship with your Highness, and we have ordered our Governor and council of Fort Marlborough to send our ship *Edgbaston*, Capt. Stephen Cobham, Commander to Benjar, for a lading [cargo] of pepper; we desire your Highness will cause the Great Men and merchants to trade with us upon the same terms as the Hollanders, and that Quick dispatch may be given to our ships.

By this conveyance we send you according to your Highness's Desire two of the largest guns procurable, being two and thirty-pounders, with some gunpowder and shot, which we present to your highness as a Free Gift, and beg you will please to accept them as a token of our affection, assuring you that so long as pepper is procurable at Benjar upon moderate reasonable terms, we shall carry on a trade with your territories.

Our sincere and hearty prayer is that God Almighty will always bless you with health and happiness and also establish a lasting Friendship between us.

In witness whereof we affix our great seal this 27th day of the month of March in the year of our Lord one thousand seven hundred and forty [1740].

* * *

To the most noble Tamjeed Alha, lawful successor to the Kingdom of Benjar where he governs in wisdom and preserves the country in peace, therefore is beloved by his princes and people.

We the English East India Company, your Majesty's faithful friends, received your letters by the two ships *Severn* and *Neptune* and are very glad the horse we sent pleased you, therefore according to your desire we will send you another by a ship that will sail soon after this, and also a betel box made of Philosopher's stone, if it can be got ready.

We will also as far as it is in our power defend your majesty's river from Sea Robbers, and all our ships shall have orders so to do, and shall lie in the river if your Majesty desires it, and if you will let us have eight thousand peculs [unit of c. 150 lb] of pepper yearly, at the agreed price, we will send you a ship of proper force for that purpose, which shall remain when the other ships are laden, but this charge we cannot bear if you let us have but six thousand pecul, which we mention because we will keep our word with your majesty and will not engage with more than we can perform. We wish your majesty all happiness, and that your Kingdom of Benjar may prosper, and we will endeavor by our trade to enrich your people and send such money as you desire, and therefore we request your majesty will ordain that your merchants may deliver us good and clean pepper.

In witness whereof we affix our great seal this 25th day of the month of April in the year of our Lord 1744.

Examining the Evidence

1. What are the English East India Company officials asking for in these letters, and what do they offer in exchange?
2. Why do the company officials discourage Sumatran royalty from visiting England?
3. What explains the flattery expressed in these letters to the princes?

MAKING CONNECTIONS

1. From the documents included in this chapter, how are trade, religion, and warfare interrelated across the Indian Ocean region in this era?

2. What do Fernández de Figueroa's account of Sofala, Barbosa's account of Vijayanagara, and the English East India Company letters suggest about the breadth and variety of Indian Ocean trading at this time?

3. How do the cities and royal courts of the Indian Ocean basin compare with those of western Africa and the Americas, based on the documents included in this and the preceding chapters?

CHAPTER 19

Consolidation and Conflict in Europe and the Greater Mediterranean, 1450–1750

Another ancient global crossroads transformed in early modern times was the Mediterranean basin, which was far more compact and less resource rich than that of the Indian Ocean but quite culturally diverse. In this period, the Ottoman Empire, centered at Istanbul, deployed weapons using gunpowder and an effective administrative apparatus to encompass much of Southwest Asia, the Arabian peninsula, and North Africa. The Ottomans were also a formidable sea power, particularly in the sixteenth century. As Sunni Muslims, the Ottomans clashed with the Shi'ite Safavids to their east and with mostly Catholic Christians, especially the Habsburgs, to their west. Relations with orthodox Russians to the north were somewhat friendlier. Other Europeans, meanwhile, split into nationalistic and schismatic Christian camps, mostly Protestants against Catholics. Long wars fueled by religious and ethnic differences nearly filled the early modern period. Caught in between, the Jews of Europe and the Mediterranean remained mobile and were often subject to persecution. Many fled to Ottoman territories, but others found havens in Amsterdam and a few other Protestant-dominated cities. In the midst of general conflict and a number of natural crises, science flourished in Europe. The resulting discoveries revolutionized the pursuit of knowledge worldwide.

19.1 GUNPOWDER AND HIGH STAKES: OTTOMANS VERSUS PRINCE DRACULA

Konstantin Mihailovic, *Memoirs of a Janissary* (1462)

Konstantin Mihailovic (c. 1435–1501) was a Serbian captive drafted into the Ottoman janissary (slave soldier) corps in the mid-fifteenth century. Mihailovic claimed to have served with a Serbian contingent during the fall of Constantinople in 1453 to Ottoman Sultan Mehmet II, "the Conqueror," under whom he served after his capture in 1455. After eight years' service as a low-ranking janissary, Mihailovic was captured by the Hungarian king Matthew Corvinus (or Matyas) in Bosnia in 1463. Once back in Christian Europe, he related his life story and offered recommendations as to how to beat the Ottomans on the battlefield. Mihailovic's memoir circulated in manuscript before being published in several languages in the sixteenth century. The following excerpt, an eyewitness account of Mehmet II's 1462 campaign against the Wallachian prince Vlad II, also known as Count Dracula the Impaler, was translated from a 1565 Czech edition. Dracula's loss to Mehmet's forces led to the reduction of his domain, now southern Romania, to full tributary status under Ottoman rule.

[Prince Vlad I, or Dracula] had two sons. He gave them to Emperor Mehmet II for his court. Dracula, their father, then died; and Emperor Mehmet, having heard that their father had died, immediately gave the older brother gifts of money, horses, robes, and tents, as befit a lord, and dispatched him with great honor to the Wallachian land [lower Moldavia, now southern Romania] to rule in place of his father, with the stipulation that each year he would come to him and report to him and pay him tribute, as his father had previously. But he left his second brother at court.

This son of Dracula had come twice in succession to the emperor's court, but then did not want to come any more for several years, until the emperor sent after him a lord called Hamza Bey who commanded the emperor's hawks. And Hamza Bey having arrived there in his land in a city called Braila, [Prince Dracula, Vlad II] did not want to report to him, but ordered his servants to detain the emperor's emissary until he returned home. And having departed from there he assembled an army, and it was winter, and the Danube had frozen very hard. Prince Dracula the younger rode across the Danube on the ice with his whole army to the emperor's land below Nikopolis. And there he released his men to plunder and kill both Turks and Christians in the villages and open towns. And there he did great damage to the emperor, and he had the noses cut off all those living and dead, male and female. And he sent those noses to Hungary, boasting that as many Turks had been defeated as there were these noses. Then, having returned, he arrived at Braila to see the emissary of the Turkish emperor, the emissary not knowing anything of what had happened. He had the emissary seized with all his servants—they were thirty in number—and he ordered them to be taken to a very secure stronghold isolated by waters, called Tirgoviste. And he had Hamza Bey, the emperor's emissary, impaled first, and around him all his servants.

Then the news came to the Turkish emperor of what Dracula—for they called him Dracula after his father—had done. Then the emperor sent for [Dracula's] brother to come to court, and when he arrived at the emperor's court, the highest lords, two viziers of the emperor's council, one whom they called Mahmut Pasha and the other Ishak Pasha—went to meet him and took him between them and led him to the emperor, where the emperor was sitting on his throne. Having risen, the emperor took him by the hand and seated him alongside himself

Konstantin Mihailovic, *Memoirs of a Janissary*, trans. Benjamin Stoltz (Ann Arbor: University of Michigan Press, 1975), 129, 131, 133.

on the right side in another somewhat lower chair and ordered that a purple garment of gold cloth be brought and placed on him. Then he ordered that a red banner be brought, and he gave it to him and in addition money, horses, and tents, as befit a lord, and he immediately dispatched with him 4000 cavalry horses ahead to Nikopolis, in order that he await him there. And the emperor having assembled an army without delay, marched after him.

And when we were in Nikopolis on the bank of the Danube, and also on the far side of the Danube Prince Dracula was encamped with his army so that he guarded against a crossing, Emperor Mehmet spoke to his janissaries, saying: "My sweet lambs, what is mine is also yours, and especially my treasures. Give me advice, for it depends on you. How could I cross to the other side against my enemy?" They answered to the emperor: "Fortunate Lord, order boats prepared or made ready and immediately in the night we will risk our necks and cross to the other side."

Then the emperor immediately ordered that they be given eighty large and well-rigged boats and other necessities for shooting: guns [i.e., cannons], mortars, field-pieces, and pistols. And when it was already night we boarded the boats and shoved off downstream in the river so that oars and men would not be heard. And we reached the other side some furlongs below where the prince's army lay, and there we dug in, having emplaced the cannon and having encircled ourselves with shields and having placed stakes around ourselves so that cavalry could do nothing against us. Then the boats went to the other side until the janissaries had all crossed to us.

Then having fallen into formation we moved a little toward the army, keeping the stakes, shields, and cannon. And when we had approached quite close to them, having halted we emplaced the cannon, for they killed 250 janissaries with cannon fire. And the emperor himself must have been very sad, seeing such a battle on the other side and not being able to do anything about it himself. And he was greatly afraid, fearing that all his janissaries would be killed. Then, seeing that so many of us

were dying, he quickly prepared, and having 120 cannon, immediately began to fire them heavily and thus we drove all the army from the battlefield and established and fortified ourselves. Then the emperor released the other infantry, which is called the *azapi*, like [Christian] footsoldiers, to come to us as quickly as possible. And Dracula, seeing that he could not prevent the crossing, moved away from us. Then the emperor himself with all his might crossed the Danube and there gave us 30,000 gold pieces to divide among ourselves; and, in addition, all the janissaries who were not free he made free to leave their property after death to whomever they wished.

And from there we marched forward to the Wallachian land after Dracula, and his brother ahead of us; for we were greatly afraid although the Wallachian prince had a small army, and therefore we were always on the lookout for them and every night surrounded ourselves with stakes. Despite this we could not always protect ourselves, for striking us in the night they beat and killed men, horses, and camels and cut down tents, so that they killed several thousand Turks and did the emperor great harm. And other Turks fleeing before him toward the janissaries, the janissaries also beat back and killed so as not to be trampled by them. And then the next morning the Turks brought in several hundred Wallachians, and the emperor ordered them all cut in two. The Wallachians, seeing that it was going badly, abandoned [Prince Dracula] and joined his brother. And he himself rode away to Hungary to King Matyas of glorious memory, and King Matyas had him put in prison for the cruel deeds he had committed.

Examining the Evidence

1. How does Mihailovic describe Dracula's resistance to Ottoman rule?

2. What does the sultan do to stop Dracula's forces?

3. Based on Mihailovic's account, what role did technology serve in the struggle between the Ottoman forces and those of Dracula, and how is booty distributed?

19.2 TWO ACCOUNTS OF A CONFLAGRATION

Marcantonio Barbaro, *Fire Engulfs Istanbul* (1569)

Marcantonio Barbaro (1518–1595) was a Venetian diplomat, or *bailo*, living in the Ottoman capital of Istanbul from 1568 to 1574, during the reign of Sultan Selim II. The Venetian government was among those very few Western entities that maintained close diplomatic ties with the Ottomans, primarily to continue its citizens' long-standing trade interests in Asia. Barbaro's letter to the doge, or Venetian prince, although its subject is a disastrous fire of tremendous proportions, provides a uniquely detailed look at the cosmopolitan city of Istanbul at the height of Ottoman power. The use of wood as the city's main building material throughout Ottoman times rendered it highly susceptible to such fires.

Letter from Pera, 1 October 1569

Serene Prince, etc. With the present letter I would now like to be able to convey fully to your Serenity the most miserable sight that has been revealed here during these days, so that you will be able, at least partly, to imagine in your mind such a marvelous [i.e., stunning] and terrible event. Yet I am afraid that since our own eyes, those trustful testimonies of our selves, could not assure us that what we have seen was not a mere dream impression, but a reality. I am afraid that presenting the truth to you in good writing would not be sufficient to make your Serenity and your Excellencies understand it in the way I would wish you to, and to grasp it as it really happened. With all that, I must not abstain from reporting truthfully what has happened.

And firstly, for your better understanding, I would like to tell you that this enormous city of Constantinople [Istanbul], built on various hills in a triangular shape, had never been so fully built,

populated, and enriched by the ruin of other provinces, especially that part facing Pera. Your Serenity should believe that presently it has been at its highest peak since many years. Truly, one may say that it is almost entirely built of wood. Because besides the structure of the houses, which is all wood (except for the mosques, the baths, and a few palaces of pashas built of stone walls as in Christendom), those few walls with which this wood is covered, are also made of bricks of plain earth mixed with straw [i.e., adobe]. Thus, one may say that everything is made of wood.

Since there has been no rain for five months, all these houses were arid and dry when fire broke out on Wednesday, the 28th of the past month (September), at the first hour of the night [i.e., just after sunset]. This happened in the most crowded, most densely built and richest part of the city, where the Jews were living, just opposite Pera. The fire spread so quickly and became so big that one could say: "And the night has become like day in its brightness." Flames propagated in every direction, and it seemed as if a rain of fire was showering from the sky. This sight, accompanied by innumerable cries of miserable men and women who saw their belongings ablaze, and their life and that of their children in danger, brought terror and boundless pity to everybody.

His Excellency the Grand Vizier [Sokolu Mehmet Pasha] and all his colleagues assembled there, assisted by men and by any possible means; but these were of no avail, since they had no practice, and the fire only expanded every hour in several directions with such fury, and to such terror of everyone, that it can be stated firmly that never before has something like that been seen or memorialized in history.

This horrendous spectacle could not have been better observed than from my dwelling, since it is

Minna Rozen and Benjamin Arbel, eds. and trans., "Great Fire in the Metropolis: The Case of the Istanbul Conflagration of 1569 and Its Description by Marcantonio Barbaro," in *Mamluks and Ottomans: Studies in Honour of Michael Winter*, ed. David J. Wasserstein and Ami Ayalon (London: Routledge, 2006), 145, 155–158.

situated on the hillside opposite the center of Constantinople [Istanbul], where the most beautiful and most densely built area of the city is spread out. Fire broke out precisely in this part, spreading longitudinally from the walls of the Grand Seigneur's palace to under Sultan Suleiman's mosque [the Suleimaniye], and in latitude from the Bedestan town down to that part of the sea separating Pera from Constantinople, in a circumference of about 3 to 4 miles. But more importantly, all this area was full of big houses and shops with various goods and merchandise, so that being more densely populated and richer than all the rest of the city, one could truly say that over half of Constantinople has been consumed. . . . And your Serenity can be assured that every single inflammable house within the aforementioned space, in width and length, was burned to ashes, because the wind, blowing alternately from different directions, caused the fire to reach every corner within that circumference, and it is no wonder that all has been burnt down.

And truly, one cannot imagine an action of lesser intelligence or of greater negligence than what has been seen on this important occasion. For considering the number of people involved and the other means that could have been employed, particularly in view of the presence of all the pashas and other magnates of the Porte, one could expect to put it under control within an hour. In this respect I would like to tell your Serenity that blames and complaints against his Excellency Mehmet Pasha are reaching the sky. For usually, when a great fire breaks out, the Janissaries bring a handkerchief or another sign to the Grand Vizier or to their Aga [Chief Commander], to indicate their presence, and afterwards, each one turning to identify his own sign, they are gratified with raises in their pay. This time, however, his Excellency Mehmet refused to accept any sign from the Janissaries. The anger of the latter, who could not give it even to their Aga, he being on his deathbed, was so great that, when requested to help they refused to collaborate. Because of such disorder the city remained at the mercy of the fire, and it is no wonder that so much damage has been done, for the conflagration continued not only the whole night and the entire following day, increasing incessantly so as to dim the sun and to cast an almost blood-red color over the entire city, but also continued all through the following night, spreading at the same time in different directions, which is undoubtedly difficult to imagine, and even more so to describe, but this spectacle was witnessed by all of us, as we were watching it from our windows.

In view of this commotion and confusion, and the dissatisfaction of the Janissaries, there was also great fear that all the rest of the city would be sacked. But by God's grace, no further incidents occurred. However, while during the second night the conflagration, with greater vigor than ever, was advancing tremendously, threatening to burn the entire city, the Most Serene Seigneur, having heard about the Janissaries' dissent caused by the lack of generosity on the part of the Illustrious Pasha, and since their Aga, son-in-law of the said Pasha, was absent owing to his illness, [the Seigneur] was so upset that he sent a message at midnight to inform the Pasha that he deprived his son-in-law of the office of Aga of the Janissaries, nominating in his place Siyavus, head of the stables and of the kapici basis [imperial gatekeepers], who was greatly favored by his Majesty. This caused considerable humiliation to the Illustrious Pasha, and opened further the way for complaints against him, since his rivals and enemies felt free to hurt him. His Majesty also issued an order, promising a certain rise in the allowance of well-behaved Janissaries. It is claimed that, being encouraged by this provision, the Janissaries started to act effectively, gaining ground against the fire, but I believe that remedy arrived not through their actions, but rather because of the wind, which turned in such a direction that it pushed the fire towards that part of the city that had already been burnt, so that after not having anything more to consume, it was extinguished by itself about the middle of the following day; there is no doubt that if a northerly or easterly wind had continued to blow as in the beginning, the entire world would not have been able to prevent the descent into ashes of this great and most famous city.

It is generally believed that the fire started in a bakery, though there is a rumor, also spread among important people, that it had been intentionally ignited in more than one place by a few Persians, and that one of them had been caught. But to date, there is no confirmation of that.

The damage caused by this memorable fire has been boundless and incredible, especially among the Jews, for in the whole of Constantinople there have not remained even two houses of Jews that have not been burnt. Having all resided within that area that has been burnt, all of them have suffered enormous damage, either by fire or by theft. Many of them have lost whatever they possessed, so that now it is heartbreaking to witness so many desperate Jewish and Turkish families with children and women weeping and crying while passing in the streets, with nothing or very little to support themselves. Our own merchants will also be hurt, for these Jews usually buy their goods and merchandise on credit for four or five months, so that many of our merchants, to a greater or smaller extent, will have to incur losses because of their ruin. . . .

Letter from Pera, October 15, 1569

. . . It is also said that the Jewish quarter in [the city of] Salonika has been burnt, and that another great fire has likewise broken out in Bursa. But the degree of certainty with respect to these occurrences in Salonika and Bursa is similar to the one regarding [the city of] Tana. It is strongly suspected here that both in Constantinople and in Pera the fire was the consequence of deliberate action, and indeed during the third night fire broke out here in Pera at three or four places, but without causing any damage. Therefore many provisions and security measures are being taken, and all through the night, both in Constantinople and in Pera, the *subasis* [city constables] are patrolling with a great number of men because of this suspicion. And, as a measure against fire, they have caused all shops to remove certain wooden coverings that are used outside houses and shops over the street, for those allowed the fire to run all through the city. They have also issued an order to the effect that when re-building new construction in the devastated area, streets should be enlarged by half a yard on each side, and the houses should not have more than two stories of eight feet each, because the Janissaries claimed that

the height of the houses rendered it difficult to ruin them, when fighting the fire.

These Janissaries, however, remain highly dissatisfied, since, as I have mentioned, a new Aga was nominated to replace the son-in-law of his Excellency Mehmet Pasha, and they were promised a raise in their pay as recompense for their efforts. However, the expectation that this promise would be put into effect in one of the recent meetings of the Divan [or Imperial Council] has not materialized, and they are suspecting that nothing will be done. Therefore it is feared that on the next occasion of a fire or any other event, they will be the cause of some trouble, or even that they will set a fire themselves as a form of revenge.

The damage of the last fire has really been tremendous, and in some parts of the city it is still not totally extinguished. Thus it seems to be inextinguishable, since it has been 18 days since its outbreak. I myself, having inspected the ravage in situ, have discovered that it is much greater than what I estimated when reporting about it to your Serenity. The circumference of the devastated area is a little less than four miles, in a nearly circular form. The destroyed buildings include 20 mosques, 15 Jewish synagogues, and 12 public baths, as well as innumerable large buildings, among them the house of the physician Amon [Mosheh Amon, physician to the Sultan], where the honorable ambassadors of your Serenity used to reside on their missions here, an impressive building, especially in this country. And although rebuilding has already started in many parts, and one gets the impression that a new city is being constructed, many years will pass before a place comparable to the one existing before the fire will arise.

Rabbi Yitzhaq ben Avraham 'Aqrish, *Three Interpretations of* Canticum Canticorum (c. 1575)

Fires were often blamed on minority populations, such as the Jews who suffered most in this case. Rabbi Yitzhaq ben Avraham 'Aqrish, who survived the fire, settled in

Minna Rozen and Benjamin Arbel, eds. and trans., "Great Fire in the Metropolis: The Case of the Istanbul Conflagration of 1569 and Its Description by Marcantonio Barbaro," in *Mamluks and Ottomans: Studies in Honour of Michael Winter*, ed. David J. Wasserstein and Ami Ayalon (London: Routledge, 2006), 145, 155–158.

Istanbul in 1553 after being forced to leave Spain in 1492 and Naples (a Spanish possession) in 1541. From 1541 to 1553, he lived in Egypt. Unlike Barbaro, 'Aqrish was directly victimized by the fire. The following is 'Aqrish's account of the fire, from his book *Three Interpretations of* Canticum Canticorum (c. 1575).

. . . and I had set out and came to [Istanbul], a great city of many people, a metropolis of Israel, and its inhabitants great men, wise and sage, people of great name, may the Lord guard them and redeem them. And I have been living here, doing my work, the work of God, and I have not been cheating in my work either. And one day, a day of misfortune and storm, a day of curse and rebuke, [Istanbul] has been burnt, and everything in it, all her palaces aflame, all houses full of beauty and precious objects. And the great fire was burning day and night, and no one could extinguish it. And myself in the midst of the conflagration, close to the altar, a place from which the fire started, may the altar be the atonement of all the children of Israel. And I have escaped like a bird from the trap, leaving my house, and all my books dear to my heart have been burnt, and no one could save them, since I myself am lame. And I have been lying stranded on the beach, five days and five nights, and no one was looking for me, and so many others like me. I saw the earth in utter chaos, and the birds wandered away, and all the land turned into a desert and wasteland, and its name would be from now on "Conflagration." And the people were going to and fro, one looking for his wife, the other looking for his sons and daughters, and one departs from his brother. I was crying for my house, for my wife and for my daughter, and especially for my precious and priceless books. And after five days I went to the mansion of the lady called Kira Esther [a Jewish woman in the service of the imperial harem living in nearby Galata], may she be blessed of all females, the widow of Eliyah Handali, may he rest in paradise, since she gave rescue and comfort to many, both rich and poor, as she had also assisted me before the fire with her donations and presents. And upon arriving at her house, I found my wife and daughter there, and some of my books, which my wife and my brother were able to save, and I found consolation with the books; although they were not many, they were among the best. Only one in fifty remained. One month later I returned to [Istanbul], to a place that the havoc did not reach, called Kastoria [now in Greece], where I found a few people from the Holy Congregation of Romania [i.e., Greek-speaking Jews], and I have been staying with them for four years, naked and needy, feeding on meager bread and scanty water.

Examining the Evidence

1. How do Barbaro and 'Aqrish describe Istanbul's great fire of 1569?
2. What role were the Janissaries alleged to have played with regard to the fire?
3. How do the observer's and survivor's accounts reflected in these document passages differ?

19.3   THE BATTLE OF BAGHDAD

Iskandar Munshi, *History of Shah 'Abbas the Great* (1625–1626)

Court historian Iskandar Munshi (c. 1557–c. 1642) composed his massive *History of Shah 'Abbas the Great* in Persian between 1616 and 1629, in the midst of his patron's rule. As his name suggests, Abbas was arguably the greatest of the Safavid emperors, and even his simplest deeds were regarded as momentous. Abbas was a fighter, at pains to hold his own against the neighboring Ottomans. In the following passages, Munshi relates key incidents on the field of battle in Baghdad, a frequent site of conflict between the Safavid and Ottoman empires.

Iskandar Munshi, *History of Shah 'Abbas the Great*, trans. and ed. Roger M. Savory, vol. 2 (Boulder, CO: Westview Press, 1978 [orig. written 1616–1629]), 648–649, 1038–1039, 1268–1272.

"The Battle of Baghdad," Year of the Tiger (1625–1626)

The Safavid garrison at Baghdad was of considerable size and had more than two thousand horses within the fort, so supplies of food for both men and animals had become scarce because of the length of that siege. Every day, some of the impoverished local people and indigent persons of the lower classes slipped out of the fort and departed. As a result of loose talk, the Ottomans learned that the defenders were short of food, and confidently expected the garrison to surrender at any minute. The month of Ramazan (May–June 1626) came, and the price of food rocketed because the townspeople, although they had certain stocks of food, in their fear of the soldiery kept it hidden, and there was little trading in the city and the markets.

Finally, Safiqoli Khan sent a report on the situation to the Shah. The Shah decided to collect all the stores in the royal camp that could be spared and attempt to get them into the fort by sending them by water to the west gate, opposite Old Baghdad, where a bridge crossed the river. The Shah hoped in this way both to raise the morale of the garrison and to give confidence to the local inhabitants so that they would once more bring their produce to market. At the same time, he hoped Ottoman morale would be lowered, and the Ottomans would cease to hope that the garrison would be starved into surrender, that last resort of a military commander.

The operation was going to be an extremely difficult one, because the Ottoman camp lined the Tigris at this point along the banks for a distance of about half a *farsak* [i.e., half an hour's walk] from the west gate. The Shah's supply boats would thus have to run the gauntlet of Ottoman troops who, becoming short of food themselves, were keeping a sharp lookout for any supplies of food by river. To carry out this operation successfully would be a major achievement, and I have not read of anything comparable in the histories of former times. The Shah requested from Safiqoli Khan the boats which were secured within the precincts of the fort, and a body of daring musketeers and other troops ferried these down the Tigris to the Shah's camp under cover of darkness. There they were loaded with flour, wheat, barley, rice, cooking fat, chickens, sheep, and other foodstuffs including desserts, preserves, sherbets, sugar, sugar candy, and the like. The boats were then dispatched at intervals, and Kalaf Beg was placed in charge of the operation.

There were not enough boats to take all the stores the Shah had collected, and so about five hundred karvars were loaded on camels and mules, and this supply train set off along the bank of the Tigris. The plan was to transfer the stores to boats when this supply train neared the west gate, because the Ottomans who were stationed in Old Baghdad had completely cut off traffic along the west bank by erecting breastworks, digging ditches, and placing groups of musketeers to guard these defenses. When Kalaf Beg and his men reached these defenses, after fierce fighting during which they inflicted heavy casualties on the Janissaries, they drove the Ottomans back behind the wall of Old Baghdad and cleared the bank of the enemy. All the stores were then transported into the fort without the Ottomans on the east bank being able to do anything to prevent the success of the operation. Kalaf Beg himself entered the fort and had a friendly conversation with Safiqoli Khan before returning to the Shah's camp, where he was warmly congratulated by the Shah.

The Shah was still camped at the confluence of the Diala and Tigris rivers. The Safavid field commander, Zeynal Beg, who had led his men across the Tigris to the west bank, eventually got tired of the inaction and determined to engage the enemy again. He received the Shah's permission to do this, the only stipulation being that he should exercise caution and not risk undue casualties. This time, the Ottomans came out to fight; Hafez Ahmad Pasha, in view of the stout defense put up by the Safavid garrison and the success of the Safavid resupply operation, had decided to try a pitched battle. A gap was made in the artillery lines and gun-carriage defenses to enable his troops to march out and draw up for battle in front of the ditch. The Safavid advance troops engaged the enemy at several points on the flanks and were getting the worst of it when Zeynal Beg and Kalaf Beg launched a tremendous charge which drove the Ottomans back to their ditch with the loss of about one thousand men. A strong wind sprang up at this point and stirred up clouds of dust, which so obscured the battlefield that it was impossible to distinguish friend from foe. Zeynal Beg called off his men, and the Ottomans made their way back to their own lines in confusion. Some Janissaries, who were of course on foot, were trampled down by the cavalry, and others missed the way across the ditch because of the poor visibility and wandering aimlessly around. The only Safavid officer of note killed in this engagement was Mohebb Ali Beg Sahi-sevan Samlu.

The Safavid blockade of the Ottoman supply routes was now having its effect. Not only were the Ottomans short of food, but sickness broke out in their camp, and every tent had its quota of sick men. The enemy now began to think of withdrawing from Baghdad, but were in no fit state to do so because of their losses and the incidence of sickness. Moreover, as a result of the depredations of the *qezelbash* [Safavid militiamen] and the scarcity of fodder, there was a shortage of donkeys for transport purposes and horses to ride. In these conditions, the Ottomans sent an envoy to the Shah, Mostafa Aqa, to ask him to appoint a negotiator. In compliance with their request, the Shah appointed the centurion Takta Beg Ostajlu, who returned to the Ottoman camp with Mostafa Aqa. The Ottoman commander in chief and his troops were at loggerheads, but after a great deal of argument and after everyone had had his say, they agreed to ask the Shah to overlook their misdeeds and allow them to retreat unmolested.

Takta Beg returned with a different Ottoman envoy, Mohammad Aqa, and reported this to the Shah. The Shah agreed to the Ottoman request, but while Takta Beg was still at the Ottoman camp and Mohammad Beg in the Shah's camp, and the terms of the agreement had not yet been finalized, the Ottoman troops, acting without orders, began to disperse in all directions. The Ottoman commander in chief and his officers were forced to retire on 9 Savval 1035 (July 4, 1626). They did not even have enough donkeys to pull a few of their heavy guns, which were cast in the time of Sultan Suleiman, and they abandoned their artillery and other weapons from the arsenal either on the spot, or at their campsite on the first night of their retreat. Various Safavid officers who found themselves in the Ottoman camp (Takta Beg, together with

Barkordar Beg Zu'l-Qadar, a retainer of Emamqoli Khan, and Mirza Ma'sum Arab Galizi Korasani, who had been taken prisoner at night near the fort) were returned. A group of Safiqoli's men emerged from the fort and proposed to annihilate the retreating Ottomans, but the Shah, sticking to his word, ordered Zeynal Beg to shadow them for a few days but not to molest them.

Ottoman commanders in chief had frequently invaded Iran and been forced to retreat in disorder without having achieved their object, but none had retreated in such a sorry state as Hafez Ahmad Pasha. Several thousand sick and dying men were abandoned around the fort. The Shah ordered that they be given medical care, but the majority of them died. Large quantities of weapons and equipment were also abandoned by the retreating Ottomans, and these were distributed among the garrison as their portion of the spoils. Although the Safavid troops did not molest the Ottomans, the same was not true of the Arabs and the Kurds, who harassed them all the way to Mosul, cutting off stragglers and releasing them after stripping them of all their clothes and equipment. At every stage along the journey, some of the Ottoman troops who were sick died.

Thus the province of Arab Iraq remained in Safavid hands, swept clean of Ottoman troops. The Shah sent letters announcing his victory to all parts of the frontier. Then, since the physicians advised that he should not remain longer at Baghdad because of the heat, the Shah sent votive offerings and alms to the residents and the poor of Karbala and Najaf, and after paying another visit to the shrine at Kazemeyn, began his return march to Iran, choosing the Mandali route because it was cooler. A Tabrizi poet devised the following chronogram to commemorate this campaign: 'Ali b. Taleb annihilated the Ottomans.'

Examining the Evidence

1. How does Iskandar Munshi explain the situation in Baghdad under Ottoman siege?
2. In Munshi's account, what do the Safavid forces do to turn the situation to their favor?
3. What role do gunpowder weapons play, and how are the defeated Ottomans treated?
4. How might we assess the accuracy of a document composed to praise Safavid greatness?

19.4 THE GLOBAL SPREAD OF SCIENTIFIC KNOWLEDGE

Galileo Galilei, *The Discovery of Jupiter's Moons* (1610)

Aside from the embrace of careful observation and deductive reasoning (plus a strong dose of skepticism), the Scientific Revolution in Europe was the result of many material factors, including improvements in optics, metal-smithing, and clock making, but also printing and long-distance transport. Galileo Galilei (1564–1642) was aided by all of these factors when he discovered four of Jupiter's moons in January 1610.

We have briefly explained our observations thus far about the Moon, the fixed stars, and the Milky Way. It remains for us to reveal and make known what appears to be most important in the present matter: four planets never seen from the beginning of the world right up to our day, the occasion of their discovery and observation, their positions, and the observations made over the past two months concerning their behavior and changes. And I call on all astronomers to devote themselves to investigating and determining their periods. Because of the shortness of time, it has not been possible for us to achieve this so far [Galileo published these in 1612]. We advise them again, however, that they will need a very accurate glass [telescope] like the one we have described at the beginning of this account, lest they undertake such an investigation in vain.

Accordingly, on the seventh day of January of the present year 1610, at the first hour of the night, when I inspected the celestial constellations through a spyglass, Jupiter presented himself. And since I had prepared for myself a superlative instrument, I saw (which earlier had not happened because of the weakness of the instruments) that three little stars were positioned near him—small but yet very bright. Although I believed them to be among the number of fixed stars, they nevertheless intrigued me because they appeared to be arranged exactly along a straight

line and parallel to the ecliptic, and to be brighter than others of equal size. And their positions among themselves with regard to Jupiter was as follows:

East   *   * ◯   *   West

That is, two stars were near him on the east and one on the west; the more eastern one and the more western one appeared a bit larger than the remaining one. I was not in the least concerned with their distances from Jupiter, for, as we said above, at first I believed them to be fixed stars. But when, on the eighth, I returned to the same observation, guided by I know not what fate, I found a very different arrangement. For all three little stars were to the west of Jupiter and closer to each other than the previous night, and separated by equal intervals, as shown in the adjoining sketch.

East   ◯   *   *   *   West

Even though at this point I had by no means turned my thought to the mutual motions of these stars, yet I was aroused by the question of how Jupiter could be to the east of all the said fixed stars when the day before he had been to the west of two of them. I was afraid, therefore, that perhaps, contrary to the astronomical computations, his motion was direct and that, by his proper motion, he had bypassed those stars. For this reason I waited eagerly for the next night. But I was disappointed in my hope, for the sky was everywhere covered with clouds.

Then, on the tenth, the stars appeared in this position with regard to Jupiter. Only two stars were near him, both to the east.

East   *   * ◯   West

The third, as I thought, was hidden behind Jupiter. As before, they were in the same straight line with Jupiter and exactly aligned along the zodiac.

Galileo Galilei, *Sidereus Nuncius; or, The Sidereal Messenger*, trans. and ed. Albert van Helden (Chicago: University of Chicago Press, 1989), 64–66.

When I saw this, and since I knew that such changes could in no way be assigned to Jupiter, and since I knew, moreover, that the observed stars were always the same ones (for no others, either preceding or following Jupiter, were present along the zodiac for a great distance), now, moving from doubt to astonishment, I found that the observed change was not in Jupiter but in the said stars. And therefore I decided that henceforth they should be observed more accurately and diligently.

And so, on the eleventh, I saw the following arrangement:

East   *   *   ◯   West

There were only two stars to the east, of which the middle one was three times as far from Jupiter than from the more eastern one, and the more eastern one was about twice as large as the other, although the previous night they had appeared about equal. I therefore arrived at the conclusion, entirely beyond doubt, that in the heavens there are three stars wandering around Jupiter like Venus and Mercury around the Sun. This was at length seen clear as day in many subsequent observations, and also that there are not only three, but four wandering stars making their revolutions about Jupiter. . . .

Alvaro Alonso Barba, *On the Number of Metals, and Places Where They Are Begotten* (1640)

The Scientific Revolution was not limited to Europe, and indeed news of scientific discovery traveled rapidly in the age of sail, even to lands where controversial findings came under close scrutiny from censors. In faraway Potosí, in present-day Bolivia, the priest and experimental metallurgist Alvaro Alonso Barba (1569–1662) referred to Galileo's Latin publication *Sidereus Nuncius* in relation to his own geological and metallurgical observations in the high Andes. Although both his work and Galileo's were suppressed by Spanish and Italian branches of the Inquisition, these scientists continued to question authority, arguing for improved understanding through reasoned experiment and use of improved tools.

Those who humbly attribute to the stars and planets special influence and dominion (besides the general effect exercised by the heavens) over all sublunar things, credit the formation of precious stones to the fixed stars; for these the precious stones appear to imitate, not only in the splendor and luster with which they shine, but also, and principally, in their fineness and permanency; on the other hand, lack of stability and constancy characterize metals; they are found sometimes molten and sometimes coagulated, which shows that they are under special control of the planets, called (on account of the variety of their movements) moveable stars. Thus, symbolically gold was designated as the Sun; silver, the Moon; copper, Venus; iron, Mars; lead, Saturn; tin, Jupiter; and quicksilver, Mercury. Nevertheless, as the last mentioned is not a metal [*sic*], some have replaced it in this last category by electrum, a natural mixture of gold and silver which at one time was considered the most precious of all metals. But this subordination or application of names is not logical, nor is it a fact that the number of metals is limited to seven. On the contrary, it is highly probable that in the interior of the Earth, there are more metals, differing from one another, than we commonly know of. Bismuth was discovered a few years ago, in the Sudnos mountains of Bohemia; it is a metal somewhat like a cross between tin and lead, without being either of the two; it is known only to a few, as may be true of many others. When we wish to attribute something of subordination or concordance of the metals to the planets, we should remember that it is not even certain that there are only seven planets; today, with optical instruments such as telescopes, others are seen; see the treatise of Galileo Galilei on the satellites of Jupiter; wherein the number and movements of these planets are carefully described.

Examining the Evidence

1. How does Galileo come to the conclusion that he is observing Jupiter's moons?
2. What role does technology play in Galileo's discovery?
3. How does Barba incorporate this new knowledge into his description of metals?

From Alvaro Alonso Barba, *Arte de los Metales (Metallurgy)*, trans. and ed. Ross E. Douglass and E. P. Mathewson (New York: John Wiley and Sons, 1923), 55–56.

19.5 | LIFE IN AN EARLY MODERN GERMAN-JEWISH COMMUNITY

Glückel of Hameln, *Memoirs* (1690)

Born in the German merchant crossroads of Hamburg at the end of the Thirty Years' War, Glikl Bas Judah Leib (1646–1724), also known as Glückel of Hameln, spent the remainder of the seventeenth century coming of age, marrying, having children (fourteen of them, twelve surviving), and learning to manage her family's jewel business. As a widow in her forties, she began composing a memoir in Yiddish for her children's sake, and it serves as one of the very few diaries from the period not written by a noblewoman at court. As an observant Jew and member of the Ashkenazi community, Glückel weaves her faith and providential understanding of history closely together. She also chronicles both the good fortunes and hardships faced by European Jews in an age of severely limited religious tolerance.

Book II

That which I have written and shall write comes from my troubled heart after the death of your father, peace unto him. He was our faithful shepherd. Surely because of our sins God took him to Himself.

While I am yet in good health I shall with God's help, leave all in seven small books. I shall begin with my birth.

It was in the year of Creation 5407 [1646–47], I think, in Hamburg, that my pure, pious mother, with the help of merciful God, brought me into the world. And though our Sages have well said, it were better that man had not been born because man must suffer much, I thank and praise my Creator who has made me according to His will.[1]

[*One page is here missing from the manuscript. The missing page apparently described the household and charity of Glückel's parents.*]

. . . (whoever) came into the house hungry, went out satisfied. He had his daughters taught religious and worldly things. I was born in Hamburg and as my parents and others told me, I was not yet three when Jews were driven thence[2] and went to Altona which then belonged to the King of Denmark, where they enjoyed many privileges. Altona is about a quarter of an hour's distance from Hamburg. Some twenty-five Jewish families lived there at that time and had a synagogue and cemetery. They lived there for a time and through the efforts of prominent men of the Community obtained permits to trade in the town. Each was valid for one month and cost one ducat, and had to be renewed at the end of the month. But the four weeks were always eight because they knew the burgomaster and the officials. Still, it was a very hard life especially for the poor and needy, who risked going without a pass; if they were caught they were imprisoned. This meant ransoming them and called for much expense and trouble before they were released. In the mornings, as soon as the men came from the synagogue, they went to town, returning to Altona towards evening when the gates were closed. When they passed through the gates, their lives were in continual peril from attacks by sailors, soldiers and all sorts of hooligans. Each woman thanked God when her husband returned safely home. Counting those that had come from Hamburg, there were at that time about forty householders. There were then

---

[1] This quotation is in reality from the morning prayers and is recited by women only as an offset to that by men who say: "Blessed be He who has not made me a woman." [Original note.]

[2] On August 16, 1648, the Council of Aldermen issued an order expelling all German Jews (Hochdeutsche Juden) from Hamburg. [Original note.]

The Life of Glückel of Hameln, 1646–1724: Written by Herself, ed. and trans Beth-Zion Abrahams (New York: Thomas Yoseloff, 1963), 13–15, 42–45.

no very wealthy men and each earned his living in an honest way. Chaim Fürst, peace unto him, possessor of 10,000 reichstaler, was the wealthiest; my father, peace unto him, had 8000, and there were others with 6000, some 3000— all lived well and at peace with one another; even people who possessed only 500 taler were content with their portion, not as the wealthy of these days, who are never content. Of them it has been said: No person before he dies receives half his desires.[3] I remember my father as a God-fearing man, without equal. Though he suffered from gout he brought his children to good positions and settled us all comfortably.

When I was about ten there was a war between the Swedes and Danes. I cannot write much of it as I was in *Cheder*[4] all day. The winter that year was the coldest for fifty years and is still known as the Swedish winter. Everything was so frozen that the Swedes were able to come right into Altona. Suddenly, one Sabbath day, the cry arose, "The Swede is coming!" It was early. We were still in bed. We sprang up, half clad as we were, and rushed into the town seeking help from the Sephardi Jews[5] and partly from the citizens. We were refugees for a short while. After a time, through great exertion on his part, and influence, my father received permission to resettle in Hamburg. He was the first German Jew to return. Later the other Jews returned from Altona, apart from those who had been living in Altona before. At that time government taxes were very low. We had no synagogue in Hamburg and no privileges and lived only by the grace of the town council. Still, Jews met together and held services in private rooms. This town council looked at it "through their fingers." But when the priests learnt of this they would not allow it and we were driven, like timid sheep, to attend the Altona synagogue. This lasted a long while: we crept back to our little synagogue, had peace for a time,

and then were driven away again, and so on, just as it is today.[6] I am afraid that this will last as long as we are in Hamburg and the town council rules. May God be gracious and send our Messiah that we may serve Him with good hearts and once more offer Him prayer in Jerusalem. Amen.

So we lived in Hamburg. My father traded in jewellery and, like a Jew, in anything else which could be profitable. The war between Denmark and Sweden grew fiercer till the King of Sweden was victorious and took everything he could from the King of Denmark and marched on the capital and besieged it. He would have succeeded if the Danish King had not had such good advisers and subjects who gave their blood and lives for him. This was God's reward to him, for he was a just monarch and treated Jews well. Although they lived in Hamburg, every Jewish householder had to pay a tax of 6 reichstaler to the Danish Government. Later the King of Holland came to the aid of the Danes by bringing his ships through the strait and thus ended the war. But though the Swedes and Danes may be friendly and intermarry, they never remain on good terms for long but always peck away at one another. . . .

Book III

Who can write and who can tell of the wonders that happen to mortals? I was about twenty-five years old at the time of which I write. My husband was very energetic in business and I, too, helped. It is not to praise myself that I mention that he took advice from no one but me, and did nothing until we had talked it over together.

At this time a young man, Mordecai, from Hanover—may the Lord avenge his blood—who worked for my brother-in-law Lipman, came to Hamburg and was our guest. We took a liking to him and engaged him to travel for us in such places

---

[3] Talmud. [Original note.]

[4] *Cheder*, literally chamber or room, and to this day a colloquial term for the old-fashioned Jewish elementary school, in which children are taught the elements of Hebrew and religion. It was only in Germany that Jewish girls and boys attended *Cheder* together. [Original note.]

[5] The Sephardi Jewish community had right of residence in Hamburg. [Original note.]

[6] Glückel refers to the prohibition of synagogue services for the German Jews. The Hamburg archives testify to the strict scrutiny to which Jewish houses suspected of serving as synagogues were subjected. The Sephardi community, however, were allowed synagogues. [Original note.]

where business could be done. He was a native of Poland and knew the language well. We sent him to Danzig to buy seed pearls, for we had heard that there were several parcels to be bought there, and seed pearls were then the most important article in the jewellery trade. We gave him a credit note for a few hundred reichstaler and instructed him how to buy the pearls. Had we sent jewelry to Danzig to be sold there and bought in return, we should have made handsomer profits, but we were so deep in the pearl business that we did not think of this.

Mordecai went to Danzig, bought the pearls and sent them on to us. He bought well and we made a good profit. But he was a young man, and desiring to marry did not wish to remain in Danzig. He therefore returned to Hamburg, became engaged to the daughter of Tall Nathan and the marriage was fixed for six months later.

My husband wished him to return to Danzig until his wedding. As if decreed from heaven, he refused. He said, "It is less than six months to my wedding day. Before I go there and return the time will have gone. I will go instead to Germany to buy wine." My husband then said, "How do you come to buy wine? I want nothing to do with that business." And Mordecai answered, "Then I'll buy it on my own account."

My husband did not approve, and tried to dissuade him, first in a friendly and then an angry way, from this business, but it was of no avail. He remained quite firm and no one could move him. My husband sent for his future father-in-law to get him to use his influence to dissuade him from the ill-fated journey, but to no effect. It was just as though the good man had to go to make room for others. If God had prolonged his life, perhaps Judah Berlin, and Issacher Cohen would never have come to their wealth, as I will relate later.

Thus Mordecai set out on his journey carrying with him about 600 reichstaler. This money he handed to my brother-in-law Reb Lipman, when he reached Hanover, to be forwarded to those places where he bought wine. Thence he had to go to Hildesheim. Mordecai was a stingy man who grudged the money that taking the post would have cost him. He made the distance from Hanover to Hildesheim, three miles, on foot. When he was

about 2000 feet[7] distant from the latter place, he came face to face with a poacher, who said to him, "Jew, give me money for a drink, otherwise I will shoot you!" Mordecai laughed at him, for he knew that the highway between Hanover and Hildesheim is safer than that between Hamburg and Altona. The poacher addressed him. again, "You Jew carcase! Why do you think so long? Say yes or no!" and took his gun and shot him in the head. Mordecai fell dead immediately.

This road was rarely deserted for as long as a quarter of an hour, but on this occasion, unfortunately, it just happened that no one passed. Thus the upstanding, noble and honest young man met an early end and instead of celebrating his marriage, he had to creep into dark earth, though so innocent. My God! When I remind myself of this, my hair stands on end. He was a truly good, God-fearing man, and had his life been spared, he would have done great things and it would have been better for us. God knows how pained we were over his death, and how much sorrow we suffered, as will be revealed later. He had not lain long wallowing in his young blood when people coming from Hildesheim found him in this miserable plight. He was recognized immediately, for he was well-known in that district. The grief is indescribable! But what did it help? We received letters from Hanover and Hildesheim, for people knew that he was our partner and thought he had had much of our money with him. All that he had was a few reichstaler for immediate needs. I can remember how upset my husband and I were when the news reached us, for at that time I was pregnant with my daughter Mattie, peace unto her. We could have done much business with him—but what has come to pass cannot be changed, especially death. Though efforts were made in Hildesheim and Hanover to find the murderer, he was never discovered. May his name be blotted out! and may the Lord avenge the guiltless blood, with the rest of the holy and pious martyrs.

We were left without anyone to help us in our business. A short time after, the wealthy Reb Judah Berlin, then a very young man, was brought by

---

[7] The Sabbath walking distance, permitted by Rabbinical law. [Original note.]

Jacob Oberkirchen, the matchmaker, as a possible suitor for Pinches Harburg's daughter. Nothing, however, came of this match, through whose fault I cannot say. Judah, who was related to us on my husband's side—he was a cousin to my brother-in-law, Lipman—remained with us as our guest for a short time. He pleased us in every way; he was well read, understood business very well, and was, besides, very intelligent. One day, my husband said to me, "Glückelchen, what do you say to our engaging the youth and sending him to Danzig for us? He seems to be a very sharp fellow." "I have already thought the same," I replied. "We must have someone."

We spoke to him and he was very pleased to travel for us. Before eight days passed he was on his way to Danzig. All that he had of his own was amber to the value of 20–30 reichstaler, which he left with my husband to sell or hold for him. See, my dear children, if God wishes to help anyone, He makes much out of little, for from this small capital, which really amounted to next to nothing, He brought Judah to great riches, and today he is a great man.

Reb Judah was in Danzig some time and did good business, buying up seed pearls. He did not strive much after deals, for we did not enjoy such big credits in Hamburg as we do now, we were still young and had no great fortunes. Still, we supplied him with letters of credit and promissory notes so that he was not short of money. He was in Danzig about two years. On his return my husband went over the accounts with him and gave him 800 reichstaler as his share of the profits. With this he moved to Hanover, intending to marry and settle there.

During this time I was brought to bed with my daughter Mattie; she was a beautiful child.

Examining the Evidence

1. How does Glückel describe the situation of Jews living in Hamburg at this time?
2. What glimpses do we get from Glückel's memoirs of everyday life for a European woman of the seventeenth century?
3. What does Glückel's history convey about the risks and opportunities of doing international business in this period?

19.6 VENICE ON A DUCAT A DAY

Peter Tolstoi, *Travel Diary* (1698)

Peter Tolstoi (1645–1729), an ancestor of the great nineteenth-century novelist Leo Tolstoi, was a Russian nobleman sent by Peter the Great to Venice to study the science of shipbuilding. Tolstoi spent the years 1697 to 1699 living in Venice and traveling through Europe, mostly in Italy and Habsburg Austria. Already in his early fifties by this time, Tolstoi was not the typical intrepid young traveler, nor was he very interested in learning how to build and arm ships. He had a keen eye for detail when it came to people and customs, however, and his account of Venice is rich and surprisingly modern, as if intended as a guide for other Russian travelers on a budget. Tolstoi went on to serve as Russian ambassador in the Ottoman

capital of Istanbul from 1701 to 1714 and held many other government posts before his death in 1729 at age eighty-four.

Venice is a very large and marvelous place, and it is twice as big as the [Habsburg] imperial capital of Vienna. Around Venice there are no town walls or passage towers or [other] walls. The domestic structures are all of stone and most marvelous and very large, and such expensive and well-built homes one seldom encounters in this world. In Venice along all the streets and along all the lanes everywhere is sea water, and they ride to all the homes in boats; but for one who wishes to go by foot there are

Max J. Okenfuss, trans., *The Travel Diary of Peter Tolstoi: A Muscovite in Early Modern Europe* (DeKalb: Northern Illinois University Press, 1987), 73–78, 149–150, 152–154, 159.

also fine footpaths along all the streets and lanes to every home for walkers, and every house has two gates, one to the water street and one to the land path. And many streets and lanes are divided into two halves: a water route, and one on land. In Venice there are no horses or cattle at all, and no coaches, carriages, or carts at all, and they do not know sledges [horse-drawn sleds]. In Venice along the streets over the water are built a multitude of stone and wooden bridges. . . .

Close to [the] church [of San Marco] right by the altar is built the home of the Venetian prince, whom the Venetians call in their language *principe*. This residence is built of fine craftsmanship, is all of stone, and in the rooms of this residence are many stone carvings of marvelous Italian work, and around the residence are also many fine carvings. These rooms are built around a courtyard and instead of being walled off, these rooms are built as offices for conducting all kinds of business. On this princely court, great stone gates are built from the palace to the square, which is called the Piazza San Marco; inside these gates sit many scribes like the Muscovite scribes of the square, who write petitions and all other necessary matters that someone might require. Goods for eating, that is, bread and all foodstuffs, meat, fish, and all poultry are plentiful in Venice, only all are expensive [compared to] Moscow; there is especially a great quantity of all kinds of fruits and vegetables, and they are always in abundance; likewise, there are flowers all year round, and they sell many flowers every day, because the Venetian women and girls use flowers in their attire and around their heads, and around their dresses. . . .

Venetians of the male sex wear black clothes, and the female sex also love to dress themselves in black; but Venetian men dress appropriate to their rank. . . . They clip their heads and beards and mustaches, and they wear large and very fine wigs, and instead of a hat they wear a black cloth cap, trimmed with black sheepskin, and they never put it on their heads but only carry it in their hands. . . . Those of the female sex and maidens of every rank dress themselves very finely in a particular Venetian style of dress, and they conceal themselves with a black taffeta [veil or scarf] from the top of the head to the waist, but many others dress in the French manner. In women's costume they use colored brocade of silk, and the women folk in Venice are very well formed and upright and politic, tall, thin, and fine in all ways, and they do not willingly do handiwork, but spend their time in idleness. There are always a great number of traveling people in Venice: Spanish, French, German, Italian, English, Dutch, Swedish, Scottish, Armenian, Persian, and all others, who come here not only for the business of trade or for study, but also just to stroll around and for all kinds of amusements. In the present year no Turks are here, because they have a war with them; but formerly, they say, there were many Turks in Venice, and for the Turkish trading people a large stone house was built, with a multitude of rooms in it, and now this house stands empty. And of Greeks in Venice, who live in residences and who do business by bargaining, there are more than five or six thousand, and also many Arabs, Hungarians, Indians, and Croats.

And of all the peoples there are especially many Jews, who have their own special place in Venice, enclosed by Hebrew houses of the same kind, and there are two gates to this place. In those places are built their two stone hospitals, and their homes are very rich, built all of stone and immeasurably high, to a height of eight or nine stories, and there are almost ten thousand Jews in Venice, and the Hebrews here are very rich, and have a great trade, and many Jews go to sea in their own ships. One Jew may have seven or eight ships of his own, and most of all they trade in expensive goods, diamonds, sapphires, emeralds, rubies, Burmese seed pearls and pearls, gold, silver, and other similar things. The Jews wear black attire, its form like that which Venetian merchants wear, and they wear fine wigs, cut their beards and mustaches; but only for recognition they wear a scarlet cloth cap, so that it is known that they are of the Hebrew race. Any Jew who does not wish to wear a scarlet cap must pay to the treasury of the republic five ducats per person per year in Venetian money, and then he is free to wear a black cap. Many Jews in Venice dress in the French mode, and their wives and the Jews' daughters dress finely and very richly in the Venetian and French mode, and many wear diamonds and Burmese seed pearls and other fine stones and expensive buttons.

The Jewish people in Venice, the male and female sex, are well formed, and the Hebrews may never have any kind of weapon on them.

The Greeks who inhabit Venice are rather wealthy, and all the Greeks dress in clothing like that worn by the Venetian trading people; and few people dress in the Greek fashion in caftans, but their wives all dress in the Venetian fashion, but others in the French mode. The Greek people in Venice of the male and female sex are not of a beautiful likeness and are very untruthful in all matters, and they are hardly firm or constant in their blessed Greek faith.

And no Venetian, noble or merchant, who goes about in the customary Venetian costume wears a sword or any kind of weapon on himself, but they have only on themselves, secretly, under their clothes, a small stiletto, or sharp-pointed knife; but those who wear French dress have swords with them. And when a Venetian who carries a sword must go to his prince or to a chancellery or to the senate, he must leave his sword in the passageway. . . .

In Venice the air causes distress, and there is a very foul wind from the seawater. . . .

Many of the Venetians are wise, politic, and learned; however, in their outward behavior they are not affectionate, although they are receptive to visiting foreigners. Among themselves they do not love to make merry, and they do not come together at home at dinner or for an evening, and they are a very sober people and never does one see a drunk anywhere. They have all kinds of drinks, many fine grape wines, and also many fine liqueurs and anise waters made of fine substantial grape wines, only they use little of them. Most take as drink lemonades, barley water, coffee, chocolate, and such drinks, from which it is impossible to get drunk.

For visiting foreigners they have stop-over houses, which in the Italian language they call *osteria*. There are many rooms in these houses, and when a foreigner arrives to stay in the inn, they give him his own room. In this room will be a bedstead, a table, an armchair and chairs, a chest for clothes, a large mirror, and everything else one could need, and each day they prepare dinner and supper for him, and every night they bring a tallow candle and also a lamp with wood oil. And for all of this the visiting man, even though he eats like a cavalier, pays a Venetian ducat a day. . . .

There are many shops of all kinds in Venice, and they are marvelously furnished as nowhere else in the world, except perhaps in France. There are a multitude of all sorts of wares fine and marvelous, in Venice. It is difficult to describe the commodities of the Venetian markets, as they are supplied every day with goods. Among the markets and amid the shops there are many fine pharmacies, in which there are all kinds of drugs, and they are so well stocked that it is impossible to describe them. There are many imported goods in the Venetian shops: French, English, Dutch, Turkish, Persian, and all other kinds.

There are many marvelous master craftsmen in Venice—gold and silver smiths, sketch-artists, joiners, sculptors, painters, master stone carvers, those who mold plaster, and others. There are many fine brass and tin and iron master craftsmen, and there are fine masters of carved and smooth ivory work; there are also masters of fine brass and wooden mathematical [i.e., scientific] instruments, and all of the works of Venetian masters are fine, even those of the arms makers. In Venice they make gold and silver and silk brocades, fine velvets, marvelous thick crimson fabrics and woolens, and various other brocades; and patterned and smooth taffeta, silks and satins, and patterned fabrics and fine patterned silks, and good gold cloth; they also make silk stockings in Venice. . . .

In the middle part of the square, male and female astrologers sit on high stages on chairs with long tin pipes, and he who wants to know something from these astrologers gives one a certain amount of money, and the astrologer whispers into his ear through that pipe. Many people are in this square all day for amusement; puppets perform, trained dogs dance, monkeys also dance, and other people play with *bandiera*, that is, with flags, and others play with brass plates and one stick very well and all together: one throws that plate high in the air with the stick, and from the height it falls down on that stick; and other people eat fire, and other people swallow large stones and many others do all kinds of tricks to amuse the people, and for this they take the money from those who watch them. On this same square at the time of the fair they erect many wooden shops and trade in them; at this time in these shops there are a great multitude of all kinds of the most marvelous and rich wares. All day at this time, the honorable Venetian people and women and girls in marvelous attire stroll through these shops, as do *forestiere*, that is all sorts of [foreign] visitors, and they walk and stroll and buy what they need at that fair, and at times from caravans.

On this square by the sea they set up large tents and sheds; in these tents men and women dance on ropes most marvelously, as do also the girls, among whom I saw one wife pregnant and close to birth, and she danced on the rope most marvelously. In another tent puppets performed a comedy just like living people. In other tents they showed marvelous things, among which I saw a man who had two heads, one in the place it should be, and he is called Jacob, and the other on the left side, called Matthew; also that one on the side has long hair, and eyes and a nose and mouth and lips, only he does not speak or eat, but constantly stares; and they say that it squeaks, but that the real head of that man speaks and drinks and eats. And he who wants to see such a man should look at its faces, for they are seldom encountered any longer in Russia; and if someone wants to see him for himself, he must travel to Italy. I also saw a bull with five legs there, and also a ram with two heads, having six legs and two tails, and many other natural marvels. And whoever wants to see them pays five *soldi* per person in Venetian money. . . .

There are operas and marvelous comedies in Venice that are impossible to describe adequately, and nowhere in the whole world are there such marvelous operas and comedies. During my stay in Venice, opera was performed in five places. The palaces where operas are performed are large and round, and the Italians call them teatrum. They build many boxes five tiers high in these palaces, and in one theater there are 200 and in another 300, and all the boxes inside the theater are done of marvelous gilt-work; others are covered with thick imprinted paper so that it is impossible to know that it is not the marvelous work of men who sketched them. Everything in this theater is gilded, and the floor is inclined so that one person sitting behind another in the chairs can see the opera; and for these chairs and benches they pay a price, and he who wishes to sit in a special

box, he must pay a higher price for the box, but for general admission to this theater the price is all the same. Over one side of this theater is a large, long hall in which the opera is performed. In this hall they sometimes have marvelous scenery, and in one opera there are 100 to 150 or more men and women in costume. The costumes they wear are of fine gold and silver, and they have many stones: crystals and jewels, and also diamonds and seed pearls. They play in these operas wearing the costumes of ancient history, and such things are presented in this theater for him who loves this history. The marvelous music in these operas is played by 50 different instruments or more, and one opera costs 30,000 or 40,000 ducats per year in Venetian money, and each ducat is 15 Muscovite altyns. The comedy in Venice is not as good as the opera, but very amusing. In Venice the opera begins on the first of November, and, having played a little, it stops and begins again at the time of the November carnival at the end of November or beginning of December; it runs until Lent every evening except Sundays and Fridays. And they begin to play in these operas in the first hour of night, and they end in the fifth or sixth hour of the night, and they never play during the day.

Many people come to these operas in masquerade, [or] in masks, so that no one will recognize them if they are at the opera, because many come with their wives, and visiting foreigners also come with girls; and because of this men and women put on masks and strange clothes, so that they are not recognized together. Also all through the carnival all the men and women and girls walk in masks, and they stroll about freely, wherever they please, and no one knows anybody. And this is how they always make merry in Venice, and they never want to be without amusement, and in this gaiety they sin much and, when they come together on the square at San Marco, many girls in masquerade hold hands with visiting foreigners, and stroll with them and amuse themselves without shame. Also at this time in many places in the square they make music and dance in the Italian fashion, and Italian dances are not very orderly; one skips around another, and they do not hold hands together.

Also many people amuse themselves by tormenting great bulls with Milanese dogs and other such fun, and they go along the sea in gondolas and barques with music, and they constantly make merry and no one is dishonored being together in this, and no one has any kind of fear in doing this; all do whatever they wish according to their own will. This freedom is always present in Venice, and Venetians always live in this ease and without fear, without injury, and without painful obligations. . . .

The womenfolk of Venice are very well attired and given to fashion and not inclined to do any kind of business, but they always love to stroll and be amused, and are weak to the sins of the flesh not only because of their wealth, but because having gotten rich, they have nothing further to do with business. And many wenches live in their own homes—of these there are more than 10,000 in Venice—and they do not regard themselves to be in sin or in shame, and they set themselves up as a business venture. Others who do not have their own homes live in special streets in little low rooms, and each room has a door on the street, and when they see a man approaching them, each solicits him over to herself with great diligence. The days when many men approach are days of great happiness for them. From this they suffer the French diseases [i.e., syphilis], and also they get rich quickly, from those who come to them. And the clergy particularly prohibits this in its sermons, but they do not constrain them. But they treat the French diseases very cleverly in Venice; when a man who has just learned of it tells a doctor, they cut out that disease and in a few days he is cured, so that no one learns of the disease; and a man who goes with this disease without treatment will be under treatment a long time, but it will be completely cured.

Examining the Evidence

1. What impresses Peter Tolstoi most about Venice, and, based on his account, what makes the city so interesting to a visitor?
2. What comparisons does Tolstoi make with Moscow, his home city?
3. How does Tolstoi describe Venetian women?

MAKING CONNECTIONS

1. What drew so many people to cities like Istanbul and Venice, and what opportunities did such urban societies offer?
2. What sense do you get from the documents in this chapter about the place of Jews in these Mediterranean and European societies at this time?
3. How does material life in the greater Mediterranean basin and Europe compare with that in other world regions in early modern times?

CHAPTER 20

Expansion and Isolation in Asia, 1450–1750

In the same way that the Mediterranean and North Atlantic trading spheres linked a wide range of producers and consumers, so too did the northwest Pacific Ocean and China Sea connect to the monsoon trade of the eastern Indian Ocean, bringing spices to China and silk and porcelain to Southeast Asia. As in the Mediterranean, pirates sailed these seas in search of valuable goods and captives, and no empire managed to gain a monopoly on violence or trade in early modern times. On land, the Russian Empire began its march east across northern Asia, reaching Pacific shores not long after the Qing seized China from the Ming dynasty in the 1640s. The islands of Japan, meanwhile, underwent consolidation in a period of extreme isolation, while the Philippines became a mostly Catholic Christian stronghold claimed by Spain, but with a significant Muslim population in the south. More isolated than open, Korea developed a unique, hierarchical society that included the widespread enslavement of native Koreans. These extremes of expansion and isolation persisted well beyond the early modern period in East Asia.

20.1 MOSCOW IN THE TIME OF IVAN THE TERRIBLE

Heinrich von Staden, *The Land and Government of Muscovy* (1578–1579)

Heinrich von Staden (1542–?) was a youth from the German province of Westphalia who made his way to Moscow in the late 1560s. He lived there as a translator and tavern keeper until the early 1570s and seems to have been favored by Tsar Ivan IV, later known as "the Terrible." Staden's account is most valuable for its descriptions of the *oprichnina*, Ivan's "state within a state" constructed between 1565 and 1572 to hobble Russian nobles. Staden also offers some wry observations on what it was like to be a freewheeling German youth in the Baltic States during the later sixteenth century. He eventually fled Russia when the Khan of Crimea attacked Moscow in 1572. He later presented his observations to Holy Roman Emperor Rudolf II in 1578, along with a proposal (never followed) on how to topple Ivan the Terrible and reduce Russia to tributary status.

I, Heinrich von Staden, the son of a burgher, was born in the city of Ahlen, which is in the bishopric of Münster, and is one mile from Beckum, three miles from the city of Münster, one mile from Hamm, and two miles from Warendorf. Many of my relatives, the von Stadens, live in the city of Ahlen and in other neighboring towns.

My father was a simple, good, pious, and honorable man who was called Old Walter, because my cousin Walter von Staden was called The Younger. The latter is presently mayor of Ahlen. My father, however, has peacefully passed on to God the Almighty with a happy expression and a smile on his lips. My mother's name was Kattarina Ossenbach. She died during the plague. They lived in the first house on the right, as one goes into the city by the east gate. Three houses are built as one. My late parents dwelt there as befits a pious Christian married

couple. My sister now lives in the same house, and is married to a nobleman named Johann von Galen. My brother, Herr Bernhardus von Staden, is the pastor in Untrop and the vicar in Ahlen.

When I had studied in Ahlen long enough that I could plan to become a priest, an unexpected accident occurred: at school I was accused of stabbing a student with an awl. As a result our parents sued each other.

Meanwhile, my cousin Steffan Hovener, a citizen of Riga, arrived from Livonia [present-day Latvia]. He said to me, "Cousin, come with me to Livonia. You will not be disturbed there." . . .

In [the German port city of] Lübeck I stayed at the house of my cousin Hans Hovener. He sent me with a wheelbarrow to work on the [city] walls, where I had to wheel earth. Every evening I had to turn in my work slip [to my cousin] so that none would be missing when he demanded payment.

Six weeks later I sailed with my cousin to Riga in Livonia. There I was in the service of Philip Glandorf, a city councilor and a strict man. I had to work on the walls again. It was awfully hard work. Because the Grand Prince [Ivan the Terrible] was advancing, the walls had to be put up quickly [in 1560]. The distributor of the work marks then became ill, and he entrusted me with his job. I secured so many work marks for myself that I did not have to work on the walls any longer. So I simply walked back and forth on the walls and looked things over. My cousin Steffan Hovener then said to me, "You are a ne'er-do-well." I therefore ran away, and went to the city of Valmiera.

Here I found work with the bailiff Heinrich Müller and had to learn Livonian farm procedure. I was often flogged with rods, and therefore I ran away. . . .

I then went with one horse to Prince Aleksandr Polubenski, the commander in Valmiera. He continually raided the bishopric of Dorpat with Polish

Heinrich von Staden, *The Land and Government of Muscovy: A Sixteenth-Century Account*, trans. and ed. Thomas Esper (Stanford, CA: Stanford University Press, 1967), 17–19, 97–99, 101–103, 108.

soldiers, and we often captured Russian boyars along with their money and possessions. The booty was divided unequally, so I did not want to give up what I had taken. I was therefore taken into the city and thrown into prison, and they threatened to hang me.

To be brief, having seen enough of the Livonian government, which was ruining Livonia, and realizing with what cunning and craftiness the Grand Prince [Ivan IV] was taking the country, I ran away and came to the border. I had to worry about the hangman there, too, because all those who were deserting to the Grand Prince and were caught at the border were killed, and so were their entire families. Likewise, those from Livonia who wanted to join the Grand Prince were hanged if they were caught. The important people of Livonia were now going over to Moscow and serving the Grand Prince.

At the border, I stuck a pen in my hatband and put a piece of clean paper and an inkpot in my shirt, so that I could make a plea if I was caught. When I crossed the border, the Ema River, I went to a nearby village and wrote to Joachim Schröter in Dorpat. He was to make inquiries of the Grand Prince's commander. I was prepared to serve the Grand Prince if he would pay me; otherwise I would go to Sweden, but I needed an answer soon. The commander sent a boyar, Atalyk Kvashnin, to me with eight horses. He received me in a friendly way and said, "You will get everything from the Grand Prince that you ask."

When I came to the commander, Prince Mikhail Morozov, at the castle in Dorpat, he received me in a friendly manner and said, "If you wish to serve the Grand Prince, we will give you estates in his name. You know conditions in Livonia and its language?" "No," I said, "I want to see the Grand Prince." "Where in Poland is the king now?" he then asked me. "I have never been in Poland," I answered. . . .

I was taken to the Chancellery for Ambassadors, and questioned about various things by the clerk Andrei Vasilievich. All this was written down at once for the Grand Prince. Very soon I was given a *pamiat'* or chit. With this I could demand and get a quart-and-a-half—or a pail—of mead, and four *den'gi* allowance, at the post station every day. At the same time I was given a silk caftan, cloth for clothes, and a coin as a present.

When the Grand Prince came to Moscow, I was brought before him as he was going from church to the palace. The Grand Prince laughed and said, "Khleba est'," and with these words he invited me to dine. Then I was given a *pamiat'* or chit in the Land Chancellery. I received the estate of Tesmino with all its villages. It had belonged to Andrei Kholopov, Prince Vladimir's treasurer. . . .

I began at the top. The Grand Prince knew me, and I knew him. I began to study. I already knew the Russian language fairly well.

There were only four of us Germans in the court of the Grand Prince's *oprichnina*—two Livonian noblemen, Johann Taube and Elert Kruse, I, Heinrich von Staden, and Caspar Elverfeld, who had been an official at Petershagen in Germany and was a doctor of law. The hearts of the two Livonian noblemen always longed for the Kingdom of Poland. They eventually managed to get to King Sigismund August with all their possessions, wives, and children. . . .

Caspar Elverfeld and I turned our hearts toward the [Holy] Roman Empire. Elverfeld had been with the Grand Prince at the *oprichnina* court before I arrived. . . .

When the Grand Prince took Staritsa into the *oprichnina* [in late 1569], he placed me on an equal level with the princes and boyars of the fourth degree. The former estates of the princes Menshik and Rudok Obolenskii, all their votchiny [hereditary lands] and pomestia [lands granted in exchange for service], were added to my other estates. The villages of Krasnoye and Novoye were *votchiny*, and six villages were *pomestia*. In addition, I had a yearly income in proportion to the number of my estates. The Grand Prince gave me a house in Moscow. A priest formerly lived there. He had been taken prisoner in the city of Polotsk and sent to the city of Vladimir. This house was excluded from the municipal records, and was painted white because it was free of civil obligations. . . .

How the *Oprichnina* Began

A number [of deceased grand princes] began the *oprichnina* action [before Ivan IV] but were unable to accomplish anything. The present Grand Prince likewise could not accomplish anything until [in 1561] he married [Maria,] the daughter of Prince [Temriuk Cherkasskii], from the Circassian region. She advised the Grand Prince to choose 500 harquebusiers [predecessors of musketeers] from among his people and generously provide them with clothes and money. They were to ride with him daily and guard him day and night. Ivan Vasilievich, Grand Prince of all Russia, thereupon undertook this and chose from his own and foreign nations a hand picked order, thus creating the *oprichnina* and the *zemschina*.

The *oprichnina* was [composed of] his people; the *zemschina*, of the ordinary people. The Grand Prince thus began to inspect one city and region after another. And those who, according to the military muster rolls, had not served [the Grand Prince's] forefathers by fighting the enemy with their *votchiny* were deprived of their estates, which were given to those in the *oprichnina*.

The princes and boyars who were taken into the *oprichnina* were ranked not according to riches but according to birth. They then took an oath not to have anything to do with the *zemskiya* people [members of the *zemschina*] or form any friendships with them. Those in the *oprichnina* also had to wear black clothes and hats; and in their quivers, where they put their arrows, they carried some kind of brushes or brooms tied on the ends of sticks. The *oprichniks* [members of the *oprichnina*] were recognized in this way.

Examining the Evidence

1. What do we learn of von Staden's early life, and why does he go to Russia?
2. How does von Staden become a favored person at Ivan's court?
3. How does the *oprichnina* work, according to von Staden?

20.2 MOUNTAIN TRAVELS

Hsü Hsia-k'o, *Travel Diaries* (1616)

Hsü Hsia-k'o (a.k.a. Hsü Hung-Tsu, 1586–1641) was an outdoors enthusiast and pioneer geographer of late Ming China. He spent over twenty years traversing the interior, climbing mountains, exploring caves, and navigating rivers. He kept careful diaries of nearly every trip, commenting mostly on natural beauty and geographical oddities. As for people, Hsü, like many modern nature lovers, had little to say. His guides were often similarly asocial Taoist hermits and Buddhist monks who lived in remote monasteries and caves. A new acquaintance described him in 1624 as follows: "He has a dark complexion and snowy white teeth. At a height of six feet, he looks as spare as a Taoist priest. His outward comportment is that of a mountain recluse, but there resides in him a rich spirit and the essence of courage."

My uncle Hsün-yang and I reached Hsiu-ning in Anhwei on March 3, 1616. We left its west gate and followed the stream coming from Ch'i-men county. Crossed it, headed south, and we reached Mei-k'ou where the stream joins the one from the city on its course to Chekiang. Followed the stream for twenty li [0.5 km] to South Ferry and crossed the bridge. Then we walked along the base of the mountain until dusk when we reached the Crag of Equaling Clouds.

We climbed five li, borrowed a lantern from a temple, and continued the ascent in a snowstorm, treading on ice. Passed Heaven's Gate after two li, also Pearl Curtain, but could not spare time to look for them in the darkness. All that we were aware of was the clinking of icicles among the trees. Finally I reached Lang-mei Temple and turned in for the night.

A heavy snowstorm came afresh after I had arrived at the monastery, but Hsün-yang and the servants had fallen behind and had still not come. I slept alone in the mountain abode and listened to the water dripping from the eaves all night without being able to sleep.

March 14. Rose and saw one color permeating the whole scene. The white snowy mountainsides were covered with ice flowers and jade trees. I stayed in the upstairs room until Hsün-yang and the servants

Hsü Hsia-k'o, *The Travel Diaries of Hsü Hsia-k'o*, ed. Li Chi (Hong Kong: Chinese University of Hong Kong Press, 1971), 63–64.

came. The figure of Yuan-ti, the presiding god of the monastery, is of a rugged black. Legend has it that birds carrying bits of mud they had brought made the figure, so it is rugged and dark. It is said to have been made during the Sung Dynasty, but the monastery was rebuilt in 1559 and the inscription of the stone in the courtyard was a composition of the emperor Shih-tsung. On either side of the central hall is a side hall, one dedicated to the Wang god and the other to Chao the general. The architecture of the monastery is grandly beautiful.

Jade Screen is at the back of the monastery and Incense Burner Peak is in front of it. The latter rises abruptly for several hundred feet like an inverted bell, a sight impressive to those who have not seen the more wonderful peaks of T'ien-t'ai and Yen-tang.

Going left from the monastery, we reached Self-Surrender Crag. Farther up is Purple Jade Screen, while west of it is Purple Heaven Crag. Both rise to enormous heights. Farther west are Three Maidens Peak and Five Old Men Peak with Pavilion of Literary Effusions in front of them. The peaks of the Five Old Men stand shoulder to shoulder, not very pointed but shaped like a brush supporter.

Returned to Lang-mei Temple, following the path by which we had come the night before. Descended the Sky Ladder and came to a place enclosed on three sides by crags which are hollow near the base and protruding above so as to form a covered corridor. Walked along the crag. A waterfall called Pearl Curtain Water flows down on its outside. In its recesses is Arhat's Cave which opens wide at the entrance and has a depth of fifteen li, its southeastern end being connected with South Ferry. At the end of the crag is Heavenly Gate whose hollow lower part allows men to walk in and out like a city gate. Outside the gate, tall *nan* trees rear their proud heads in the sky and stretch out their thousand green boughs. Inside the Gate, a range of crags forms the back of the Pearl Curtain, making a beautiful sight.

Went back to the monastery for the night and made plans to go to Five Wells and Bridge Crag. The Taoist monk Wang Pong-hua promised to accompany us in the morning.

March 15. Hear some voice in my dream calling "heavy snow." Made the servant hasten to get up and see, and heard the report that snow was covering hill and dale. Therefore I stayed in bed until nine when I got up and walked with Po-hua for two li to Pavilion of Literary Effusions. Although our plan for visiting Five Wells was frustrated, we were more than compensated by the wonderful sight of the whole universe covered in snow.

Examining the Evidence

1. How does Hsü describe his trekking and climbing adventures in China?
2. How does Hsü interact with the natural environment?
3. What is Hsü's relation to monasteries and religious figures?

20.3 CHINA UNDER SIEGE

Wang Xiuchu, *The Qing Attack on Yangzhou* (1645)

Wang Xiuchu is unknown to us except through his gripping account of the siege of the city of Yangzhou during the Qing takeover of China (Beijing was captured in 1644). Yangzhou was an opulent commercial crossroads located on the Grand Canal just east of the old capital of Nanjing. Qing forces under General Dodo, Prince of Yu, laid waste to the city as an example to neighboring cities, including Nanjing, where Ming holdouts remained steadfast. Wang's account of Manchu pillaging serves as a chilling reminder of the violence of the Ming fall, one often characterized as fairly uneventful. Yangzhou was defended by the viceroy Shi Kefa (1601–1645), who was killed in the siege.

Lynn A. Struve, ed. and trans., *Voices from the Ming-Qing Cataclysm: China in Tigers' Jaws* (New Haven, CT: Yale University Press, 1993), 32–37.

[May 20, 1645] One or two persons having told me that Qing troops had entered the city, I rushed out to ask others, and someone said that it was just the arrival of reinforcements from the Marquis of Jingnan, General Huang Degong. Soon I saw that the guards atop the city wall were still in disciplined order, but farther on, in the market, people were talking clamorously as a group of disheveled, barefoot people arrived in a trail of dust. Gasping in alarm, they didn't know what to say when queried. Suddenly a wave of several dozen horsemen was seen galloping desperately from north to south, protecting one man in their midst—the viceroy Shi Kefa. They had probably fled to the eastern wall but found the outside troops pressing close, so now, wanting to escape by the southern gate, they had come through here. When I saw them, I had no doubt that enemy troops had entered the city. Presently a single horseman came back, riding slowly with slack reins, his face turned upwards, wailing in anguish. In front of the horse walked two soldiers, who couldn't bear to leave the rider. To this day the sight remains before my eyes, and I regret that the rider's name has not been passed down. When he had gone some distance away, the men guarding the wall came down, making a commotion, and scurried for cover, throwing off their helmets and spears, some even cracking their heads or spraining their ankles. When I looked back at the turrets on the wall, I saw that they were completely empty.

Prior to this time the viceroy had found the city wall was too narrow to mount cannon on top. So he ordered platforms placed at certain ramparts—the fronts perpendicular to the wall and the backs connecting with the roofs of people's residences just inside the wall—to provide more room for mounting the cannon. But the work had not been finished. When the first enemy soldiers climbed over the wall, brandishing bows and slashing about wildly with swords, the soldiers who'd been keeping watch on the wall jostled against one another, trying frantically to escape. The way ahead being jammed, they all made for those platforms, crawling and pulling, hoping to reach the roofs of the houses. But the new platforms, not yet stable, collapsed underfoot, and people fell like leaves, eight or nine out of ten being killed. Those who made it to the rooftops broke tiles with each step, so that altogether it sounded like swords striking shields in a melee or like a hail of bullets, and the clatter went out infinitely in all four directions. The people in the houses underneath ran forth, startled out of their wits. Soon every room in those homes, from the outer reception halls to the inner apartments, was totally filled with soldiers and people who'd been on the wall and were now desperately seeking any nook or cranny in which to hide, oblivious to the owners' protestations.

In one house after another, people closed the doors to their outer rooms and held their breath. Directly in back of the central hall of my home was the city wall, so by peering out through a crack in the window I could see soldiers atop the south wall going westward. They marched in an orderly manner and didn't mind the soaking rain, so I thought they were the well-regimented troops [of the viceroy's command]. But just as I'd regained my composure somewhat, there came an urgent knocking at my door. Some neighbors were organizing a joint welcome for the Qing troops, and they were setting up a bench on which to burn incense to show that they dared not resist. Seeing that things were so far beyond help and being loath to go against the majority view, I lamely uttered a string of [yeses]. Then I changed into another style of clothing and waited, neck craned, watching apprehensively.

When quite a while passed and no troops came, I again peered through the back window to the top of the wall, where the military unit was spreading out, some soldiers walking on and some stopping. Suddenly I saw some women dressed in the Yangzhou fashion being bundled along among them, and for the first time I was taken aback. I turned to my wife and said, "Enemy soldiers have entered the city. If things go awry, you should cut short your own life." "Yes," she said, "Let me give you my few pieces of silver to keep." And then she sobbed, "Women like me in situations like this no longer think to live in the human world." . . . Just then someone from the countryside rushed in exclaiming, "They've come! They've come!"

I ran out and saw several cavalrymen approaching from the north, all leading their horses by the reins and walking slowly. . . . At this point people were looking out for themselves, and there was no communication among neighbors. Although we were only feet apart, not a sound could be heard.

When the soldiers got somewhat closer, I began to see that they were going from door to door soliciting silver. But they weren't being greedy, and they let people alone after getting small amounts. If someone refused to give anything, the soldiers would raise their swords threateningly, but they still hadn't struck anyone. (Later I learned that someone had donated 10,000 taels, but goaded by some Yangzhou natives, the Qing soldiers had him killed anyway.) When they got to my door, one horseman pointed to me and said to another, "Get something for me from this one dressed in blue." But before the second horseman could let go of his reins, I was in flight, so he gave me up and rode away on his steed. I wondered why they had wanted to get me even though I was wearing coarse clothes like a villager.

When my younger and eldest brothers arrived, we put our heads together, saying, "All those who live near here are wealthy merchants, so they look on us as wealthy merchants, too. What can we do?" The upshot was that I relied on my two brothers to brave the rain and hurriedly take the womenfolk through back-alley shortcuts to my second elder brother's house. It was located behind the He family graveyard, and close by on either side lived only very poor people. I alone stayed behind at my place to keep an eye on developments. But in no time my eldest brother came back and said, "Blood has been spilled on the main streets. What are you waiting here for? If all four of us brothers face life or death in the same place, then whatever happens, we'll have no regrets." So, respectfully carrying our ancestral tablets, I accompanied him to my elder brother's house, where we hid along with his wife and son, our youngest brother, my own wife and son, and two of my wife's sisters, and her younger brother.

By dusk the sound of Qing soldiers slaying people had penetrated to the doorstep, so we climbed onto the roof for temporary refuge. The rain was heavy, and several of us huddled under one blanket, so every strand of our hair got soaked. The sounds of lamentation and pain outside struck terror from the ears to the soul. Not until the stillness of late nighttime did we dare let ourselves down from the roof by the eaves, light the stove, and cook something to eat.

Fires had started all over the city—more than ten close by and innumerable ones farther away. The red glare was reflected in the sky like lightning; the crackling of the fires bombarded my ears incessantly. Faintly one could also hear the most pitiful sounds, and the mournful aura was extremely chilling—horrid beyond description. When our rice was ready, we just looked at each other, so anxious and tearful that we couldn't use our chopsticks, nor could we think of what to do. My wife took the silver that she had given me previously and broke it into four portions, one for each of us brothers to keep, and we hid the pieces in our topknots, shoes, and waistbands. She also found a tattered robe and a pair of shoes. After I changed into those, I lay wide awake till dawn. . . .

On [May 21] the force of the flames abated somewhat, and the sky also gradually cleared. So again we ascended to our rooftop hideout and found more than ten people already concealing themselves in the rain gutters. Suddenly a man emerged from a chamber to the east and climbed straight up the wall with a saber-wielding soldier in fleet pursuit. But when the soldier saw my group, he let that man go and began chasing me. Terrified, I fled downward off the roof, followed by my brothers, and we ran more than a hundred paces before stopping. After this incident I was separated from my wife and son and no longer knew if they were alive or dead.

The shrewd soldiers, fearing that many were in hiding, tricked people with a "warrant to assuage the populace," which stated that no one who came out voluntarily would be executed. So those who'd been hiding vied to comply, and soon fifty or sixty people had gathered, half of them women. One of my elder brothers said, "If the four of us alone run into fierce soldiers, we won't be able to avoid calamity. It would be better to cast our lot with that group, for larger numbers make it easier to avoid harm. Even if the worst happens, we'll have been together in both life and death and have no regrets." Because our minds had become muddled and we had no better idea for saving our lives, the other three of us perfunctorily agreed, and together we joined the larger group. The three Manchu soldiers in charge searched my brothers and got all their silver, but they didn't search me.

Some women came up, and two among them called out to me. I recognized them as the concubines of my friend Zhu Shu, and I anxiously stopped them. The two concubines' hair had fallen loose, they were partially naked, and they stood in mud so deep that it reached their calves. One was embracing a girl, whom a soldier lashed and threw into the mud before driving her away. One soldier hoisted a sword and led the way, another leveled his spear and drove us from behind, and a third moved back and forth in the middle to make sure no one got away. Several dozen people were herded like cattle or goats. Any who lagged were flogged or killed outright. The women were bound together at their necks with a heavy rope—strung together like pearls. Stumbling with each step, they were covered with mud. Babies lay everywhere on the ground. The organs of those trampled like turf under horses' hooves or people's feet were smeared in the dirt, and the crying of those still alive filled the whole outdoors. Every gutter or pond that we passed was stacked with corpses, pillowing each other's arms and legs. Their blood had flowed into the water, and the combination of green and red was producing a spectrum of colors. The canals, too, had been filled to level with dead bodies.

We came to the residence of the police chief, the Honorable Yao Yongyan, and went straight in the back entrance. The place was spacious, and there were piles of corpses everywhere. I thought that this would be my place of death. But we wended our way through to the front door, out onto the street, and to another house—that of a merchant from the west named Qiao Chengwang—which was the lair of the three soldiers herding our group. Upon entering, we saw a soldier who had detained several young women and who had been rifling the chests and hampers, making mountains of varicolored silks and satins.

When he saw the other three soldiers arrive, he laughed heartily and then drove the few dozen of us into the back hall. The women were put into a side room wherein were two small square tables, three dressmakers, and a middle-aged woman, who was also working on some garments. She was a local person, heavily made up and gaudily dressed, who gestured, talked, and laughed smugly. Every time the soldiers ran across some good item, she would beg them for it, brazenly using her fawning charms. One of the soldiers at one point remarked, "When we campaigned in Korea [1627 and 1636–1637], we captured women by the tens of thousands, and not one lost her chastity. How is it that wonderful China has become so shameless?" Alas, this is why China is in chaos. Then the three soldiers stripped the women of all their wet clothes, from outer to inner wear and from head to heel, and they ordered the middle-aged woman to take measurements and make alterations so the others could change into fresh gowns. Needless to say, the women, relentlessly forced to expose their naked bodies, felt so ashamed and awkward that they wanted to die. After the women had finished changing clothes, the soldiers cuddled them while drinking wine and eating meat, doing all sorts of things with no regard for propriety.

Examining the Evidence

1. How does Wang Xiuchu explain the fall of Yangzhou to Qing forces?
2. What do Wang and other city-dwellers do to try and save themselves?
3. What does this passage say about the methods used in the Qing takeover of China in the 1640s?

20.4 A GERMAN VISITOR DESCRIBES JAPAN

Engelbert Kaempfer, *People You Meet on the Road in Japan* and *The Prostitutes' Quarter of Nagasaki* (1691)

Engelbert Kaempfer (1651–1716) was a German physician from Westphalia who worked for the Dutch East India Company for much of his adult life. He attended high school for a short time in the town of Hameln when the Jewish gem merchant Glikl Bas Judah Leib (Glückel of Hameln) (see Document 19.5) was establishing her prosperous clan there. Unlike most early modern European travel writers, Kaempfer was not a missionary, merchant, or government official. He was a secular-minded medical doctor who considered himself a scientist. His methodical approach to the cultures he observed in Safavid Iran, Romanov Russia, and Tokugawa Japan prefigure modern ethnographies far more than even the most sympathetic missionary's writings. Kaempfer's *History of Japan*, based on his journals from two years' residence in the country between 1690 and 1692, was first published in English translation in 1727. Some potentially scandalous passages were omitted.

People You Meet on the Road in Japan

Pilgrims to Ise

When on a pilgrimage to Ise [a major Shinto religious shrine]—which takes place throughout the year but especially in spring—people have to use a stretch of this great road, regardless of from what province they come. So it is crowded with such travelers during the said season as people of both sexes, old and young, rich and poor, embark on this meritorious journey and act of devotion, attempting to the best of their ability to make their way on foot. Many of them have to beg for their board and food along the way; because there are so many of them, travelers are constantly accosted, and this is a great nuisance for people going to the court, even though they approach with bare head and meek voice and say only once: "My dear lord, please give the pilgrim to Ise a coin for his journey." The inhabitants of the city of Edo and the provinces of Oshu are in the habit of making this journey more often than others, apparently without permission of their superiors. Yes, even unruly children who are to be punished for their misdeeds run away from their parents to Ise, and when they return with a letter of indulgence, they must be absolved from any punishment. Because there are so many of them and they are so poor, one often sees them sleeping in the fields; on occasion they are lying at the side of the road, sick or dead. Others pick up the box with the letter of indulgence they drop and attach it to the next tree or bush.

There are also a number of slippery customers who pretend that they are on this pilgrimage, and for as long as they are doing well spend most of the year on the road begging. Others manage to perform this pilgrimage in a rather theatrical and amusing fashion, to more successfully attract people's attention and money. Generally they make up a party of four people and dress in a wide, white linen robe like that of the *kuge* [aristocrats] or the courtiers of the *dairi* [royal compound]. Two of them, walking slowly and often stopping, carry a litter decorated with pine branches and strips of white paper, on top of which sits a lightweight replica of a large bell, cauldron, or any other object that features and is significant in the old tales of their ancestors and gods. The third man carries a commandant's staff, which, however, is decorated with a white paper mop to indicate the propriety of this pious performance. He walks ahead, and they sing a song about the object on display in a rough falsetto voice. The fourth man visits houses or approaches charitable travelers, collecting alms. They travel only a short distance each day, for they have all summer to undertake their begging journey.

Engelbert Kaempfer, *Kaempfer's Japan: Tokugawa Culture Observed*, ed. and trans. Beatrice M. Bodart-Bailey (Honolulu: University of Hawai'i Press, 1999) 142–143, 274–275.

Junrei

Here and there one finds the so-called *junrei*, that is, those who visit the thirty-three most important Kannon temples throughout the country. They drift around in twos or threes and at each house sing a pitiful Kannon tune; occasionally they also play a fiddle or zither not unlike the vagrants in Germany, but they do not approach travelers for alms. They carry small boards around their necks, each inscribed separately with the name of a temple they have not yet visited and arranged in proper order. They have a linen cloth around their chests and other accouterments peculiar to their pilgrimage. Some like this pious vagabond life so much that they have no desire to earn their living by any other occupation but spend their time traveling the country in a never-ending pilgrimage.

Vows

Occasionally in winter one comes across the strange spectacle of a number of naked people, girded only with a bunch of straw to cover their private parts. They have made a vow to a certain temple and deities to pay a visit in this difficult fashion so that their parents, close friends, or they themselves may regain their health or some other favor. They lead a life of austerity and poverty on their journey, and always walk along the road by themselves without much rest.

Shorn Beggars

This large road is, moreover, full of a variety of other beggars: often they are young and have their heads shorn. The custom of shaving the head was introduced by Shotoku Taishi when he zealously spread the worship of *hotoke*, or foreign gods, and has been kept till the present day. When his sworn enemy Moriya violently opposed his spreading the teachings of these gods, Shotoku Taishi ordered that all men who had adopted this heathen religion shave half their head to distinguish them from those supporting Moriya and that poor children should be shorn completely like the priests. This meant that, by being shorn, they had a monopoly on seeking alms.

Among those who shave their heads is an extraordinary number of young wenches called *bikuni*, or nuns, because they are under the authority and protection of convents at Kamakura and Miyako, to which annually they must pay a part of their earnings; others pay temples in Ise or Kumano. They usually reside in the vicinity of these temples and hence are called *Kumano no bikuni* to distinguish them from religious nuns. They are nearly the prettiest wenches we have seen on our travels through Japan, because the privilege to collect alms as a nun is generally requested, and easily obtained, by those poor girls who are beautiful and blessed with an attractive figure, since it is well known that these are the most suitable weapons for plundering the pockets of travelers. The begging *yamabushi* make their daughters enter this profession, and they themselves also marry the *bikuni*. Among them are some who have been trained in houses of prostitution and have bought their freedom after having served their term to spend the remaining part of their youth in this fashion. These *bikuni* move in groups of two or three, walk daily one or several miles from their home, and approach genteel travelers who pass in *kago* [palanquin, or sedan chair] or on horseback. Each of them attaches herself to one particular traveler, starts up a rustic tune, and as long as it is to her advantage, she accompanies and amuses him for several hours. They look neither religious nor poor, for they cover their shorn heads with black silk hoods and adorn themselves nicely and neatly in secular dress, covering their hands with fingerless gloves and protecting their faces, generally decorated with makeup, with large sun hats. They carry a small walking stick and look like romantic shepherdesses. Moreover, their speech and manner are neither insolent, woeful, vulgar, nor affected but open and modestly restrained. But not to praise these female beggars and their modesty inordinately, I have to mention that, following the custom of the country and their order, they are not too modest to expose their breasts to a generous traveler on the open road. So I can hardly exclude them from the category of loose women and prostitutes, however much they adopt religious tonsure [hairstyle].

The Prostitutes' Quarter of Nagasaki

According to the custom of this country, we will pass from the temples to the *keiseimachi*, or prostitutes' quarter. For politeness' sake it is also called *maruyama*, after the name of the hill on which it is located, and it is frequented no less than the temples.

This quarter makes up the southernmost part of the city, and according to Japanese calculation consists of two streets, but to our way of counting, of several streets. It is situated on the slope of a hill and includes the finest houses of the commoners' city, occupied by no one else but the keepers of this profession. Except for a smaller one in Chikuzen, the quarter is the only one on Saikoku where the poor of this island (which, except for Miyako, produces the most beautiful people of Japan) can secure a living for their pretty daughters. On account of the good living that can be earned from the foreigners and locals (the most debauched of all cities), the quarter is well supplied and, next to that of Miyako, is considered the most famous in the country. The girls are traded for a sum of money when still children for a certain number of years (ten, twenty). A well-to-do brothel keeper keeps seven to thirty girls, old and young, under the same roof in separate rooms and daily has them assiduously instructed in dancing, playing instruments, writing letters, and other skills becoming to this sex and appropriate to a life of luxury. The youngest are both students and servants to the oldest and most experienced. As the girls improve in these arts and in good deportment in company, and profit their keeper by being much in demand and frequently asked out, he also rewards them higher ranks and gives them better accommodation. Also the fee the keeper charges to their admirers increases. For an elegant affair of one night the price starts from two mace

[c. 7.5 g of silver] and goes up to two *bu* [c. 9 g of gold], the highest permissible by law. One of the lowliest, either someone considered past service or condemned to this job for some crime, has to keep the evening and night watch in a specially designated anteroom of the house and for one mace light a candle for passersby. If these prostitutes marry honest people, they pass as honest women among the commoners, since they are not responsible for their profession and furthermore have been well educated. The brothel keepers, on the contrary, however rich they may be, cannot pass as and associate with honest people. They are called by the derogatory and thought-provoking term *kutsuwa*, meaning "horse-bit," and are considered to be subhuman, of the same status as the *eta*, or leather tanners, who are the executioners and knackers in this country. Consequently the brothel keepers must bear the burden of making their male servants or day laborers available to execute the courts' punishment and lend them to the *eta*.

Examining the Evidence

1. What kinds of people does Kaempfer encounter on the road as he travels in Japan?
2. What aspects of female behavior strike Kaempfer as most notable?
3. How does Kaempfer describe the lives of prostitutes and procurers in the trading enclave of Nagasaki?

20.5 NOTES FROM A KOREAN QUEEN'S DIARY

Lady Hong, *Diary* (c. 1750)

Lady Hong (1735–1815) was a member of Korea's high nobility who married Crown Prince Sado in 1745, at the age of ten. By the age of twenty, she had given birth to two daughters and a son. Lady Hong's husband grew so mentally unstable and violent that he would today be called a serial killer. As a result of his behavior, his father, King Yongjo, killed his own son in 1762. Lady Hong's only son took the throne as King Chongjo in 1776, and her

grandson succeeded him as King Sunjo, who ruled from 1800 to 1834. In her memoir, begun in 1796, in part to clarify the events leading to her husband's death, she recalls the many vicissitudes of her life as a princess, queen, and mother, as well as the many intrigues of Korea's Neo-Confucian Yi dynasty court. Unlike most surviving writings from the period, typically composed and published in Chinese, Lady Hong's memoir was written using the Korean han'gul alphabet.

Lady Hong, *Memoirs of a Korean Queen*, ed. and trans. Choe-Wall Yang-hi (Boston: Routledge, 1985), 47–49.

Although what follows is something I should not record, I cannot help but do so. When I was pregnant with Uiso, I often saw [my sister-in-law] Princess Hwap'yong in my dreams. She would come into my bedroom, sit beside me, and laugh. In my immature way I thought it was because Princess Hwap'yong had died in childbirth, and since she appeared so regularly in my dreams, I was concerned about my own well-being, for I understood that the spirit of delivery is merciless. When Uiso was born and washed, I found he had a red spot on his shoulder and a blue spot on his stomach. At first I did not pay special attention to this, but King Yongjo was supposed to proceed to Onyang on 11 October 1750, and on the tenth he and Lady Sonhui came to see us, their faces half happy and half sad. Suddenly, they undid the baby's coat collar and bared his shoulders, discovering the red spot immediately. They seemed to be very moved and really to think that Princess Hwap'yong had been reincarnated. From that time on, they treasured the baby just as they had treasured my sister-in-law, Hwap'yong. When the child was newly born, the king had never taken any special precautions toward him, and had come to see the baby in the robe he had worn for his audience with the government officials. But from that day forth, he was most careful about anything he felt might harm the baby, indulging in groundless and obscure superstitions which I could not understand. His behavior was probably affected by something he had seen in his dreams.

One hundred days after the baby's birth, the king ordered repairs to be made to the Hwan'gyong-jon Mansion, where he used to give audience to the people, and moved the baby into this palace. As King Yongjo loved the baby so much, I implored him to treat the baby's father [Lady Hong's husband, the crown prince] better. But the fact is that the king loved the baby because he thought it was the reincarnation of Hwap'yong and, as its parents, we were treated no better than before—a thing I could not understand. In the fifth month, 1751, when the baby was only ten months old, the king invested him with the title of royal grandson. Although this was motivated by his extreme love for his grandson, I thought he was overdoing things, and when Uiso died in the spring of 1752, the king's agony exceeded description.

In January 1752, with the help and influence of heaven and the royal ancestors, I again became pregnant and in the ninth month, 1752, I bore another son. This was the future King Chonjo. In view of the few blessings I had received up till then, it was an unexpected happiness. When the baby was born, his appearance was impressive, his bone structure outstanding, and he really was the True Man of Taoism, the heaven-sent one. Around the time of the baby's conception, the crown prince had roused from sleep and said, "I dreamt about a dragon; it must be an omen that I shall beget a noble son." He had asked me to get a strip of white silk for him, and he had drawn the dragon he had seen in his dream and hung it on the wall. Naturally, there ought to be an unusual omen before the birth of a sage.

After the bitter loss of Uiso, King Yongjo was delighted to regain a foundation for the state, and said to me, "Since the royal grandson is so outstanding, he must be a blessing sent by the divine spirits of the royal ancestors. You, a descendant of Princess Chongmyong, became the crown prince's consort, and your body was blessed so that you were able to make this meritorious contribution to the state." He also said, "Please rear the child carefully yet modestly, for in this way you may spin out his happiness." Naturally, I held these royal instructions in high regard, never forgetting such royal favor and keeping these in mind all the time. The crown prince too was overjoyed, and everyone in the country rejoiced, even more so than before. My parents congratulated me, clapping their hands in joy. Whenever they saw me, they congratulated me on giving birth to the royal grandson. I was very happy and proud to think that at the age of less than twenty, my body had been blessed that I was able to ensure the happiness of the state, and that my future was secured. I prayed that in my old age I might long be able to enjoy my son's filial devotion.

Examining the Evidence

1. How does Lady Hong describe her experience as the mother of Korea's future king?
2. What was the role of religion in Lady Hong's interpretation of events?
3. How does Lady Hong's writing reflect Neo-Confucian ethics?

20.6   MANILA: GLOBAL COMMERCIAL CROSSROADS

Antonio de Morga, *Account of the Philippine Islands* (c. 1600)

Antonio de Morga (1559–1636) graduated from the University of Salamanca and after teaching law for several years spent the rest of his life as a judge in Spain's overseas colonies. He began his work as a civil magistrate in 1582 in northern Spain but was sent, along with his wife, children, and numerous servants, to the Philippines in 1594. The voyage, which included an overland trek across Mexico, took fifteen months. De Morga served briefly as lieutenant governor before heading up Manila's newly reinstated high court of appeals, or *audiencia*, in 1598. After an ill-advised fight with Dutch pirates in 1600 that nearly got him killed, the judge was called away to serve in the Audiencia of New Spain, in Mexico City. His last post, taken up in 1615, was as president of the Audiencia of Quito, in what is now Ecuador. De Morga's keen observations of commerce in Manila in its heyday are among the most detailed to survive. They were published in Mexico City in 1609.

A considerable number of junks (which are large ships) come as a rule laden with goods from Great China to Manila. Every year thirty, sometimes forty, of these ships come, though they do not enter together as a fleet or armada, but in squadrons, with the monsoon and in settled weather, which ordinarily comes with the March new moon. These vessels belong to the provinces of Canton, Chincheo, and Ucheo, whence they come. They make the journey to Manila in fifteen or twenty days, sell their merchandise and return in good time, before the strong southwesterly winds set in at the end of May, or the first days of June, so as not to run into danger on their voyage.

These vessels come laden with merchandise, with their owners, who are rich men, together with servants and factors representing others who remain in China. These men leave there with permission and license of their provincial viceroys and mandarins, and the goods they usually bring with them, for sale to the Spaniards, are bundles of raw silk of the thickness of two heads and other silk of lesser quality, soft and unspun; these are white and of all other colors, in small skeins; they also bring quantities of velvet, some plain, some embroidered with all sorts of fancywork, colors and patterns; Others have a background of gold overlaid with a gold embroidery; there are stuffs and light brocades of gold and silver, woven into silks of different colors and patterns; quantities of gold and silver, wound in skeins over thread and silk. But all the tinsel glitter of this gold and silver is false, and only [deserves to be called gold and silver] on paper. They bring, too, damasks, satins, taffetas, grogram [rough-textured silk fabric], silk stuff, and other cloths of every color, some finer and better than others; also a good deal of cloth made from leaves [i.e., plant fibers], which they call "linen gauze," and white cotton cloth of different kinds and sorts, suitable for every possible use. Besides these they bring musk, benzoin, ivory, many covers for beds; hangings, coverlets, drapery of embroidered velvet; damasks and grogram of different shades, tablecloths, cushions, carpets, caparisons [festive cloth covers] for horses made of the same stuff and decorated with glass beads or pearl trimmings; pearls, rubies, sapphires, and crystal-stones; metal basins, kettles, and other vessels of copper and cast iron; large assortments of nails of all kinds, sheet iron, tin, lead, saltpeter, and gunpowder; wheat, flour, preserves of oranges, peaches, black parsnips, pears, nutmeg, ginger, and other fruits from China; salt hams and other meats, live fowls of good stock, excellent capons; plenty of green fruit, all kinds of oranges, very good chestnuts, nuts, pears, chicueys, both green and ripe, which is a delicious fruit; every variety

Antonio de Morga, *Sucesos de las Islas Filipinas*, trans. and ed. J. S. Cummins (London: Hakluyt Society, 1971), 305–310.

of fine thread, needles, and knick-knacks; little boxes and writing cases; beds, tables, chairs, gilt couches, decorated with many designs and patterns; tame buffaloes, geese like swans in appearance; horses, mules, and donkeys, even caged birds some of which talk, while others sing, and they make them play lots of tricks; thousands of other gewgaws and trifles of little value and worth, yet which are rated highly by the Spaniards; and in addition a great deal of fine [porcelain] crockery of all sorts, cangans, and sines [vessel types], besides black and blue robes; tacley, which are beads of all kinds, strings of cornelians, and other beads and stones of all colors; pepper and other spices; and rarities, to recount all of which would mean never finishing, nor would even masses of paper suffice for the task.

As soon as the ship reaches the mouth of Manila Bay, the watchman stationed on the island of Miraveles goes out in a light vessel to inspect it, after which he puts two or three soldiers on board her as guards so that she may anchor above the bar, near the city, and so that no one shall either board or disembark from the ship until the vessel has been examined. A fire-signal is set off by the watchman on his island, and the news rushed to the city so that even before the ship anchors the governor and citizens generally know all about it: what vessel it is, whence it comes, what people and merchandise it carries on board.

When the ship arrives and anchors, the royal officials carry out their inspection of the cargo. At the same time a formal valuation is made of the worth of the goods according to Manila prices, for the vessel immediately pays three percent on everything to the royal exchequer. As soon as the examination is over and the valuation concluded, then the cargo of merchandise is unloaded by another official and placed on board sampans [small skiffs] and taken to the parian [market], or to other establishments and warehouses outside the city where it is sold freely.

No Spaniard, Sangley [Chinese], or any other person whatever is permitted to board the vessel to buy or bargain for goods and supplies, nor for anything else either. Nor, when the goods are on land in warehouses and stores, is it allowed to take anything

violently or to force them to sell: all the trading has to be voluntary and the Sangleyes are allowed to do as they wish with their property.

The ordinary price of silks (both raw and woven) and the cloths which form the bulk of their cargoes is settled in a leisurely way and by persons who understand the business, on both the Spanish and the Sangley sides. The price is paid in silver [ingots] and in reales [silver coins] for they do not wish to accept gold or other methods of payment, and will not take anything else to China. All the business has to be finished by the month of May, more or less, so that the Sangleyes can return and so that the Spaniards may have their purchases ready to load on to the galleons bound for New Spain at the end of June. However, most of the more thrifty traders and richer men do their bargaining at a later date, and at lower prices, holding their goods over until the following year's galleon. Some of the Sangleyes remain at Manila with a portion of their cargo if the price offered them is not right, and they gradually sell it off in a leisurely manner. The Sangleyes are very skilful and intelligent traders, patient and level-headed, so as to do their business the better. They are ready to allow credit and give liberal terms to those whom they know will deal squarely with them and will not fail in paying them in due time. On the other hand, however, since they are a people without any religion or conscience, and so greedy, they commit innumerable frauds and tricks in their dealings, so that it is necessary to be sharp, and to know the goods one is buying, so as not to be cheated. But buyers get even with them by playing tricks in their turn as well as by their faulty payments. So between one side and the other the judges and the *audiencia* are kept busy.

Likewise some Japanese and Portuguese merchant ships come annually from the port of Nagasaki in Japan with the north winds at the end of October and March. They enter and anchor in Manila in the same way as that described above. The bulk of their cargo is very good quality wheat flour and highly rated salt meats, for supplying Manila; they also bring fine woven silk materials of different colors; beautiful and prettily decorated screens done in oil and gilt; all sorts of cutlery; many suits of armor, lances, swords, and some finely wrought weapons like halberds; writing cases, boxes and smaller wooden containers, varnished and delicately worked, besides other pretty looking trinkets; excellent fresh pears; barrels and kegs of good salt tunny [fish]; cages of very fine larks, called fimbaros; and other trifles besides. Some of this is also purchased without royal dues being levied on the ships; most of the goods brought are consumed here, but part of them are exported to New Spain. As a rule the price is paid in *reales* although, since they have silver in Japan, they are not as greedy for them as are the Chinese. Indeed they usually bring a quantity of sheets of silver as merchandise and they sell these at moderate rates.

These ships go back to Japan with the southwest winds in June and July, taking with them their purchases: raw Chinese silk; gold; deer hides; brazilwood for dyeing; honey; manufactured wax; palm and Spanish wine; civet cats; china jars for keeping their tea in; glass; cloth, and various novelties from Spain.

Some Portuguese ships sail to Manila annually, southwest with the winds, from Maluku, Melaka, and India, bringing merchandise consisting of spices, such as cloves, cinnamon, pepper; slaves (blacks and kaffirs); all sorts of cotton cloths, fine thin muslins, gauzes, stiff cotton stuffs and woolen rambutis [bristly cloth] and other delicate and costly cloths; amber and ivory; cloths bordered with agave fiber to be used as bedcovers; rich hangings and quilts from Bengal, Cochin, and other countries; many gilt articles and curiosities; precious stones such as diamonds, rubies, sapphires, topazes, dark colored rubies and other fine stones, both set and loose; many jewels and novelties from India; wine; raisins, almonds, and delicious preserves, and other fruit brought from Portugal and prepared in Goa; carpets and lengths of tapestry from Persia and Turkey made of silks and first-rate wools; beds; writing cases; parlor armchairs, and other fine gilt articles made in Macao. Then there is needle-work, both colored and plain white, chain-stitch and in royal point, and other work of beauty and perfection. All this is sold in Manila, and paid for in silver coin and in gold. These ships return with the January

northeast monsoon winds, carrying to Maluku rice, wine, porcelain, and other items needed there. To Melaka they take only gold and silver money, besides some special trinkets and novelties from Spain, and emeralds. Royal duties are not collected from these vessels.

Some smaller vessels come from Borneo with the southwest winds. They belong to the natives of that island, and return with the first northeast winds. They enter the river of Manila to sell their merchandise from on board their vessels. Their cargoes consist of some fine, beautifully worked palm mats; slaves for the natives [i.e., for Filipino buyers]; sago—a sort of food of theirs made from the pith of palm trees; china-ware jars; large and small jars, glazed black and well made, which are both lasting and serviceable; and fine camphor, which is produced in that island. And although excellent diamonds are found on the opposite coast [i.e., in Borneo] they are not brought to Manila by these ships, for they are sold to the Portuguese of Melaka along that coast. These goods from Borneo are bought by the Filipinos rather than by the Spaniards. And what the ships carry back thence are supplies of wine and rice, cotton goods, and other trinkets from these islands which are not to be found in Borneo.

Very occasionally ships come here to Manila from Siam and Cambodia. They bring benzoin, pepper, ivory, cotton cloths, rubies and sapphires (though badly cut and set), some slaves, rhinoceros horns, hides, hoofs and teeth, and other trinkets. On the return journey they carry whatever is to be found in Manila. Their coming and their return journey is between the north-easterlies and south-westerlies during the months of April, May, and June.

The Spaniards do their trading, make their investments, and assemble their cargoes for New Spain on the basis of these imported goods and from the products of these [Philippine] islands, namely: gold, cotton cloth, cloth for padding, cakes of white and yellow wax. In this business each man does as best suits his convenience, loading his goods on the ships that are to make the voyage. The cargoes are valued and inspected, since they pay to the royal exchequer of Manila, before they set sail, the two percent in royal dues levied on all exports; and this besides the freight charges on the ship, which amount to forty Castilian ducats per ton. This is paid into the royal exchequer in the port of Acapulco in New Spain, besides the ten percent due on entry and first sale in New Spain.

Examining the Evidence

1. What accounted for the high volume of trade in Manila, according to de Morga?
2. According to de Morga's account, what sorts of goods were exchanged in Manila at this time and by whom?
3. To what extent was this Manila trade in Asian versus European hands?

MAKING CONNECTIONS

1. What do the documents in this chapter convey about the variety of societies and lifestyles in East Asia in this era?
2. How do women's lives compare in these Asian societies, based on the glimpses provided in this chapter's readings?
3. How do the descriptions of East Asian cities found in this chapter's documents compare with descriptions of cities in other world regions around this time?

CHAPTER 21

Transforming New Worlds: The American Colonies Mature, 1600–1750

The Americas were perhaps the region of the world most transformed in early modern times. In many places, from Mexico to Brazil to the Caribbean to French Canada, lives and livelihoods settled into radically new patterns under colonial rule. Indigenous societies conquered by the Spanish adjusted to tribute, draft labor, and other demands of colonial life, and enslaved Africans and their descendants also carved out new spaces for themselves far from their original homelands. Some resisted slavery and established long-lasting runaway communities in the backlands, while others found spaces within colonial societies, including convents and other religious institutions. At the same time, most European settlers and their descendants established rural and urban enclaves in which they sought to produce cash crops or simply subsist, and others sought fortunes in mining, trade, and manufacture. For all early modern "Americans," the world was connected. American silver, sugar, tobacco, furs, and even diamonds paid for Chinese silk, Sumatran pepper, and many other imports, both exotic and mundane.

21.1 ARRIVAL OF THE JAPANESE EMBASSY IN MEXICO CITY

Domingo Chimalpahin, *Annals* (1610)

Domingo Chimalpahin (1579–c. 1631) was an indigenous Mexican scholar who left behind a long history of his times in Nahuatl, the language of the vanquished Aztecs that continued to be the dominant tongue in Mexico's Central Highlands throughout colonial times. Chimalpahin described a wide range of important events, such as the arrivals of viceroys, funerals of archbishops, miraculous cures, and natural disasters like earthquakes and volcanic eruptions. The following selection, translated directly from the Nahuatl in 2006, relates the arrival in Mexico City of an embassy sent by the Japanese shogun Tokugawa Ieyasu.

Today, Thursday in the afternoon, the 16th of the month of December of the year 1610, at 6 o'clock, was when perhaps as many as nineteen people from Japan, in China [*sic*], arrived and entered here in the city of Mexico. A noble, their lord, the ambassador, from the court of the great ruler the emperor in Japan, who brought them, came to make peace with the Christians so that they would never make war but always be at peace and esteem each other, so that Spanish merchants will be able to enter Japan and none of the people there will be able to impede them. And likewise the people of Japan will be able to come enter Mexico here to do business, to come here to sell their goods that are made there, and no one here will be able to impede them, for thus the lord Viceroy don Luis de Velasco, Marquis of Salinas, whom they came to see, informed them. Don Rodrigo de Vivero . . . had gotten lost on the ocean as he was coming here to Mexico, as became known today. A year ago, in the year 1609, when he was already expected, no one came. Later it was said that perhaps the ship was lost, or broke up somewhere

on the ocean, or sank in it with the goods as happens sometimes. It was really thought that the ship in which don Rodrigo was coming was lost and sank. It turns out that a sea storm arose over them in the ocean, and they went along driven by the winds of the storm, and they threw all their goods they were bringing in the water, and in that condition the storm carried them to where they landed in the great royal *altepetl* [i.e., kingdom] of Japan, where the people of Japan met them in peace; the ruler, the emperor of Japan [and don Rodrigo] met together. It became known that he went to reside at his palace; he made much of him, fed him, and there don Rodrigo borrowed from the emperor in Japan; he came having borrowed very many thousand [pesos] belonging to him that don Rodrigo brought here to Mexico. And also because of that don Rodrigo came bringing people of Japan to come get the so and so many thousand pesos that he borrowed. And some of the said people of Japan who came here were already Christians and some still idolaters who were not yet baptized. And they came gotten up as they are gotten up there; they wear something like an ornamented jacket, doublet, or long blouse, which they tie at their middle, their waist; there they place a *catana* [Asian cutlass] of metal, which counts as their sword, and they wear something like a mantilla [light women's headscarf]. And their footwear is soft, softened leather called chamois, counting just like foot-gloves that they put on their feet. They seem bold, not gentle and meek people, going about like eagles. And their foreheads are very bare because they closely shave their foreheads, making the shaving of their foreheads reach to the middle of their heads. Their hair just begins at their temples, all going around toward the nape of their necks. They are long-haired; their hair reaches to their necks

Don Domingo de San Antón Muñón Chimalpahin Quautlehuanitzin, *Annals of His Time*, ed. and trans. James Lockhart, Susan Schroeder, and Doris Namala (Stanford, CA: Stanford University Press, 2006), 170, 173.

from their letting it grow long. They cut only the tips; they look like girls because of the way they wear their hair. Their hair is rather long at the neck; they put together something like a *piochtli* [tail on the nape of the neck], which they tie in twisted, intertwined fashion, reaching to the middle of the head with close shaving. It really looks like a tonsure that they display on their heads, because long hair goes around from their temples to the nape of their neck. And they do not have beards, and they have faces like women, and they are whitish and light, with whitish or yellowish faces. All the people of Japan are like that, that is how their corporal aspect is, and they are not very tall, as everyone saw them. When they entered Mexico here, the nobleman from there who came appointed as leader of the Japan people was greatly honored. The carriage of the viceroy, his very own property, went to Chapultepec to meet him as he was passing by on the road. He sent to him, sitting in the coach together, a Discalced [Franciscan] friar whom they brought from Japan, who came

to interpret for them, and a judge of the Audiencia [royal appeals court] who went to Chapultepec to meet him, when the Japanese came by on the way here. And when they came from Chapultepec, inside the said carriage rode all three of them, the nobleman from Japan, the Discalced friar, and the judge. When they entered the city of Mexico, they came to establish themselves in the Augustinian church, and not until the next day did they see the lord viceroy; and while they stayed here in Mexico, it was the viceroy who fed them.

Examining the Evidence

1. How does this native Mexican author describe the dangers of the trans-Pacific voyage between Japan and Mexico?
2. How does Chimalpahin describe the clothing, physical appearance, and attitude of the Japanese visitors?
3. What does this document suggest about relations between Mexico and Japan around 1610?

21.2 THE WEALTH OF SPANISH AMERICA

María de Carranza and Nicolás de Guevara, *Letters from the Spanish Indies* (1589–1590)

Spanish immigrants in the Americas in the sixteenth century were as concerned as modern immigrants about keeping in touch with their families back home. However, letters had to travel great distances, and their bearers were often involved in long, perilous journeys to transport them. Despite this hardship, hundreds of copies of early letters have survived, some sent in duplicate, others undeliverable for one reason or another. The following letters, one from a textile-factory owner's wife in the Mexican city of Puebla and the other from a mine owner in Potosí (in present-day Bolivia) are typical of this early

time when silver flowed and commerce was highly profitable. Both writers seem flush with cash and optimism, and encourage their loved ones to flee the "poverty and hunger" of Spain to join them in the New World.

María de Carranza, A Letter from Puebla, Mexico, to a Brother in Seville (1589)

Desired and beloved brother of my heart,

I have never had a reply to the many letters I have written you, except one, and it gave me great joy to know of the health of yourself and my sister-in-law and my nephews, whom I hope our Lord someday lets me see, as I desire. My husband Diego Sánchez Guadalupe was no less happy than I, though for him as well as for

James Lockhart and Enrique Otte, trans. and eds., *Letters and People of the Spanish Indies: The Sixteenth Century* (Cambridge, UK: Cambridge University Press, 1976), 85–86, 136–138.

me, after our having desired it, and put so much into sending to call you here, it would be a greater happiness to see you; yet you want to stay there in that poverty and need which people suffer in Spain. I ask you for the love of God to spare me such pain from your absence, and yourself such necessity, when I have the means to give you relief. Do be sure to come quickly now, and don't make your children endure hunger and necessity. I would have sent money for your trip, but since I have had no reply to your letters, I didn't dare. Go to [the town of] Ronda and collect the rent from my houses, and if you wish to, mortgage them and take four or five years' income in advance; I leave it to your discretion. And invest all except what you need for travel in fine cloths, in Rouen and Dutch linens; be sure you do it yourself, and don't trust it to others.

Be aware that anyone who brings children must come very well prepared; six hundredweight of hardtack will be enough, but better have over that than under, and make it yourself, since you know how. And buy four cured hams from Ronda, and four cheeses; twelve pounds of rice; chickpeas and beans, rather too much than too little; all the spices; vinegar and olive oil, four jugs of each; jerked beef and mutton, plenty of it and well dressed; and as much linen and woolen clothing for you to wear as you can bring, because here it is very expensive.

Do everything in your power to bring along with you two masters of weaving coarse woolens and carding, for they will profit us greatly, and also a candlemaker, who should be an examined journeyman and good at his trade. Buy their provisions and make a contract with them from the day they sail, and I will fulfill whatever you agree to; I will pay their passage and any debts they have when they arrive. And you can do all this much better than I could. Your brother-in-law Diego Sánchez Guadalupe, to whom you owe more than to me, shares my desires; to make me happy he would have gone there [to Spain] himself, and I was tempted to let him for the sake of you and my sister-in-law and my nephews, but in order not to be left here alone and because he is an older man, I didn't let him go.

Tell the sister of my soul to consider this letter hers; how is it that her heart doesn't melt like mine for us to see each other? I understand that she is the reason you haven't come, yet she is the one who loses and has lost in not enjoying a land where food is plentiful and she can give me a good old age. I ask her, since it is in her own favor, to come quickly and make my old age happy with her arrival and that of my longed-for nephews.

Cristóbal de Velasco, my brother-in-law, was here, and I gave him hospitality that he enjoyed considerably, but then he went to Panama and left me disconsolate in his absence, and I will not be satisfied until he comes back. Our Lord fullfil my desires, so that you can find relief, and I happiness.

I greet Aunt Ana de Ribera and Aunt Ana Ruiz, and when you come here, leave them where you can send them some presents, money and other things to help them, because we owe it to them, since they are sisters of our mother. Diego Sánchez de Guadalupe is not writing because he is tired of sending letters and peevish that you don't answer, so he only gave permission for me to write. Maybe I will have more luck than he has had. I am sorry that so much is necessary for your own redemption.

I will send you power [of attorney] to collect on the property in Ronda or sell it, and I do not send it now because I am not sure it will reach your hands, for I think that if my letters had arrived, I would already have had some letter from you to enjoy. And if you decide not to come with this fleet because you aren't outfitted yet, write me, and give the letter to Francisco López de Olmos to be directed to the house of Alonso de Casas in Puebla. Trusting our Lord will give me this happiness, I and mine continue in our hope, and we greet my sister-in-law and my beloved nephews. And as to my beloved daughter Mencía Gómez, I have reserved a very rich marriage for her. May God arrange it for his holy service as I wish. From Puebla, 2nd of October, 1589.

María de Carranza

Nicolás de Guevara, A Letter from Potosí to a Friend in Medina del Campo, Spain (1595)

Very magnificent sir,

You will consider it something new to see a letter of mine from such remote parts, but recognizing the kinship there is between us, I wanted to take advantage of your favor on this occasion. I had a sister in the town of Belorado, married to an honorable man there named Andrés Ruiz, and my uncle Licenciate Pedro de Guevara has written me from Madrid that she died and left four children. To help bring them up, I thought I would send, through you, 350 gold pesos, to be delivered entire in Medina del Campo, the charges borne as appears in the authenticated bill of lading that accompanies this. A great friend of mine called Juan de Guesala is taking the money and will be very careful to deliver it when he arrives; he is going to live in Durango, Biscay, where I was born and raised. I beg you, when you receive this, to send the accompanying letter to Andrés Ruiz, and tell him that when Juan de Guesala arrives the amount will be sent to him. Since that is a land of scarcity, they are doubtless in need.

Now that I am writing you, it seems proper to give you an account of my life. I came to Peru in the year of '81 and soon came up here to the imperial town of Potosí, where I have lived the whole time, occupying myself in the business of extracting silver. I have many very good mining sites in the Rich Mountain, and a mill where I grind the ore. I also bought the office of municipal council secretary and notary public of this town, for 42,000 ducats in cash; it is the most profitable office having to do with

papers that the king our lord offers in all his realms, and as to honor, it is the best thing here. I have or am gaining a great stock of ore to process, and if it yields well, with our Lord's aid, I mean to go back to Spain within three years. When I arrive, I will come to pay you my respects.

I married a second cousin of mine named doña Francisca de Lantadilla, from this land here, daughter of Martín de Ayales, with a dispensation from Rome. I wanted to give you such a long account of everything because it would not be right to neglect to give it to a person such as yourself. I beg you to do me the great favor of answering my letter and telling me in what way I might serve your grace, whose person I greatly desire that our Lord guard and increase.

Written in Potosí, 4th of April, 1595.

Nicolás de Guevara

Examining the Evidence

1. How do these writers describe life in the Spanish colonies versus life in Spain itself?
2. What kind of advice do they give to their loved ones?
3. How did these letter writers seek to manage family business across such great distances?

21.3   LIFE IN A PERUVIAN CONVENT

Ursula de Jesús, *Visions of the World to Come* (c. 1650)

Born a slave of African descent in Lima, Peru, Ursula de Jesús (1604–1666) served in a Roman Catholic convent for most of her life. When de Jesús was forty-one years old, several nuns purchased her freedom, in part to unburden their own consciences, but de Jesús remained in the convent to devote the remaining years of her life to prayer and spiritual contemplation. As a former slave and

woman of color, de Jesús was not allowed to become a nun herself, but she was given space as a layperson of chaste devotion, or *beata*. She also continued to work in the convent's kitchen, where most enslaved women of African descent labored. In line with Baroque Catholic teachings of the time, de Jesús was deeply concerned about the fate of the souls of dead Christians, most of whom were said to suffer in purgatory, a hell-like place where sins were purged. Around 1650, de Jesús began to have visions, and thanks to her rare literacy and candor

Ursula de Jesús, *The Souls of Purgatory: The Spiritual Diary of a Seventeenth-Century Afro-Peruvian Mystic, Ursula de Jesús*, trans. and ed. Nancy E. van Deusen (Albuquerque: University of New Mexico Press, 2004), 80, 82, 84–85, 88, 96–97.

we gain some insight into the class and racial tensions of the convent as well as the deep religiosity of its "cell-mates."

Stairway to Heaven

On Wednesday morning, [the nun] doña Antonia de Serrantes sent her slave to ask me to cook for her. I told her black female slave, "Go with God, your owner only remembers me to give orders." But then, I called her back again to do what she asked me. During the siesta I went to pray, and the voices said, *If you have left the world behind why do you complain? Was it not better to accept that without becoming angry and do it out of compassion and love of God?*, and other things of this sort.

Thursday. Some days my heart races, and everything tires me out. I went before God to ask Him for His grace. There I saw a stairway extending from earth to heaven, and one path leading off to my right and another to my left. The voices explained that the stairway was the path of those who carry the cross. The right path is for those going to purgatory, and the left one for the condemned, and those who do not fear God and disobey His holy commandments. The latter fall into this tremendous place and drop down precipitous cliffs. I saw extreme darkness there. Moreover, they said that although these two paths came together, and those in purgatory suffered the same torture as those in hell, still they have hope because it is not forever and they are consoled. Those who climb the stairway carry the cross that our Lord Jesus Christ carried first. Only those who follow Him can take this path. . . .

On Tuesday while doing my spiritual exercises, I saw a wretched [nun], a thousand depths below. She was in that wretched place [hell], lying flat on her back on something like a barbecue, surrounded by many demons who tormented her. Flames came out of her mouth, eyes, and ears, just as when flames burst from a firework that is not allowed to leave the ground. She had that noise in her head, and they touched her head, using a thousand different methods of torture. Others came and placed horrible pieces of iron around her feet. The voices said, *See, this is how the indulgent and lazy ones live. They turn their backs on everything and pay attention to nothing.*

They do not fear God, but only feed their appetites, spending their time jeering and causing a ruckus. God offers them the help they need. In speaking of the woman who was [lying] there, God said that He had provided her with memory, understanding, and will so that she could make the appropriate choice. She had chosen that life, in spite of her confessors, preachers, the inspirations, and books. Our Lord Jesus Christ said, *Be vigilant and pray in order to avoid temptation. She had made that choice and fallen into temptation.* . . .

Hope for Black Women

On the day of the Epiphany I was in a state of recollection after having taken communion. I do not know whether these are tricks of the big-footed one [the devil], or from my head, but I recalled María Bran, a slave of the convent who had died suddenly some fourteen years ago: one of the things most forgotten for me in this world. At the same time, I saw her in a priest's vestment, the whitest of whites, beautifully embellished and gathered together with a short cord with elegant tassels. She also wore a crown of flowers on her head. The celestial beings arranged for me to see her from the back, although I could still see her face and she was quite lovely, and her face a resplendent black. I said, "How is it that such a good black woman, who had been neither a thief nor a liar, had spent so much time in purgatory?" She said she had gone there because of her character, and because she slept and ate at the improper time. Although she had been there a long time, her punishment had been mild. She was very thankful to God, who with His divine providence had taken her from her land and brought her down such difficult and rugged roads in order to become a Christian and be saved. I asked whether black women went to heaven and she said they did if they were thankful and heeded His beneficence, and thanked Him for it. They were saved because of His great mercy. When I ask these questions I do not do so because I want to but, just as soon as I see them, they speak to me without my wishing it to happen, and they make me speak without wanting to. . . .

Monday, as soon as I had gone to the choir and prostrated myself before the Lord, I saw two black women below the earth. In an instant, they were beside me. One of them said to me, "I am Luisa, the one who served [the nun] Ana de San Joseph, and I have been in purgatory for this long, only because the great merciful God showed compassion toward me. No one remembers me." Very slowly, she spoke of God's goodness, power, and mercy, and how we should love and serve Him. Luisa had served this [convent] community in good faith, but sometimes they had accused her of certain things, and at times she suffered her penance where she tended to cook. For the love of God, would Ursula please commend her spirit to God. Before Luisa died, she had endured awful hardships, and because of them they had discounted much of the punishment. . . .

Another time, after I had taken communion the voices told me to commend the spirit of a black woman to God. She had been in the convent and had been taken out to be cured because she was gravely ill but died a few days later. This had happened more than thirty years ago, and I had forgotten about her as if she had never existed. I was frightened and thought to myself, "So long in purgatory?" The voices responded, *For the things she did.* Here, the voices led me to understand that she had illicitly loved a nun and the entire convent knew about it, but that my father, Saint Francis, and my mother, Saint Clare, had gotten down on their knees and prayed to our Lady to secure the salvation of that soul from her Son. That is because she had served His house in good faith.

Examining the Evidence

1. What does de Jesús see in her visions or dreams that relate to her everyday life?
2. Were the nuns and slaves of nuns spared the rigors of hell and purgatory in de Jesús's visions?
3. What does this document say about race and gender relations in seventeenth-century Lima, Peru?

CONTRASTING VIEWS

EXPLOITATION OR OPPORTUNITY IN THE PERUVIAN ANDES?

21.4 | GUAMAN POMA DE AYALA, *THE FIRST NEW CHRONICLE* (C. 1610)

Felipe Guaman Poma de Ayala (c. 1550–1620) was a native Quechua speaker who came of age in highland Peru during the Potosí silver boom. He apparently served as translator for several Spanish priests and magistrates in the 1580s and 1590s. Literate in Spanish, intensely religious, and well traveled, as an older man he sat down to compose a nearly 1200-page letter to King Philip III of Spain. In it, Guaman Poma argued forcefully for a separate kingdom ruled by noble Andean native lords; Spanish abuses, he felt, were atrocious and too deeply rooted to be reformed. In the following passage, Guaman Poma denounces the abuses of forced draft workers sent to the mines of Huancavelica, which supplied the silver refineries of Potosí with mercury for large-scale amalgamation.

The quicksilver mines of Huancavelica are where the poor Indians are so harshly punished, where they are tortured and so many Indians die; it is there that the noble caciques [village headmen] of this kingdom are finished off and tortured. The same is true in all the other mines: the silver mines of Potosí, the silver mines of Chocllo Cocha, the gold mines of Carabaya, and the other mines elsewhere in the kingdom [of Peru]. The owners and stewards of the mines, whether Spaniards, mestizos, or Indians, are such tyrants, with no fear of God or justice, because they are not audited and are not inspected twice a year. And thus there is no remedy.

They hang one noble cacique by his feet, and they seat another one on a llama and whip him. Others are bound stark naked to the whipping post, where they are punished and their hair is roughly shorn. Still others are kept in the

Felipe Guaman Poma de Ayala, *The First New Chronicle and Good Government*, trans. and ed. David Frye (Indianapolis, IN: Hackett, 2006), 179–181.

public jail in stocks and fetters, without being given any food or water or being allowed to provide their own. All of this abuse and shaming is done to them under the excuse that a few Indians are missing from the mita [forced labor draft]. These punishments are carried out against the lords of the land in this kingdom, who hold their titles by His Majesty. They are punished most cruelly, as if they were thieves or traitors. Because of these troubles, they have died in shame, and there is no remedy.

And they are not paid for the labor of traveling to and from the mines or for the time they spend at the mines. The Indians, under the pretext of mining chores, are made to spend their workdays herding cattle and conveying goods; they are sent off to the plains, and the Indians die. Some have to make [fine woolen cloth]; others are ordered to weave coarse cloth; and others are [forced to seek money by selling useless goods]—these Indians are not paid for their labor, and their work is kept hidden.

And [the mine owners] keep Indian cooking women in their residences; they use cooking as a pretext for taking concubines. They and their stewards force their way on some of the daughters of their Indian servants and de-flower them, and they force their way on their servants' wives by sending their husbands off to the mines at night, or by sending them somewhere far away. And they oblige the Indians to accept corn or meat or chicha [corn beer] or cheese or bread at their own expense, and they deduct the price from their labor and their workdays. In this way, the Indians end up very poor and deep in debt, and they have no way to pay their tribute.

There is no remedy for all this, because any *corregidor* [royal magistrate], governor, or judge who enters comes to an agreement with the mine owners, and all the owners join forces in bribing him. When he sees the gold with his own eyes, he would rather tell them to kill all the poor Indians. Even the protector of the Indians [a court-appointed public defender] is useless; he is, instead, against the Indians. He does not defend them against these torments from hell, nor does he warn Your Majesty or your royal Audiencia [appeals court] about the harms done to the poor Indians.

Your Majesty should know: where do the mine owners get the means to dress up all in silk and gold and silver, other than from the labor of the poor Indians and from what they steal from Your Majesty? Therefore, it would be good that these mine owners be inspected every six months and audited and held to account, and that the mines be inspected. Because they whip the Indian women in their husbands' absence, and they also whip their husbands, their clothes hiked up and their shameful parts exposed—they whip them as if they were small children, on their bottoms; and they beat other Indians as if they were animals, horses, or as if they were their black slaves; and they commit so many other offenses that it would take too long to write them all, which we leave to God and to your judges and justices.

Because of all these offenses, the Indians leave their pueblos to avoid going to the mines, where they would suffer torments and martyrdom. To avoid suffering the de-monic pains and torments of that inferno, some flee the mines, while others flee the highway that would bring them to the mines, to keep from dying a sudden death. Those who go would rather die than live, and they beg to be finished off once and for all, because, when they get the quicksilver poisoning, they dry up like sticks, they get asthma, and they cannot live by day or by night. They last a year or two like that, and then they die.

Therefore, for my part, I recommend that Your Majesty have your governor and your Audiencia report to you, write to you, and inform you, so that some Christian might stand up for the poor of Jesus Christ, in order that this might be remedied and that all the ills and harm done in the mines of this kingdom might cease to grow.

21.5 BERNARDO DE VARGAS MACHUCA, *DEFENSE OF THE WESTERN CONQUESTS* (1618)

A contemporary of Peru's Guaman Poma de Ayala, Bernardo de Vargas Machuca (c. 1555–1622) was a Spaniard who arrived in the Americas too late to participate in the conquests of the Aztecs and Incas. An accomplished horseman, Vargas Machuca was recruited to search for Eldorado in what is today Colombia in the early 1580s, but he spent more time attempting to conquer "rebellious" gatherer-hunter peoples throughout northwest South America, mostly without

Bernardo de Vargas Machuca, *Defending the Conquest: Bernardo de Vargas Machuca's Defense and Discourse of the Western Conquests*, ed. Kris Lane, trans. Timothy Johnson (University Park: Pennsylvania State University Press, 2010), 109–111.

(continued)

success. He nevertheless wrote a manual for conquistadors published in 1599 and followed it with a rebuttal of Bartolomé de las Casas's famous 1558 tract, *A Very Brief Account of the Destruction of the Indies*, which he felt defamed both Spain and the conquistadors. This selection from Vargas Machuca's *Defense of the Western Conquests* attempts to justify the conquest of the Incas more than eighty years after the capture of Atawallpa.

They [native Andeans] recognize the benefits gained from the Spaniards and enjoy more freedom than they had with their own lords, who deprived them of what they hunted in order to eat, and from wearing fine blankets, as only the nobles and the privileged could dress as they liked, hunt, and eat freely all that they wanted, and these were few, and the rest required particular license, and unheard-of cruelties were found among [them], because there was an Inca who, in order to clear the land of useless people, gathered all the lame, one-armed, blind, and old people from his realm and put them into great straw huts and set them on fire. There are some opinions that this happened but once, and others, many times, and though they were pagans it is great cruelty nevertheless. And so it is true that [native Andeans] have escaped from tyrannies such as those mentioned and others even greater, and because of these [tyrannies] the Incas were lords. And now, they have found the monarchs of Spain to have great clemency and justice, and their [government] ministers and Spaniards much love and kind reciprocity, such as they have had from the first day; and to merit this [treatment], the Spanish-speaking natives need no understanding, though there are some who are quite subtle and of great ingeniousness; we refer to those who cannot speak Spanish well as barbarians. This is why when a Spaniard wishes to insult someone he says, "So-and-so is an Indian." One of the Incas [i.e., surviving Inca nobles] in the kingdom of Peru, a lord over part of it, knew this expression quite well, for having received a letter from the viceroy and governor at the time, he called upon a Spaniard to read it to him. When the Spaniard told him he did not know how to read, [the Inca noble] responded, "You are as much an Indian as I.'" If I had to pass judgment, I would switch the nationalities by calling the Indian a Spaniard and the Spaniard an Indian, which he did so keenly. And though I may stray a bit from the purpose, in order to see the inventiveness that some of the lords and caciques have, I will tell what happened to one cacique.

A mestizo, son of a Spaniard and an Indian and a people respected by the Spaniards, was passing through his town. An Indian from that town, to whom the mestizo owed a hundred pesos, went to the cacique because he could not collect [the debt]. He related his circumstances

and asked him to order the [mestizo] to pay. The cacique sent a constable to call upon him at the *tambo* or inn where he was lodged, and when he saw that the cacique was calling upon him and ordering him to appear, he laughed heartily, as any mestizo or Spaniard would do, it being an extraordinary thing to convince them to appear before Indian justice. And arguing with him, he responded with harsh words saying, like a violent brute, that if the cacique wanted anything of him, he should come to the inn himself. Upon receiving the answer, the cacique sent one of the jailors with more than fifty Indians to him, and though he resisted, he was brought in with his hands tied, and they accused him in the presence [of the cacique] where he pompously confessed to the debt. They put him in the stocks and condemned him to pay half his debt before he would be freed, for his being part Indian; and for his other [i.e., Spanish] half, they sent him to the closest Spanish chief magistrate in case justice would be done because of his being part Spaniard. This sentence pronounced, the mestizo sent a dispatch to the royal *audiencia* [appeals court] complaining about the cacique; once the case was heard by the judges and well understood, they confirmed the sentence, which was greatly celebrated because the cacique had demonstrated such great subtlety in the case. And if truth be told, some of the Spanish-speaking Indians who have spent time around our Spaniards, both humble and noble, acquire understanding.

COMPARING THE EVIDENCE

1. How do Guaman Poma and Vargas Machuca characterize the Spanish colonial justice system in the Peruvian Andes?

2. How do Guaman Poma and Vargas Machuca portray the everyday lives of native Andean commoners and their caciques, or regional headmen?

3. What examples do these authors draw from to make their points?

4. How can we gauge the validity of the arguments presented by these anticolonial and procolonial writers? Which one do you find more believable, and why?

21.6 DESCRIPTION OF QUEBEC CITY AND A CHRISTIAN HURON VILLAGE

Pehr Kalm, *Travels into North America* (1749)

Pehr (or "Peter") Kalm (1716–1779) was a Swedish naturalist who visited Canada in the mid-eighteenth century. Like any outsider, he missed or misunderstood some features of the societies he visited, but he was unusually thorough in his descriptions of everything from river courses to dietary habits. Kalm had also visited the Sami homeland of northern Scandinavia prior to his trip to North America and offers some comparisons between Canadians and "Laplanders." In the following passages, translated from the Swedish in the 1770s, Kalm describes the capital of French Canada, Quebec City, and the nearby Christian Huron village of Lorette.

Most of the houses in Quebec are built of stone, and in the upper city they are generally but one story high, the public buildings excepted. I saw a few wooden houses in the town, but they must not be rebuilt when decayed. The houses and churches in the city are not built of bricks, but the black limeslates of which the mountain consists, whereon Quebec stands. . . . The roofs of the public buildings are covered with common slates, which are brought from France, because there are none in Canada. . . .

Quebec is the only seaport and trading town in all Canada, and from thence all the produce of the country is exported. The port is below the town in the river, which is there about a quarter of a French mile broad, twenty-five fathoms deep, and its ground [i.e., bottom] is very good for anchoring. The ships are secured from all storms in this port; however, the northeast wind is worst, because it can act more powerfully. When I arrived here, I reckoned thirteen great and small vessels, and they expected more to come in. But it is to be remarked, that no other ships than French ones can come into the port, though they may come from any place in France, and likewise from the French possessions in the West Indies. All the foreign goods found in Montreal and other parts of Canada must be taken from thence. The French merchants from Montreal on their side, after making six months stay among several Indian nations, in order to purchase the skins of beasts and furs, return about the end of August, and go down to Quebec in September or October, in order to sell their goods there. The privilege of selling the imported goods, it is said, has vastly enriched the merchants of Quebec; but this is contradicted by others, who allow that there are a few in affluent circumstances, but that the generality possess no more than absolutely necessary for their bare subsistence, and that several are very much in debt, which they say is owing to their luxury and vanity. The merchants dress very finely, and are extravagant in their repasts; and their ladies are every day in full dress, and as much adorned as if they were to go to court. . . .

August 12th. This afternoon I [and my servant] went out of town, to stay in the country for a couple of days that I might have more leisure to examine the plants that grow in the woods here, and the state of the country. In order to proceed the better, the governor-general had sent for an Indian from Lorette to show us the way, and teach us what use they make of the spontaneous plants hereabouts. This Indian was an Englishman by birth, taken by the Indians thirty years ago, when he was a boy, and adopted by them, according to their custom, instead of a relation of theirs killed by the enemy. Since that time he constantly stayed with them, became a Roman Catholic and married an Indian woman: he dresses like an Indian, speaks English and French, and many of the Indian languages. In the wars between the French and English, in

Peter Kalm, *Travels into North America*, trans. John Reinold Forster, vol. 3 (Barre, MA: Imprint Society), 409–411, 423–433, 437–438, 445–446.

this country, the French Indians have made many prisoners of both sexes in the English plantations, adopted them afterwards, and they married with people of the Indian nations. From hence the Indian blood in Canada is much mixed with European blood, and a great part of the Indians now living owe their origin to Europe. It is likewise remarkable that a great part of the people they had taken during the war and incorporated with their nations, especially the young people, did not choose to return to their native country, though their parents and nearest relations came to them and endeavored to persuade them to it, and though it was in their power to do it. The licentious life led by the Indians pleased them better than that of their European relations; they dressed like the Indians and regulated all their affairs in their way. It is therefore difficult to distinguish them except by their color, which is somewhat whiter than that of the Indians. There are likewise examples of some Frenchmen going amongst the Indians and following their way of life. There is on the contrary scarce one instance of an Indian's adopting the European customs; but those who were taken prisoners in the war have always endeavored to come to their own people again, even after several years of captivity, and though they enjoyed all the privileges that were ever possessed by the Europeans in America. . . .

August 14th. Lorette is a village, three French miles to the westward of Québec, inhabited chiefly by Indians of the Huron nation, converted to the Roman Catholic religion. The village lies near a little river, which falls over a rock there, and turns a sawmill and a flourmill. When the Jesuit, who is now with them, arrived among them, they lived in their usual huts, which are made like those of the Laplanders [i.e., Sami of northern Scandinavia]. They have since laid aside this custom and built all their houses after the French fashion. In each house are two rooms, their bedroom, and the kitchen on the outside before it. In the room is a small oven of stone, covered at top with an iron plate. Their beds are near the wall, and they put no other clothes on them than those they are dressed in. Their other furniture and utensils look equally wretched. Here is a fine little church, with a steeple and bell. The steeple is raised pretty high, and

covered with white tin plates. They pretend that there is some similarity between this church in its figure and disposition and the Santa Casa, at Loretto in Italy, from whence this village got its name. Close to the church is a house built of stone, for the clergymen, who are two Jesuits, that constantly live here. The divine service is as regularly attended here as in any other Roman Catholic church; and I was pleased with seeing the alacrity [cheerful readiness] of the Indians, especially of the women, and hearing their good voices when they sing all sorts of hymns in their own language. The Indians dress chiefly like the other adjacent Indian nations; the men, however, like to wear waistcoats, or jackets, like the French. The women keep exactly to the Indian dress. It is certain that these Indians and their ancestors, long since, on being converted to the Christian religion, have made a vow to God, never to drink strong liquors. This vow they have kept pretty inviolable hitherto, so that one seldom sees one of them drunk, though brandy and other strong liquors are goods that Indians would sooner be killed for than part with them.

These Indians have made the French their patterns in several things besides the houses. They all plant maize; and some have small fields of wheat and rye. They plant our common sunflower in their maize fields, and mix the seed of it into their sagamite, or maize-soup. The maize they plant here is of the small sort, which ripens sooner than the other: its grains are smaller, but give more and better flour in proportion. It commonly ripens here at the middle, sometimes however at the end, of August. . . .

August 21st. Today there were some people of three Indian nations in this country with the governor-general: Hurons, Micmacs, and Anies, the last of which are a nation of Iroquois, and allies of the English, and were taken prisoners in the last war.

The Hurons are some of the same Indians with those who live at Lorette, and have received the Christian religion. They are tall, robust people, well shaped, and of a copper color. They have short black hair, shaved on the forehead from one ear to the other. None of them wear hats or caps. Some have earrings, others not. Many of them have the face painted all over with vermillion; others have only strokes of it on the forehead and near the ears; and some paint their hair with vermillion. Red is the color they chiefly make use of in painting themselves; but I have likewise seen some who had daubed their face with a black color. Many of them have figures in the face, and on the whole body, which are stained into the skin, so as to be indelible. . . . These figures are commonly black; some have a snake painted in each cheek, some have several crosses, some an arrow, others the sun, or anything else their imagination leads them to. They have such figures likewise on the breast, thighs, and other parts of the body; but some have no figures at all. They wear a shirt, which is either white or checked, and a shaggy piece of cloth, which is either blue or white, with a blue or red stripe below. This they always carry over their shoulders, or let it hang down, in which case they wrap it round their middle. Round their neck they have a string of violet wampums, with little white wampums between them. These wampums are small, of the figure of oblong pearls, and made of the shells the English call clams. At the end of the wampum strings many of the Indians wear a large French silver coin, with the king's effigy, on their breasts. Others have a large shell on the breast, of a fine white color, that they value very high, and is very dear; others, again, have no ornament at all round the neck. They all have their breasts uncovered. Before them hangs their tobacco pouch, made of the skin of an animal, and the hairy side

turned outwards. Their shoes are made of skins, and bear a great resemblance to the shoes without heels that the women in Finland make use of. Instead of stockings, they wrap the legs in pieces of blue cloth, as I have seen the Russian boyars do.

The Micmacs are dressed like the Hurons, but distinguish themselves by their long straight hair, of a jetty-black color. Almost all the Indians have black straight hair; however, I have met with a few whose hair was pretty much curled. But it is to be observed that it is difficult to judge of the true complexion of the Canada Indians, their blood being mixed with the Europeans, either by the adopted prisoners of both sexes, or by the Frenchmen who travel in the country and often contribute their share towards the increase of the Indian families, their women not being very shy. The Micmacs are commonly not so tall as the Hurons. I have not seen any Indians whose hair was as long and straight as theirs. Their language is different from that of the Hurons; therefore there is an interpreter here for them on purpose.

Examining the Evidence

1. How does Kalm describe the site and commerce of Quebec City and Montreal?
2. How does the Huron village of Lorette compare to Quebec City?
3. What does Kalm make of race relations in French Canada, based on his observations?

21.7 RUNAWAY SLAVES

John G. Stedman, *A Surinam Maroon Described* (1790)

John Gabriel Stedman (1744–1797) was a Dutch–English soldier who in his early forties traveled to the Dutch colony of Surinam, on the Wild Coast of South America, to participate in a war against runaway African slaves,

also called maroons. The Surinam maroons were divided into numerous tribes and had been fully autonomous since the 1650s. They were perhaps the Americas' most successful runaways, and they survive today in the modern nation of Suriname and neighboring French Guyana. Although Stedman was alarmed at the violent tactics of the maroons, whom he calls "the Rebels," their

Richard Price and Sally Price, eds., *Stedman's Surinam: Life in an Eighteenth-Century Slave Society* (Baltimore, MD: Johns Hopkins University Press, 1992), 200–201.

tenacious rejection of slavery and creation of their own hybrid culture won his respect. In the course of his service (1773–1777), Stedman became outraged by the cruelty of Dutch slave owners in Surinam and by the institution of slavery itself. When a much-altered version of his narrative was published in 1796, with jaw-dropping illustrations of cruel punishments by the English artist and poet William Blake, it became a key document in the British movement for the abolition of slavery. The following passage is from Stedman's 1790 manuscript.

Having frequently mentioned the Rebel Negroes, with whom we were now certain to have a rencounter, I here present the reader with the figure of one of these people upon his guard, as alarmed by supposing to hear a rustling among the bushes, and a couple of Rangers [members of an all-black regiment] at a distance ready to take him by surprise. The first is armed with a firelock and a hatchet, his hair (though woolly) may be observed to be plaited close to his head, by way of distinction from the Rangers, or any other straggling Negroes who are not accepted yet among them, and his beard is grown to a point, like that of all the Africans when they have no opportunity to shave. The whole dress of this man consists of a cotton sheet negligently tied across his shoulders, which protects him against the rain, and serves him as a bed in which to lie down and sleep in the most obscure places he can find. The rest are his camisa [shirt], his pouch (which is made of some animal's skin), a few cotton strings for ornament around his ankles and wrists, and a superstitious obia or amulet tied about his neck, in

which case he places all his hope and confidence. The skull and ribs are supposed to be some of his enemies scattered upon a sandy savanna. The two Rangers who make their appearance at a distance may be distinguished by their red caps, while I must observe the Rebels many times have availed themselves of capturing one of these scarlet distinctions, which by clapping on their own heads in an engagement has not only saved their lives, but given them an opportunity to shoot their enemies.

Another stratagem of theirs has been discovered, viz., that firearms being scarce among them, numbers have intermixed in the crowd with only a crooked stick, shaped something like a musket to supply it in appearance, which has even more than once had the effect, when they came to ransack the [sugar] estates, of preventing proper defense by the plantation slaves, who were thus struck with panic, and whose courage damped, with the show of such superior numbers, allowing the Rebels calmly (after burning the houses) to carry away even their own wives and daughters.

Examining the Evidence

1. How does Stedman distinguish the maroons from African American soldiers sent to fight against them?
2. What tricks did the maroons use to their advantage despite their small numbers and isolation?
3. Why might this document have been used later to call for the abolition of the transatlantic slave trade?

MAKING CONNECTIONS

1. How do the perspectives of Chimalpahin, the Spanish immigrants, and de Jesús compare?
2. How would you compare the lives of runaways, or those who escaped colonial society, in Quebec and Surinam?
3. In what ways was the colonial experience in the Americas distinct from life in empires elsewhere in the world in early modern times?

The World from 1750 to the Present

CHAPTER 22

Atlantic Revolutions and the World, 1750–1830

During the Enlightenment ideas developed in Europe and spread around the world, influencing the thinking of people thousands of miles from the Continent. Calls arose for reformed government, for new standards of citizenship, and for greater equality and freedom. Revolts erupted across the Spanish Empire. North American colonists freed themselves from Great Britain, and Spanish Americans gained independence from Spain. However, as Europeans tried to bring their ideas of freedom to others, many objected to the simultaneous European goal of further foreign conquest.

22.1 THE ENLIGHTENMENT AMONG ARTISANS

Jacques-Louis Ménétra, *Journal of My Life* (1764–1802)

Jacques Ménétra (1738–c.1804) was a French glazier— that is, an artisan who cut and installed windows. In learning his trade, Ménétra led the life of a journeyman traveling the countryside to work in guilds across France. The autobiography he composed during his lifetime is an unusual document, for European workers in the eighteenth century were often not literate. Ménétra's account contains political comments and is full of adventure, including descriptions of his exploits with women he seduces and, disturbingly, even rapes. Although it had no punctuation or capitalization in the original, Ménétra's autobiography addresses some intriguing questions about what working people knew of Enlightenment values such as secularism and individual freedom.

I went to Paris to see Denongrais Madame la Police had been interfering with business she made up her mind to sell her property and to retire with her cuckold [man whose wife is unfaithful] of a husband to her native village for she'd put by quite a bit in the course of her work I was all for it She said to me I see clearly from what you've just said that you never loved me She was right for never had a woman touched my heart except for sensual pleasure and nothing else I promised her to come say farewells and they've yet to be said.

Since it was the good season we went to Champigny and went with some friends of mine to what are called *guinguettes* [open-air cafés with music and dancing—Trans.] Sundays and holidays we went to dance in front of the castle and other days usually with the people from the *guinguette* we played tennis or went visiting the local festivals One holiday in a village one league from Montigny people were playing tennis on the square when Du Tillet showed up accompanied by the lord the magistrate or sheriff and the priest I heard somebody say That's the Parisian over there I wondered what this was all about It's because they know you're good at tennis said my friend they're going to propose a match In fact six young men came and politely gave each of us a racket My friend said no since he didn't know how to play but he said But as for my friend he'll give you a good show I declined They insisted the lord the sheriff and the priest joined in I played applause hands were heard to clap They took us to the castle (and) gave us refreshment.

I was greatly applauded I promised again that the fellows from Montigny and I would be waiting for them next Sunday People came from all around I was all over the court and we had a good time we won and whatever else they were well entertained My friend went all out because M Trudaine had wanted to see me play and when I passed in front of him he and the people around him said to me Courage So I answered that that was one thing I wasn't lacking

One day I followed the game warden Since I had no rifle I let him run all over the fields and went to a village where I had seen the curate [a parish priest or his assistant] pay his respects to M Trudaine who recognized me and said I was pretty nimble at tennis and took me to his presbytery [area of church or residence reserved for the clergy] for a drink

After some idle talk we finally got onto the subject of religion We talked about the mysteries of the sacraments . . . I spoke passionately about the sufferings that had been inflicted on men who worshipped the same God except for a few matters of opinion And (I said that) the Roman religion should be tolerant if it followed the maxims of its lawgiver that because of its mysteries it was absurd and that all mysteries were in my opinion nothing but lies And that so long as they sold indulgences and gave remission for sins in exchange for money fear of hell which was like purgatory just an

Jacques-Louis Ménétra, *Journal of My Life*, intro. Daniel Roche, trans. Arthur Goldhammer (New York: Columbia University Press, 1986), 129–130.

invention of the first impostors that Jesus had never spoken of purgatory And that all those sacraments were nothing but pure inventions to make money and impress the vulgar And that he himself who was a very intelligent man was not capable of making his God chewing him and then swallowing him That we mistreated those peoples who did not share our belief (and who) according to the Church should have been damned because all the priests went around saying Outside the Church there is no salvation And that we accused those who worship idols of being idolators when we prostrate ourselves before statues We even worship a piece of dough which we eat in the firm belief that it is God And those idolators only worship all those things to keep from being hurt by them and other things in the hope of getting some good out of them while we on the other hand we were real man-eaters After praying to him and worshipping him in order to satisfy him we've got to eat him too

He answered me with objections as many others had answered me His one and only response was to say to me All these mysteries must be believed because the Church believes them he said to me My friend you are enlightened It is necessary that for the sake of government nations live always in ignorance and credulity So I answered him So be it.

Examining the Evidence

1. What aspects of Enlightenment thought does Ménétra display in this segment of his autobiography?

2. What arguments does Ménétra use to challenge Catholic Church practices and beliefs, and to support his own principles?

3. How does Ménétra see himself, and how are his ideas about his place in the world in accord with Enlightenment values?

22.2 THE SPREAD OF ENLIGHTENMENT

Sugita Gempaku, *A Dutch Anatomy Lesson in Japan* (1771)

Japanese medical theory and practice in the eighteenth century generally followed the Chinese model. The idea behind Chinese practices was to maintain or restore bodily health by balancing the opposing forces of yin and yang within the body and by ensuring a good relationship between the inner self and the outer world. Western medicine developed in a different direction during the Scientific Revolution and the Enlightenment. As news of these developments arrived in Japan, the scholar Sugita Gempaku became determined to translate Dutch medical books and to observe Western procedures—in this case dissection—for the benefit of his Japanese contemporaries. Medical men in Japan had greater freedom to experiment with foreign ideas than did other segments of the society, so they could forge ahead.

All of us arrived together in the designated place in Kotsugahara. The executed body to be dissected was of a female criminal about fifty years old, who, born in Kyoto, had earned for herself the nickname of "Aochababa" (Green Tea Hag). She had committed a heinous crime, we were told.

Toramatsu, an *eta*[1] and a skillful dissector, was expected to perform the task, but he failed to appear on account of a sudden illness. His ninety-year-old grandfather, a sturdy-looking man, took his place.

---

[1] *eta*: A member of an outcast group that did menial or unpleasant tasks.

William Theodore De Bary, Carol Gluck, and Arthur E. Tiedemann, *Sources of Japanese Tradition*, vol. 2 (New York: Columbia University Press, 2005), 372–375.

He said that he had performed a number of dissections ever since his youth. In dissecting the human body, the custom until then was to leave everything to such outcast people (such as the *eta*). They would cut open the body and point out such organs as the lungs, liver, and the kidneys while the observing doctors simply watched them and came away. All they could say then was, "We have actually viewed the innards of a human body." With no labels attached to each organ, all they could do was listen to the dissector's words and nod.

On this occasion too, the old man went on explaining the various organs such as the heart, the liver, the gallbladder, and the stomach. Further, he pointed to some other things and said, "I don't know what they are, but they have always been there in all the bodies that I have so far dissected." Checking them later with the Dutch charts, we were able to identify them to be the main arteries and veins and suprarenal glands. The old man also said, "In my past experience of dissection, the doctors present never seemed puzzled, or asked questions specifically about one thing or another."

Comparing the things we saw with the pictures in the Dutch book Ryotaku and I had with us, we were amazed at their perfect agreement. There were no such divisions as the six lobes and two auricles of the lungs or the three left lobes and the four right lobes of the liver mentioned in old medical books. Also, the positions and forms of the intestines and the stomach were very different from the traditional descriptions.

The shogun's official doctors . . . had beheld dissections seven or eight times before, but always what they saw was different from what had been taught in the past thousand years. They said they had been making sketches each time they saw something that struck them as strange. On this basis, I suppose, they had written that perhaps the Chinese and Japanese were different in their internal structures. This I had read.

After the dissection was over, we were tempted to examine the forms of the bones, too, and picked up some of the sun-bleached bones scattered around the ground. We found that they were nothing like those described in the old books but were exactly as represented in the Dutch book. We were completely amazed.

On our way home, three of us . . . talked of what a startling revelation we had seen that day. We felt ashamed of ourselves for having come this far in our lives without being aware of our own ignorance. How presumptuous on our parts to have served our lordships and pretended to carry out our duties as official doctors when we were totally without knowledge of the true makeup of our bodies, which should be the foundation of the art of healing! Based on today's experience, suppose we should, by some means, learn even the barest outline of the truth about the body and practice our medicine according to that knowledge, we should be able to justify our claim as medical professionals.

Thus we talked and sighed. Ryotaku, too, said all of this was very true, and he was in complete agreement. I broke the spell by saying, "even this one volume of *Ontleedkundige Tafeln*—suppose we translate it—many facts about the body will be clarified and the art of healing will be greatly benefited. I would like, in some way or another, to read this book without the aid of a Nagasaki interpreter."

Ryotaku replied, "I have had the cherished idea of reading a Dutch book, but I have not found a friend to share that purpose, and I have been passing the days in regret. However, if you are all for it—I have been to Nagasaki and learned something of the language—shall we then make mine the seed of our knowledge and start work on the book?"

"That makes me glad!" I said. "If you would join forces as comrades, I too will show you I can rouse myself to action!"

Ryotaku, very much elated, said, "'For good purpose, do not dally,' the proverb says. Let us meet at my home tomorrow. We will find some way to go at the work."

I promised earnestly to follow his words, and we parted.

The next day, we gathered at Ryotaku's house. We talked over the experience of the day before. Then we faced the book.

But it was as though we were on a boat with no oar or rudder adrift on the great ocean—a vast expanse and nothing to indicate our course. We just gazed at each other in blank dismay.

Ryotaku, however, had studied the Dutch language for some years. He had been to Nagasaki and learned something of the Dutch words and syntax. He was also an old man ten years my senior. So we decided to make him our leader and respect him as our teacher.

As far as I was concerned, I knew nothing of the Dutch language, not even the twenty-five letters of the alphabet. As the project was such a sudden event, I had to begin by learning the letters and gradually familiarize myself with the language.

We conferred and discussed together how to approach the translation and put it into proper and intelligible Japanese.

We thought it too difficult to attack the internal structure of the body at the incipient stage of our work. At the beginning of the book, there were illustrations of the full view of the human body, front and back. As we were familiar with all parts of the body's outside, we thought it would be easy to pair off the signs on the illustrations and on the explanatory notes, thus to learn the names of the parts of the body; at any rate, these were the first of the illustrations—we decided to begin with them. The result of this work was the compilation of the volume called *Atlas and Nomenclature of the Human Body* (*Keitai-meimokuhen*) in *A New Book of Anatomy* (*Kaitai Shinsho*). . . .

Needless to say, we did take questions to the interpreters who came to Edo annually. Also, between times we attended the dissections of human bodies, and more often we opened animal bodies to confirm what we read.

When I first obtained that book of anatomy and ascertained its accuracy by actual observation, I was struck with admiration by the great difference between the knowledge of the West and that of the East.

And I was inspired to come to the determination that I must learn and clarify the new revelation for applying it to actual healing and also for making it the seed of further discoveries among the general physicians of Japan. I was anxious to bring the work to completion as fast as possible. I had no other thought in those days than to write down in the evening what we had deciphered in the day's meeting. I considered the forms of expression in many ways, trying and retrying, and in the four years, I rewrote the manuscript eleven times over before feeling ready to hand it to the printers. Thus the work *A New Book of Anatomy* (*Kaitai Shinsho*) was completed.

Examining the Evidence

1. What do Sugita Gempaku and his Japanese colleagues see when attending the dissection that amazes them and spurs them to action?

2. What do Gempaku's attitudes toward dissection suggest about his sympathy with Enlightenment ideas?

3. What does the author say about medical education in Japan versus such training elsewhere?

4. What does Gempaku's account of witnessing the dissection and his subsequent work on the translation of the Dutch medical book reveal about the global reach of the Enlightenment and science generally in the last third of the eighteenth century?

22.3	# AN EGYPTIAN'S VIEW OF NAPOLEON AND THE FRENCH INVASION

'Abd-al-Rahmân 'al-Jabarti, *Diary* (1798–1801)

Napoleon's invasion of Egypt in 1798 was a horrific experience for its inhabitants. The fleet of 400 boats and 36,000 men behaved with staggering brutality and brought great fear in the land. Egyptians could never predict when French soldiers would suddenly appear to pillage, rape, and murder them or torch their homes. 'Abd-al-Rahmân 'al-Jabarti (1753–1825), a Muslim scholar and author, carefully recorded the events connected with

Al-Jabarti's Chronicle of the First Seven Months of the French Occupation of Egypt, Muharram-Rajab 1213/15 June–December 1789, ed. and trans. by S. Moreh (Leiden, The Netherlands: Brill, 1975), 49, 50, 78, 81–82, 115–117.

the French invasion, including his appraisal in the following section describing both the Mamluk officials of Egypt and the French. He chronicled and deplored French habits, including their violence. Yet, even after the French army withdrew from his country, 'al-Jabarti remained curious about Europeans' excavations in Egypt and commented on their tourism and scholarly observations. This curiosity begins to shed light on why the brief French invasion became so influential in future Egyptian policies, many of which aimed to build European-style institutions.

The Ghuzz [a name for Turkish tribal groups of fighters], the soldiers, and the Mamluks [powerful slave armies] gathered on the two banks, but they were irresolute, and were at odds with one another, being divided in opinion, envious of each other, frightened for their lives, their well-being, and their comforts; immersed in their ignorance and self-delusion, arrogant and haughty in their attire and presumptuousness; afraid of decreasing in number, and pompous in their finery, heedless of the results of their action; contemptuous of their enemy, unbalanced in their reasoning and judgment. They were unlike the other group, that is the French, who were a complete contrast in everything mentioned above. They acted as if they were following the tradition of the Community (of Muhammad) in early Islam and saw themselves as fighters in a holy war. They never considered the number of their enemy too high, nor did they care who among them was killed. Indeed they considered anyone who fled a traitor to his community, and an apostate to his faith and creed. They follow the orders of their commander and faithfully obey their leader. Their only shade is the hat on their head and their only mount their own two feet. Their food and drink is but a morsel and a sip, hanging under their arms. The baggage and change of clothing hang on their backs like a pillow and when they sleep they lie on it as is usual. They have signs and signals among themselves which they obey to the letter. . . .

That same day they [the French] also announced that lamps should be lit all night in the streets and markets. Each house was required to have a lamp as well as every third shop. The people were to sweep,

splash water, and clean the streets of the rubbish, filth, and dead cats. This was in spite of the fact that the streets and houses where the French lived, were full of filth, infected earth mixed with bird feathers, the entrails of animals, garbage, the stench of their drinks, the sourness of their alcoholic beverages, their urine and excrement, such that a passer-by was obliged to hold his nose. . . .

And on that day the French looted the property of the soldiers of the galleon who had served the Amirs [chieftains]. They also plundered the caravanserai of 'Ali Bey which was situated on the bank of the Bulaq and another at al-Jamaliyya, seizing their wares and those of their partners, on the pretext that they had fought against them on the side of the Mamluks, and escaped with them (the Mamluks). . . .

On that day they ordered the inhabitants of the Citadel to vacate their homes and move into town and live there. Thus the inhabitants left the Citadel and the French brought up cannons which they positioned in various places. They further demolished some buildings and erected walls. Thus they pulled down the high places and raised up the low places. They built on the foundations of Bab al-'Azab [gates to the citadel in Cairo] in al-Rumayla and changed its features and disfigured its beauties and wiped out the monuments of scholars and the assembly rooms of sultans and great men and took what works of art were left on its great gates and in its magnificent sitting-rooms (*iywan*) such as arms, shields, axes, helmets, and Indian lances and balls with chains of the warriors (*ukar al-fidawiyya*). They demolished the palace of Yusuf Salah al-Din and the council halls of kings and sultans which had high supports and tall pillars, as well as the mosques and chapels (*zawaya*) of religious orders and shrines. They disfigured the Great Mosque, the lofty distinguished one which was built by the man of glorious deeds, Muhammad ibn Qalawun al-Malik al-Nasir. They removed its *minbar* (pulpit), wrecked its *iywan*, took its wood, shook its pillars, and removed its iron stool near its praying area (*maqsura*) a wondrously wrought work in which the Sultan used to pray. Thus they behaved as the enemies of the religion would behave but "Our trust is in God alone, and He is an excellent protector." . . .

On that day they told the people to desist from burying the dead in cemeteries close to dwellings, such as the cemeteries of al-Azbakiyya, and al-Ruway'i and to bury them only in graveyards far (from the populated areas). Those who had no vaults in the cemetery should bury their dead in the vaults of the Mamluks. And when they buried someone they were required to increase the depth of the graves. They further ordered people to hang out their clothing, furnishings, and bedding on their roofs for several days and to fumigate their houses with fumes which would remove the putrescence. All this was out of fear, as they claimed, of the smell and contagion of the plague. The French said that the putrescence is imprisoned in the depths of the earth. When winter sets in and the depths of the earth become cold because of the flow of the Nile, the rain, and the dampness, what is imprisoned in the earth comes out with its rotten vapors and the air becomes rotten, so epidemic and plague occur.

As for the French it is their custom not to bury their dead but to toss them on garbage heaps like the corpses of dogs and beasts, or to throw them into the sea. Among the other things which they said is that when someone becomes sick they must inform the French who then send an authorized representative to examine him and to find out whether he has the plague or not. Then they decide what to do with him. . . .

To the administrators of affairs (managers), the astronomers, scholars, and scientists in mathematics, geometry, astronomy, engraving and drawing, and also to the painters, scribes, and writers they [the French] assigned al-Nasiriyya quarter and all the houses in it, such as the house of QasimBey, the Amir of the Pilgrimage known as AbuSayf, and the house of Hasan Kashif Jarkas which he founded and built to perfection, having spent upon it fantastic sums of money amounting to more than a hundred thousand dinars. When he had completed plastering and furnishing it, the French came and he fled with the others and left all that it contained, not having enjoyed it for even a whole month. The administrators, astronomers, and some of the physicians lived in this house in which they placed a great number of their books and with a keeper taking care of them and arranging them. And the students among them would gather two hours before noon every day in an open space opposite the shelves of books, sitting on chairs arranged in parallel rows before a wide long board. Whoever wishes to look up something in a book asks for whatever volumes he wants and the librarian brings them to him. Then he thumbs through the pages, looking through the book, and writes. All the while they are quiet and no one disturbs his neighbor. When some Muslims would come to look around they would not prevent them from entering. Indeed they would bring them all kinds of printed books in which there were all sorts of illustrations and *cartes* (*kartat*) [maps] of the countries and regions, animals, birds, plants, histories of the ancients, campaigns of the nations, tales of the prophets including pictures of them, of their miracles and wondrous deeds, the events of their respective peoples and such things which baffle the mind. I have gone to them many times and they have shown me all these various things and among the things I saw there was a large book containing the Biography of the Prophet, upon whom be mercy and peace. In this volume they draw his noble picture according to the extent of their knowledge and judgment about him. He is depicted standing upon his feet looking toward Heaven as if menacing all creation. In his right hand is the sword and in his left the Book and around him are his Companions, may God be pleased with them, also with swords in their hands. In another page there are pictures of the Rightly Guided Caliphs. On another page a picture of the Midnight Journey of Muhammad and al-Buraq and he, upon whom be mercy and peace, is riding upon al-Buraq from the Rock of Jerusalem. Also there is a picture of Jerusalem and the Holy Places of Mekka and Medina and of the four Imams, Founders of the Schools and the other Caliphs and Sultans and an image of Islambul [another name for Istanbul] including her Great Mosques like Aya Sofya and the Mosque of Sultan Muhammad. In another picture the manner in which the Prophet's Birthday is celebrated and all the types of people who participate in it (are shown); also (there are) pictures of the Mosque of Sultan Sulayman and the manner in which the Friday prayers are conducted in it, and the Mosque of Abii Ayyub al-Ansari and the manner in which prayers for the dead are performed in it, and pictures of the countries, the coasts, the seas, the Pyramids, the ancient temples of Upper Egypt including the pictures, figures, and inscriptions which are drawn upon them. Also there are pictures of the species of animals, birds, plants and herbage which are peculiar to each land. The glorious Qur'an is translated into their language! Also many other Islamic books. I saw in their possession the *Kitab al-Shifa'* of Qadi Iyad, which they call *al-Shifa al-Sharif* and *al-Burda* by Abu Siri, many verses of which they know by heart and which they translated into French. I saw some of them who know chapters of the Qur'an by heart. They have a great interest in the sciences, mainly in mathematics and the knowledge of languages, and make great efforts to learn the Arabic language and the colloquial. In this they strive day and night. And they have books especially devoted to all types of languages, their declensions and conjugations as well as their etymologies. They possess extraordinary astronomical instruments of perfect construction and instruments for measuring altitudes of wondrous, amazing, and precious construction. And they have telescopes for looking at the stars and measuring their scopes, sizes, heights, conjunctions, and oppositions, and the clepsydras [an ancient water clock] and clocks with gradings and minutes and seconds, all of wondrous form and very precious, and the like.

In a similar manner they assigned the house of Ibrahim Katkhuda al-Sinnari and the house of the former Katkhuda Zayn al-Fiqar and neighboring houses to the studious and knowledgeable ones. They called this *al-Madaris* (the Schools) and provided it with funds and copious allowances and generous provisions of food and drink. They provided them with a place in the house of the above-mentioned Hasan Kashif and built in it neat and well-designed stoves and ovens, and instruments for distilling, vaporizing, and extracting liquids and ointments belonging to medicine and sublimated simple salts, the salts extracted from burnt herbs, and so forth. In this place there are wondrous retorts [vessels] of copper for distillation, and vessels and long-necked bottles made of glass of various forms and shapes, by means of which acidic liquids and solvents are extracted. All this is carried out with perfect skill and wondrous invention and the like.

Examining the Evidence

1. What are 'al-Jabarti's negative views of the French?
2. What positive views does 'al-Jabarti express in his description of the French?
3. What values does 'al-Jabarti express in his account?
4. How would you characterize 'al-Jabarti as an evaluator of French behavior?

22.4 HAITI AND THE REVOLUTIONARY TRADITION

The Haitian Constitution (1801)

The Haitian Revolution, which erupted in the 1790s, was both slave revolt and racial uprising against white supremacy. Ideas from the French Revolution of 1789 motivated many reformers in Haiti, even as those reformers hoped to free themselves from French rule. In the process of gaining their independence, which was finally achieved in 1804, Haitian reformers produced liberal constitutions guaranteeing the rule of law and

Laurent Dubois and John D. Garrigus, eds., *Slave Revolution in the Caribbean, 1789–1804: A Brief History with Documents* (Boston: Bedford/St. Martin's, 2006), 167–170.

human rights. The Constitution of 1801, major excerpts of which appear in this document, was written by a committee and announced by the leader of the uprising, Governor-General Toussaint Louverture, who sent the Constitution to Napoleon. Napoleon found fault with the Constitution, and he and Louverture became enemies.

The deputies of the departments of the colony of Saint-Domingue, united in a Central Assembly, have decided on and laid out the constitutional foundation of the regime of the French colony of Saint-Domingue, which are as follows:

Title 1: Of the Territory

Article 1. Saint-Domingue in its entirety, and Samana, la Tortue, la Gonâve, les Cayemites, l'Île-à-Vache, La Saône, and other adjacent islands, form the territory of a single colony, which is part of the French empire, but submitted to particular laws.

Article 2. The territory of this colony is divided into departments, districts, and parishes.

Title 2: Of Its Inhabitants

Article 3. There can be no slaves in this territory; servitude is abolished within it forever. All men who are born here live and die free and French.

Article 4. All men, whatever their color, are eligible for all positions.

Article 5. There exist no distinctions other than those based on virtues and talents and no superiority other than that granted by the law to the exercise of a public function.

The law is the same for all, whether it punishes or protects.

Title 3: Of Religion

Article 6. The Catholic, Apostolic and Roman religion is the only one that is publicly professed. . . .

Article 8. The governor of the colony will assign to each minister of the religion the extent of his spiritual administration, and these ministers can never, under any pretext, form a body within the colony.

Title 4: Of Morals

Article 9. The civil and religious institution of marriage encourages the purity of morals, and therefore those spouses who practice the virtues their status demands of them will always be distinguished and specially protected by the government.

Article 10. Divorce will not be allowed in the colony.

Article 11. The status and the rights of children born in marriage will be fixed by laws meant to spread and maintain social virtues and encourage and cement familial ties.

Title 5: Of Men in Society

Article 12. The Constitution guarantees individual liberty and security. No one can be arrested except by virtue of a formally expressed order, emanating from an administrator that the law grants the right to arrest and to detain in a publicly designated location.

Article 13. Property is sacred and inviolable. All persons, either by themselves or through their representatives, are free to dispose of and administer what is recognized as belonging to them. Anyone who attacks this right commits a crime against society and is guilty toward the person whose property they have troubled.

Title 6: Of Cultivation and Commerce

Article 14. Since the colony is essentially agricultural, it cannot be allowed to suffer even the slightest interruption in the work of cultivation.

Article 15. Each plantation is a factory that requires the union of cultivators and workers; it is the peaceful refuge of an active and faithful family, where the owner of the property or his representative is of necessity the father.

Article 16. Each cultivator and worker is a part of the family and receives a portion of its revenues.

All change in residency on the part of cultivators leads to the ruin of cultivation. . . .

Article 17. Since the introduction of cultivators is indispensable to the reestablishment and the growth of crops, it will take place in Saint-Domingue; the

Constitution charges the governor to take appropriate measures to encourage and favor this increase in the number of hands, to stipulate and balance various interests, and to assure and guarantee the execution of the respective obligations that will be the result of this introduction.

Article 18. Since the commerce of the colony consists entirely in the exchange of the commodities and products of its territory, the introduction of those of the same kind as its own is and will remain prohibited.

Title 7: Of Legislation and Legislative Authority

Article 19. The administration of the colony will be determined by laws proposed by the governor and pronounced by an assembly of inhabitants, who will meet at fixed dates in the center of the colony, under the title of the Central Assembly of Saint-Domingue. . . .

Article 24. The Central Assembly votes on the adoption or the rejection of the laws that are proposed by the governor; it votes on regulations that have been made and on the application of laws that are already in place, on abuses to be corrected, on improvements to be pursued in all aspects of the services of the colony.

Article 25. On the basis of the report of the tax receipts and spending presented to it by the governor, the Central Assembly determines, if necessary, the amount, the length, and the mode of collection of the tax, and its increase or decrease; these reports will subsequently be printed. . . .

Title 8: Of the Government

Article 27. The administrative reins of the colony are confided to a governor who will correspond directly with the government of the metropole for everything relative to the interests of the colony.

Article 28. The Constitution names as governor the citizen Toussaint Louverture, the general-in-chief of the army of Saint-Domingue and, in consideration of the important services he has rendered the colony, in the most critical circumstances of the revolution, and on the request of its thankful inhabitants, the reins [of government] are confided to him for the rest of his glorious life.

Article 29. In the future, each governor will be named for five years and will be allowed to continue every five years if he has overseen a good administration.

Article 30. To affirm the tranquillity that the colony owes to the firmness, activity, and tireless zeal and rare virtues of General Toussaint Louverture, and as a sign of the unlimited confidence of the inhabitants of Saint-Domingue, the Constitution attributes to him the exclusive right to choose the citizen who, in the unfortunate event of his death, will replace him. This choice will be secret. . . .

Article 31. The citizen chosen by General Toussaint Louverture to take over the reins of the government will take an oath before the Central Assembly, at his death, to execute the Constitution of Saint-Domingue and to remain attached to the French government.

Examining the Evidence

1. What Enlightenment ideas and reform principles does the Constitution of 1801 reflect?
2. What prerevolutionary and authoritarian principles remain in the Constitution?
3. Why would Napoleon, to whom it was submitted, declare that it had provisions that undermined the "dignity" of France?
4. Given the complexities of the situation in Haiti, especially its status in 1801 as a colony of France, what were the reformers trying to achieve in this Constitution?

Manuel Belgrano, *Autobiography* (1814)

Manuel Belgrano (1770–1820) was the son of well-to-do parents who sent him away from his Buenos Aires home to be educated in Spain, where he obtained his law degree in 1793. There he also picked up a great many Enlightenment ideas about the importance of reforming laws, opening up trade, and improving education. When Belgrano returned to Buenos Aires, his talent and connections helped him obtain a good job with the colonial government there. Gradually, he became a rebel when the Spanish bureaucracy rejected his ideas, and in 1810, he was elected a member of a junta established that same year to replace the Spanish colonial administration. A leader in the cause of Argentinean independence, Belgrano is considered one of the most important national heroes of Argentina.

I was born in Buenos Aires; my parents were Don Domingo Belgrano y Peri, known as Perez, a native of Onella [Spain], and Dona Maria Josefa Gonzalez Casero, a native of Buenos Aires. My father was a merchant, and since he lived in the days of monopoly [guaranteed by Spanish laws against competition] he became sufficiently wealthy to live comfortably and to give his children the best education to be had in those days.

I learned my first letters, Latin grammar, philosophy, and a smattering of theology in Buenos Aires. I was then sent to Spain to become a lawyer, and there I studied at Salamanca, graduated at Valladolid, continued my studies in Madrid, and was admitted to the bar in Valladolid.

I must confess that I was less interested in a legal career than in the study of modern languages, political economy, and public law and when I was fortunate enough to meet men dedicated to the common good who introduced me to their useful ideas, I was seized with the desire to promote public welfare and to enhance my reputation in working for such an important object, to the advantage especially of my own country.

Since I was in Spain in 1789 at a time when the French Revolution was causing a change in ideas, particularly among the men of letters with whom I associated, the ideas of liberty, equality, security, and property, took a firm hold on me, and I saw only tyrants in those who would prevent a man, whatever his origin, from enjoying the rights with which God and Nature had endowed him, and which even human societies had agreed, directly or indirectly, to establish. At the time when I completed my training in 1793 political economy enjoyed great popularity in Spain, and I think that this was the reason why I was appointed secretary of the consulate of Buenos Aires, . . . though I had not made the slightest attempt to obtain the post, and the official of the department concerned with these matters even asked me to nominate well-qualified persons who could be appointed to similar bodies to be established in the chief commercial centers in America.

When I understood that these bodies would be, in effect, societies concerning themselves with agriculture, industry, and commerce, a vast field of activity unfolded itself to my imagination, for I was ignorant of Spain's administration of its colonies. I had heard muffled rumors of complaint and discontent among Americans, but I attributed these to their failure to secure their claims, and not at all to a perverted policy of the Spaniards which had been systematically pursued since the conquest. . . .

Finally I left Spain for Buenos Aires. I cannot sufficiently express the surprise I felt when I met the men appointed by the king to be members of the junta that was to deal with agriculture, industry, and commerce and promote the welfare of the provinces composing the viceroyalty of Buenos Aires. All were Spanish

Manuel Belgrano, "The Making of an Insurgent" in *Latin American Revolutions, 1808–1826: Old and New World Origins*, ed. John Lynch (Norman: University of Oklahoma Press, 1994), 258–262.

merchants. With the exception of one . . . they knew nothing but their monopolistic business, namely, to buy at four and sell for eight. An idea of their knowledge and of their "liberal" attitude towards the country, as well as of their determination to preserve the monopoly from which they drew their wealth, can be learned from one incident, without need of further proof, the Court of Spain, as I have since appreciated, vacillated in the methods by which it exploited its colonies: and thus we have seen liberal and illiberal measures applied simultaneously, proof of the . . . fear of losing the colonies. On one occasion it decided to enrage agriculture; to provide labor it adopted the cruel slave trade, and gave its operators certain privileges, including permission to export agricultural produce to foreign countries. . . .

I became discouraged, and realized that the country could expect nothing from men who placed their private interests above the common good. But since my position gave me an opportunity to write and speak about some useful topics, I decided at least to plant a few seeds that some day might bear fruit, either through the efforts of others or through the passage of time.

I wrote various reports about the establishment of schools. The scarcity of pilots, and the direct interest of the merchants in the project, presented favorable circumstances for the establishment of a school of mathematics, and I obtained agreement to this on condition of getting approval of the Crown. But this it never gave. On the contrary, it did not rest until the school was abolished, because although the Spaniards recognized the justice and utility of such establishments in America, they were openly opposed to them because of a mistaken view, in my opinion, of how the colonies might best be retained.

I was no more successful with a drawing school which I also managed to establish without it costing even half a *real* for the master. The fact is that neither these nor other proposals to the Crown for the development of the three important branches of agriculture, industry, and commerce with which the consulate was concerned, met with official approval. The sole concern of the Crown was with the revenue that it derived from each. It was said that all these establishments were luxuries, and that Buenos Aires was not yet in a condition to support them.

I promoted various other useful and necessary projects, with more or less the same results. It will be for the future historian of the consulate to describe

them. For myself I shall only say that from the beginning of 1794 to July 1806 I passed my time in futile efforts to promote the public good. All foundered on the opposition of the government of Buenos Aires, of Madrid, or of the merchants who composed the consulate, for whom there was no other reason, justice, utility, or necessity than their commercial interest. Anything that came into conflict with that interest was vetoed and that was that.

It is well known how General Beresford [who fought for the British] entered Buenos Aires with about 1400 men in 1806. At that time I had been a captain in the militia for ten years, more from caprice than from any particular liking for military matters. My first experience of war came at that time. The marquis of Sobremonte, then viceroy of the Rio de la Plata, sent for me several days before Beresford's unfortunate entrance and asked me to form a company of cavalry from among the young men engaged in commerce; he said that he would give me professional officers to train them. I sought recruits but could not find any, because of the great hostility felt for the militia in Buenos Aires, at once a blow to the authorities and a sign of their weakness.

The general alarm was sounded, and, moved by a sense of honor, I flew to the fort, the point of assembly. There all was disorder and discord, the inevitable result with groups of men unaccustomed to discipline or authority. Companies were formed and I was attached to one of them. I was ashamed of my ignorance of the most trivial details of military affairs, and I had to rely on the instructions of a veteran officer, who also joined voluntarily, for he was given no assignment.

This was the first company which marched to occupy the *Casa de las Filipinas*. Meanwhile the others argued with the viceroy himself that they were obliged only to defend the city and not to go out into the country; consequently they would agree only to defend the Barrancas. The result was that the enemy, meeting with no opposition from veteran troops or disciplined militia, forced all the entrances with the greatest ease. There was some feeble firing on the part of my company and some others in an effort to stop the enemy, but in vain, and when the order came to retreat and we were falling back I myself heard someone say: "They did well to order us to retreat, for we were not made for this sort of thing."

I must confess that I grew angry, and that I never regretted more deeply my ignorance, as I have already said, of even the rudiments of military affairs. My distress was all the greater when I saw the entrance of the enemy troops, and realized how few of them there were in comparison with a city the size of Buenos Aires. I was obsessed by this . . . and almost went out of my mind, for it was painful to me to see my country under foreign domination, and above all in such a state of degradation that it could be conquered by the daring action of the brave and honorable Beresford, whose valor, in so perilous an undertaking, I admired and always shall admire.

On the other hand let me recall the record of the consulate in these moments, protesting as it did its loyalty to the king of Spain. It proved . . . the well-established truth that the only country, king, or religion that the merchant knows is his self-interest; he works only for that; and his present opposition to the liberty and independence of America has no other motive. . . .

. . . [H]e [General Craufurd[1]] told me of his ideas about our independence, perhaps in the hope of forming new links with this country, since that of conquest had failed. I described our condition to him, and made it plain that we wanted our old master or none; that we were far from possessing the means required for the achievement of independence; that even if it were won under the protection of England, she should abandon us if she saw some advantage in Europe, and then we would fall under the Spanish sword; that every nation sought its own interest and did not care about the misfortunes of others. He agreed with me, and when I had shown how we lacked the means for winning independence, he was of the opinion that it would take a century to achieve, such are the calculations of men! A year passed, and behold, without effort on our part to become independent, God himself gave us our opportunity. . . . Then it was that the ideals of liberty and independence came to life in America, and Americans for the first time began to speak openly of their rights.

Examining the Evidence

1. How had Belgrano and his family benefited from Spanish colonial rule in Argentina? After he finished his education, why did the Spanish authorities probably consider Belgrano a "safe" choice to work in their colonial administration of Argentina?

2. How does Belgrano characterize Spanish colonial policy in Latin America? According to Belgrano, why did the Spanish colonial leaders and local Argentine business elites tied to the colonial leadership refuse to embrace economic reforms?

3. What are Belgrano's own values? How did those values contribute to his turning against the very colonial government he served?

4. What are Belgrano's attitudes toward the Argentine independence movement, and how do these attitudes change?

---

[1] **General Craufurd:** Like Beresford, Craufurd was another British general fighting to help Argentine rebels against Spain, as the French and Spanish had fought to help rebels against Britain in the American Revolution.

MAKING CONNECTIONS

1. Despite many differences in their circumstances, in what ways are Ménétra, Gempaku, and Belgrano kindred spirits?

2. Whether in 'al-Jabarti's observations of the French invasion of Egypt, the Haitian Constitution of 1801, or Belgrano's description of his frustrations with Spanish colonial rule in Argentina, what underlying attitudes about the social order and powerful authorities are being expressed?

3. How do all of the documents in this chapter testify to the global spread of Enlightenment ideas and the revolutionary spirit in this era? In what ways do they express opposition to revolutionary change?

CHAPTER 23

Industry and Everyday Life, 1750–1900

The Industrial Revolution began in the eighteenth century, setting the world on the path to replacing human energy with machine power and dramatically expanding productivity. This course continues to the present day. Beginning in Europe and then spreading across the globe, the Industrial Revolution affected people's lives directly as it led to urbanization and often to wretched living and working conditions for many. Disease spread rapidly in urban settings and among workers crowded together in factories where conditions were physically dangerous, if not lethal. The Industrial Revolution was a source of conflicting interests and even warfare over the conditions of everyday life and trade, and over making a profit. Leaders debated whether or not to industrialize. As industrialists and merchants increasingly sought profits, the poor were often caught in the crossfire between innovation and warfare.

23.1 THE EXPERIENCE OF JAPANESE FACTORY LIFE

Song of the Living Corpses (1890s)

Industrialization rapidly took hold in Japan after the Meiji Restoration of 1868 and was part of the government program of modernization. Families whose traditional livelihoods had been hurt by the end of the old court system with its retainers and needs for many luxury goods, as well as patriotic peasants who wanted the country to prosper, sent their children and especially their daughters to the new factories. For many, conditions in these newly industrialized cultures were as harsh as they were in England, the United States, and almost every industrializing nation. This song, popular with women factory hands, describes arriving at a factory in Japan and setting out to work there.

My family was poor,
At the tender age of twelve
I was sold to a factory.
Yet though I work for cheap wages
My soul is not soiled.
Like the lotus flower in the midst of mud,
My heart too
Will one day blossom forth.

I was carried away by sweet-sounding words.
My money was taken and thrown away.
Unaware of the hardships of the future,
I was duckweed in the wind.

Excited I arrived at the gate,
Where I bowed to the doorman,
I was taken immediately to the dormitory,
Where I bowed to the room supervisor.
I was taken immediately to the infirmary,
Where I risked my life having a medical examination.
I was taken immediately to the cafeteria,
Where I asked what was for dinner.
I was told it was low-grade rice mixed with sand.

When I asked what the side dish was,
I was told there weren't even two slices of
    pickle to eat.
Then I was taken immediately to the factory,
Where I donned a blue skirt and blue shirt,
And put on hemp-straw sandals and blue socks.
When I asked where I was to work
I was told to fasten threads on the winder.

Because my parents were good-for-nothings,
Or because my parents weren't good-for-nothings
But I was a good-for-nothing myself,
I was deceived by a fox without a tail.
Now I'm awakened at four-thirty in the morning;
First I fix my face, then go to the cafeteria;
Then it's off to the factory
Where the chief engineer scowls at me.

When I return to my room,
The supervisor finds all manner of fault with me,
And I feel like I'll never get on in this world.
When next I'm paid
I'll trick the doorkeeper and slip off to the station,
Board the first train
For my dear parents' home.
Both will cry when I tell them
How fate made me learn warping,
Leaving nothing but skin and bone on my soul.

We friends are wretched,
Separated from our homes in a strange place,
Put in a miserable dormitory
Woken up at four-thirty in the morning,
Eating when five o'clock sounds,
Dressing at the third bell,
Glared at by the manager and section head,
Used by the inspector.
How wretched we are!

E. Patricia Tsurumi, *Factory Girls: Women in the Thread Mills of Meiji Japan* (Princeton, NJ: Princeton University Press, 1990), 157–159.

Though I am a factory maid,
My heart is a peony, a cherry in double blossom.
Though male workers make eyes at me,
I'm not the kind to respond.
Rather than remain in this factory,
I'll pluck up my courage,
And board the first train for Ogawa;
Maybe I'll even go to the far corners of Manchuria.

Examining the Evidence

1. What conditions were most oppressive for the young textile workers?
2. What are the hopes and fantasies of these workers, based on this song's popularity?
3. How might this song have come into being?
4. What are the positive aspects of the lives of these women factory workers?

23.2 THE CHINESE CASE AGAINST OPIUM

Edict of Commissioner Lin Zexu (1839)

Commissioner Lin Zexu (1785–1850) was a Chinese scholar–official delegated by the government to deal with the country's opium problem. The issue of opium was multifaceted because it was a much-used product around the world, especially for the relief of pain before the days of aspirin and other modern painkillers. Opium addiction particularly affected many Chinese in the early nineteenth century, costing them money and making them lethargic and even depressed—a real concern to Chinese officials. The British used the trade in opium to finance their own purchases of highly desirable goods from China and the rest of the world, especially tea purchases that kept the working population stimulated. Silver drained from China despite the influx of wealth created by the purchase of tea. The 1830s brought a standoff: the Chinese outlawed the opium trade to protect their balance of trade and stabilize their working population, but British drug smugglers—that is, British "merchants"—were just as determined to keep their profits and products flowing and called in the government to protect their drug smuggling. Lin Zexu explained the Chinese position to Queen Victoria of England in a strongly worded, public letter.

Lin, high imperial commissioner [and others] . . . , hereby conjointly addresses this public dispatch to the queen of England for the purpose of giving her clear and distinct information (on the state of affairs) &c.

It is only our high and mighty emperor, who alike supports and cherishes those of the Inner Land [*Inner Land* and *Central Land* both refer to China], and those from beyond the seas—who looks upon all mankind with equal benevolence. . . . You, the queen of your honorable nation, sit upon a throne occupied through successive generations by predecessors, all of whom have been styled respectful and obedient. Looking over the public documents accompanying the tribute sent (by your predecessors) on various occasions, we find the following: "All the people of my country, arriving at the Central Land for purposes of trade, have to feel grateful to the great emperor for the most perfect justice, for the kindest treatment," and other words to that effect. Delighted did we feel that the kings of your honorable nation so clearly understood the great principles of propriety, and were so deeply grateful for the heavenly goodness (of our emperor):—therefore, it was that we of the heavenly dynasty nourished and cherished your people from afar, and bestowed upon them redoubled proofs of our urbanity and kindness. It is merely from these circumstances, that your country—deriving immense advantage from its commercial intercourse with us, which has endured now two hundred years—has become the rich and flourishing kingdom that it is said to be!

William H. McNeill and Mitsuko Iriye, eds., *Modern Asia and Africa, Readings in World History*, vol. 9 (New York: Oxford University Press, 1971), 111–118. Previously published in *Chinese Repository* 8 (February 1840): 497–503.

But, during the commercial intercourse which has existed so long, among the numerous foreign merchants resorting hither, are wheat and tares [a grass resembling wheat whose seeds are poisonous], good and bad; and of these latter are some, who, by means of introducing opium by stealth, have seduced our Chinese people, and caused every province of the land to overflow with that poison. . . . This is a principle which heaven's Providence repugnates; and which mankind conjointly look upon with abhorrence! Moreover, the great emperor hearing of it, actually quivered with indignation, and especially dispatched me, the commissioner, to Canton, that in conjunction with the viceroy and lieut.-governor of the province, means might be taken for its suppression!

Every native of the Inner Land who sells opium, as also all who smoke it, are alike adjudged to death. Were we then to go back and take up the crimes of the foreigners, who, by selling it for many years have induced dreadful calamity and robbed us of enormous wealth, and punish them with equal severity, our laws could not but award to them absolute annihilation! But, considering that these said foreigners did yet repent of their crime, and with a sincere heart beg for mercy; that they took 20,283 chests of opium piled up in their store-ships, and through Elliot, the superintendent of the trade of your said country, petitioned that they might be delivered up to us, when the same were all utterly destroyed, of which we, the imperial commissioner and colleagues, made a duly prepared memorial to his majesty; — considering these circumstances, we have happily received a fresh proof of the extraordinary goodness of the great emperor, inasmuch as he who voluntarily comes forward, may yet be deemed a fit subject for mercy, and his crimes be graciously remitted him. But as for him who again knowingly violates the laws, difficult indeed will it be thus to go on repeatedly pardoning! He or they shall alike be doomed to the penalties of the new statute. We presume that you, the sovereign of your honorable nation, on pouring out your heart before the altar of eternal justice, cannot but command all foreigners with the deepest respect to reverence our laws! If we only lay clearly before your eyes, what is profitable and what is destructive, you will then know that the statutes of the heavenly dynasty cannot but be obeyed with fear and trembling!

We find that your country is distant from us about sixty or seventy thousand miles [a Chinese li or mile is about a third of a British mile; even so, this is an inaccurate estimate], that your foreign ships come hither striving the one with the other for our trade, and for the simple reason of their strong desire to reap a profit. Now, out of the wealth of our Inner Land, if we take a part to bestow upon foreigners from afar, it follows, that the immense wealth which the said foreigners amass, ought properly speaking to be [a] portion of our own native Chinese people. By what principle of reason then, should these foreigners send in return a poisonous drug, which involves in destruction those very natives of China? . . .

We have heard that in your own country opium is prohibited with the utmost strictness and severity: — this is a strong proof that you know full well how hurtful it is to mankind. Since then you do not permit it to injure your own country, you ought not to have the injurious drug transferred to another country, and above all others, how much less to the Inner Land! Of the products which China exports to your foreign countries, there is not one which is not beneficial to mankind in some shape or other. There are those which serve for food, those which are useful, and those which are calculated for resale; — but all are beneficial. Has China . . . ever yet sent forth a noxious article from its soil? Not to speak of our tea and rhubarb, things which your foreign countries could not exist a single day without, if we of the Central Land were to grudge you what is beneficial, and not to compassionate your wants, then wherewithal could you foreigners manage to exist? And further, as regards your woolens, camlets, and longells [textiles], were it not that you get supplied with our native raw silk, you could not get these manufactured! . . . Our other articles of food, such as sugar, ginger, cinnamon, &c., and our other articles for use, such as silk piece-goods, chinaware, &c., are all so many necessaries of life to you; how can we reckon up their number! On the other hand, the things that come from your foreign countries are only calculated to make presents of, or serve for mere amusement. It is quite the same to us if we have them, or if we have them not. If then these are of no material consequence to us of the Inner Land, what difficulty would there be in prohibiting and shutting our market against them? It is only that our heavenly dynasty most freely permits you to take off her tea, silk, and other commodities, and convey them for consumption everywhere, without the slightest stint or grudge, for no other reason, but that where a profit exists, we wish that it be diffused abroad for the benefit of all the earth!

Your honorable nation takes away the products of our central land, and not only do you thereby obtain food and support for yourselves, but moreover, by re-selling these products to other countries you reap a threefold profit. Now if you would only not sell opium, this threefold profit would be secured to you: how can you possibly consent to forgo it for a drug that is hurtful to men, and an unbridled craving after gain that seems to know no bounds! Let us suppose that foreigners came from another country, and brought opium into England, and seduced the people of your country to smoke it, would not you, the sovereign of the said country, look upon such a procedure with anger, and in your just indignation endeavor to get rid of it? Now we have always heard that your highness possesses a most kind and benevolent heart, surely then you are incapable of doing or causing to be done unto another, that which you should not wish another to do unto you! We have at the same time heard that your ships which come to Canton do each and every of them carry a document granted by your highness' self, on which are written these words "you shall not be permitted to carry contraband goods;" this shows that the laws of your highness are in their origin both distinct and severe, and we can only suppose that because the ships coming here have been very numerous, due attention has not been given to search and examine; and for this reason it is that we now address you this public document, that you may clearly know how stern and severe are the laws of the central dynasty, and most certainly you will cause that they be not again rashly violated!

Moreover, we have heard that in London the metropolis where you dwell . . . no opium whatever is produced. It is only in sundry parts of your colonial kingdom of Hindostan . . . where the very hills are covered with the opium plant, where tanks are made for the preparing of the drug; month by month, and year by year, the volume of the poison increases, its unclean stench ascends upwards, until heaven itself grows angry, and the very gods thereat get indignant! You, the queen of the said honorable nation, ought immediately to have the plant in those parts plucked up by the very root! . . .

Suppose the subject of another country were to come to England to trade, he would certainly be required to comply with the laws of England, then how much more does this apply to us of the celestial empire! Now it is a fixed statute of this empire, that any native Chinese who sells opium is punishable with death, and even he who merely smokes it, must not less die. Pause and reflect for a moment: if you foreigners did not bring the opium hither, where should our Chinese people get it to re-sell? It is you foreigners who involve our simple natives in the pit of death, and are they alone to be permitted to escape alive? . . . Therefore it is that those foreigners who now import opium into the Central Land are condemned to be beheaded and strangled by the new statute, and this explains what we said at the beginning about plucking up the tree of evil, wherever it takes root, for the benefit of all nations. . . .

Our celestial empire rules over ten thousand kingdoms! Most surely do we possess a measure of godlike majesty which ye cannot fathom! Still we cannot bear to slay or exterminate without previous warning, and it is for this reason that we now clearly make known to you the fixed laws of our land. If the foreign merchants of your said honorable nation desire to continue their commercial intercourse, they then must tremblingly obey our recorded statutes, they must cut off for ever the source from which the opium flows, and on no account make an experiment of our laws in their own persons! . . .

Let your highness immediately, upon the receipt of this communication, inform us promptly of the state of matters, and of the measure you are pursuing utterly to put a stop to the opium evil. Please let your reply be speedy. Do not on any account make excuses or procrastinate. A most important communication.

Examining the Evidence

1. Describe the tone of Commissioner Lin Zexu's letter to Queen Victoria.
2. How does Commissioner Lin Zexu describe the products China has to trade in comparison with the products that Britain trades?
3. What arguments does Lin Zexu offer for ending the opium trade?
4. What values does Lin Zexu express in his letter to the queen, and why do you think the British ultimately ignored his arguments?

23.3   CHOLERA STRIKES RAILWAY WORKERS IN INDIA

Official Report to the British Government (c. 1889)

Regions of active industrial development, such as railroad construction sites, became breeding grounds for the spread of disease because of crowding and deficiencies in sanitation due to rapid population growth. Medical observations and attempts at disease control were growing functions of imperial expansion, in large part to protect European officials and soldiers. Western officials, whether in Europe or in regions being colonized, sent reports of disease and general well-being to ensure progress on projects such as railroad building. Often these reports described horrendous conditions, as in the report on the spread of cholera and other illnesses in India.

All the year round the whole country is very feverish, the months of January and February being slightly less so. The "Lanias" who come down from "Purtabgarh," "Jownpur" and other adjacent districts in Oudh die in great numbers from fever, dysentery and ulcers. These latter are caused by the slightest abrasion of the skin from a flying stone or other slight cause, and in a few days whatever the reason may be, the part becomes a foul ulcer which unless treated at once takes months to cure, if indeed they do not prove incurable. Men may be seen with their legs or arms almost rotting off with these sores. Between the months of March and July the water-supply fails almost entirely for miles, the streams either dry up or become so foul from rotting

vegetation that the water is undrinkable. The rainfall of 1888 was much less than the average and the water-supply failed in April; hence in May cholera broke out at "Pali" and spread over the whole length of the district, the mortality being terrible, some 2500 or 3000 labourers and petty contractors being carried off by it; the scare was such that people hurrying away at the first sign of its approach were left by their relatives to die all along the line, giving the staff (the Assistant Engineers having in dozens of instances to drag the bodies away themselves, make the funeral piles and light them with their own hands) as much as they could do and more to keep the road clear. None of the natives, with but the rarest exceptions, would touch the corpses or go within fifty yards of them. (It may be mentioned as a curious fact that during the outbreak of cholera no vultures, the usual useful scavengers, were to be seen either at their work or on the wing.) In one gang of 30 men employed breaking ballast, 14 were carried off in two days, also Sub-Overseer. At the Gorchetta Bridge on which the girder erection was going on at the time some 50 men were carried off; the contractor himself was taken ill, but ultimately recoved [sic]. The whole line was deserted throughout the district. Mr Thomason, Assistant Engineer, after giving medicine &c., to a number of his men who were down at Anukpur, where the foundations were being taken for a bridge, himself succumbed in about six hours before any of his brother officers could reach him. Even now, nearly three months

Ian J. Kerr, *Building the Railways of the Raj, 1850–1900* (Delhi: Oxford University Press, 1995), 159–160.

after the cholera has practically ceased, on pulling down the little grass shelters erected by the coolies [menial laborers, often Asians], numbers of skeletons have been found. The greatest difficulty was experienced in procuring provisions as all the petty villages within 5 or six miles of the line were closed to outsiders, the villagers declining to allow even a European inside, and ready even to use their axes and latties [a tool] to prevent it. One village or rather hovel containing originally eighty people all told, now contains 28; the rest are dead.

Examining the Evidence

1. What specific conditions does the official note in his report?
2. What attitudes does the official display in his description of villagers and the cholera epidemic?
3. How did the changes brought about by industrialization affect health and well-being?
4. What conclusions can you draw from this description of villagers about the Indians' actual attitudes and behaviors?

CONTRASTING VIEWS

DEBATES OVER INDUSTRIALIZATION

23.4 ADAM SMITH, *OF THE DIVISION OF LABOR* (1776)

Scottish philosopher Adam Smith (1723–1790) was one of the great economic and social thinkers of the eighteenth century. His powerful writing influenced people to adopt "free trade" or "laissez-faire" beliefs that government restrictions on trade should be lifted so that people could act in their own self-interest and thus prosper. At the same time, Smith also advocated that self-interest should not override concern for the general good of all in society—an important point that is often omitted from discussions of Smith's thinking. In this excerpt, Smith turns his attention to a major component of industry and manufacturing: the division of labor.

Book I, Chapter 1: The greatest improvement in the productive powers of labor, and the greater part of the skill, dexterity, and judgment with which it is anywhere directed, or applied, seem to have been the effects of the division of labor. . . .

To take an example, therefore, the trade of the pin-maker; a workman not educated to this business, . . . nor acquainted with the use of the machinery employed in it, could scarce, perhaps, with his utmost industry, make one pin in a day, and certainly could not make twenty. But in the way in which this business is now carried on, not only the whole work is a peculiar trade, but it is divided into a number of branches, of which the greater part are likewise peculiar trades. One man draws out the wire, another straights it, a third cuts it, a fourth points it, a fifth grinds it at the top for receiving the head; to make the head requires two or three distinct operations; to put it on, is a peculiar business, to whiten the pins is another; it is even a trade by itself to put them into the paper; and the important business of making a pin is, in this manner, divided into about eighteen distinct operations, which, in some manufactories, are all performed by distinct hands, though in others the same man will sometimes perform two or three of them.

I have seen a small manufactory of this kind where ten men only were employed, and where some of them consequently performed two or three distinct operations. But though they were very poor, and therefore but indifferently accommodated with the necessary machinery, they could, when they exerted themselves, make among them about twelve pounds of pins in a day. There are in a pound upwards of four thousand pins of a middling size. Those ten persons, therefore, could make among them upwards of forty-eight thousand pins in a day. Each person, therefore, making a tenth part of forty-eight thousand pins, might be considered as making four thousand eight hundred pins in a day. But if they had all wrought separately and independently, and without any of them having been educated to this peculiar business, they certainly could not each of them have made twenty, perhaps not one pin in a day; that is, certainly, not the two hundred and

Adam Smith, *An Inquiry into the Nature and Causes of the Wealth of Nations*, ed. Edwin Cannan, vol. 1 (New York: G. P. Putnam's Sons, 1904), 5–7, 9, 12–13, 15–16.

fortieth, perhaps not the four thousand eight hundredth part of what they are at present capable of performing, in consequence of a proper division and combination of their different operations. . . .

The division of labor, so far as it can be introduced, occasions, in every art, a proportionable increase of the productive powers of labor. The separation of different trades and employments from one another seems to have taken place in consequence of this advantage. This separation too is generally called furthest in those countries which enjoy the highest degree of industry and improvement; what is the work of one man in a rude state of society being generally that of several in an improved one. . . .

This great increase of the quantity of work which, in consequence of the division of labor, the same number of people are capable of performing, is owing to three different circumstances; first, to the increase of dexterity in every particular workman; *secondly*, to the saving of the time which is commonly lost in passing from one species of work to another; and *lastly*, to the invention of a great number of machines which facilitate and abridge labor, and enable one man to do the work of many. . . .

It is the great multiplication of the productions of all the different arts, in consequence of the division of labor, which occasions, in a well-governed society, that universal opulence which extends itself to the lowest ranks of the people. Every workman has a great quantity of his own work to dispose of beyond what he himself has occasion for; and every other workman being exactly in the same situation, he is enabled to exchange a great quantity of his own goods for a great quantity, or, what comes to the same thing, for the price of a great quantity of theirs. He supplies them abundantly with what they have occasion for, and they accommodate him as amply with what he has occasion for, and a general plenty diffuses itself through all the different ranks of the society. . . .

Book I, Chapter 2: This division of labor, from which so many advantages are derived, is not originally the effect of any human wisdom, which foresees and intends that universal opulence to which it gives occasion. It is the necessary, though very slow and gradual consequence of a certain propensity in human nature which has in view no such extensive utility; the propensity to truck, barter, and exchange one thing for another. . . .

Man has almost constant occasion for the help of his brethren, and it is in vain for him to expect it from their benevolence only. He will be more likely to prevail if he can interest their self-love in his favor, and show them that it is for their own advantage to do for him what he requires of them. Whoever offers to another a bargain of any kind, proposes to do this. Give me that which I want, and you shall have this which you want, is the meaning of every such offer; and it is in this manner that we obtain from one another the far greater part of those good offices which we stand in need of. It is not from the benevolence of the butcher, the brewer, or the baker that we expect our dinner, but from their regard to their own interest.

23.5 FRIEDRICH ENGELS, *THE CONDITION OF THE WORKING CLASS IN ENGLAND* (1844)

German-born industrialist Friedrich Engels (1820–1895) collaborated with Karl Marx (1818–1883) in the development of socialist activism and theory—a theory of workers' triumph over the oppression of factory owners that was influential in the development of socialist political parties. Engels also was a partner in a large textile manufacturing firm in Manchester, which was an important hub of English industrialization. Manchester's population grew rapidly from under 20,000 in 1760 to over 300,000 in 1851, thanks to the availability of factory work in the new textile industries there. Engels thus described conditions in an industrial city that he knew very well when he published this book.

Here the streets, even the better ones, are narrow and winding, . . . the houses dirty, old, and tumble-down, and the construction of the side streets utterly horrible. . . .

The first court below Ducie Bridge, known as Allen's Court, was in such a state at the time of the cholera that the sanitary police ordered it evacuated, swept, and disinfected with chloride of lime. . . . The view from this bridge, mercifully concealed from mortals of small stature by a parapet as high as a man, is characteristic for the whole district. At the bottom flows, or rather stagnates, the Irk, a narrow, coal-black, foul-smelling stream, full of débris and refuse, which it deposits on the shallower right bank. In dry weather,

Frederick Engels, *The Condition of the Working-Class in England in 1844*, trans. Florence Kelley Wischnewetzky (London: Swan Sonnenschein & Co., 1892), 48–52.

(continued)

CONTRASTING VIEWS *(continued)*

a long string of the most disgusting blackish-green, slime pools are left standing on this bank, from the depths of which bubbles of miasmatic gas constantly arise and give forth a stench unendurable even on the bridge forty or fifty feet above the surface of the stream. . . . Above the bridge are tanneries, bonemills, and gasworks, from which all drains and refuse find their way into the Irk, which receives further the contents of all the neighbouring sewers and privies [toilets]. . . . Below the bridge you look upon the piles of débris, the refuse, filth, and offal from the courts on the steep left bank; here each house is packed close behind its neighbour and a piece of each is visible, all black, smoky, rumbling, ancient, with broken panes and window frames. The background is furnished by old barrack-like factory buildings. On the lower right bank stands a long row of houses and mills; the second house being a ruin without a roof, piled with débris; the third stands so low that the lowest floor is uninhabitable, and therefore without windows or doors. Here the background embraces the pauper burial-ground, the station of the Liverpool and Leeds railway, and, in the rear of this, the Workhouse, the "Poor-Law Bastille" of Manchester, which, like a citadel, looks threateningly down from behind its high walls and parapets on the hilltop, upon the working-people's quarter below.

Above Ducie Bridge, the left bank grows more flat and the right bank steeper, but the condition of the dwellings on both banks grows worse rather than better. He who turns left here from the main street, Long Millgate, is lost; he wanders from one court to another, turns countless corners, passes nothing but narrow, filthy nooks and alleys, until after a few minutes he has lost all clue, and knows not whither to turn. . . . Everywhere before the doors refuse

and offal; that any sort of pavement lay underneath could not be seen but only felt, here and there, with the feet. This whole collection of cattle-sheds for human beings was surrounded on two sides by houses and a factory, and on the third by the river, and besides the narrow stair up the bank, a narrow doorway alone led out into another almost equally ill-built, ill-kept labyrinth of dwellings.

Enough! The whole side of the Irk is built in this way, a planless, knotted chaos of houses, more or less on the verge of uninhabitableness, whose unclean interiors fully correspond with their filthy external surroundings. And how could the people be clean with no proper opportunity for satisfying the most natural and ordinary wants? Privies are so rare here that they are either filled up every day, or are too remote for most of the inhabitants to use. How can the people wash when they have only the dirty Irk water at hand, while pumps and water pipes can be found in decent parts of the city alone? In truth, it cannot be charged to the account of these helots [serfs or slaves, as in ancient Sparta] of modern society if their dwellings are not more cleanly than the pig-sties which are here and there to be seen among them. The landlords are not ashamed to let dwellings like the six or seven cellars on the quay directly below Scotland Bridge, the floors of which stand at least two feet below the low-water level of the Irk that flows not six feet away from them; or like the upper floor of the corner-house on the opposite shore directly above the bridge, where the ground floor, utterly uninhabitable, stands deprived of all fittings for doors and windows, a case by no means rare in this region, when this open ground floor is used as a privy by the whole neighbourhood for want of other facilities!

23.6 JOSÉ MANUEL BALMACEDA, *ON THE NEED TO DEVELOP NATIONAL INDUSTRY* (1880s)

The new Latin American nations that fought and won their freedom from colonial rule during the 1800s depended on plantation and mining economies as they sought to establish secure governments. Most of these nations exported their less expensive raw materials and imported more expensive manufactured goods from industrial states, such as Great Britain. During the unstable conditions of the nineteenth century, local Latin American politicians and social critics observed or studied the economic relationships with Europe and the United States that worked to their own disadvantage. Other Latin Americans closely observed the effects of the rise of industry across the West itself because wealth allowed the West to become stronger militarily and enforce its will. Here is the opinion of Chile's president José Manuel

Benjamin Keen, ed., *Latin American Civilization: History and Society, 1492 to the Present*, 6th ed. (Boulder, CO: Westview Press, 1996), 276.

Balmaceda (1840–1891) about industrialization in Chile—an opinion that upset the powerful British and eventually led to Balmaceda's ouster and suicide.

Economic developments of the last few years prove that, while maintaining a just balance between expenditures and income, we can and should undertake productive national works that will nourish, more especially, our public education and our national industry.

And since I speak of our national industry, I must add that it is weak and uncertain because of lack of confidence on the part of capital and because of our general resistance to opening up and utilizing its beneficial currents.

If, following the example of Washington and the great republic of the North, we preferred to consume our national production, even if it is not as finished and perfect as the foreign production; if the farmer, the miner, and the manufacturer constructed their tools and machines whenever possible in our country's workshops; if we broadened and made more varied production of our raw materials, processing and transforming them into objects useful for life or personal comfort; if we ennobled industrial labor, increasing wages in proportion to the greater skill of our working class; if the state, while maintaining a balance between revenues and expenditures, devoted a portion of its resources to the protection of national industry, nourishing and supporting it during its first trials; if the state, with its resources and legislation, and all of us together, collectively and singly, applied ourselves to producing more and better consuming what we produce, then a more vigorous sap would circulate through the industrial organism of the Republic, and increased wealth and well-being would give us the possession of that supreme good of an industrious and honorable people; the capacity to live and clothe ourselves by our own unaided efforts.

23.7 LI HUNG-CHANG, *A REPORT TO THE EMPEROR: PROBLEMS OF INDUSTRIALIZATION* (1872)

After China lost a series of wars with Britain and other European powers in the 1840s and 1850s, some Chinese officials became interested in the role that industry played in Europe's swift rise to global eminence. The scholar–official Li Hung-Chang (1823–1901) was one of these officials, especially because he had fought in the Taiping Rebellion and had seen the force of Western guns up close. His concerns were the "self-strengthening" that the Chinese government had called for in the aftermath of the Opium War and Taiping Rebellion, and he supported change, as we see in this excerpt from a report he wrote in defense of steamship building. Other Chinese officials, however, had a vested interest in preserving China's social system: industrialization for them would throw people out of work, lead to banditry, and provoke the kinds of rebellions and war that erupted in Europe in the nineteenth century.

We have seen with admiration the Sacred Emperor's vigorous striving for self-strengthening and for laying down broad far-reaching plans. Our admiration is beyond telling. Your minister has been thinking that the various European countries in the last several decades have advanced from India to the southern oceans, from the southern oceans to the northeast, and have invaded China's frontiers and interior land. Peoples never recorded in previous histories, who have had no contact with us since ancient times, have come to our points of entry to ask for trade relations. Our Emperors have been as generous as the sky and have made treaties with all of them for international trade in order to control them. People from a distance of ninety thousand *li*, from the cardinal points of the globe, are gathering together in China; this is the greatest change during the last three millennia and more!

The Westerners particularly rely upon the excellence and efficacy of their guns, cannon, and steamships, and so they can overrun China. The bow and spear, small guns, and native-made cannon which have hitherto been used by China cannot resist their rifles, which have their bullets fed from the rear opening. The sailing boats, rowboats, and the gunboats which have been hitherto employed

Reprinted by permission of the publisher from *China's Response to the West: A Documentary Survey, 1839–1923*, by Ssu-yü Têng and John K. Fairbank, pp. 108–109. Cambridge, MA: Harvard University Press. Copyright © 1954, 1979 by the President and Fellows of Harvard College. Copyright renewed 1982 by Ssu-yü Têng and John K. Fairbank.

(continued)

cannot oppose their steam-engined warships. Therefore, we are controlled by the Westerners.

To live today and still say "reject the barbarians" and "drive them out of our territory" is certainly superficial and absurd talk. Even though we wish to preserve the peace and to protect our territory, we cannot preserve and protect them unless we have the right weapons. They are daily producing their weapons to strive with us for supremacy and victory, pitting their superior techniques against our inadequacies, to wrangle with and to affront us. Then how can we get along for one day without weapons and techniques?

The method of self-strengthening lies in learning what they can do, and in taking over what they rely upon. Moreover, their possession of guns, cannons, and steamships began only within the last hundred years or so, and their progress has been so fast that their influence has spread into China. If we can really and thoroughly understand their methods—and the more we learn, the more improve—and promote them further and further, can we not expect that after a century or so we can reject the barbarians and stand on our own feet? Japan is just a small nation. Recently she has begun to trade with Europe; she has instituted iron factories and built many steamships. She has changed to the use of Western weapons. Does she have the ambition to plot and invade the Western nations? Perhaps she is merely planning for self-protection. But if Japan seeks only self-protection, she is nevertheless oppressing and looking down on our China. Should not China plan for herself? Our scholars and officials have confined themselves to the study of stanzas and sentences and are ignorant of the greatest change of the last several thousand years; they are accustomed to the temporary security of the present, and so they forget why we received the heavy blow and deep suffering of twenty or thirty years ago [the Opium War], and how we can obtain the domestic security and control the foreigners within several centuries. That is how this talk of stopping steamship construction has originated.

COMPARING THE EVIDENCE

1. What values do advocates of industrialization see in its impact?
2. How do Adam Smith and Friedrich Engels differ concerning industrialization's benefits and the overall effects on society?
3. What are both the obvious and more hidden drawbacks to the growth of industry?
4. How do the Balmaceda and Hung-Chang documents highlight industrialization as a political issue about national independence?

MAKING CONNECTIONS

1. According to the various commentators in this chapter's documents, why are commerce and industry such important topics of debate at this time? How do Commissioner Lin Zexu's public letter to Queen Victoria and Hung-Chang's report reflect contrasting views?
2. What are the various interests of the commentators regarding industry and commerce, and how does their status affect their opinions, if at all?
3. What are the common negative experiences of industrialization and commerce expressed in the documents?
4. What is the changing nature of society—both globally and locally—as noted by the authors of these documents?

CHAPTER 24

Nation-States and Their Empires, 1850–1900

Nation building in the modern era entailed welding diverse peoples and interests into a common whole. Because the nation-state could increasingly mobilize citizen support, especially in the form of taxes to build military power, it became a much-admired form of government, even using war to create national unity. A variety of political forms coexisted, including monarchies, chieftaincies, and overseas empires—some of them extensions of cohesive nations. Competition among nations in Europe, Japan, and the United States to conquer foreign lands and appropriate their resources surged as the nineteenth century progressed. People in colonized regions suffered violence, famine, and increased demands on them for physical labor—all in the cause of fortifying national power and wealth. For their part, local leaders often spoke their minds about the so-called civilization imperialists claimed to represent.

24.1   NATION BUILDING IN THE UNITED STATES

Abraham Lincoln, *First Inaugural Address* (March 4, 1861)

Abraham Lincoln (1809–1865) was elected to lead his troubled country in 1860, and ultimately, his presidency turned out to be one that built the United States into a solid nation with fewer fundamental divisions within its economic and political leadership than before Lincoln became president. When campaigning for the U.S. Senate in 1858, Lincoln had maintained that "a house divided against itself cannot stand. . . . This government cannot endure, permanently half slave and half free." When he took office, pro-slavery advocates believed that Lincoln would set out to destroy their way of life, and fearing this very outcome, seven Southern states had already seceded from the Union to form the Confederate States of America. In his inaugural address of 1861, excerpted here, Lincoln tried to reason away those fears, proclaiming a political culture of national unity and promising the South that their way of life was not threatened. Leaders of the Southern states were unmoved, however, and within six weeks of the inauguration, the U.S. Civil War erupted, and four more states seceded. When the war was over—four long and bloody years later—the two sides reunited into an increasingly powerful nation-state, albeit one with racial, gender, and emotional divisions.

The Chief Magistrate derives all his authority from the people, and they have conferred none upon him to fix terms for the separation of the States. The people themselves can do this also if they choose, but the executive, as such, has nothing to do with it. His duty is to administer the present government, as it came to his hands, and to transmit it, unimpaired by him to his successor. . . .

My countrymen, one and all, think calmly and *well*, upon this whole subject. Nothing valuable can be lost by taking time. If there be an object to *hurry* any of you, in hot haste, to a step which you would never take *deliberately*, that object will be frustrated

by taking time; but no good object can be frustrated by it. Such of you as are now dissatisfied, still have the old Constitution unimpaired, and, on the sensitive point, the laws of your own framing under it; while the new administration will have no immediate power, if it would, to change either. If it were admitted that you who are dissatisfied, hold the right side in the dispute, there still is no single good reason for precipitate action. Intelligence, patriotism, Christianity, and a firm reliance on Him who has never yet forsaken this favored land are still competent to adjust in the best way, all our present difficulty.

In your hands, my dissatisfied fellow-countrymen, and not in *mine*, is the momentous issue of civil war. The government will not assail *you*. You can have no conflict without being yourselves the aggressors. *You* have no oath registered in heaven to destroy the government, while *I* shall have the most solemn one to "preserve, protect, and defend" it.

I am loath to close. We are not enemies, but friends. We must not be enemies. Though passion may have strained, it must not break our bonds of affection. The mystic chords of memory, stretching from every battlefield and patriot grave, to every living heart and hearthstone, all over this broad land, will yet swell the chorus of the Union, when again touched, as surely they will be, by the better angels of our nature.

Examining the Evidence

1. What attitudes does Lincoln urge U.S. citizens to adopt as he is being inaugurated, and who is he addressing most especially in this speech?
2. How does Lincoln describe his own position and powers as president?
3. How does Lincoln describe the United States as a nation?
4. What is the tone of Lincoln's address on the eve of civil war?

Joseph R. Fornieri, ed., *The Language of Liberty: The Political Speeches and Writings of Abraham Lincoln* (Washington, DC: Regnery Publishing, 2003), 573–574.

24.2 IMAGINING THE PERFECT NATION

Rokeya Sakhawat Hossain, *Sultana's Dream* (1905)

Sultana's Dream outlined a brief utopia imagined by an outsider to the nation-state—and one doubly so because she was a Muslim woman and also a subject of the British Empire in South Asia in 1905. Written by Rokeya Sakhawat Hossain (1880–1932), the young wife of an Indian official, *Sultana's Dream* was published in English in an Indian women's magazine. Hossain's husband was proud of her accomplishments in learning the English language so well. Made confident by his support, she went on to write essays, establish a school for girls, and participate in other women's causes. Such activism went against the custom of seclusion for women that was common in many parts of the world, including the general conviction in Europe and the United States that women were not "evolved" enough to act outside the home. Her belief in women's ability to contribute to society kept her active in the public sphere, even though many in India and Britain were against such participation by women.

One evening I was lounging in an easy chair in my bedroom and thinking lazily of the condition of Indian womanhood. I am not sure whether I dozed off or not. But, as far as I remember, I was wide awake. I saw the moonlit sky sparkling with thousands of diamondlike stars, very distinctly.

All on a sudden a lady stood before me; how she came in, I do not know. I took her for my friend, Sister Sara.

"Good morning," said Sister Sara. I smiled inwardly as I knew it was not morning, but starry night. However, I replied to her, saying, "How do you do?"

"I am all right, thank you. Will you please come out and have a look at our garden?"

I looked again at the moon through the open window, and thought there was no harm in going out at that time. The menservants outside were fast asleep just then, and I could have a pleasant walk with Sister Sara. . . .

When walking I found to my surprise that it was a fine morning. The town was fully awake and the streets alive with bustling crowds. I was feeling very shy, thinking I was walking in the street in broad daylight, but there was not a single man visible.

Some of the passersby made jokes at me. Though I could not understand their language, yet I felt sure they were joking. I asked my friend, "What do they say?"

"The women say that you look very mannish. . . . They mean that you are shy and timid like men."

"Shy and timid like men?" It was really a joke. I became very nervous, when I found that my companion was not Sister Sara, but a stranger. Oh, what a fool had I been to mistake this lady for my dear old friend, Sister Sara.

She felt my fingers tremble in her hand, as we were walking hand in hand.

"What is the matter, dear?" she said affectionately.

"I feel somewhat awkward," I said in a rather apologizing tone, "as being a purdahnishin [living in purdah or seclusion] woman I am not accustomed to walking about unveiled."

"You need not be afraid of coming across a man here. This is Ladyland. . . . "

"How nice it is," said I . . .

I became very curious to know where the men were. I met more than a hundred women while walking there, but not a single man.

"Where are the men?" I asked her. . . .

"O, I see my mistake, you cannot know our customs, as you were never here before. We shut our men indoors."

"Just as we are kept in the zenana [area of seclusion for women]?"

"Exactly so."

digital.library.upenn.edu/women/sultana/dream/dream.html (accessed April 6, 2018)

"How funny," I burst into a laugh. Sister Sara laughed too.

"But dear Sultana, how unfair it is to shut in the harmless women and let loose the men."

"Why? It is not safe for us to come out of the zenana, as we are naturally weak."

"Yes, it is not safe so long as there are men about the streets, nor is it so when a wild animal enters a marketplace. . . . Suppose some lunatics escape from the asylum and begin to do all sorts of mischief to men, horses, and other creatures; in that case what will your countrymen do?"

"They will try to capture them and put them back into their asylum."

"Thank you! And you do not think it wise to keep sane people inside an asylum and let loose the insane?"

"Of course not!" said I laughing lightly.

"As a matter of fact, in your country this very thing is done! Men, who do or at least are capable of doing no end of mischief, are let loose and the innocent women, shut up in the zenana! How can you trust those untrained men out of doors?"

"We have no hand or voice in the management of our social affairs. In India man is lord and master, he has taken to himself all powers and privileges and shut up the women in the zenana."

"Why do you allow yourselves to be shut up?"

"Because it cannot be helped as they are stronger than women."

"A lion is stronger than a man, but it does not enable him to dominate the human race. You have neglected the duty you owe to yourselves and you have lost your natural rights by shutting your eyes to your own interests." . . .

By this time we reached Sister Sara's house. It was situated in a beautiful heart-shaped garden. It was a bungalow with a corrugated iron roof. . . .

We sat side by side. She brought out of the parlor a piece of embroidery work and began putting on a fresh design. . . .

"How can you find time to do all these? You have to do the office work as well? Have you not?"

"Yes. I do not stick to the laboratory all day long. I finish my work in two hours." "In two hours! How do you manage? In our land the officers, magistrates, for instance, work seven hours daily."

"I have seen some of them doing their work. Do you think they work all the seven hours? . . . No, dear Sultana, they do not. They dawdle away their time in smoking. Some smoke two or three choroots [a type of cigar] during the office time. They talk much about their work, but do little. Suppose one choroot takes half an hour to burn off, and a man smokes twelve choroots daily; then you see, he wastes six hours every day in sheer smoking. . . .

"Will you care to see our kitchen?" she asked me.

"With pleasure," said I, and we went to see it. . . . There was no sign of coal or fire.

"How do you cook?" I asked.

"With solar heat," she said, at the same time showing me the pipe, through which passed the concentrated sunlight and heat. And she cooked something then and there to show me the process. . . .

"Thirty years ago, when our present Queen was thirteen years old, she inherited the throne. She was Queen in name only, the Prime Minister really ruling the country.

"Our good Queen liked science very much. She circulated an order that all the women in her country should be educated. Accordingly a number of girls' schools were founded and supported by the Government. Education was spread far and wide among women. And early marriage also was stopped. No woman was to be allowed to marry before she was twenty-one. I must tell you that, before this change we had been kept in strict purdah. . . . In a few years we had separate universities, where no men were admitted. . . . While the women were engaged in scientific research, the men of this country were busy increasing their military power. When they came to know that the female universities were able to draw water from the atmosphere and collect heat from the sun, they only laughed at the members of the universities and called the whole thing 'a sentimental nightmare'!"

"Your achievements are very wonderful indeed! But tell me how you managed to put the men of your country into the zenana. . . ."

"By brain. . . . Women's brains are somewhat quicker than men's. Ten years ago, when the military officers called our scientific discoveries 'a sentimental nightmare,' some of the young ladies wanted to say something in reply to those remarks. But both the Lady Principals restrained them and said they should reply not by word, but by deed, if ever they got the opportunity. And they had not long to wait for that opportunity. . . . Soon afterward certain persons came from a neighboring country and took shelter in ours. . . . The King, who cared more for power than for good government, asked our kind-hearted Queen to hand them over to his officers. She refused, as it was against her principle to turn out refugees. For this refusal the king declared war against our country. . . .

"A meeting of a number of wise ladies was held at the Queen's palace to advise as to what should be done to save the land.

"Some proposed to fight like soldiers; others objected and said that women were not trained to fight with swords and guns, nor were they accustomed to fighting with any weapons. A third party regretfully remarked that they were hopelessly weak of body.

"'If you cannot save your country for lack of physical strength,' said the Queen, 'try to do so by brain power.' . . .

"Then the Lady Principal of the second university (who had collected sun-heat), who had been silently thinking during the consultation, remarked that they were all but lost; and there was little hope left for them. There was, however, one plan which she would like to try, and this would be her first and last effort; if she failed in this, there would be nothing left but to commit suicide. All present solemnly vowed that they would never allow themselves to be enslaved, no matter what happened. . . . The Lady Principal rose again and said, 'Before we go out the men must enter the zenanas. I make this prayer for the sake of purdah.' 'Yes, of course,' replied Her Royal Highness.

"On the following day the Queen called upon all men to retire into zenanas for the sake of honor and liberty.

"Wounded and tired as they were, they took that order rather for a boon! They bowed low and entered the zenanas without uttering a single word of protest. They were sure that there was no hope for this country at all.

"Then the Lady Principal with her two thousand students marched to the battle field, and arriving there directed all the rays of the concentrated sunlight and heat toward the enemy. The heat and light were too much for them to bear. They all ran away panic-stricken, not knowing in their bewilderment how to counteract that scorching heat. When they fled away leaving their guns and other ammunitions of war, they were burnt down by means of the same sunheat.

"Since then no one has tried to invade our country any more."

"And since then your countrymen never tried to come out of the zenana?"

"Yes, they wanted to be free. . . .

"Her Royal Highness sent them a circular letter intimating to them that if their services should ever be needed they would be sent for, and that in the meanwhile they should remain where they were.

"Now that they are accustomed to the purdah system and have ceased to grumble at their seclusion, we call the system *mardana* instead of zenana. . . .

"Since the mardana system has been established, there has been no more crime or sin; therefore we do not require a policeman to find out a culprit, nor do we want a magistrate to try a criminal case." . . .

"You are a lucky people!" ejaculated I. "You know no want. What is your religion, may I ask?"

"Our religion is based on Love and Truth." . . . I somehow slipped down and the fall startled me out of my dream. And on opening my eyes, I found myself in my own bedroom still lounging in the easy chair!

Examining the Evidence

1. Describe the tone of this story. Why does the author describe it as a dream?

2. In Hossain's account of this dream, what factors allow women to become powerful in this society?

3. What do you see as the author's purposes in writing this story, aside from the personal aspect of showing her husband that she could write in English?

4. How does Hossain's story contribute to building national sentiment?

24.3   A PLACE IN THE SUN

Kaiser William II of Germany, *Speech to the North German Regatta Association* (1901)

Germany, like Japan and the United States, was a new-comer to establishing an overseas empire. Whereas England, France, and the Netherlands had consolidated themselves as nations over the centuries and had long crossed the seas for access to trade and territory, this was not the case for Germany. Only in 1871 had Chancellor Otto von Bismarck accomplished the unification of numerous German states under a single government. Reluctantly, he allowed German adventurers and businessmen to advance in Africa, Asia, and the Middle East. Bismarck's own preference was to consolidate German power on the European continent. Such was not the case with William II (1859–1941), who became Kaiser (emperor) in 1888 at the age of twenty-nine. He fired Bismarck and set out to build up Germany militarily and territorially abroad, explaining his national ambitions in 1901 in what has become a famous speech.

In spite of the fact that we have no such fleet as we should have, we have conquered for ourselves a place in the sun. It will now be my task to see to it that this place in the sun shall remain our undisputed possession, in order that the sun's rays may fall fruitfully upon our activity and trade in foreign parts, that our industry and agriculture may develop within the state and our sailing sports upon the water, for our future lies upon the water. The more Germans go out upon the waters, whether it be in races of regattas, whether it be in journeys across the ocean, or in the service of the battle-flag, so much the better it will be for us.

For when the German has once learned to direct his glance upon what is distant and great, the pettiness which surrounds him in daily life on all sides will disappear. Whoever wishes to have this larger and freer outlook can find no better place than one of the Hanseatic cities[1]. . . . We are now making efforts to do what, in the old time, the Hanseatic cities could not accomplish, because they lacked the vivifying and protecting power of the empire. May it be the function of my Hansa during many years of peace to protect and advance commerce and trade! . . .

As head of the empire I therefore rejoice over every citizen, whether from Hamburg, Bremen, or Lübeck, who goes forth with this large outlook and seeks new points where we can drive in the nail on which to hang our armor. Therefore, I believe that I express the feeling of all your hearts when I recognize gratefully that the director of this company who has placed at our disposal the wonderful ship which bears my daughter's name has gone forth as a courageous servant of the Hansa, in order to make for us friendly conquests whose fruits will be gathered by our descendants!

Examining the Evidence

1. What are William's announced goals for Germany?
2. How does the Kaiser explain the benefits of expansion?
3. What role do you see for the German navy in Kaiser William's speech?
4. What is the importance of Kaiser William's message?

[1] **Hanseatic cities:** Those cities belonging to the traditional commercial alliance of northern German towns.

C. Gauss, *The German Kaiser as Shown in His Public Utterances* (New York: Charles Scribner's Sons, 1915), 181–183.

24.4 WORKING FOR THE IMPERIALISTS

Roger Casement, *Report on the Administration of the Independent State of the Congo* (1903)

Work anywhere in regions dominated by foreign powers usually entailed hardship and an attempt by imperialists to overturn local traditions and values. Old livelihoods, often involving crafts, subsistence farming, and trade, disappeared as private businesspeople, backed by imperial governments, demanded that colonized peoples work on plantations or in mines. In the Belgian Congo, the government agents of King Leopold set quotas for the collection of rubber and punished those who could not meet those quotas. When news of these punishments became public knowledge, the Irish diplomat Roger Casement (1864–1916) went to the Congo to investigate. Conducting interviews with the Congolese themselves, he reported back to the British government on the conditions there in the early twentieth century.

The town of N * consists approximately of seventy-one K * houses and seventy-three occupied by L *. These latter seemed industrious, simple folk, many weaving palm fibre into mats or native cloth; others had smithies, working brass wire into bracelets, chains and anklets; some iron workers making knives. Sitting down in one of these blacksmith's sheds, the five men at work ceased and came over to talk to us. I counted ten women, six grown-up men and eight lads and women in this shed of L *. I then asked them to tell me why they had left their homes. Three of the men sat down in front of me, and told a tale which I cannot think can be true, but it seemed to come straight from their hearts. I repeatedly asked certain parts to be gone over again while I wrote in my note-book. The fact of my writing down and asking for names, etc., seemed to impress them, and they spoke with what certainly impressed me as being great sincerity.

I asked, first, why they had left their homes, and had come to live in a strange, far-off country among the K * where they owned nothing, and were little better than servitors. All, when this question was put, women as well, shouted out: "On account of the rubber tax levied by the Government posts" . . .

I asked, then, how this tax was imposed. One of them, who had been hammering out an iron collar on my arrival, spoke first. He said:—

"I am N. N. These two beside me are O. O. and P. P. all of us Y **. From our country each village had to take twenty loads of rubber. These loads were big; they were as big as this. . . ." (Producing an empty basket which came nearly up to the handle of my walking stick)."That was the first size. We had to fill that up, but as rubber got scarcer the white man reduced the amount. We had to take these loads in four times a month."

Q.: "How much pay do you get for this?"

A. (entire audience): "We got no pay. We got nothing."

And then N. N., whom I asked again, said:—

"Our village got cloth and a little salt but not the people who did the work. Our Chiefs ate up the cloth; the workers got nothing. The pay was a fathom of cloth and a little salt for every basket full, but it was given to the Chief, never to the men. It used to take ten days to get the twenty baskets of rubber—we were always in the forest and then when we were late we were killed. We had to go further and further into the forest to find the rubber vines, to go without food, and our women had to give up cultivating the fields and gardens. Then we starved. Wild beasts—the leopards—killed some of us when we were working away in the forest, and others got lost or died from exposure and starvation and we begged the white men to leave us alone, saying we could get no more rubber, but the white men and

William H. Worger, Nancy Clark, and Edward Alpers, *Africa and the West: A Documentary History*, 2d ed., vol. 2, *From Colonialism to Independence, 1875 to the Present* (New York: Oxford University Press, 2010), 14, 16–18.

their soldiers said: 'Go! You are only beasts your-selves, you are only nyama (meat).' We tried, always going further into the forest, and when we failed and our rubber was short, the soldiers came to our towns and killed us. Many were shot, some had their ears cut off; others were tied up with ropes round their necks and bodies and taken away. The white men sometimes at the posts did not know of the bad things the soldiers did to us, but it was the white men who sent the soldiers to punish us for not bring-ing in enough rubber."

Here P. P. took up the story from N. N:—

"We said to the white man: 'We are not enough people now to do what you want of us. Our country has not many people in it and we are dying fast. We are killed by the work you make us do, by the stoppage of our plantations, and the breaking up of our homes.' The white man looked at us and said: 'There are lots of people in Mputu' (Europe, the white man's country). 'If there are lots of people in the white man's country there must be many people in the black man's country.' The white man who said this was the chief white man at F. F.*, his name was A. B., he was a very bad man. Other white men of Bula Matadi who had been bad and wicked were B. C., C. D., and D. E. These had killed us often, and killed us by their own hands as well as by their sol-diers. Some men were good.". . .

"These ones told them to stay in their homes, and did not hunt and chase them as the others had done, but after what they had suffered they did not trust more anyone's word and they had fled from their country and were now going to stay here, far from their homes, in this country where there was no rubber."

Q.: "How long is it since you left your homes, since the big trouble you speak of?"

A.: "It lasted three full seasons, and it is now four seasons since we fled and came into the K * country."

Q.: "How many days is it from N * to your own country?"

A.: "Six days of quick marching. We fled because we could not endure the things done to us. Our Chiefs were hanged and we were killed and starved and worked beyond endurance to get rubber."

Q.: "How do you know it was the white men them-selves who ordered these cruel things to be done to you? These things must have been done without the white men's knowledge by the black soldiers."

A. (P. P.): "The white men told their soldiers: 'You kill only women; you cannot kill men.

You must prove that you kill men.' So then the soldiers when they killed us" (here he stopped and hesitated, and then pointing to the private parts of my bulldog—it was lying asleep at my feet) he said: "then they cut off those things and took them to the white men, who said: 'It is true, you have killed men.'"

Q.: "You mean to tell me that any white man or-dered your bodies to be mutilated like that and those parts of you carried to him?"

P. P., O. O., and all (shouting): "Yes! many white man. D. E. did it."

Q.: "You say this is true? Were many of you so treated after being shot?"

All (shouting out): "Nkoto! Nkoto!" (Very many! Very many!)

There was no doubt. Their vehemence, their flashing eyes, their excitement was not simulated. Doubtless they exaggerated the numbers, but they were clearly telling me what they knew and loathed.

Examining the Evidence

1. What are the working conditions described by the Congolese?
2. What specific grievances do the Congolese have about their treatment?
3. What is the attitude of the interviewer toward his Congolese informants?
4. Do you believe this report? Why or why not?

24.5 AMAR SINGH, *DIARY* (1898–1901)

Amar Singh (1879–1942) served in the British army, as did many hundreds of thousands of Indians. In fact, the British had the largest standing army in the world at the end of the nineteenth century because of loyal Indian soldiers like Singh and men from other colonized countries. Singh and his contemporaries benefited from the steady military jobs, but despite British dependence on Indian and African fighting men, all was not well with the relationship. In this excerpt, Singh describes the treatment of Indian soldiers by the British even as the Asians were serving to put down other Asians—the Boxers—on behalf of the Europeans.

. . . The Indians are looked upon as inferiors in the scale of humanity. The British are better treated, supplied, fed, clothed, and paid than the Indians. Even they are better armed though they have now found the mistake and are arming them on the same principle. No Indian can rise above the rank of a rissaldar or subadar major, and however young or junior a British officer may be he always looks down upon the other as an ignorant fellow, even though he may be much [more] experienced and possessed of [a] better head. . . .

As an example I will write on my own regiment, with which I am well acquainted and which is on a better footing than any other composed of Indians. The lieutenants, Alexander and Gaussen, always commanded over our captains. Captain Hughes always considered himself much more senior to Jasjee and even went so far as to take away his sword without any trial. Hughes is merely a captain while Jasjee is a major. The difference lies [in] that the one is British while the other is an Indian. [The princely states and the British officers in the Indian Army give different interpretations to the same ranks. Jamadar, rissaldar, rissaldar major and subedar major, the titles carried by the Jodhpur officers, are read in the princely state forces as equivalent to lieutenant, captain, and major; the British officers of the Indian Army consider them titles of noncommissioned officers, such as sergeants.]

The taking away of Jasjee's sword is a great blow to our pride. There was clearly written in the orders that the special service officers [Hughes, Turner] had no other business than to see that the orders of the general officer commanding [Sir Pratap] are understood and to give counsel and not to interfere in any way at all. The charge against Jasjee being that he was drinking on the line of march. He had no doubt drunk a little, which every other British officer does. He was quite sane, and yet Capt. Hughes took away his sword. Just fancy a junior punishing a senior. Nowhere, either in the British or foreign armies, a junior can punish a senior. Then what business Hughes had? If Jasjee is not to be considered a major, why does the government allow or empower the states to confer these ranks in the Imperial Service Forces? Either there ought to be no captains and majors in the imperial service or, if they ought, then they must be treated on the same footing which is rather difficult. . . .

Had it not been for Sarkar this thing would have gone too high. Major Turner never objected to it. On the other hand he sent a bad report of Jasjee to Jodhpore. I do not know what would have happened to the regiment if Sarkar had not been with it. Hurjee would never be considered on the same footing as a British colonel nor I as a lieutenant. Whatever may happen, I for myself will never serve in the army except in imperial service [meaning the princely state forces, which are commanded by Indian officers]. Even if any one offered me a direct rissaldar majorship in the British Indian Army I would straight away reject. I would not like to be treated like a coolie.

Examining the Evidence

1. What is Singh's opinion of the British officers and soldiers?
2. What are his ideas of military order?
3. Describe Singh's relationship as a member of the military to the British nation.

Amar Singh, *Reversing the Gaze: Amar Singh's Diary; A Colonial Subject's Narrative of Imperial India*, ed. Susanne Rudolph et al. (New York: Oxford University Press, 2000), 187–188.

MAKING CONNECTIONS

1. What common concerns about the nation-state as a political form or as the base for imperial expansion are evident in these documents?

2. Based on the documents in this chapter, what do Abraham Lincoln, Rokeya Sakhawat Hossain, and Amar Singh see as their role in or relationship to the nation-state?

3. How might you reconcile the positive aspects of the nation-state with the harm seen to be caused by its representatives abroad? How might Kaiser William II respond to criticisms of imperialist policies expressed in the documents?

4. What emotions, if any, do the commentators show in their judgments of imperialists?

CHAPTER 25

Wars, Revolutions, and the Birth of Mass Society, 1900–1929

The years from the Boxer Rebellion at the turn of the twentieth century to the Great Depression in 1929 saw immense turmoil, warfare, and revolutionary violence. Tensions erupted under the burden of imperial competition for wealth and territory. Ordinary people were impoverished, as the mighty empires did everything in their power to win the battle against their imperial rivals. Rebellions and civil wars erupted around the world in Mexico, China, the Russian Empire, and across Europe—before, during, and following World War I. While World War I itself took a massive toll in death, disability, and disease, it also destabilized much of the world both politically and economically. At the same time, leaders and theorists developed differing plans for a better society, including programs to implement communism and a League of Nations. The world after the "Great War" was different from that preceding it, as dynasties collapsed and mass society came into being.

25.1   REVOLUTIONARY PLANS FOR THE MEXICAN FUTURE

The Plan de Ayala (1910)

As Boxers, Turks, Vietnamese, and others challenged the imperial status quo, the Mexican Revolution broke out in 1910 to oppose the authoritarian ruler Porfirio Diaz, who had arranged for the arrest of his middle-class political opponent Francisco Madero. Madero escaped to San Antonio, Texas, where he called for an uprising of the people against Diaz's government in his Plan de San Luis Potosí. Madero's plan, however, made little mention of any reforms that would benefit the ordinary people of Mexico. It did nothing to ensure their livelihoods—particularly against the large plantation owners and foreign businessmen who had a large share in running the country and who had bought up property confiscated from the poor. Madero's takeover of the Mexican government in 1911 seemed to many an outrage because of his lack of concern for society as a whole. Emilio Zapata, the popular leader of peasants, traders, and artisans, and his supporters (called *Zapatistas*) issued this counterproposal for reform and called for the ouster of Madero.

Liberating Plan of the sons of the State of Morelos, affiliated with the Insurgent Army which defends the fulfillment of the Plan of San Luis, with the reforms which it has believed proper to add in benefit of the Mexican Fatherland.

We who undersign, constituted in a revolutionary junta to sustain and carry out the promises which the revolution of November 20, 1910 just past, made to the country, declare solemnly before the face of the civilized world which judges us and before the nation to which we belong and which we call [*sic, llamamos*, misprint for *amamos*, love], propositions which we have formulated to end the tyranny which oppresses us and redeem the fatherland from the dictatorships which are imposed on us, which [propositions] are determined in the following plan:

1. Taking into consideration that the Mexican people led by Don Francisco I. Madero went to shed their blood to reconquer liberties and recover their rights which had been trampled on, and not for a man to take possession of power, violating the sacred principles which he took an oath to defend under the slogan "Effective Suffrage and No Reelection," outraging thus the faith, the cause, the justice, and the liberties of the people: taking into consideration that that man to whom we refer is Don Francisco I. Madero, the same who initiated the above-cited revolution, who imposed his will and influence as a governing norm on the Provisional Government of the ex-President of the Republic Attorney Francisco L. de Barra [*sic*], causing with this deed repeated sheddings of blood and multiplicate misfortunes for the fatherland in a manner deceitful and ridiculous, having no intentions other than satisfying his personal ambitions, his boundless instincts as a tyrant, and his profound disrespect for the fulfillment of the preexisting laws emanating from the immortal code of '57, written with the revolutionary blood of Ayutla.

Taking into account that the so-called Chief of the Liberating Revolution of Mexico, Don Francisco I. Madero, through lack of integrity and the highest weakness, did not carry to a happy end the revolution which gloriously he initiated with the help of God and the people, since he left standing most of the governing powers and corrupted elements of oppression of the dictatorial government of Porfirio Díaz, which are not nor can in any way be the representation of National Sovereignty, and which, for being most bitter adversaries of ours and of the principles which even now we defend, are provoking the discomfort of the country and opening new wounds in the bosom of the fatherland, to give it its own blood to drink; taking also into account that the aforementioned Sr. Francisco I. Madero, present President of the Republic, tries to avoid the fulfillment of the promises which he made to the Nation in the Plan of San Luis Potosí, being [*sic, siendo,* misprint for *ciñendo,* restricting] the above-cited promises to the agreements of Ciudad Juárez, by means of false promises and numerous intrigues against the Nation nullifying, pursuing, jailing, or killing revolutionary elements who helped him to occupy the high post of President of the Republic;

Taking into consideration that the so-often-repeated Francisco I. Madero has tried with the brute force of bayonets to shut up and to drown in blood the pueblos who ask, solicit, or demand from him the fulfillment of the promises of the revolution, calling them bandits and rebels, condemning them to a war of extermination without conceding or granting a single one of the guarantees which reason, justice, and the law prescribe; taking equally into consideration that the President of the Republic Francisco I. Madero has made of Effective Suffrage a bloody trick on the people, already against the will of the same people imposing Attorney José M. Pino Suárez in the Vice-Presidency of the Republic, or [imposing as] Governors of the States [men] designated by him, like the so-called General Ambrosio Figueroa, scourge and tyrant of the people of Morelos, or entering into scandalous cooperation with the científico party, feudal landlords, and oppressive bosses, enemies of the revolution proclaimed by him, so as to forge new chains and follow the pattern of a new dictatorship more shameful and more terrible than that of Porfirio Díaz, for it has been clear and patent that he has outraged the sovereignty of the States, trampling on the laws without any respect for lives or interests, as has happened in the State of Morelos, and others, leading them to the most horrendous anarchy which contemporary history registers.

For these considerations we declare the aforementioned Francisco I. Madero inept at realizing the promises of the revolution of which he was the author, because he has betrayed the principles with which he tricked the will of the people and was able to get into power: incapable of governing, because he has no respect for the law and justice of the pueblos, and a traitor to the fatherland, because he is humiliating in blood and fire Mexicans who want liberties, so as to please the científicos, landlords, and bosses who enslave us, and from today on we begin to continue the revolution begun by him, until we achieve the overthrow of the dictatorial powers which exist.

2. Recognition is withdrawn from Sr. Francisco I. Madero as Chief of the Revolution and as President of the Republic, for the reasons which before were expressed, it being attempted to overthrow this official.

3. Recognized as Chief of the Liberating Revolution is the illustrious General Pascual Orozco, the second of the Leader Don Francisco I. Madero, and in case he does not accept this delicate post, recognition as Chief of the Revolution will go to General Don Emiliano Zapata.

4. The Revolutionary Junta of the State of Morelos manifests to the Nation under formal oath: that it makes its own the plan of San Luis Potosí, with the additions which are expressed below in benefit of the oppressed pueblos, and it will make itself the defender of the principles it defends until victory or death.

5. The Revolutionary Junta of the State of Morelos will admit no transactions or compromises until it achieves the overthrow of the dictatorial elements of Porfirio Díaz and Francisco I. Madero, for the nation is tired of false men and traitors who make promises like liberators and who on arriving in power forget them and constitute themselves as tyrants.

6. As an additional part of the plan we invoke, we give notice: that [regarding] the fields, timber, and water which the landlords, científicos, or bosses have usurped, the pueblos or citizens who have the titles corresponding to those properties will immediately enter into possession of that real estate of which they have been despoiled by the bad faith of our oppressors, maintaining at any cost with arms in hand the mentioned possession; and the usurpers who consider themselves with a right to them [those properties] will

deduce it before the special tribunals which will be established on the triumph of the revolution.

7. In virtue of the fact that the immense majority of Mexican pueblos and citizens are owners of no more than the land they walk on, suffering the horrors of poverty without being able to improve their social condition in any way or to dedicate themselves to Industry or Agriculture, because lands, timber, and water are monopolized in a few hands, for this cause there will be expropriated the third part of those monopolies from the powerful proprietors of them, with prior indemnization, in order that the pueblos and citizens of Mexico may obtain ejidos [cooperative farming rights], colonies, and foundations for pueblos, or fields for sowing or laboring, and the Mexicans' lack of prosperity and well-being may improve in all and for all.

8. [Regarding] The landlords, científicos, or bosses who oppose the present plan directly or indirectly, their goods will be nationalized and the two third parts which [otherwise would] belong to them will go for indemnizations of war, pensions for widows and orphans of the victims who succumb in the struggle for the present plan.

9. In order to execute the procedures regarding the properties aforementioned, the laws of disamortization and nationalization will be applied as they fit, for serving us as norm and example can be those laws put in force by the immortal Juárez [former president of Mexico] on ecclesiastical properties, which punished the despots and conservatives who in every time have tried to impose on us the ignominious yoke of oppression and backwardness. . . .

14. If President Madero and other dictatorial elements of the present and former regime want to avoid the immense misfortunes which afflict the fatherland, and [if they] possess true sentiments of love for it, let them make immediate renunciation of the posts they occupy and with that they will with something staunch the grave wounds which they have opened in the bosom of the fatherland, since, if they do not do so, on their heads will fall the blood and the anathema of our brothers.

15. Mexicans: consider that the cunning and bad faith of one man is shedding blood in a scandalous manner, because he is incapable of governing; consider that his system of government is choking the fatherland and trampling with the brute force of bayonets on our institutions; and thus, as we raised up our weapons to elevate him to power, we again raise them up against him for defaulting on his promises to the Mexican people and for having betrayed the revolution initiated by him, we are not personalists, we are partisans of principles and not of men!

Examining the Evidence

1. What characteristics of the Zapatistas' plan give it political importance?
2. What are the Zapatistas' main complaints as announced in this plan?
3. What are the main complaints connected to the livelihoods of Mexicans?
4. What provisions in this plan would make the ruling classes determined to defeat the Zapatistas?

25.2 AN AUSTRALIAN SOLDIER FIGHTS FOR BRITAIN

E. P. F. Lynch, *War Memoir* (1916–1919)

Australian Edward Lynch (1898–1980) was only eighteen years old when he volunteered to go to Europe to fight for the Allies in World War I. His memoir opens with a lighthearted departure from his hometown and quickly becomes a grim account of the war on the western front. Lynch was one among thousands of men and women who wrote about the war, seeing in his officers "cooks

E. P. F. Lynch, *Somme Mud: The War Experiences of an Infantryman in France, 1916–1919*, ed. Will Davies (London: Doubleday, 2006), 178–180, 184–190.

inspecting the geese." Like his compatriots, some of whom saw the war differently, he set down true-to-life descriptions in several dozen school notebooks immediately after the war ended. Some believe that he did so to purge himself of the horrors of the experience. This excerpt describes the battle at Passchendaele (Belgium) in 1916. Almost a century passed before this memoir was brought to light and published.

We come through Ypres, once a fine city now smashed and burned to a crumbling shell. We see all that is left of the Ypres Cathedral and the famous Cloth Hall, a few shell-riddled broken walls precariously balanced around a heap of rubble that was once the architectural glory of Ypres. On we march through the town, hushed by the ghost of a fallen city's calamity. Out through the Menin Gate—just two great shattered walls converging on a torn and broken road that we know is the Menin Road. . . .

The whole road is bordered by dead mules and mud-splattered horses, smashed wagons and limbers [wagons drawing artillery] and freshly killed men who have been tossed off the track to leave the corduroy [road] open for the never-ending stream of traffic.

For six days and six nights we work under shellfire most of the time, in and around the reserve lines doing repair work on the road leading to Zonnebeke. Our casualties never cease to mount up, but the work goes on for the lines of communication must ever be kept open. . . .

An officer is here now. "We're in for it, men. The 2nd Division has made a couple of attacks and have been badly cut up. We're to take over the front line tonight."

We're to be thrown into the front line just when we least expected it!

"Where is the front line?"

"No one knows just where the line is, but they've been fighting on Broodseinde Ridge all day. That's all we can gather."

We move off. All night we force march along narrow corduroy roads getting five minutes' spell in each hour. The place is a stream of traffic. Wounded are coming back in hundreds—pale, quiet, drawn-looking men from the big attacks. . . .

Still we move on, passing our dead and certain we'll attack today. Machine-gun bullets are flying around. Now and again we see one of our men going back wounded. Several stretcher cases come by as we move on toward the flares.

Now we are passing dead Fritz [Germans] in dozens so know we are on territory recently taken from the enemy. Again we halt. The guides from the line have met us, so at last the uncertainty is lifting. [Several days go by in the mud with on and off shelling, amid which the narrator is sent on patrol and then as a messenger through the fire and back. Then the battle begins.]

Hundreds of men are quietly lying in the mud just behind our outpost line and waiting to launch themselves through to the attack. There's a keyed-up feeling amongst us all. Men waiting for the blow to fall, expecting it to fall on them. . . .

These men are the second wave of the attack and are to take the second objective wherever that is. . . .

Whish! Whish! Whist! Whizz! Whizz! and *Crash! Crash! Crash! Bang! Bang! Crash! Crash! Crash!* Our barrage is just clearing our heads and bursting on the enemy wire and on his forward positions and back areas. Out in front of us, shells are landing in a jumping, flashing glowing roar of vivid lightning. The very night is afire.

Enemy flares are going up everywhere. Fritz machine-guns are barking savagely. *Whonk! Bang!* And the enemy barrage is down upon us as we crouch in our little post knowing that one direct hit will fix us all. We glance behind—the enemy shells are everywhere. Blinding flashes of bursting fireballs.

Slush, slush, slush, the men of the first wave are jumping our post and steadily and slowly advancing toward where our shells are bursting. The enemy shells are falling everywhere, but their machine-guns are quiet. The advancing men are well ahead and cannot now be seen.

Suddenly our barrage lifts and we can now hear the slushing patter of running men as the first wave charge for the enemy. Flares go up in dozens, the machine-guns are fairly spluttering again out in front, shouts float back from ahead where we can see the first streaks of daylight creeping over the eternal mud.

Enemy shells are crashing everywhere and through the flashing flames of their roaring bursts, we can see the second wave of the advance coming through at the run. We give a yell of encouragement as they jump our trench and they are gone on toward the more distant point where our shells are now tearing into Fritz.

The first batches of the wounded are coming back. Walking, staggering, lurching, limping back. Men with blood-stained bandages and men with none. Men carrying smashed arms, others painfully limping on shattered legs. Laughing men and shivering men. Men with calm, quiet faces and fellows with jumping blood-shot eyes above strangely lined pain-racked and tortured faces. Men walking back as if there's nothing left to harm them and others who flinch and jump and throw themselves into shell holes at every shell burst and at each whistle of a passing bullet. Wounded men who have done their job.

Man after man slides down into our little post and we get their field dressings out, bandage their bleeding wounds and they pass on to the rear, joking or suffering silently. Our teeth and lips are brown with iodine stains from biting through the tops of iodine bottles. . . .

A wounded man is wandering about out in front. A man goes out and leads him in and we bandage his shoulder where a piece of shell hit him. He says he's not going out just yet and sits down on the floor and tells us about how the first objective was taken.

"Saw a terrible thing up there. A few of us rushed a Fritz post, but as we were right on top of it, a Fritz fired a flare gun at us and the flare went into a man's stomach. God! He screamed and screamed! He was running round and round trying to tear that burning flare out of his inside and all the time we could smell his flesh burning, just like grilled meat. He gave an awful scream and fell dead, but that horrible smell of burning flesh kept on. I can smell it still." And he shudders and shakes at the memory of it all.

"Did you get the Fritz?"

"Too true we got him. Seven or eight bayonets got him, the flamin' mongrel!" And the man gets up and goes away, vomiting. . . .

Four Fritz are coming back. They are bloodstained and plastered in mud and have the terrified appearance of men at the end of their tether. One of them sees our trench and runs straight into it, whining as he comes.

Longun jumps in front of him

"Get to blazes out of this! Keep going!" but the Fritz seems to misunderstand Longun and throws his arms about and pokes his face up as he tries to kiss him. Longun's great fists snap out; *crack, crack* on the Fritz's face and *thud!* He is over on his back then up and running after the other three, whimpering like a frightened child. . . .

It is night now—we're to be relieved before morning and glad of it. We've been in here for three days and although we haven't done any hop-overs, we have had nearly two hundred casualties. Fritz has been shelling our posts and working parties heavily, but our artillery has been pelting everything they have at Fritz and they must be as badly shaken as we are.

The night is very dark. Enemy fire is intense and our casualties are mounting up. I have had a hard, grueling day running messages mostly under snipers' rifles, but they haven't got me yet. The runners are now working in pairs to ensure the messages get through. I am running with a man we call "Turk" who's a stranger to me. We've been together all day and now are in the first objective taken in the big attack and have been told to wait for another message to go back.

Suddenly an enemy barrage is down around us. *Crash! Crash!* as the shells explode, sending spouts of mud skywards at each blast. . . .

Turk and I make to climb out.

"No, don't go through that. Go along and follow the new sap back, it's safer." And we run along the trench till we reach the sap and begin rushing down it. I have the message in my pocket and Turk is on my heels. We're a quarter of the way down the sap and all hell breaks loose. Enemy shells are crashing and killing and wounding men every few yards. None can escape as the enemy barrage has caught the sap absolutely full of men from a big working and carrying parry.

"Stretcher-bearers! Pass the word for bearers! Men hit!"

"Bearers wanted!" The urgent calls are being shouted from end to end of the sap.

Turk and I are shoving and fighting our way over dead and wounded men. We can't wait to help anyone. Our message must go through.

We're now halfway down the sap. Here it is full of men carrying duckboards, "A" frames and sheets of corrugated iron. *Bang! Bang!* And the shells are crashing in an unending stream of flames and whistling roars all about us, as we forge ahead ducking and diving and shoving our way along. The scene is terrible. Men are lying in agony everywhere. Some reach out to us to be helped along. We brush them off and struggle and climb over "A" frames and up-ended duckboards for a few more yards.

Crash! And just behind us another shell lands fair into the trench. We know what now lies where it burst, and shove along, but *Crash! Crash!* and two more land a few yards ahead. The flame lights up everything. A rush of air and another phosphorus-laden blast is in our faces. It's only a minute and we must catch a shell. We can't last. We're barely making a metre a minute so dense is the jam of men and material along the trench.

Bang! Crash! Bang! We're fair in the centre of a terrific shelling. I turn to Turk and roar, "Give it a go over the top?"

He nods and in a far-away, hopeless, despairing voice his shout comes back, "Can't be any worse." . . .

Above the shouts of Turk, above the roar of the shell bursts, my terrified ears catch the wailing shriek of a shell coming fair for me! I screw and twist in my stride, trying to fling myself down. *Whizz! Crash!* The ground under my feet is heaving upwards. I'm surrounded by a shower of mud and blue, vicious flame. My feet are rising, rising, my head is going down, down, I'm falling, falling, falling through a

solid cloud of roaring sound. *Smack!* And I am on my back, winded. My head and back have had an awful thud. I'm dazed.

Clatter, clatter, clatter, someone is coming to me, someone running on wood. A man's boot lands hard on my chest.

"Wait! Wait!" comes from above the boot. *Clatter, clat, clat,* the sounds are going from me now.

"Wait! Wait!" drifts back to me from away ahead. Pain, gnawing pain, shoots through me. My hip, my knee, my leg, my foot. I come to my senses and, getting my breath back, realize that Turk has stamped on me, over me, and gone tearing on ahead in a frenzy of fear. I look about and am lying on my back in a deep trench, lying on hard wooden duckboards. I realize that a shell has burst under me and tossed me into the trench. I know my leg is smashed, it's numb, and now a shooting mass of jumping pain. I must examine it, must bandage it, must stop the bleeding, but somehow all I can do is to roll and roll on that leg, pressing it harder and harder into the boards.

Hands are pressing my shoulders, hands are forcing me to my back.

"Steady, steady, where're you hit?" And two or three men are holding me.

Examining the Evidence

1. What images of war does Lynch convey?
2. According to Lynch's account, what emotions and thoughts do the soldiers feel?
3. What is the role of technology in this scene from World War I?
4. What are Lynch's feelings about enemy soldiers?
5. Does this description from Lynch's diary convey the sense of World War I being a "great war"? Why or why not?

25.3 PROCLAIMING THE SOVIET ALTERNATIVE TO WAR-WEARY RUSSIANS

V. I. Lenin, *April Theses* (1917)

In the spring of 1917, Bolshevik leader V. I. Lenin (1870–1924) returned to revolutionary Russia after years in exile as a propagandist and journalist. A new, revolutionary administration called the Provisional Government had just been installed after the abdication of Tsar Nicholas II. To develop his political ideas, Lenin had read widely, including not only Karl Marx but also Nicolo Machiavelli, Charles Darwin, Aristotle, and Harriet Beecher Stowe. Now he had an opportunity to direct his programs toward the masses at home. Virtually his first act on arriving from his exile in the West was to issue his "April Theses," a program for immediate action to determine Russia's future. Lenin's followers were stunned at his extreme position, and many believed that the April Theses sounded a call for civil war. "Peace, land, and bread" was a platform, however, that appealed to those who had been serving as cannon fodder in World War I and suffering from shortages. "All power to the Soviets"— another of his programs—sounded the call for the masses finally to take power.

(1) In our attitude towards the war, which under the now government of Lvov and Co. unquestionably remains on Russia's part a predatory imperialist war owing to the capitalist nature of that government, not the slightest concession to "revolutionary defencism" is permissible.

The class-conscious proletariat can give its consent to a revolutionary war, which would really justify revolutionary defencism, only on condition: (a) that the power pass to the proletariat and the poorest sections of the peasants aligned with the proletariat; (b) that all annexations be renounced in deed and not in word; (c) that a complete break with all capitalist interests be effected in actual fact.

In view of the undoubted honesty of those broad sections of the mass believers in revolutionary defencism who accept the war only as a necessity, and not as a means of conquest, in view of the fact that they are being deceived by the bourgeoisie, it is necessary with particular thoroughness, persistence and patience to explain their error to them, to explain the inseparable connection existing between capital and the imperialist war, and to prove that without overthrowing capital *it is impossible* to end the war by a truly democratic peace, a peace not imposed by violence.

The most widespread campaign for this view must be organized in the army at the front.

Fraternization.

(2) The specific feature of the present situation in Russia is that the country is *passing* from the first stage of the revolution—which, owing to the insufficient class-consciousness and organization of the proletariat, placed power in the hands of the bourgeoisie—to its *second* stage, which must place power in the hands of the proletariat and the poorest sections of the peasants.

This transition is characterized, on the one hand, by a maximum of legally recognized rights (Russia is *now* the freest of all the belligerent countries in the world); on the other, by the absence of violence toward the masses, and, finally, by their unreasoning trust in the government of capitalists, those worst enemies of peace and socialism.

This peculiar situation demands of us an ability to adapt ourselves to the *special* conditions of Party work among unprecedentedly large masses of proletarians who have just awakened to political life.

(3) No support for the Provisional Government; the utter falsity of all its promises should be made clear, particularly of those relating to the renunciation of annexations. Exposure in place of the

V. I. Lenin, *Revolution at the Gates: A Selection of Writings from February to October 1917*, ed. Slavoj Žižek (New York: Verso, 2002), 56–60.

impermissible, illusion-breeding "demand" that *this* government, a government of capitalists, should cease to be an imperialist government.

(4) Recognition of the fact that in most of the Soviets of Workers' Deputies our Party is in a minority, so far a small minority, as against *a bloc of all* the petty-bourgeois opportunist elements, from the Popular Socialists and the Socialist-Revolutionaries down to the Organizing Committee (Chkheidze, Tsereteli, etc.), Steklov, etc., etc., who have yielded to the influence of the bourgeoisie and spread that influence among the proletariat.

The masses must be made to see that the Soviets of Workers' Deputies are the *only possible* form of revolutionary government, and that therefore our task is, as long as *this* government yields to the influence of the bourgeoisie, to present a patient, systematic, and persistent *explanation* of the errors of their tactics, an explanation especially adapted to the practical needs of the masses.

As long as we are in the minority we carry on the work of criticizing and exposing errors, and at the same time we preach the necessity of transferring the entire state power to the Soviets of Workers' Deputies, so that the people may overcome their mistakes by experience.

(5) Not a parliamentary republic—to return to a parliamentary republic from the Soviets of Workers' Deputies would be a retrograde step—but a republic of Soviets of Workers', Agricultural Laborers' and Peasants' Deputies throughout the country, from top to bottom.

Abolition of the police, the army and the bureaucracy.

The salaries of all officials, all of whom are elective and displaceable at any time, not to exceed the average wage of a competent worker.

(6) The weight of emphasis in the agrarian program to be shifted to the Soviets of Agricultural Labourers' Deputies.

Confiscation of all landed estates.

Nationalization of *all* lands in the country, the land to be disposed of by the local Soviets of Agricultural Laborers' and Peasants' Deputies. The organization of separate Soviets of Deputies of Poor Peasants. The setting up of a model farm on each of the large estates (ranging in size from 100 to 300 dessiatines, according to local and other conditions, and to the decisions of the local bodies) under the control of the Soviets of Agricultural Laborers' Deputies and for the public account.

(7) The immediate amalgamation of all banks in the country into a single national bank, and the institution of control over it by the Soviet of Workers' Deputies.

(8) It is not our *immediate* task to "introduce" socialism, but only to bring social production and the distribution of products at once under the control of the Soviets of Workers' Deputies.

(9) Party tasks:
    (a) Immediate convocation of a Party congress;
    (b) Alteration of the Party Program, mainly:
        (i) On the question of imperialism and the imperialist war;
        (ii) On our attitude toward the state and our demand for a "commune state";
        (iii) Amendment of our out-of-date minimum program.
    (c) Change of the Party's name.
(10) A new International.

Examining the Evidence

1. What elements of Marxism do you find in Lenin's program?
2. What is Lenin's attitude toward the war and Russia's involvement in it?
3. What differences does Lenin have with the Provisional Government?
4. What proposals and plans would appeal most to ordinary Russian people during World War I?

CONTRASTING VIEWS

THE POSTWAR MIDDLE EAST

25.4   *SYKES–PICOT AGREEMENT (1916)*

With the consent of Russia, the nations of France and Britain secretly agreed to divide the Middle Eastern territories of the Ottoman Empire after what the two powers believed would be the Ottoman defeat in the war. The agreement went against earlier promises of independence and rights to established Arab leaders, and the Bolsheviks were quick to make the agreement public after the November Revolution of 1917. Negotiated by French diplomat François-Georges Picot and British envoy Sir Mark Sykes, the agreement was visualized in this map.

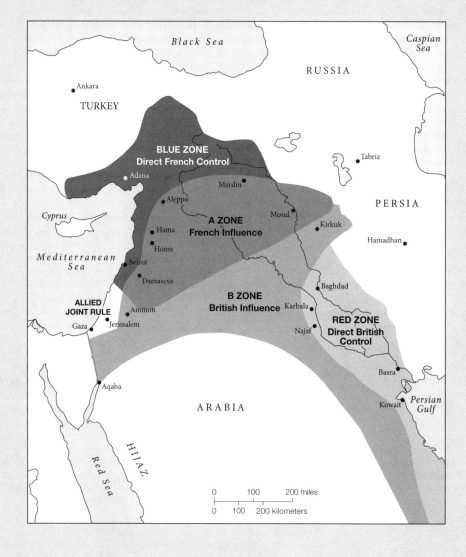

25.5 THE BALFOUR DECLARATION (1917)

Arthur Balfour (1848–1930) was the British foreign secretary during World War I. The goal of the Allies during the war was to build support from as many groups as possible, including the Jews, but statesmen and influential citizens were full of plans for the future of the Middle East, where lands ruled by the Ottoman Empire were at stake and where oil was an increasingly important commodity. The Allied powers promised independence to these Ottoman citizens in return for fighting against the empire, while it also promised Jewish members of the European Zionist movement that their people could have settlements in Palestine. The Balfour Declaration was addressed to Lord Rothschild, head of the British Zionist Organization and himself an influential financier and political personality.

I have much pleasure in conveying to you, on behalf of his Majesty's Government, the following declaration of sympathy with Jewish Zionist aspirations which has been submitted to and approved by the Cabinet:—

His Majesty's Government view with favor the establishment in Palestine of a national home for the Jewish people, and will use their best endeavors to facilitate the achievement of this object, it being clearly understood that nothing shall be done which may prejudice the civil and religious rights of existing non-Jewish communities in Palestine, or the rights and political status enjoyed by Jews in any other country.

I should be grateful if you would bring this declaration to the knowledge of the Zionist Federation.

J. C. Hurewitz, *Diplomacy in the Near and Middle East, a Documentary Record: 1914–1956*, vol. 2 (New York: D. Van Nostrand, 1956), 26.

25.6 RESOLUTION OF THE GENERAL SYRIAN CONGRESS AT DAMASCUS (1919)

The Allies had promised Arab leaders across the Middle East that in return for fighting against the Ottoman Empire, they would be granted independence following the war. Some of those leaders, notably King Faisal, who had spearheaded Arab resistance to the Ottomans for the Allies, attended the postwar peace conference in Paris in 1919 to ensure the fulfillment of those promises by the Allied victors of World War I. It became apparent, however, that the Allies had no intention of honoring their word to those who had contributed to victory—not to Italy, to Africans, or to Arabs in the Middle East. This document is the official resolution of an Arab congress that met in the summer of 1919 to address the situation.

We the undersigned members of the General Syrian Congress, meeting in Damascus on Wednesday, July 2nd, 1919, made up of representatives from the three Zones, viz., the Southern, Eastern, and Western, provided with credentials and authorizations by the inhabitants of our various districts, Muslims, Christians, and Jews, have agreed upon the following statement of the desires of the people of the country who have elected us to present them to the American Section of the International Commission; the fifth article was passed by a very large majority; all the other articles were accepted unanimously.

1. We ask absolutely complete political independence for Syria within these boundaries. The Taurus System on the North; Rafah and a line running from Al Jauf to the south of the Syrian and the Hejazian line to Akaba on the south; the Euphrates and Khabur Rivers and a line extending east of Abu Kamal to the east of Al Jauf on the east; and the Mediterranean on the west.

J. C. Hurewitz, *Diplomacy in the Near and Middle East, a Documentary Record: 1914–1956*, vol. 2 (New York: D. Van Nostrand, 1956), 63–64.

(continued)

CONTRASTING VIEWS *(continued)*

2. We ask that the Government of this Syrian country should be a democratic civil constitutional Monarchy on broad decentralization principles, safeguarding the rights of minorities, and that the King be the Emir Feisal, who carried on a glorious struggle in the cause of our liberation and merited our full confidence and entire reliance.

3. Considering the fact that the Arabs inhabiting the Syrian area are not naturally less gifted than other more advanced races and that they are by no means less developed than the Bulgarians, Serbians, Greeks, and Romanians at the beginning of their independence, we protest against Article 22 of the Covenant of the League of Nations, placing us among the nations in their middle stage of development which stand in need of a mandatory power.

4. In the event of the rejection by the Peace Conference of this just protest for certain considerations that we may not understand, we, relying on the declarations of President Wilson that his object in waging war was to put an end to the ambition of conquest and colonization, can only regard the mandate mentioned in the Covenant of the League of Nations as equivalent to the rendering of economical and technical assistance that does not prejudice our complete independence. And desiring that our country should not fall a prey to colonization and believing that the American Nation is farthest from any thought of colonization and has no political ambition in our country, we will seek the technical and economical assistance from the United States of America, provided that such assistance does not exceed 20 years.

5. In the event of America not finding herself in a position to accept our desire for assistance, we will seek this assistance from Great Britain, also provided that such assistance does not infringe the complete independence and unity of our country and that the duration of such assistance does not exceed that mentioned in the previous article.

6. We do not acknowledge any right claimed by the French Government in any part whatever of our Syrian country and refuse that she should assist us or have a hand in our country under any circumstances and in any place.

7. We oppose the pretentions of the Zionists to create a Jewish commonwealth in the southern part of Syria, known as Palestine, and oppose Zionist migration to any part of our country; for we do not acknowledge their title but consider them a grave peril to our people from the national, economical, and political points of view. Our Jewish compatriots shall enjoy our common rights and assume the common responsibilities.

8. We ask that there should be no separation of the southern part of Syria, known as Palestine, nor of the littoral western zone, which includes Lebanon, from the Syrian country. We desire that the unity of the country should be guaranteed against partition under whatever circumstances.

9. We ask complete independence for emancipated Mesopotamia and that there should be no economical barriers between the two countries.

10. The fundamental principles laid down by President Wilson in condemnation of secret treaties impel us to protest most emphatically against any treaty that stipulates the partition of our Syrian country and against any private engagement aiming at the establishment of Zionism in the southern part of Syria; therefore we ask the complete annulment of these conventions and agreements.

The noble principles enunciated by President Wilson strengthen our confidence that our desires emanating from the depths of our hearts, shall be the decisive factor in determining our future; and that President Wilson and the free American people will be our supporters for the realization of our hopes, thereby proving their sincerity and noble sympathy with the aspiration of the weaker nations in general and our Arab people in particular.

We also have the fullest confidence that the Peace Conference will realize that we would not have risen against the Turks, with whom we had participated in all civil, political, and representative privileges, but for their violation of our national rights, and so will grant us our desires in full in order that our political rights may not be less after the war than they were before, since we have shed so much blood in the cause of our liberty and independence.

We request to be allowed to send a delegation to represent us at the Peace Conference to defend our rights and secure the realization of our aspirations.

25.7 | THE MANDATE SYSTEM UNDER THE COVENANT OF THE LEAGUE OF NATIONS (1919)

Promulgated in early 1918, Woodrow Wilson's Fourteen Points articulated principles of self-determination and the rights of peoples. Wilson also lobbied hard to establish a League of Nations to protect those rights and to arbitrate disputes. The Covenant or charter of the League of Nations stated a range of aims and established a range of institutions. It also laid out the mandate system, which distributed the former colonies and territories of Germany and the Ottoman Empire to nations around the world, with Britain and France receiving the lion's share. Note, however, that those colonies and territories are not called colonies but mandates. Given this settlement, many today believe that the League of Nations should more accurately be described as the League of Empires.

Article 22

To those colonies and territories which as a consequence of the late war have ceased to be under the sovereignty of the States which formerly governed them and which are inhabited by peoples not yet able to stand by themselves under the strenuous conditions of the modern world, there should be applied the principle that the well-being and development of such peoples form a sacred trust of civilization and that securities for the performance of this trust should be embodied in this Covenant.

The best method of giving practical effect to this principle is that the tutelage of such peoples should be entrusted to advanced nations who by reason of their resources, their experience or their geographical position can best undertake this responsibility, and who are willing to accept it, and that this tutelage should be exercised by them as Mandatories on behalf of the League.

The character of the mandate must differ according to the stage of the development of the people, the geographical situation of the territory, its economic conditions and other similar circumstances.

Certain communities formerly belonging to the Turkish Empire have reached a stage of development where their existence as independent nations can be provisionally recognized subject to the rendering of administrative advice and assistance by a Mandatory until such time as they are able to stand alone. The wishes of these communities must be a principal consideration in the selection of the Mandatory.

Other peoples, especially those of Central Africa, are at such a stage that the Mandatory must be responsible for the administration of the territory under conditions which will guarantee freedom of conscience and religion, subject only to the maintenance of public order and morals,

The Covenant of the League of Nations, from the *Avalon Project: Documents in Law, History and Diplomacy* (New Haven, CT: Yale Law School, Lillian Goldman Law Library), avalon.law.yale.edu/20th_century/leagcov.asp.

(continued)

the prohibition of abuses such as the slave trade, the arms traffic and the liquor traffic, and the prevention of the establishment of fortifications or military and naval bases and of military training of the natives for other than police purposes and the defense of territory, and will also secure equal opportunities for the trade and commerce of other Members of the League.

There are territories, such as South-West Africa and certain of the South Pacific Islands, which, owing to the sparseness of their population, or their small size, or their remoteness from the centers of civilization, or their geographical contiguity to the territory of the Mandatory, and other circumstances, can be best administered under the laws of the Mandatory as integral portions of its territory, subject to the safeguards above mentioned in the interests of the indigenous population.

In every case of mandate, the Mandatory shall render to the Council an annual report in reference to the territory committed to its charge.

The degree of authority, control, or administration to be exercised by the Mandatory shall, if not previously agreed upon by the Members of the League, be explicitly defined in each case by the Council.

A permanent Commission shall be constituted to receive and examine the annual reports of the Mandatories and to advise the Council on all matters relating to the observance of the mandates.

Comparing the Evidence

1. According to the documents, in what ways are the Allied positions and promises to various groups about postwar treatment contradictory?
2. What are the competing interests in the Middle East as described in these documents?
3. What arguments do the Arabs muster against the Allied powers?
4. What does the Mandate System do to resolve the competing interests?

25.8   **AN ALLY CRITIQUES ATATÜRK**

Halide Edib Adivar, "Dictatorship and Reform in Turkey" (1929)

Halide Edib Adivar (1884–1964) was a prominent political activist, novelist, and, later in her life, professor of literature at the University of Istanbul. During the difficult postwar years, as the Ottoman Empire was dismantled and occupied by the victorious Allies, Adivar became a major political figure on the side of Turkish independence. In public speeches and writing, she aided Atatürk (Mustafa Kemal) in his struggle to turn back the Allied-directed Greek invasion of Turkey and to prevent an Allied takeover of the country. However, once Atatürk succeeded and assumed virtually

dictatorial power, Adivar moved abroad as an exile, only to return in 1939 after her former ally's death. In this passage, Adivar considers Atatürk's accomplishments, the history of the "new" Turkey, and the political state of the world more generally.

[W]hat is of supreme interest is the change of a democratic state, of five years' standing, into a dictatorial one without even an altering of the form or the closing of the National Assembly. . . . Mustafa Kemal Pasha possessed the lightning power of seizing favorable circumstances at the right moment. After all, the Turkish dictatorship was not and is not unique in the world. The postwar world favors

---

Halidé Edib, *Turkey Faces West: A Turkish View of Recent Changes and Their Origin*, (Yale University Press, 1930).

dictatorship. Bitterly disillusioned about the old institutions which were not sufficient to stop the great catastrophe of 1914, it seeks something new. The old broke down, crushing what was good as well as what was rotten. The new generation is morbidly impatient to see a new world rise overnight. Hence such words as "liberalism" and "freedom of thought," which lead to a slow growth, are now out of favor in politics. . . . Dictatorships have the appearance of "doing" all the time, whether they accomplish lasting changes and effect internal reconstruction or not. Accordingly, they are the latest fashion in politics. . . .

But the continuation under the dictatorial regime of 1925 to 1929 in Turkey of reforms—some of them begun long ago—and especially the nature of these reforms, are more interesting and profitable to consider than the terrorist methods by which they are supposed to have been made possible.

This process of reform has been going on for nearly a century, but within the last twenty years it has moved with tremendous rapidity. The story in the Western press, usually the outcome of the most superficial and hurried observation after a pleasant Mediterranean trip, is that Turkey was changed overnight from an Eastern into a Western country. This view is more than superficial; it is false. Whether the recent reforms could have been carried out by other than terrorist methods is a question to be seriously discussed. . . .

The first and most spectacular of these was the so-called "hat law," passed in 1925. It was also the most futile and superficial in comparison with the others which followed. But it was the *only one* which accomplished a change overnight even in outside appearances. In a week it made the Turks don European hats (the only part of the city-dweller's outfit which was still un-Westernized) and made them look like Westerners, although the manner in which it was accomplished was utterly un-Western. The Westernization of Turkey is not and shall not be a question of mere external imitation and gesture. It is a much deeper and more significant process. To tell the Turk to put on a certain headdress and "get civilized" or be hanged, or imprisoned, is absurd, to say the least. The opposition of individuals among the men on the street, really much more Westernized than the

people who carried the measure through, had a note of wounded self-respect rather than an objection to the wearing of hats. Among all the recent measures, this was the most seriously opposed in the country itself. Any opposition to the hat law was labeled as reactionary. The interesting fact connected with the substitution of the hat for the Turkish fez is that of all the changes of the last four years it attracted the greatest attention in the Western world. . . .

In Turkey, the first substantial result of the hat law was that it enriched European hat factories at the expense of the already impoverished Turks. Broadly one can say that the hat law could not have passed in 1925 without a regime of terror. The Islamic reactionaries, the liberals, the people who understand the spirit of the West were all opposed to it for different reasons. What would otherwise have happened is this: a very small number of Turks who had worn hats in the summer in Constantinople would have gradually increased, and in a generation the hat-wearers would have been in a majority in the cities. But the Turkish peasant would have stuck to his old headdress.

The adoption of the Swiss code in place of the Islamic family law in 1926 was an act of a much more serious nature. This could have been put through without much coercion, although there would have been some bitter criticism.

The prevalent journalistic stuff published in the West about Turkish women declaring that they were freed from harems in thousands, that their veils were lifted, and that they were first allowed to enter public life as a result of this law, is both absurd and untrue. All Turkish men of the progressive type, regardless of the political party to which they belonged, especially from 1908 on, have been in favor of the progress of women and have helped to give them rights and opportunities—educational, economic, and social. From the moment Turkish women entered the economic field there has been no discrimination whatever of the kind which European feminists complain of. Women in Turkey have always received the same salaries or wages as the men, and the fact of their being married or unmarried has never hampered them in their search for work. Lately, women have also had good facilities for education. In 1916 the University of Istanbul opened its doors to them, and among the large number of students who have been sent to Europe, especially to Germany, there were a considerable number of women. Naturally, the Great War gave these movements a practical turn. The governmental departments as well as financial houses and trades then had to employ a great number of women. Not only in the big cities but also in smaller places women were forced to take up some trade and go to work in order to support their families. As breadwinners they became vital and important to the nation as a whole. The large amount of public work which women were thus obliged to do led to a natural social freedom and did away entirely with their partial seclusion in the majority of cities.

A very significant event of the Young Turk regime was the passing of a revised family law in 1916. The Islamic law concerning women had two weak points: polygamy and divorce. In the cities the right of polygamy, outside of the court circle and that of the conservative rich, was not widely exercised. General public opinion banned it, and urban economic conditions were making it an impossibility for a Turk to have even a single wife. But in certain rural districts, especially in Eastern Anatolia, the scarcity of men and the scarcity of labor both led men to take more than one wife whenever they could do so.

As to divorce, a man had the right, up to 1916, to repudiate his wife at any moment while a woman had to go to court and prove certain things before she could obtain a divorce. Before that time, the family law had been within the special jurisdiction of the *Sheih-ul-Islam*, then the judicial head of the Islamic religion in Turkey; and the extreme conservatives as well as the religious bodies were opposed to any change in this situation. The family belonged with religion, they argued, and a change might lead to the entire disintegration of society. Nevertheless, in 1916, the Islamic courts were placed under the authority of the Ministry of Justice, and the family law was revised in favor of women—in the spirit of Islam, although the execution of the law was no longer subject to its control. Marriage in Islam is a mutual contract between man and woman, and the revised law interpreted marriage from that particular point of view. Women were allowed to insert into their marriage contracts every right, including that of divorce. From that time on, educated Turkish women could, and did in a small number of cases, take advantage of this freedom under the law, but the vast number of uneducated women naturally could not profit by it.

A year after the Sultan's government had been abolished in Constantinople, it was seriously discussed whether the revised family law of 1916 should be restored with or without alterations. In 1924 the National Assembly took up the question, and it aroused great interest especially among the women of the cities, and of Constantinople in particular. At a large meeting of women in the Nationalist Club, a committee of women was chosen to study the situation and send a petition to the National Assembly. . . . This committee made a study of the family laws of Sweden, France, England, and Russia, and having found the Swedish law most desirable, sent a translated copy with a petition attached to it to the National Assembly. . . . Their petition at the time had no definite result. But there was a group of very keenly interested young deputies who worked for the adoption of a Western code rather than the restoration of the revised family law of 1916. Mahmoud Essad Bey, the deputy from Smyrna, who became Minister of Justice in 1925, was one of the leading spirits in this movement. In 1926 the new law following the Swiss code was passed. It can be termed, perhaps, one of the two most significant and important changes that have taken place during the dictatorial regime. This particular law will mean the final social unification of the Turks with the European nations, since it gives the Turkish family that kind of stability which constitutes the Western ideal of the family. The decision to adopt the Swiss law, which is entirely Western, instead of to revise and alter the old Islamic family law, which could have made marriage a freer if a less stable institution and brought it nearer to the present Russian law, was one more triumph in Turkey of the Western ideal over the Eastern ideal, and one of more importance for the future than is presently realized.

The educational rights that Turkish women have gained are no longer questioned even by the smallest minority, and the sphere of their work has been constantly widening. It is perhaps a blessing that they have not obtained the vote. Thus they have been protected from the danger of being identified with party politics, and their activities outside the political world could not be stopped for political reasons. [Turkish women received the right to vote in 1934.]

In the Turkish home, women continue to be the ruling spirit, more so, perhaps, because the majority contribute to the upkeep by their labors. At the present time, offices, factories, and shops are filled with women workers in the cities; and in addition to their breadwinning jobs, and sometimes in connection with them, women have interested themselves in child welfare and hygiene, and in organizing small associations to teach poor women embroidery, sewing, weaving, and so on. The favorite profession of Turkish women today, after teaching, is medicine. All this is the city aspect of the situation. In the rural districts, women still continue to live their old life with its old drudgery, and will continue to live under these conditions until a more up-to-date agricultural system is adopted and the rudiments of education can be taught them. It would not be an underestimate to say that something like ninety percent of the Turkish women are very hard workers; the question is not how to provide more work for them but how to train them better for their work and to give them more leisure. The small percentage of the idle rich (much smaller in Turkey than elsewhere) do on a miniature scale what the idle rich of other countries do. Unfortunately, Turkey is judged by the life and attitude of these idlers, who are conspicuous to the eyes of the traveler, rather than by the hardworking majority.

In 1928 the clause in the Turkish constitution which declared Islam the state religion was abolished. This act was again the culmination of a process that had been going on for a number of years. As far back as 1908 the Young Turks had adopted a definite policy tending to the separation of church and state.

Examining the Evidence

1. What are Halide Edib Adivar's judgments about the times in which she lives and in particular the changes in Turkey?
2. What is Adivar's attitude toward European countries to the west?
3. What are Adivar's arguments about both outsiders' and reformers' concern for women?
4. What is Adivar's broad view of reforms in Turkey?

MAKING CONNECTIONS

1. How and in what specific ways did World War I serve as a major catalyst for change, as evidenced in many of these documents?
2. What kinds of plans and programs did the Zapatistas in Mexico and V. I. Lenin in Russia lay out for remaking society?
3. Although in different ways, how do E. P. F. Lynch's diary, the General Syrian Congress resolution, and Halide Edib Adivar's critique of Atatürk all reflect a certain disillusionment about how events unfolded during these decades?
4. In what ways do the programs put forward and the criticisms expressed in this chapter's documents reflect issues associated with the status of imperialism and empires?

CHAPTER 26

Global Catastrophe: The Great Depression and World War II, 1929–1945

The Great Depression was a global event that drove down agricultural prices, saw the global financial system collapse, and led to unemployment as high as 30 percent of the workforce in countries like Germany. Around the world, authoritarian rulers came to power, promising muscular responses to the turmoil, which they blamed on the feebleness of both democracy and the rule of law. To solve economic and social problems at home, Germany, Italy, and Japan all sought to expand and pursued aggressive policies to create larger empires. The ultimate result was World War II — an event so horrendous and riveting that today it still dominates our thinking about history and the meaning of the past. Civilians died in larger numbers than did soldiers, and while the devastation advanced, the old imperial world order began to collapse.

26.1 AUTHORITARIAN MAN OF THE PEOPLE

Getulio Vargas, *New Year's Address* (1938)

Authoritarian rulers took over globally as a response to the deep economic crises faced by so many nations. Brazil suffered great turmoil in the 1930s, not unlike other countries facing the perils of the Great Depression. The result was the rise to power of the dictator Getulio Vargas (1882–1954), who was backed by the military. Vargas set up a corporatist state similar to that of Benito Mussolini in Italy, and like many dictators he appealed to patriotism and the poor in his speeches, stating that his aim was to provide them with social assistance and good jobs. Vargas suppressed his opposition ruthlessly, but he continued to work actively to put programs in place to alleviate poverty. This document is Vargas's public statement as he suspended the Brazilian constitution in 1938.

At the dawn of the new year, when in the hearts and souls the call of hope and happiness is more lively and crackling, and we feel more strongly, and overwhelmingly the aspiration for victory, achievement, and progress, I come to communicate with you and speak directly to everyone, without distinction of class, profession, or hierarchy, so that united and in brotherhood, we might lift quite high the idea of an irrevocable vote for the greatness and happiness of Brazil.

I have received from the Brazilian people, in grave and decisive moments, unequivocal proof of a perfect communion of ideas and sentiments. And for that very reason, more than ever, I judge myself obligated to transmit to the people my word of faith, so much more opportune and necessary if we consider the responsibilities arising out of the recently instituted regime, in which patriotism is measured by sacrifice and the rights of individuals have to be subordinate to the obligations to the nation.

It was imperative, for the good of the majority to change procedures and agree to a labor policy, consonant with our realities and the demands for the country's development.

The Constitution of November 10 is not a document of simple, legal regulation of the state, made to order, according to fashions in vogue. It is adapted concretely to the current problems of Brazilian life, considered in origins of formation, defining, at the same time, the directions toward its progress and enrichment.

The actions practiced, in these fifty days of government, reflect and confirm the decisive will to act inside of the principles adopted.

We are suspending payment of the foreign debt, because of the imposition of circumstances alien to our desires. . . .

We are modifying the onerous policy followed in relation to coffee, and in the same manner the monetary regimen, which was in force for our trade. . . .

Alongside these resolutions of an economic and financial character, there figured others of not lesser significance, in the political-administrative sphere. I want to allude to the acts of abolition of political parties, of organization of the national court, and regulation of pensions in the public, civil service.

By the first, there was had in view elimination of the interference from factious interests and groups in the solution of the problems of government. The state, according to the new order, is the nation, and because of that, ought to dispense with political intermediaries in order to maintain contact with the people, and consult their aspirations and needs. By the second, there were created national courts, causing the disappearance of organizational contradictions and anomalies in which we had as many courts as existing federated units. The codification of national law, already initiated, will come

Robert M. Levine and John J. Crocitti, eds., *The Brazil Reader: History, Culture, Politics* (Durham, NC: Duke University Press, 1999), 186–189.

to complete these measures of notable reach for the strengthening of the ties of national cohesion. Just as a single flag supremely protects all Brazilians, the law also ought to assure, by a uniform method, the rights of citizenship in the entire national territory. By the last, it is fitting to refer to the law that prohibits accumulation of public offices. For more than a century, this provision challenged the legislators of good intention. The solution encountered is, without doubt, strict. It will bring about sacrifices to some people, but it represents a benefit for the collectivity and demonstrates, in an undeniable manner, the moralizing proposal of abolishing all situations of privilege. Permitting more equitable distribution for access to the public offices, it implicitly benefits more people and offers an opportunity to assure equivalent remuneration for services rendered.

We will persist in the willingness to eliminate the barriers that separate zones and isolate regions, so that the national economic body might be able to evolve homogeneously, and the expansion of the internal market might be done without restraints of any type. . . .

In the regimen of the revoked Constitution, it was not possible to take these initiatives, nor assume the responsibilities of such heavy duties. . . .

Until recently, our equipment for teaching was limited to the minimum necessities for individual competence. . . . There was an abundance of Ph.D.s and a lack of qualified technicians; the man competent in his trade was rare; artistic technique declined in front of the machine, without us being able to make free use of industrial workers.

The national government resolved to undertake, in this respect, a decisive task. In addition to modernizing the existing establishments, increasing their capacity and efficiency, it initiated the construction of large professional schools, which ought to constitute a vast network of popular teaching, radiating throughout the country. It will attend, also, to the initiatives of local governments, by means of auxiliary materials and technical guidance. . . .

The sentiment of human solidarity is one of the most noble and highest manifestations of the Christian spirit. When the state takes the initiative of projects of economic assistance and supports the struggle of the worker, it is to attend to an imperative of social justice, giving an example to be observed by all, without need of compulsion. . . .

The multiplicity of sectors in which the state acts does not exclude, but instead affirms, a fundamental rule: that of security for the work and achievements of general interest. The public order and tranquility will be maintained without vacillation. The government continues vigilant in the repression of extremism and is going to segregate, in fortified military prisons and agricultural colonies, all those agitating elements, recognized by their seditious activities or condemned by political crimes. We will not permit that the struggle and patriotic dedication of the good Brazilians might come to endure turmoil and alarms originated by personalistic ambitions, or the ideological craziness of false prophets and vulgar demagogues . . . Brazilians! In the hour of cheerfulness and promise, I bring to you my friendly greeting.

Like you, I believe in the high destiny of the fatherland and, like you, I work to achieve it. In the New State there will be no place for the skeptics and the hesitant, unbelieving in themselves and others. There are those who, at times, interrupt your journey's repose honestly earned, with the alarm of their fears and the rumor of slanderous negativism. With trustful heart and uplifted enthusiasm, you devote yourselves to the daily labor and to the cares of the home, where you have guarded the hopes of happiness and find the comforting shelter of dear ones.

To all those who live under the bright protection of the Southern Cross, I give, in this dawn of the new year, the best vows of good fortune and prosperity. And from all of you — Brazilians! — I ask and hope, at this moment, for the solemn promise to well serve the fatherland and to do everything for its enrichment.

Examining the Evidence

1. What reforms is Vargas undertaking in Brazil?
2. What are Vargas's announced goals for Brazil, and how does he characterize his critics?
3. How does Vargas justify making so many changes? Is he convincing?
4. Describe the overall tone and message of Vargas's pronouncement.

Factory Worker Joana de Masi Zero, *Reminiscences* (1930s)

Dictators advanced their own interests and often those of the wealthy. However, through the mass media, many were able to build widespread appeal. Brazilian workers and the poverty-stricken in these desperate years of the Great Depression often called Getulio Vargas the "Father of the Poor." Like many dictators, Vargas had broad support as a savior and strong man. This reminiscence of a Brazilian worker provides evidence of that popular support for Vargas.

I was five when my father died. My grandfather came to live with us, but he died, too. Only the women remained, my mother, my grandmother, and we three sisters.

The house was my mother's, but the rest? For food and clothing we had to work. First, my mother went to work in a chicken coop; later, she started to sew men's clothing at home. My oldest sister started working when she still was a girl. She was the first, when she was twelve. Then I went to work, and finally Carmela. At first, she stayed at home, doing chores: she would prepare lunch and keep house. My older sister worked in a textile factory, going from one to another. My first job was sewing carpets by hand. I was twelve. I worked for a year and a half. It was in a private house, and they hired girls to work. Then I went to a factory. . . . When I went to work there my mother had to get me a work permit because I was still a minor, fourteen years of age. Actually, I was younger; I started in July, but my birthday was in October. Only then I worked legally. Only my sisters and I left school. Our other friends continued because their parents could afford it. . . . When I was fifteen, I moved to a more difficult machine in the factory, but earned more. . . . I went from factory to factory . . . finding different jobs. . . . I worked in one factory for twenty-five years. Getulio was president. Many people said that he was a dictator, but he did many things for us

workers. His labor laws were good. There were no strikes, at least never at places where I was working. Sometimes, to avoid strikes, the bosses dismissed us early, saying to us; "You go home; we're going to stop the machines so we won't have any fights at the door." They meant with the militants. All the laws we have today were thanks to [Vargas]. . . . Then they started to withhold payments for pensions. . . . Everyone paid whether they wanted to or not. Later, this system changed for the worse; retirement paid almost nothing. Every time the politicians changed the laws they took more from us. Getulio's time was good; later, I don't know. We earned well and prices didn't go up. You went out to buy milk, for example, and the price was always the same. We didn't live in luxury; we made our own clothes — we knew how to sew — we were well dressed, we had money to go to the movies every week, sometimes twice. We ate well, we lived well. They say he was a dictator, but for us he was good. . . .

When Getulio died it was like a death in the family. People were sad. No one talked; everyone was quiet. It was a really sorrowful day, especially for the workers. Things were closed for, I think, three days.

I retired when I turned sixty-five. The first month I earned the same as I had made when I was working, and after that, for a while as well. Then they began to take a little here and there, and the government took more and more, and now I earn almost nothing.

Examining the Evidence

1. What is the social position of Joana de Masi Zero?
2. Describe Zero's education and work life.
3. What reasons does Zero give for supporting Vargas?
4. What specific benefits in her life does Zero attribute to Vargas?
5. Given the document, how do you explain the widespread support for dictators in the 1930s?

Robert M. Levine and John J. Crocitti, eds., *The Brazil Reader: History, Culture, Politics* (Durham, NC: Duke University Press, 1999), 220–221.

26.2 THE FATE OF ETHIOPIA

Haile Selassie, *Appeal to the League of Nations* (1936)

Fascists believed that they were entitled to take over as many nations as they wanted, as did imperial powers such as Britain and France. Simultaneously, the League of Nations was committed to upholding the rights of people to self-determination. In 1935, Benito Mussolini's Italy attacked Ethiopia, one of the few African countries to have maintained its independence during the heyday of imperialism. Ethiopian emperor Haile Selassie (1892–1975) resisted militarily and additionally took his cause to the one body pledged to guarantee freedom—the League of Nations. Although the League condemned Italy's aggression, it took no forceful action, and soon Britain and France accepted the Italian takeover of this African land. Haile Selassie made this impassioned plea for help in person to members of the League.

I, Haile Selassie I, emperor of Ethiopia, am here today to claim that justice which is due to my people, and the assistance promised to them eight months ago, when fifty nations asserted that an aggression had been committed in violation of international treaties.

There is no precedent for a head of state himself speaking in this assembly. But there is also no precedent for a people being victim of such injustice and being at present threatened by abandonment to its aggressors. Also, there has never before been an example of any government proceeding to the systematic extermination of a nation by barbarous means, in violation of the most solemn promises made to all the nations of the earth that there should be no resort to a war of conquest, and that there should not be used against innocent human beings the terrible poison of harmful gases. It is to defend a people struggling for its age-old independence that the head of the Ethiopian Empire has come to Geneva to fulfill this supreme duty, after having himself fought at the head of his armies.

I pray Almighty God that he may spare nations the terrible sufferings that have just been inflicted on my people, and of which the chiefs who accompany me here have been the horrified witnesses.

It is my duty to inform the governments assembled in Geneva, responsible as they are for the lives of millions of men, women, and children, of the deadly peril which threatens them, by describing to them the fate which has been suffered by Ethiopia.

It is not only upon warriors that the Italian government has made war. It has above all attacked populations far removed from hostilities, in order to terrorize and exterminate them.

At the beginning, towards the end of 1935, Italian aircraft hurled upon my armies bombs of tear gas. Their effects were but slight. . . .

The Italian aircraft then resorted to mustard gas. Barrels of liquid were hurled upon armed groups. But this means also was not effective; the liquid only affected a few soldiers, and barrels upon the ground were themselves a warning to troops and to the population of the danger.

. . . Special sprayers were installed on board aircraft so that they could vaporize, over vast areas of territory, a fine, death-dealing rain. Groups of nine, fifteen, eighteen aircraft followed one another so that the fog issuing from them formed a continuous sheet. It was thus that, as from the end of January 1936, soldiers, women, children, cattle, rivers, lakes, and pastures were drenched continually with this deadly rain. In order to kill off systematically all living creatures, in order the more surely to poison waters and pastures, the Italian command made its aircraft pass over and over again. That was its chief method of warfare.

The very refinement of barbarism consisted in carrying ravage and terror into the most densely populated parts of the territory—the points farthest removed from the scene of hostilities. The object

William Safire, ed., *Lend Me Your Ears: Great Speeches in History* (New York: W. W. Norton, 1997), 297–300.

was to scatter fear and death over a great part of the Ethiopian territory.

These fearful tactics succeeded. Men and animals succumbed. The deadly rain that fell from the aircraft made all those whom it touched fly shrieking with pain. All those who drank the poisoned water or ate the infected food also succumbed in dreadful suffering. In tens of thousands the victims of the Italian mustard gas fell. It is in order to denounce to the civilized world the tortures inflicted upon the Ethiopian people that I resolved to come to Geneva. . . .

In October 1935, the fifty-two nations who are listening to me today gave me an assurance that the aggressor would not triumph, that the resources of the Covenant would be employed in order to ensure the reign of right and the failure of violence.

I ask the fifty-two nations not to forget today the policy upon which they embarked eight months ago, and in faith of which I directed the resistance of my people against the aggressor whom they had denounced to the world. Despite the inferiority of my weapons, the complete lack of aircraft, artillery, munitions, hospital services, my confidence in the League was absolute. I thought it to be impossible that fifty-two nations, including the most powerful in the world, should be successfully opposed by a single aggressor. Counting on the faith due to treaties, I had made no preparation for war, and that is the case with certain small countries in Europe. . . .

War then took place in the atrocious conditions which I have laid before the assembly. In that unequal struggle between a government commanding more than forty-two million inhabitants, having at its disposal financial, industrial, and technical means which enabled it to create unlimited quantities of the most death-dealing weapons, and, on the other hand, a small people of twelve million inhabitants, without arms, without resources, having on its side only the justice of its own cause and the promise of the League of Nations. What real assistance was given to Ethiopia by the fifty-two nations who had declared the Rome government guilty of a breach of the Covenant and had undertaken to prevent the triumph of the aggressor? . . .

What have become of the promises made to me? . . . The Ethiopian government never expected other governments to shed their soldiers' blood to defend the Covenant when their own immediate personal interests were not at stake. Ethiopian warriors asked only for means to defend themselves. On many occasions I have asked for financial assistance for the purchase of arms. That assistance has been constantly refused me. What, then, in practice, is the meaning of Article 16 and of collective security?

Apart from the Kingdom of the Lord there is not on this earth any nation that is superior to any other. Should it happen that a strong government finds it may, with impunity, destroy a weak people, then the hour strikes for that weak people to appeal to the League of Nations to give its judgment in all freedom. God and history will remember your judgment. . . .

Representatives of the world, I have come to discharge in your midst the most painful of the duties of the head of a state. What reply shall I have to take back to my people?

Examining the Evidence

1. How does Haile Selassie explain the League of Nations' responsibilities?
2. What are Selassie's stated grievances?
3. What specifically does Selassie want from the League of Nations, and why might members of the League have been unwilling to act on his request?
4. What larger arguments, beyond the fate of Ethiopia, does Selassie present in his plea to the League of Nations?

Kwame Nkrumah, *Autobiography* (1957)

In the 1930s, Kwame Nkrumah (1909–1972) left the British colony of the Gold Coast, where he was born, to study first in the United States and then in England. African and Caribbean local people often went to the metropole to study and then returned to their homeland as leaders of

---

Kwame Nkrumah, *Ghana: The Autobiography of Kwame Nkrumah* (New York: Thomas Nelson & Sons, 1957), 29.

those under imperial rule. While in London, Nkrumah worked in political circles that were rapidly changing in character. More and more students became activists and took up the cause of decolonization and Pan-African unity. In his autobiography, Nkrumah describes the impact that the Italian invasion of Ethiopia had on him. After the war, he returned to the Gold Coast and led the anti-British movement there. In 1957, the region became the independent state of Ghana.

On arrival in Liverpool I was met by the agent of George Grant, a Nzima timber merchant. I stayed in a hotel for the first week, then I traveled up to London in order to have my passport visaed for the United States. Bewildered and very much out of my depth I began to wonder if it would not be better to give the whole thing up and return home. But just as I was feeling particularly depressed about the future, I heard an excited newspaper boy shouting something unintelligible as he grabbed a bundle of the latest editions from a motor van, and on the placard I read :

"*MUSSOLINI INVADES ETHIOPIA.*" That was all I needed. At that moment it was almost as if the whole of London had suddenly declared war on me personally. For the next few minutes I could do nothing but glare at each impassive face wondering if those people could possibly realize the wickedness of colonialism, and praying that the day might come when I could play my part in bringing about the downfall of such a system. My nationalism surged to the fore; I was ready and willing to go through hell itself, if need be, in order to achieve my object.

Examining the Evidence

1. Why did Nkrumah, upon learning of the Italian invasion of Ethiopia, suddenly see London in a different light?
2. Based on Nkrumah's account, how is the Italian invasion of Ethiopia linked to broader movements for decolonization following World War II?

26.3 INDIA'S PUSH FOR INDEPENDENCE

Mohandas Gandhi, *Quit India Declaration* (1942)

Mohandas Gandhi (1869–1948) was a powerful voice for anti-British resistance leading to an independent India. He served as a leader alongside the pro-independence Indian National Congress, and he gathered a mass following by urging Indians to give up their belief in Western values such as materialism and violence. Gandhi also advocated nonviolence based on *satyagraha*, or soul-force, again, a tactic in stark contrast to Western militarism. As World War II progressed, Gandhi became admired worldwide as one of the most respected voices calling for the British to "Quit India." At the same time, he spoke across India to guide his followers in the ways of civil disobedience to imperial rulers. This is one of his wartime speeches.

There are people who ask me whether I am the same man that I was in 1920, or whether there has been any change in me. You are right in asking that question.

Let me, however, hasten to assure that I am the same Gandhi as I was in 1920. I have not changed in any fundamental respect. I attach the same importance to nonviolence that I did then. If at all, my emphasis on it has grown stronger. There is no real contradiction between the present resolution and my previous writings and utterances.

Occasions like the present do not occur in everybody's and but rarely in anybody's life. I want you to know and feel that there is nothing but purest *Ahimsa* [the idea of doing no harm] in all that I am saying and doing today. The draft resolution of the Working Committee is based on *Ahimsa*;

Shriman Narayan, ed., *The Selected Works of Mahatma Gandhi*, vol. 6, *The Voice of Truth* (Ahmedabad-14, India: Navajivan Publishing House, 1968), 50–54.

the contemplated struggle similarly has its roots in *Ahimsa*. If, therefore, there is any among you who has lost faith in *Ahimsa* or is wearied of it, let him not vote for this resolution. . . .

Ours is not a drive for power, but purely a non-violent fight for India's independence. In a violent struggle, a successful general has been often known to effect a military coup and to set up a dictatorship. But under the Congress scheme of things, essentially non-violent as it is, there can be no room for dictatorship. A non-violent soldier of freedom will covet nothing for himself, he fights only for the freedom of his country. The Congress is unconcerned as to who will rule, when freedom is attained. The power, when it comes, will belong to the people of India, and it will be for them to decide to whom it should be entrusted. . . .

I know how imperfect our *Ahimsa* is and how far away we are still from the ideal, but in *Ahimsa* there is no final failure or defeat. . . .

I believe that in the history of the world, there has not been a more genuinely democratic struggle for freedom than ours. I read Carlyle's *French Revolution* while I was in prison, and Pandit Jawaharlal[1] has told me something about the Russian revolution. But it is my conviction that inasmuch as these struggles were fought with the weapon of violence they failed to realize the democratic ideal. In the democracy which I have envisaged, a democracy established by nonviolence, there will be equal freedom for all. Everybody will be his own master. It is to join a struggle for such democracy that I invite you today. Once you realize this you will forget the differences between the Hindus and Muslims, and think of yourselves as Indians only, engaged in the common struggle for independence.

Then, there is the question of your attitude toward the British. I have noticed that there is hatred toward the British among the people. The people say they are disgusted with their behavior. The people make

no distinction between British imperialism and the British people. To them, the two are one. This hatred would even make them welcome the Japanese. It is most dangerous. It means that they will exchange one slavery for another. We must get rid of this feeling. Our quarrel is not with the British people, we fight their imperialism. The proposal for the withdrawal of British power did not come out of anger. It came to enable India to play its due part at the present critical juncture. It is not a happy position for a big country like India to be merely helping with money and material obtained willy-nilly from her while the United Nations [at the time, another name for the Allied Powers] are conducting the war. We cannot evoke the true spirit of sacrifice and valor, so long as we are not free. I know the British Government will not be able to withhold freedom from us, when we have made enough self-sacrifice. We must, therefore, purge ourselves of hatred. Speaking for myself, I can say that I have never felt any hatred. As a matter of fact, I feel myself to be a greater friend of the British now than ever before. One reason is that they are today in distress. My very friendship, therefore, demands that I should try to save them from their mistakes. As I view the situation, they are on the brink of an abyss. It, therefore, becomes my duty to warn them of their danger even though it may, for the time being, anger them to the point of cutting off the friendly hand that is stretched out to help them. People may laugh, nevertheless that is my claim. At a time when I may have to launch the biggest struggle of my life, I may not harbor hatred against anybody.

Examining the Evidence

1. What values does Gandhi promote in this speech?
2. What future does Gandhi see for India?
3. What problems does Gandhi see in his society?
4. What are Gandhi's attitudes toward the British, and why is it significant that he is making this "Quit India" declaration in 1942?
5. What are the intentions of Gandhi's speech?

---

[1] **Pandit Jawaharlal Nehru:** Became the first prime minister of India.

26.4   THE BATTLE OF STALINGRAD

Vera Ivanovna Malakhova, *Interview* (1990s)

Stalingrad was perhaps the most horrific single battle of World War II and the war's turning point on the European continent. The Germans and their allies were definitively defeated, although casualties in this lengthy battle were enormous on both sides (some two million dead, wounded, or imprisoned and likely to die in the camps). The battle began in July 1942 and continued into February 1943 when the German army surrendered. Combatants fought in the streets and sewers, from the air, and house to house with little relief. Soldiers starved and froze to death; at best they lost fingers and toes to frostbite. Although the Battle of Stalingrad is depicted as an entirely male event, in fact women were successfully enlisted to aid the Soviet army over the entire course of World War II as soldiers, pilots, and auxiliary personnel. Here a medical doctor, who served in the Soviet army for four years of the war, describes some aspects of her life around the time of the Battle of Stalingrad and during it.

The battle for Stalingrad was hell, literally. I was already seasoned by that time. I had already been wounded and nursed back to health in the medical battalion, and it was after that that I found myself in the battle for Stalingrad. Even so, it was absolute hell! I'll tell you how one girl, a nurse named Nadenka, perished. She was so obliging, she did so much for the wounded; when things needed to be done, she did them. Well, she and the quartermaster went to get their usual dinner. They brought it to them in thermoses. The only thing they fed us, you know, was millet gruel. We even called it PMS—perpetual millet soup. Yes. Well, they took this soup, this watery gruel, and they went and sat down to eat in a dugout. And they had just begun to eat, when there was an air raid. Every other hour, the Germans were bombing us. You

could check your watch by the bombings; they were terrible pedants. They swooped down terrifyingly, dived, and dropped anything, you name it: not only bombs, but rails, tractor wheels, tractor parts of all sorts. Everything made a noise, shrieked to the howling of sirens. In the beginning, we didn't know just what was flying, what kind of strange monsters, and then it turned out these monsters were actually metal tractor parts. And the rails, the rails were especially dangerous: They pierced the ground because they were dropped from a great height. And that time, the entire dugout caved in, and all the soldiers who were in it died instantly. They were crushed. And when they dug them out, they didn't find any survivors. That's how Nadenka perished. . . .

Real love existed at the front, too. You see this portrait of Georgii Antonovich? It was such a wonderful, good feeling. By the way, I knew he was from the Caucasus. But I didn't know what his nationality was. Well, after the encirclement, in Stalingrad, he died of peritonitis in my arms. He had been badly wounded, they had put a hole in his intestines, and we couldn't save him. And when he was dying—with peritonitis, they were always conscious to the end. Enough said—so many of them died in my arms! Oh! I don't even know how many. And you know, his last words . . . He lived another two days, and I could see him grow thinner and thinner before my very eyes, his skin darkened, and his nose became incredibly pointed! They didn't give him anything to drink, because they thought . . . , but why not give him something to drink, all the same he's going to die. And he, his last words were: "Well, how will you get along without me?" He had brought me out of the encirclement. "How will you live without me?" And he really loved me and thought that when the war was over we would be together, we would get married, and the rest.

Barbara Alpern Engel and Anastasia Posadskaya-Vanderbeck, eds., Sona Hoisington, trans., *A Revolution of Their Own: Voices of Women in Soviet History* (Boulder, CO: Westview Press, 1998), 190–194.

Well, you know, I did like him. For starters, he was two years older than me; and then, he was tall, he was serious, he kept order among the men. All the soldiers in the medical company loved him because he was a just man and brave. . . .

He was the regiment's senior physician. At that time, there were four doctors; later there were only two for each regiment. There weren't any more doctors available; all the rest had been killed. There was the regiment's senior physician; there was the commander of the medical company; there was an epidemiologist, who was the sanitation inspector; and there was the junior doctor, the one who treated patients—that was me. Although all three of them were graduates of the academy, they said very openly, Vera, we haven't the faintest idea how to use a stethoscope, how to diagnose a sick person, and so on, only you can do that. . . .

Yes, all three were men. And when we were encircled . . . Kostia Galkin, the sanitation inspector, the epidemiologist, was such a wonderful man! He loved to laugh; he was so happy-go-lucky. And, oh, the jokes he told! And you know, once when German tanks had started straight at us—they simply crushed people and fired rounds of shells—he went crazy and headed straight for the German tanks. There was a wheat field, the tanks were coming across it, and we looked and saw Kostia headed right for those tanks. We cried out, "Kostia! Kostia!" We liked him so much. "Come back!" But he did nothing of the sort.

Here's how Georgii Antonovich Khukhlaev led me out of the encirclement. He was an excellent horseman. He had an orderly, and this orderly had a horse. For two days, we had gone without water; we became completely dried out! It was June and very hot! The Germans were bombing us, they were shelling us, their tanks were coming at us. In short, everyone was completely exhausted, and the wounded were crying out, water, water, a drink of water! . . . But there was no water, not even a drop! It was the second day. And Georgii Antonovich said to his orderly, "Unsaddle the horse, take a bucket, and find me water, whatever it takes." Suddenly, tanks were coming at us. There was a small woods, Kostia went into this thicket. Georgii Antonovich said to me, "Get on the horse!" But before that, he said, "Take

off your dress!" I thought, Good God! He must have lost his mind too. Why should I . . . ? At that time, we were issued these dresses like uniforms. Well okay, he dragged out his bag—he was so tall—and gave me his second pair of pants and said, "Put on these pants!" Well, I thought, he's really crazy. I couldn't disobey him; he was the regiment's senior physician. So I pulled on the pants, and somehow he hitched them up for me. "Get on the horse!" He took me— I was small, and of course, thin, not the way I am now—and he put me on this horse, which had no bridle, no saddle, no—you know, those things you put your feet in, I can't remember what they're called—stirrups! No stirrups, nothing. He sat me on the horse, twisted the mane around my hands, and said, "If you don't want to fall into the hands of the Germans, hang on tight to the horse, dig in." Now, we had straps that we used to drag the wounded off the battlefield with. Once I had to do that. And from those straps he made me stirrups, loops, and he put me on the croup of the horse, and put my feet into those loops, in boots, and he wound the mane around my hands. And he said: "Press against the horse, grab him around the neck, dig into him. I'll do the rest." He called to his own horse, and my horse galloped after him, and that's how he rescued me from the encirclement. We dashed across the field. We escaped the tanks, but the shooting continued, shells were exploding, the horse kept rearing. How in the world did I manage to stay on? I had never ridden before, never even been close to a horse. Well, I'd seen them at the front, but I never thought I would get on a horse. It was my terrible baptism by fire!

Then we got lost and wandered into some ravine. . . .

It was the summer of 1942, the beginning of July. And when we wandered into this ravine, we found several soldiers already hiding there. Georgii Antonovich told me to get down, but he couldn't get me off the horse because I was so frightened, I had dug my nails into its neck and was holding onto it for dear life. Slowly, soldiers began to gather in the ravine; twelve or fourteen of us must have gathered there. And Georgii Antonovich said: "Vera Ivanovna is the highest ranking among you. She's a senior lieutenant. Obey her." And he whispered in my ear: "I won't abandon you. I'm going to find out where the division is and how we can get out of the encirclement." We already knew that we had been encircled by the Germans. I thought, Good God! . . .

This was near Kastornaia, the Kastornaia station. It was an important railroad junction. Well, I thought, he'll soon be gone. I said, "What if you're wounded?" He replied, "I won't be." That's just how he said it: with confidence. And so he rode off on this same horse. And the ravine was quite deep. He left, and, as soon as he left, we heard the sound of a motor. *Zhizhi* . . . A *rama* was flying overhead. Now, a rama was a German plane with two fuselages, a double tail, and a single motor. [This plane flew very low, for reconnaissance.] All the frontline soldiers knew just what it was. And this rama began to descend; it descended and landed on the very field where the tanks were—quite a distance from us. I said: "Guys, we're done for. What have you got for weapons?" It turned out one person had a carbine, some had automatics—but not everyone had them yet, not everyone had a rifle, even. And Natasha, who was in charge of medication, was there, too—I don't know how she got there—and Andrei, the medical orderly, crept up. And there were also signalmen, ordinary soldiers. "Yes," I said, "That's it. They're about to get us. They'll get out of the rama." Now, ramas could "see" everything. They had amazing sighting devices. I thought, that's it: They've spotted us; now they'll finish us off. At that moment, Andrei said to Natasha—Natasha was a member of the Komsomol [a group for Communist youth activists]—"Natasha, here, take this German leaflet. Let's crawl out of here." We all wanted water to drink something awful! We hadn't had anything to drink for two whole days. Way off in the distance, I noticed a crane standing in a village; it was a well. "Let's crawl over there and get a drink," said Andrei. "Don't you dare," I said. "I'm senior to you in rank; don't you dare." He crawled off and so did Natasha; neither of them returned. Later, after we had gotten out of the encirclement, we were told that everyone in the village had been lined up and questioned: Who is a Communist? Who is a Komsomol? Who

is a Jew? And she was a komsomolka; she had her Komsomol card with her. Well, by all accounts, they were among those who were shot. The Germans finished everyone off: all the communists, all the Jews! There were a lot of Jews in our medical battalion, and they were all shot—every last one of them. They shot all the communists and Komsomol members, too. June of '42. That's when the most horrible battles took place, that's when we retreated.

Toward evening, late in the day, Georgii Antonovich suddenly appeared.

He had found out where the rest of the unit was, and he led those of us who were left, out of the encirclement. We managed to join up with the unit, but we had to fight our way out. We were right with the soldiers, under attack. It was awful. And since we had had absolutely nothing to drink, our lips were cracked and bleeding. And my dress—I had taken off his pants—was all crumpled, all dirty, all spattered with mud. While we were fighting our way out, you know, the villagers . . . We kept going from one village to the next: That village was occupied by Germans, this village was occupied by Germans. . . . Then we ended up in another village and found "ours" there. "The Germans were here, but now they've left." "Give us some water, some water!" And when we passed by, erect, with all our automatics and carbines at the ready, you know, they poured water on us, and whoever got even a drop was so happy. They simply poured water over us. But we couldn't afford to stop; we had to break through! And that's how I got out of the encirclement.

Examining the Evidence

1. What personal relationships existed during the Battle of Stalingrad?
2. Based on Vera Ivanovna Malakhova's account, how would you describe the battlefield scene?
3. What is the tone of Malakhova's memories of the war?
4. What skills did combatants and doctors use to survive?

26.5   HOPE FOR THE POSTWAR FUTURE

United Nations, *Universal Declaration of Human Rights* (1948)

As the full deprivations of World War II became public, many leaders lobbied for a declaration that would address the wide range of harms and abuses that people had faced under the fascists. Amid outrage and lobbying, the Canadian John Peters and French human rights activists drafted the proposed declaration. When it was finished and adopted, Eleanor Roosevelt, widow of President Franklin D. Roosevelt and head of the UN Commission on Human Rights, called it an "international Magna Carta." Nonetheless, critics of the Declaration of Human Rights thought it too "universalist" in its conditions, meaning that it did not take into account cultural differences. Others believed that it did not go far enough in guaranteeing the well-being of the world's peoples.

Preamble

Whereas recognition of the inherent dignity and of the equal and inalienable rights of all members of the human family is the foundation of freedom, justice and peace in the world,

Whereas disregard and contempt for human rights have resulted in barbarous acts which have outraged the conscience of mankind, and the advent of a world in which human beings shall enjoy freedom of speech and belief and freedom from fear and want has been proclaimed as the highest aspiration of the common people,

Whereas it is essential, if man is not to be compelled to have recourse, as a last resort, to rebellion against tyranny and oppression, that human rights should be protected by the rule of law,

Whereas it is essential to promote the development of friendly relations between nations,

Whereas the peoples of the United Nations have in the Charter reaffirmed their faith in fundamental human rights, in the dignity and worth of the human person and in the equal rights of men and women and have determined to promote social progress and better standards of life in larger freedom,

Whereas Member States have pledged themselves to achieve, in co-operation with the United Nations, the promotion of universal respect for and observance of human rights and fundamental freedoms,

Whereas a common understanding of these rights and freedoms is of the greatest importance for the full realization of this pledge,

Now, Therefore The General Assembly proclaims This Universal Declaration Of Human Rights as a common standard of achievement for all peoples and all nations, to the end that every individual and every organ of society, keeping this Declaration constantly in mind, shall strive by teaching and education to promote respect for these rights and freedoms and by progressive measures, national and international, to secure their universal and effective recognition and observance, both among the peoples of Member States themselves and among the peoples of territories under their jurisdiction.

Article 1

All human beings are born free and equal in dignity and rights. They are endowed with reason and conscience and should act toward one another in a spirit of brotherhood.

Article 2

Everyone is entitled to all the rights and freedoms set forth in this Declaration, without distinction of any kind, such as race, color, sex, language, religion, political or other opinion, national or social origin, property, birth or other status. Furthermore, no distinction shall be made on the basis of the political, jurisdictional or international status of the country

. . . *And Justice for All: The Universal Declaration of Human Rights at 50*, Headline Series (New York: Foreign Policy Association, 1998), 23–30.

or territory to which a person belongs, whether it be independent, trust, non-self-governing or under any other limitation of sovereignty.

Article 3

Everyone has the right to life, liberty and security of person.

Article 4

No one shall be held in slavery or servitude; slavery and the slave trade shall be prohibited in all their forms.

Article 5

No one shall be subjected to torture or to cruel, in-human or degrading treatment or punishment.

Article 6

Everyone has the right to recognition everywhere as a person before the law.

Article 7

All are equal before the law and are entitled without any discrimination to equal protection of the law. All are entitled to equal protection against any discrimination in violation of this Declaration and against any incitement to such discrimination.

Article 8

Everyone has the right to an effective remedy by the competent national tribunals for acts violating the fundamental rights granted him by the constitution or by law.

Article 9

No one shall be subjected to arbitrary arrest, deten-tion or exile.

Article 10

Everyone is entitled in full equality to a fair and public hearing by an independent and impartial tribunal, in the determination of his rights and obligations and of any criminal charge against him.

Article 11

(1) Everyone charged with a penal offence has the right to be presumed innocent until proved guilty according to law in a public trial at which he has had all the guarantees necessary for his defense.

(2) No one shall be held guilty of any penal offence on account of any act or omission which did not con-stitute a penal offence, under national or international law, at the time when it was committed. Nor shall a heavier penalty be imposed than the one that was ap-plicable at the time the penal offence was committed.

Article 12

No one shall be subjected to arbitrary interference with his privacy, family, home or correspondence, nor to attacks upon his honor and reputation. Every-one has the right to the protection of the law against such interference or attacks.

Article 13

(1) Everyone has the right to freedom of movement and residence within the borders of each State.

(2) Everyone has the right to leave any country, including his own, and to return to his country.

Article 14

(1) Everyone has the right to seek and to enjoy in other countries asylum from persecution.

(2) This right may not be invoked in the case of prosecutions genuinely arising from nonpolitical crimes or from acts contrary to the purposes and principles of the United Nations.

Article 15

(1) Everyone has the right to a nationality.

(2) No one shall be arbitrarily deprived of his na-tionality nor denied the right to change his nationality.

Article 16

(1) Men and women of full age, without any limita-tion due to race, nationality or religion, have the right to marry and to found a family. They are en-titled to equal rights as to marriage, during marriage and at its dissolution.

(2) Marriage shall be entered into only with the free and full consent of the intending spouses.

(3) The family is the natural and fundamental group unit of society and is entitled to protection by society and the State.

Article 17

(1) Everyone has the right to own property alone as well as in association with others.

(2) No one shall be arbitrarily deprived of his property.

Article 18

Everyone has the right to freedom of thought, conscience and religion; this right includes freedom to change his religion or belief, and freedom, either alone or in community with others and in public or private, to manifest his religion or belief in teaching, practice, worship and observance.

Article 19

Everyone has the right to freedom of opinion and expression; this right includes freedom to hold opinions without interference and to seek, receive and impart information and ideas through any media and regardless of frontiers.

Article 20

(1) Everyone has the right to freedom of peaceful assembly and association.

(2) No one may be compelled to belong to an association.

Article 21

(1) Everyone has the right to take part in the government of his country, directly or through freely chosen representatives.

(2) Everyone has the right of equal access to public service in his country.

(3) The will of the people shall be the basis of the authority of government; this will shall be expressed in periodic and genuine elections which shall be by universal and equal suffrage and shall be held by secret vote or by equivalent free voting procedures.

Article 22

Everyone, as a member of society, has the right to social security and is entitled to realization, through national effort and international co-operation and in accordance with the organization and resources of each State, of the economic, social and cultural rights indispensable for his dignity and the free development of his personality.

Article 23

(1) Everyone has the right to work, to free choice of employment, to just and favorable conditions of work and to protection against unemployment.

(2) Everyone, without any discrimination, has the right to equal pay for equal work.

(3) Everyone who works has the right to just and favorable remuneration ensuring for himself and his family an existence worthy of human dignity, and supplemented, if necessary, by other means of social protection.

(4) Everyone has the right to form and to join trade unions for the protection of his interests.

Article 24

Everyone has the right to rest and leisure, including reasonable limitation of working hours and periodic holidays with pay.

Article 25

(1) Everyone has the right to a standard of living adequate for the health and well-being of himself and of his family, including food, clothing, housing and medical care and necessary social services, and the right to security in the event of unemployment, sickness, disability, widowhood, old age or other lack of livelihood in circumstances beyond his control.

(2) Motherhood and childhood are entitled to special care and assistance. All children, whether born in or out of wedlock, shall enjoy the same social protection.

Article 26

(1) Everyone has the right to education. Education shall be free, at least in the elementary and fundamental stages. Elementary education shall be compulsory.

Technical and professional education shall be made generally available and higher education shall be equally accessible to all on the basis of merit.

(2) Education shall be directed to the full development of the human personality and to the strengthening of respect for human rights and fundamental freedoms. It shall promote understanding, tolerance and friendship among all nations, racial or religious groups, and shall further the activities of the United Nations for the maintenance of peace.

(3) Parents have a prior right to choose the kind of education that shall be given to their children.

Article 27

(1) Everyone has the right freely to participate in the cultural life of the community, to enjoy the arts and to share in scientific advancement and its benefits.

(2) Everyone has the right to the protection of the moral and material interests resulting from any scientific, literary or artistic production of which he is the author.

Article 28

Everyone is entitled to a social and international order in which the rights and freedoms set forth in this Declaration can be fully realized.

Article 29

(1) Everyone has duties to the community in which alone the free and full development of his personality is possible.

(2) In the exercise of his rights and freedoms, everyone shall be subject only to such limitations as are determined by law solely for the purpose of securing due recognition and respect for the rights and freedoms of others and of meeting the just requirements of morality, public order and the general welfare in a democratic society.

(3) These rights and freedoms may in no case be exercised contrary to the purposes and principles of the United Nations.

Article 30

Nothing in this Declaration may be interpreted as implying for any State, group or person any right to engage in any activity or to perform any act aimed at the destruction of any of the rights and freedoms set forth herein.

Examining the Evidence

1. What is the range of rights announced in the declaration?
2. What rights specifically address the recent fascist past?
3. What principles from past declarations, constitutions, and political philosophies appear in the Declaration of Human Rights?
4. What particular articles in the declaration could be objected to as being too Western? What particular articles could be objected to as being too sweeping and blind to cultural differences? Are there missing guarantees?

MAKING CONNECTIONS

1. What general political attitudes of this era do the documents present?
2. How did working people feel about their lives during these times of economic and military struggle?
3. How does the UN Universal Declaration of Human Rights reflect concerns of a variety of people as seen in the documents? How might Vargas and Selassie have different reactions to the declaration?
4. Often the history of the economic depression and the growing political authoritarianism of the 1930s and of World War II are seen primarily as aspects of European and U.S. history. How do these documents challenge that limited view?

CHAPTER 27

The Emergence of New Nations in a Cold War World, 1945–1970

World War II signed the death warrant for direct imperialism as exercised by the Western powers and Japan. Except for the United States and the Soviet Union, the imperial powers were bankrupt and psychologically, if not actually, defeated. The many colonized men and women who served the imperialists had gotten yet another taste of inhumane values not only under the imperialists' rule but also during this total war. Liberation movements thrived at the war's end, and within two decades many colonies had become independent, often by withstanding violent opposition from France, Britain, Belgium, and the Netherlands. Meanwhile, the Cold War between the United States and the USSR also shaped the decolonization process, even as new authors presented powerful postcolonial literature to the world. Amidst it all, prosperity returned to many regions of the world.

27.1 DECOLONIZING THE SUEZ CANAL

Gamal Abdel Nasser, *Denouncement of the Proposal for a Canal Users' Association* (1956)

In 1952, Gamal Abdel Nasser (1918–1970) took part in the military overthrow of the Egyptian king, a puppet of the British government. The British had granted Egypt its independence in 1922 but stayed on to rule behind the scenes. The son of a postal inspector, Nasser quickly rose from being an army officer to the president of Egypt—a position that he used to improve the economic well-being of his people by redistributing land from the very wealthiest estates. In 1956, the British persuaded the United States not to provide Egypt with loans to build the projected Aswan Dam, which would create vast hydroelectric resources. Nasser's response was to nationalize the Suez Canal to return its income to Egypt. The British insisted that the Egyptians were incapable of running so complex an operation as the Suez Canal and proposed that they would head a consortium to run it. Nasser's speech of September 1956 is a response to that proposal. Nasser became a hero to both his fellow Arabs and to people in emerging nations.

In these decisive days in the history of mankind, these days in which truth struggles to have itself recognized in international chaos where powers of evil domination and imperialism have prevailed, Egypt stands firmly to preserve her sovereignty. Your country stands solidly and staunchly to preserve her dignity against imperialistic schemes of a number of nations who have uncovered their desires for domination and supremacy.

In these days and in such circumstances Egypt has resolved to show the world that when small nations decide to preserve their sovereignty, they will do that all right and that when these small nations are fully determined to defend their rights and maintain their dignity, they will undoubtedly succeed in achieving their ends. . . .

I am speaking in the name of every Egyptian Arab and in the name of all free countries and of all those who believe in liberty and are ready to defend it. I am speaking in the name of principles proclaimed by these countries in the Atlantic Charter. But they are now violating these principles and it has become our lot to shoulder the responsibility of reaffirming and establishing them anew. . . .

We have tried by all possible means to cooperate with those countries which claim to assist smaller nations and which promised to collaborate with us but they demanded their fees in advance. This we refused so they started to fight with us. They said they will pay toward building the High Dam and then they withdrew their offer and cast doubts on the Egyptian economy. Are we to declaim [disclaim?] our sovereign right? Egypt insists her sovereignty must remain intact and refuses to give up any part of that sovereignty for the sake of money.

Egypt nationalized the Egyptian Suez Canal company. When Egypt granted the concession to de Lesseps [Ferdinand de Lesseps was the French developer of the Suez Canal] it was stated in the concession between the Egyptian Government and the Egyptian company that the company of the Suez Canal is an Egyptian company subject to Egyptian authority. Egypt nationalized this Egyptian company and declared freedom of navigation will be preserved.

But the imperialists became angry. Britain and France said Egypt grabbed the Suez Canal as if it were part of France or Britain. The British Foreign Secretary forgot that only two years ago he signed an agreement stating the Suez Canal is an integral part of Egypt.

Egypt declared she was ready to negotiate. But as soon as negotiations began threats and intimidations started. . . .

The Suez Canal Problem, 26 July–22 September 1956, U.S. Department of State Publication No. 6392 (Washington, DC: U.S. Government Printing Office, 1956), 345–351.

Eden [Anthony Eden, British prime minister, 1955–1957] stated in the House of Commons there shall be no discrimination between states using the canal. We on our part reaffirm that and declare there is no discrimination between canal users. He also said Egypt shall not be allowed to succeed because that would spell success for Arab nationalism and would be against their policy, which aims at the protection of Israel.

Today they are speaking of a new association whose main objective would be to rob Egypt of the canal and deprive her of rightful canal dues. Suggestions made by Eden in the House of Commons which have been backed by France and the United States are a clear violation of the 1888 convention, since it is impossible to have two bodies organizing navigation in the canal. . . .

By stating that by succeeding, Abdel Nasser would weaken Britain's stand against Arab nationalism, Eden is in fact admitting his real objective is not Abdel Nasser as such but rather to defeat Arab nationalism and crush its cause. Eden speaks and finds his own answer. A month ago he let out the cry that he was after Abdel Nasser. Today the Egyptian people are fully conscious of their sovereign rights and Arab nationalism is fully awakened to its new destiny. . . .

Those who attack Egypt will never leave Egypt alive. We shall fight a regular war, a total war, a guerrilla war. Those who attack Egypt will soon realize they brought disaster upon themselves. He who attacks Egypt attacks the whole Arab world. They say in their papers the whole thing will be over in forty-eight hours. They do not know how strong we really are. We believe in international law. But we will never submit. We shall show the world how a small country can stand in the face of great powers threatening with armed might. Egypt might be a small power but she is great inasmuch as she has faith in her power and convictions. I feel quite certain every Egyptian shares the same convictions as I do and believes in everything I am stressing now.

We shall defend our freedom and independence to the last drop of our blood. This is the staunch feeling of every Egyptian. The whole Arab nation will stand by us in our common fight against aggression and domination. Free peoples, too, people who are really free will stand by us and support us against the forces of tyranny.

Examining the Evidence

1. What is Nasser's view of the imperial powers?
2. What is Nasser's defense of nationalization?
3. What is Nasser telling the European powers?
4. What is the tone of Nasser's declaration?
5. What ingredients of this document explain Nasser's high standing among not just Arabs but also people in other emerging nations?

27.2 A MEETING OF EMERGING NATIONS

President Sukarno of Indonesia, *Speech at the Opening of the Bandung Conference* (1955)

President Sukarno (1901–1970) of Indonesia was born Kusno Sosrodihardjo and led Indonesia's transition to independence under a wide ideological umbrella. He sought to bring together Indonesians of different ethnicities, ideologies, and religions, although he had started out as a Marxist and an ideologue himself. Sukarno had hoped Japanese control of Indonesia would bring about liberation, but this did not happen. After the defeat of Japan in World War II, the Dutch were finally driven out and Indonesia became an independent nation. Meanwhile, Sukarno sought to fortify the emerging nations during the Cold War by calling them together at the

Africa-Asia Speaks from Bandong (Jakarta: Indonesian Ministry of Foreign Affairs, 1955), 19–29. Available at Modern History Sourcebook, http://www.fordham.edu/halsall/mod/1955sukarno-bandong.html.

Bandung Conference in 1955. There, differing important speeches were made by the leaders of decolonization—all of them bringing global attention to the task ahead for emerging nations and for the entire world.

This twentieth century has been a period of terrific dynamism. Perhaps the last fifty years have seen more developments and more material progress than the previous five hundred years. Man has learned to control many of the scourges which once threatened him. He has learned to consume distance. He has learned to project his voice and his picture across oceans and continents. He has probed deep into the secrets of nature and learned how to make the desert bloom and the plants of the earth increase their bounty. He has learned how to release the immense forces locked in the smallest particles of matter. . . .

We are living in a world of fear. The life of man today is corroded and made bitter by fear. Fear of the future, fear of the hydrogen bomb, fear of ideologies. Perhaps this fear is a greater danger than the danger itself, because it is fear which drives men to act foolishly, to act thoughtlessly, to act dangerously. . . .

All of us, I am certain, are united by more important things than those which superficially divide us. We are united, for instance, by a common detestation of colonialism in whatever form it appears. We are united by a common detestation of racialism. And we are united by a common determination to preserve and stabilize peace in the world. . . .

We are often told "Colonialism is dead." Let us not be deceived or even soothed by that. I say to you, colonialism is not yet dead. How can we say it is dead, so long as vast areas of Asia and Africa are unfree.

And, I beg of you do not think of colonialism only in the classic form which we of Indonesia, and our brothers in different parts of Asia and Africa, knew. Colonialism has also its modern dress, in the form of economic control, intellectual control, actual physical control by a small but alien community within a nation. It is a skillful and determined enemy, and it appears in many guises. It does not give up its loot easily. Wherever, whenever and however it appears, colonialism is an evil thing, and one which must be eradicated from the earth. . . .

Not so very long ago we argued that peace was necessary for us because an outbreak of fighting in our part of the world would imperil our precious independence, so recently won at such great cost.

Today, the picture is more black. War would not only mean a threat to our independence, it may mean the end of civilization and even of human life. There is a force loose in the world whose potentiality for evil no man truly knows. Even in practice and rehearsal for war the effects may well be building up into something of unknown horror.

Not so long ago it was possible to take some little comfort from the idea that the clash, if it came, could perhaps be settled by what were called "conventional weapons"—bombs, tanks, cannon and men. Today that little grain of comfort is denied us for it has been made clear that the weapons of ultimate horror will certainly be used, and the military planning of nations is on that basis. The unconventional has become the conventional, and who knows what other examples of misguided and diabolical scientific skill have been discovered as a plague on humanity.

And do not think that the oceans and the seas will protect us. The food that we eat, the water that we drink, yes, even the very air that we breathe can be contaminated by poisons originating from thousands of miles away. And it could be that, even if we ourselves escaped lightly, the unborn generations of our children would bear on their distorted bodies the marks of our failure to control the forces which have been released on the world.

No task is more urgent than that of preserving peace. Without peace our independence means little. The rehabilitation and upbuilding of our countries will have little meaning. Our revolutions will not be allowed to run their course. . . .

What can we do? We can do much! We can inject the voice of reason into world affairs. We can mobilize all the spiritual, all the moral, all the political strength of Asia and Africa on the side of peace. Yes, we! We, the peoples of Asia and Africa, 1,400,000,000 strong, far more than half the human population of the world, we can mobilize what I have called the Moral Violence of Nations in favor of peace. We can demonstrate to the minority of the world which lives on the other continents that we, the majority are for peace, not for war. . . .

So, let this Asian-African Conference be a great success! Make the "Live and let live" principle and the "Unity in Diversity" motto the unifying force which brings us all together—to seek in friendly, uninhibited discussion, ways and means by which each of us can live his own life, and let others live their own lives, in their own way, in harmony, and in peace.

Examining the Evidence

1. Explain the timing and purpose of the Bandung meeting as expressed in Sukarno's speech.
2. What values is Sukarno expressing to the Bandung delegates?
3. What assessment does Sukarno make of the state of the world and the claim that "colonialism is dead"?
4. What contributions does Sukarno believe emerging nations have to make?

Richard Wright, *The Color Curtain: A Report on the Bandung Conference* (1956)

The Bandung Conference was a globally influential event. Celebrated African American author Richard Wright (1908–1960) noted the importance of Bandung for people of color and for those oppressed by varieties of colonialism. The deadly racism in the United States caused Wright, who grew up in poverty in the South, to move to France in 1945 even as the civil rights movement began a new phase of its activism. From there he continued providing shrewd observations, writing novels that shaped the drive for an improved status of people of color. Wright, like other African Americans, developed a strong interest in conditions in the decolonizing world, which caused him to attend the Bandung meeting and report on the scene.

I picked up the evening's newspaper that lay folded near me upon a table and began thumbing through it. Then I was staring at a news item that baffled me. I bent forward and read the item a second time. *Twenty-nine free and independent nations of Asia and Africa are meeting in Bandung, Indonesia, to discuss "racialism and colonialism.".* . . . What is this? I scanned the list of nations involved: China, India, Indonesia, Burma, Egypt, Turkey, the Philippines, Ethiopia, Gold Coast, etc. My God! I began a rapid calculation of the populations of the nations listed and, when my total topped the billion mark, I stopped, pulled off my glasses, and tried to think. . . .

Only brown, black, and yellow men who had long been made agonizingly self-conscious, under the rigors of colonial rule, of their race and their religion could have felt the need for such a meeting. There was something extra-political, extra-social, almost extra-human about it; it smacked of tidal waves, of natural forces. . . . *And the call for the meeting had not been sounded in terms of ideology.* The agenda and subject matter had been written for centuries in the blood and bones of the participants. The conditions under which these men had lived had become their tradition, their culture, their *raison d'être.* And they could not be classed as proletarians; they comprised princes and paupers, Communists and Christians, Leftists and Rightists, Buddhists and Democrats, in short, just anybody and everybody who lived in Asia and Africa.

I felt that I had to go to that meeting; I felt that I could understand it. I represented no government, but I wanted to go anyhow. . . .

I was now ready to go to Bandung to the conference. Rumors were rife. Everybody was guessing what each Asian and African nation was expecting to gain from its participation. . . . Pandit Nehru was hoping to emerge from the conference as some kind of acknowledged leader or spokesman for Asia. Japan was expected to walk a tightrope, bowing and smiling to all sides among people over whom she once brutally ruled . . . hoping thereby to stimulate trade and retrieve her position as the real leader of Asia. . . .

Richard Wright, *The Color Curtain: A Report on the Bandung Conference*, in *Black Power: Three Books from Exile* (New York: Harper Perennial, 2008), 437, 439–440, 532–533, 571–572, 574–575.

It was my impression that, with the exception of Nehru, Chou En-lai, and U Nu, no other delegations . . . came to Bandung but with the narrowest of parochial hopes and schemes. But when they got to Bandung, with their speeches in their pockets, something happened that no Asian or African, no Easterner or Westerner, could have dreamed of. . . .

Racial feeling manifested itself at Bandung in a thousand subtle forms. The Sten guns and the hand grenades of the brown Indonesian troops evoked deep fear in many white observers. Said one Englishwoman:

"I'd suggest that we evacuate Australia right now and settle the population in Canada."

As I watched the dark-faced delegates work at the conference, I saw a strange thing happen. Before Bandung, most of these men had been strangers, and on the first day they were constrained with one another, bristling with charge and countercharge against America and/or Russia. But, as the days passed, they slowly cooled off, and another and different mood set in. . . . As they came to know one another better, their fear and distrust evaporated. Living for centuries under Western rule, they had become filled with a deep sense of how greatly they differed from one another. But now, face to face, their ideological defenses dropped. Negative unity, bred by a feeling that they had to stand together against a rapacious West, turned into something that hinted of the positive. They began to sense their combined strength; they began to taste blood. . . . They could now feel that their white enemy was far, far away. . . . Day after day dun-colored Trotskyites consorted with dark Moslems, yellow Indo-Chinese hobnobbed with brown Indonesians, black Africans mingled with swarthy Arabs, tan Burmese associated with dark brown Hindus, dusty nationalists palled around with yellow Communists, and Socialists talked to Buddhists. But they all had the same background of colonial experience, of subjection, of color consciousness, and they found that ideology was not needed to define their relations. . . . I got the notion that ideologies were the instruments that these men had grown used to wielding in their struggles with Western white men and that now, being together and among themselves, they no longer needed them. As the importance of ideology declined, I began to feel that maybe ideology was a weapon that suited only certain hostile conditions of life. Racial realities have a strange logic of their own.

Over and beyond the waiting throngs that crowded the streets of Bandung, the Conference had a most profound influence upon the color-conscious millions in all the countries of the earth. . . .

Just how conscious were the Asian statesmen at Bandung of the racial content of what they were organizing? I discussed this problem with none less than Nehru. That Asian statesman asked me what I thought of the reactions of the West to the Conference and I said:

"Mr. Prime Minister, the West has exploited these people for centuries and such gatherings as this evoke fear deep in their hearts. There are people who ask if this is not racism in reverse—"

"Yes," Nehru said. "The West feels what you say. But what the West feels can come about. Race feeling is in these people, and if the West keeps pressuring them, they will create racism in them."

Examining the Evidence

1. What are Richard Wright's expectations as he reads about the Bandung Conference?
2. What are the problems that Wright sees facing the participants in the Bandung Conference?
3. According to Wright, why was the Bandung meeting of such importance?
4. What views do Sukarno and Wright share?

27.3   CONSUMERISM AND THE COLD WAR

British Advertisement (1950s) and *Soviet Fashion Spread* (1957)

The Cold War between the United States and the USSR has often been characterized as a political game of chess combined with a vast and costly military buildup. However, the Cold War was also fought over which side could provide the better standard of living for its citizens. This competition was put on public display in 1959, when Nikita Khrushchev of the USSR and U.S. vice president Richard Nixon held what has come to be called the "Kitchen Debate" over quality-of-life issues. The televised face-off took place at the United States Exhibition in Moscow, which showcased a typical modern American home, complete with labor-saving appliances such as the washing machine and automatic dishwasher—new conveniences that were also in demand in European households. Advertising for household products emphasized women's domestic roles while presenting them as stylish and feminine, as we see in the first image in this section, a 1950s British advertisement for the Robbialac paint company. Official communist publications also appealed to women as consumers at the end of the Stalinist era, as we see in the second image, a fashion spread that appeared in a 1957 issue of the Polish fashion magazine *Moda* (*Fashion*). Here, a chimney sweep reads the newspaper *Glos Robotniczy* (*The Workers' Voice*) while the two models behind him hold chimney brushes.

Museum of London/HIP/Art Resource, New York.

Fashion spread from *Moda*, a Polish fashion magazine, 1957.

Examining the Evidence

1. In the British paint advertisement, how do the couple's clothing, gestures, and facial expressions, combined with the kitchen setting, contribute to the image's message? What message is being conveyed?

2. What does the chimney sweep's focus on the newspaper suggest about Soviet ideals? How do you interpret the gestures and facial expressions of the models flanking him?

3. What values and ideals does each advertisement convey? Compare and contrast the values expressed in both images.

4. How do these images enrich our understanding of the Cold War? What do they reveal about gender roles at the time?

5. Fear was one emotion that many citizens on both sides felt during the Cold War. What emotions and desires might these images have aroused? What features might have appealed to their respective audiences?

27.4 LITERATURE AFTER EMPIRE

Flora Nwapa, *Efuru* (1966)

Literature, including manifestoes, journalism, poetry, and novels, flowed from the pens and typewriters of people emerging from colonialism and establishing new nations. Just as Gandhi had refocused South Asians and people in many parts of the world to think differently about resistance, so postwar African and Latin American writers, among others, created a range of characters with the potential to give readers a new vision of themselves, encouraging them to take greater control of politics, communities, and everyday life. In 1966, Nigerian author and educator Flora Nwapa (1931–1993) published *Efuru*, the first novel by an African woman. Like African women across many parts of the continent, heroine Efuru is a hard-working market woman but also one full of character and beauty and fully observant of tradition, though not paralyzed by it. Her husbands cheat on her; her only child and revered father die; and she becomes ill, as she recounts in this excerpt to a doctor friend, Difi. She gains strength and poise from the African goddess of the water. In the male-dominated political culture of the new nations, Efuru's fullness as a female literary character became an emblem of liberation and human capacity, especially for women.

"Then, I became ill. Where the illness came from, nobody knew. Everybody thought I was going to die. Many dibias were consulted and we were asked to sacrifice to the gods, our ancestors and the woman of the lake. All was in vain. I was worse. Then a rumour went round that I was guilty of adultery—that I, Efuru, the daughter of Nwashike Ogene, was guilty of adultery. My mother was not an adulterous woman, neither was her mother, why should I be different? Was it possible to learn to be left-handed at old age? Then, my husband, Eneberi, had the nerve to ask me to confess so as to live. Eneberi, my husband, of all people, asked me to confess that I am

an adulterous woman. Ajanupu saved me. I was too weak to do anything. But Ajanupu said a few home truths to Eneberi. I hear he is in hospital on account of the injury given him by Ajanupu.

"She took me to a doctor in Aba. I was cured. I came back only a month ago. I went to my husband's house and collected all my belongings. Then I called my age-group and told them formally what I was accused of. According to the custom of our people, selected members of my age-group followed me to the shrine of our goddess—Utuosu. There I swore by the name of Utuosu, she should kill me if I committed adultery. She should kill me if since I married Eneberi any man in our town, in Onicha, Ndoni, Akiri, or anywhere I had been, had seen my thighs.

"I remained for seven Nkwos and now I am absolved. Utuosu did not kill me. I am still alive. That means that I am not an adulterous woman. So here I am. I have ended where I began—in my father's house. The difference is that now my father is dead. But I have nothing to say to Eneberi. He will forever regret his act. It is the will of our gods and my chi that such a misfortune should befall me."

The doctor was silent when Efuru ended her story. Then he asked: "You will not go back to him?"

"I thought you were my friend, Difu?" Efuru said horrified.

"I am your friend. I have always been your friend."

"If you are my friend, why then do you want me to go back to the man who accused me of adultery. You don't know the seriousness of the offence."

"What will you do now?"

"What have I been doing before?"

"But, you are still young, and men will continue to seek you. If I were you, I would make up with Eneberi."

"You might as well ask me to make up with Adizua, my first husband," Efuru said, laughing.

Flora Nwapa, *Efuru* (London: Heinemann Educational Books, 1966), 279–281. Taken from Proquest online facsimile.

"Yes, where is Adizua? Any news about him?"

"I have heard nothing about him. To me, he has been dead years ago."

"So he did not return?"

"No, he did not return."

The doctor shook his head.

"Difu, I have not asked, how is your wife?"

"Oh, she is well. I left her in the country of the white people."

"All alone?"

"She lives with an elderly woman who takes great care of her and our two sons."

"That is good. I think I should be going," Efuru said, standing up.

"I think you should consider going back to your husband."

"Difu, it is not possible. Let day break."

"Let day break, Efuru."

Efuru slept soundly that night. She dreamt of the woman of the lake, her beauty, her long hair and her riches. She had lived for ages at the bottom of the lake. She was as old as the lake itself. She was happy, she was wealthy. She was beautiful. She gave women beauty and wealth but she had no child. She had never experienced the joy of motherhood. Why then did the women worship her?

Examining the Evidence

1. What examples of community appear in this excerpt, and what ends does community serve?
2. What role does Efuru's illness play in this story?
3. What is Efuru's relationship to her African heritage?
4. How does this novel fit into the history of decolonization?

CONTRASTING VIEWS

THE COLD WAR AND LATIN AMERICA

27.5 | DEAN ACHESON, *WAGING PEACE IN THE AMERICAS* (1949)

The United States had long intervened in the affairs of the Western Hemisphere, announcing as early as the Monroe Doctrine (1823) that South America was in its sphere of influence and that other powers should stay away. More than a century later, Dean Acheson (1893–1971) was secretary of state under President Harry S. Truman and, in that role, repeated U.S. concerns about foreign influence in the Western Hemisphere. In his capacity as guardian of American foreign policy, Acheson oversaw the unfolding of the Cold War as it pertained to Europe, Asia, Africa, and Latin America. In this excerpt from his speech to the Pan American Society in 1949, Acheson addressed concerns over growing unrest in the Caribbean.

There are two reasons in particular why I am glad to be able to discuss this subject tonight. The first is so obvious that we tend to take it for granted. It is that our countries are close neighbors, bound together by a common heritage of struggles for liberty and freedom.

The second reason is that the community between our countries presents us with a unique opportunity to press forward toward the positive objectives of our foreign policy. . . . We in this hemisphere have fortunately been spared the terrible destruction of war, and we are relatively remote from any direct threat against our independence. The prospects are, therefore, bright that we can continue to work together in an atmosphere of relative peace and stability. We are in a real sense waging peace, in the Americas. . . .

For more than 2 years the Caribbean area has been disturbed by plots and counterplots. These plots have in themselves been inconsistent with our common commitments not to intervene in each other's affairs. Increasingly, however, denunciations have been succeeded by

Dean Acheson, *Waging Peace in the Americas* (Department of State Publication 3647, Inter-American Series), 38, from the *Avalon Project: Documents in Law, History and Diplomacy*, (New Haven, CT: Yale Law School, Lillian Goldman Law Library), Avalon.law.yale.edu/20th_century/decad063.asp.

overt attempts at military adventure. . . . This situation is repugnant to the entire fabric of the inter-American System. The United States could not be faithful to its international obligations if it did not condemn it in the strongest terms. . . . Aggression or plotting against any nation of this hemisphere is of concern to us. Wherever it occurs, or may be threatened, we shall use our strongest efforts, in keeping with our international commitments, to oppose it and to defend the peace of the hemisphere.

27.6 NIKITA KHRUSHCHEV, *SPEECH TO THE RFSR TEACHER'S CONGRESS* (1960)

Nikita Khrushchev (1894–1971) helped de-Stalinize the Soviet Union, although he did so erratically, often changing policies on such matters as free speech. At the same time, Khrushchev kept the USSR engaged in world politics after World War II, even to the extent of being involved in Latin American affairs. The son of peasants and a former henchman of Stalin, Khrushchev had an openly brash style that seemed in keeping with Cold War rhetoric. He often shook his fist and pounded his shoe when dealing with the world's leaders, including U.S. presidents. In particular, he was insistent about the status of Cuba, which had undergone a revolution one year earlier. Yet he and U.S. President John F. Kennedy both backed down in the Cuban Missile Crisis of 1962, when neither would take the required initiative needed to blow the world to bits in a nuclear holocaust.

A few days ago the Governor of New York State, Rockefeller [Nelson Rockefeller, 1908–1979] openly called for struggle against the government of Cuba and the Cuban people. He advised that a course directed against Cuba should be taken and that the regime chosen by the people should be stifled through economic blockade.

Rockefeller's pronouncements are an obvious example of the aggressive actions of American politicians who are not accustomed to taking the will of the people into account.

But the time when the United States *diktat* [harsh, imposed settlement on weaker or defeated party] prevailed is over. The Soviet Union is raising its voice on behalf of, and is offering help to, the people of Cuba who are fighting for their independence. . . .

The peoples of the socialist countries will help their Cuban brothers to uphold their independence with the object of frustrating the economic blockade the United States of America has just declared against Cuba.

And not only we, the working people of the socialist camp, but the peoples of all countries must be vigilant against the intrigues of the American imperialists.

It is clear to everybody that economic blockade by the American monopolists can be a prelude to intervention against Cuba. Therefore we must speak up in defense of Cuba and give warning that the imperialists can no longer rob and divide the world as they please, each choosing any piece for himself, as they used to do in the past. Today the peoples of the colonial and dependent countries rebel and fight successfully to rid themselves of the shameful colonial yoke and of enslavement by the United States imperialists. For our part, we shall do everything to support Cuba and her courageous people in their struggle for the freedom and national independence which they have won under the leadership of their national leader Fidel Castro.

The socialist states and all peoples who stand for peace will support the Cuban people in their just struggle and no one will succeed in enslaving the Cubans.

It should be borne in mind that the United States is now not at such an inaccessible distance from the Soviet Union as formerly. Figuratively speaking, if need be, Soviet artillerymen can support the Cuban people with their rocket fire, should the aggressive forces in the Pentagon dare to start intervention against Cuba. And the Pentagon would be well advised not to forget that, as has been shown by the latest tests, we have rockets which land accurately in a predetermined square target 13,000 kilometers [about 8,000 miles] away. This, if you wish, is a warning to those who might like to solve international problems by force and not by reason. . . .

Soviet News 4304 (July 11, 1960): 28–29. Available at Modern History Sourcebook, www.fordham.edu/halsall/mod/1960khrushchev-cuba1.html.

(continued)

CONTRASTING VIEWS *(continued)*

27.7   JOHN F. KENNEDY, *THE LESSON OF CUBA* (1961)

John F. Kennedy (1917–1963) became U.S. president in 1961 and immediately became enmeshed in the Cold War. Kennedy used especially harsh words when discussing world affairs such as the fate of islands off China and the status of Cuba. Just a few months into his administration, the United States provided covert support for an invasion of Cuba, which turned into a miserable failure (known as the Bay of Pigs fiasco) and served only to advance the Cold War. Cold War rhetoric escalated too, causing many to fear nuclear holocaust. In a speech to the American Society of Newspaper Editors excerpted here, Kennedy presents the official U.S. view of Cuban leader Fidel Castro and offers thoughts on the failed invasion attempt that had just taken place. Kennedy and Khrushchev would become the major players in the Cuban Missile Crisis of 1962.

The President of a great democracy such as ours, and the editors of great newspapers such as yours, owe a common obligation to the people: an obligation to present the facts, to present them with candor, and to present them in perspective. It is with that obligation in mind that I have decided in the last 24 hours to discuss briefly at this time the recent events in Cuba.

On that unhappy island, as in so many other areas of the contest for freedom, the news has grown worse instead of better. I have emphasized before that this was a struggle of Cuban patriots against a Cuban dictator. While we could not be expected to lend our sympathies, we made it repeatedly clear that the armed forces of this country would not intervene in any way.

It is not the first time that Communist tanks have rolled over gallant men and women fighting to redeem the independence of their homeland. Nor is it by any means the final episode in the eternal struggle of liberty against tyranny, anywhere on the face of the globe, including Cuba itself.

Mr. Castro has said that these were mercenaries. According to press reports, the final message to be relayed from the refugee forces on the beach came from the rebel commander when asked if he wished to be evacuated. His answer was: "I will never leave this country." That is not the reply of a mercenary. . . .

Meanwhile we will not accept Mr. Castro's attempts to blame this Nation for the hatred with which his onetime supporters now regard his repression. But there are from this sobering episode useful lessons for all to learn. Some may be still obscure and await further information. Some are clear today.

First, it is clear that the forces of communism are not to be underestimated; in Cuba or anywhere else in the world, the advantages of a police state—its use of mass terror and arrests to prevent the spread of free dissent—cannot be overlooked by those who expect the fall of every fanatic tyrant. . . .

Secondly, it is clear that this Nation, in concert with all the free nations of this hemisphere, must take an even closer and more realistic look—at the menace of external Communist intervention and domination in Cuba. The American people are not complacent about Iron Curtain tanks and planes less than 90 miles from our shores. . . .

The evidence is clear—and the hour is late. We and our Latin friends will have to face the fact that we cannot postpone any longer the real issue of the survival of freedom in this hemisphere itself. . . .

Third, and finally, it is clearer than ever that we face a relentless struggle in every corner of the globe that goes far beyond the clash of armies or even nuclear armaments. The armies are there, and in large number. The nuclear armaments are there. But they serve primarily as the shield behind which subversion, infiltration, and a host of other tactics steadily advance, picking off vulnerable areas one by one in situations which do not permit our own armed intervention.

Power is the hallmark of this offensive—power and discipline and deceit. The legitimate discontent of yearning peoples is exploited. The legitimate trappings of self-determination are employed. But once in power, all talk of discontent is repressed—all self-determination disappears—and the promise of a revolution of hope is betrayed, as in Cuba, into a reign of terror. . . .

The Department of State Bulletin 44 (May 8, 1961): 659–661. Available at Modern History Sourcebook, www.fordham.edu/halsall/mod/1961-kennedy-cuba1.html.

The message of Cuba, of Laos, of the rising din of Communist voices in Asia and Latin America—these messages are all the same. The complacent, the self-indulgent, the soft societies are about to be swept away with the debris of history. Only the strong, only the industrious, only the determined, only the courageous, only the visionary who determine the real nature of our struggle can possibly survive.

27.8   FIDEL CASTRO, *SECOND DECLARATION OF HAVANA* (1962)

Fidel Castro (1926–2016) came to power in Cuba in 1959 after the fall of the country's corrupt, U.S.-backed dictatorship. Repulsed by the Americans, who sought to overthrow him, Castro turned to the Soviets and moved Cuba into the communist camp. As such, Cuba became a major player in the Cold War, and Castro assumed the position of spokesperson for those who wanted to eliminate the U.S. domination of Latin America. He attracted admirers from around the world for standing up to the great power in the Hemisphere, even as many fled Cuba for a life outside the communist state.

What is Cuba's history but that of Latin America? What is the history of Latin America but the history of Asia, Africa, and Oceania? And what is the history of all these peoples but the history of the cruelest exploitation of the world by imperialism?

At the end of the last century and the beginning of the present, a handful of economically developed nations had divided the world among themselves, subjecting two thirds of humanity to their economic and political domination. Humanity was forced to work for the dominating classes of the group of nations which had a developed capitalist economy.

The historic circumstances which permitted certain European countries and the United States of North America to attain a high industrial development level put them in a position which enabled them to subject and exploit the rest of the world. . . .

The discovery of America sent the European conquerors across the seas to occupy and to exploit the lands and peoples of other continents; the lust for riches was the basic motivation for their conduct. . . .

Since the end of the Second World War, the Latin American nations are becoming pauperized constantly. The value of their capita income falls. The dreadful percentages of [the] child death rate do not decrease, the number of illiterates grows higher, the peoples lack employment, land, adequate housing, schools, hospitals, communication systems and the means of subsistence. . . . Latin America, moreover, supplies cheap raw materials and pays high prices for manufactured articles. Like the first Spanish conquerors, who exchanged mirrors and trinkets with the Indians for silver and gold, so the United States trades with Latin America. To hold on to this torrent of wealth, to take greater possession of America's resources and to exploit its long-suffering peoples: this is what is hidden behind the military pacts, the military missions and Washington's diplomatic lobbying. . . .

The ruling classes are entrenched in all positions of state power. They monopolize the teaching field. They dominate all means of mass communication. They have infinite financial resources. Theirs is a power which the monopolies and the ruling few will defend by blood and fire with the strength of their police and their armies.

The duty of every revolutionary is to make revolution. We know that in America and throughout the world the revolution will be victorious. But revolutionaries cannot sit in the doorways of their homes to watch the corpse of imperialism pass by. . . . Each year by which America's liberation may be hastened will mean millions of children rescued from death, millions of minds freed for learning, infinitudes of sorrow spared the peoples. Even though the Yankee imperialists are preparing a bloodbath for America they will not succeed in drowning the people's struggle. They will evoke universal hatred against themselves. This will be the last act of their rapacious and caveman system. . . .

COMPARING THE EVIDENCE

1. What Cold War positions do these documents express, and how convincing do these arguments seem in retrospect?
2. What main issues concern these leaders, and what are the main points of antagonism?
3. In what ways do the Kennedy and Castro documents present a markedly different understanding of U.S. interests in Latin America and the Caribbean?
4. What is the tone of these pronouncements, and why do you suppose they were made?

James Nelson Goodsell, *Fidel Castro's Personal Revolution in Cuba: 1959–1973* (New York: Alfred A. Knopf, 1975), 264–268.

MAKING CONNECTIONS

1. Describe decolonization as seen in the documents on the Suez Canal, the Bandung Conference, and Napwa's novel.

2. What accounts for these differing experiences of national liberation?

3. Explain the simultaneous rising tide of consumerism and growing Cold War tensions.

4. How do ideas of national liberation and Third World autonomy fit with the ongoing Cold War concerns?

CHAPTER 28

A New Global Age, 1980s to the Present

Since at least the sixteenth century, the world's peoples have been linked, at first through interconnections of the hemispheres that developed through global shipping. Some five centuries later, globalization continued but at an even faster pace because of the communications innovations developed during the twentieth century. The consequences of globalization were mixed and depended on location. There were vast differences in standards of living among countries, mostly between those in the Southern Hemisphere and the wealthier nations of the Northern Hemisphere. Disease and violence spread across the globe with amazing rapidity, reminding one of the results of colonization. Seemingly local or national events had global resonance. As people became more aware of global problems, some attempted to correct them. Globalization helped people unite around religious beliefs, both for good and for ill. Helpful information was available to more people than ever before. Along with global problems, a brisk debate arose over how to shape the future.

28.1 A NEW REGIME IN IRAN

Ayatollah Ruhollah Khomeini, *The Uprising of Khurdad 15* (1979)

Ayatollah Ruhollah Khomeini (1902–1989) was an Islamic cleric from Iran and a longstanding opponent of the U.S. ally, the shah of Iran, whose government imprisoned him for this opposition. From imprisonment and then from exile, Khomeini and his followers used cassette recordings and other media to encourage Iranians to resist the shah's government, and they did so after hearing Khomeini's message. In 1979, this opposition, composed of storekeepers, teachers, and people from many walks of life, drove the shah from Iran and achieved a revolution, thus allowing Khomeini to institute a religiously based regime. This government became an inspiration to Shi'a Muslims across the globe. This document expresses his plan for the regime.

Those who are ignorant must be guided to a correct understanding. We must say to them: "You who imagine that something can be achieved in Iran by some means other than Islam, you who suppose that something other than Islam overthrew the Shah's regime, you who believe non-Islamic elements played a role—study the matter carefully. Look at the tombstones of those who gave their lives in the movement of Khurdad 15. If you can find a single tombstone belonging to one of the non-Islamic elements, it will mean they played a role. And if, among the tombstones of the Islamic elements, you can find a single tombstone belonging to someone from the upper echelons of society, it will mean that they too played a role. But you will not find a single tombstone belonging to either of those groups. All the tombstones belong to Muslims from the lower echelons of society: peasants, workers, tradesmen, committed religious scholars. . . . Those who imagine that some force other than Islam could shatter the great barrier of tyranny are mistaken."

As for those who oppose us because of their opposition to Islam, we must cure them by means of guidance, if it is at all possible; otherwise, we will destroy these agents of foreign powers with the same fist that destroyed the Shah's regime.

Your opponents, oppressed people, have never suffered. In the time of the *taghut* [a false leader, that is, the shah], they never suffered because either they were in agreement with the regime and loyal to it, or they kept silent. Now you have spread the banquet of freedom in front of them and they have sat down to eat. . . . Xenomaniacs, people infatuated with the West, empty people, people with no content! Come to your senses; do not try to westernize everything you have! Look at the West, and see who the people are in the West that present themselves as champions of human rights and what their aims are. Is it human rights they really care about, or the rights of the superpowers? What they really want to secure are the rights of the superpowers. Our jurists should not follow or imitate them.

You should implement human rights as the working classes of our society understand them. Yes, they are the real Society for the Defense of Human Rights. They are the ones who secure the well-being of humanity; they work while you talk. . . .

For they are Muslims and Islam cares about humanity. You who have chosen a course other than Islam—you do nothing for humanity. All you do is write and speak in an effort to divert our movement from its course.

But as for those who want to divert our movement from its course, who have in mind treachery against Islam and the nation, who consider Islam incapable of running the affairs of our country despite its record of 1400 years—they have nothing at all to do with our people, and this must be made clear. . . .

How much you talk about the West, claiming that we must measure Islam in accordance with Western criteria! What an error! . . .

Hamid Algar, trans., *Islam and Revolution: Writings and Declarations of Imam Khomeini* (Berkeley, CA: Mizan Press, 1981), 269–274.

It was the mosques that created this Revolution, the mosques that brought this movement into being. . . . The *mihrab* [an indentation in the wall of a mosque, indicating the direction of Mecca] was a place not only for preaching, but also for war—war against both the devil within man and the tyrannical powers without. . . .

So preserve your mosques, O people. Intellectuals, do not be Western-style intellectuals, imported intellectuals; do your share to preserve the mosques!

Examining the Evidence

1. What ideals and values does Ayatollah Khomeini advocate for Iranians?
2. How does Islam fit within the new society?
3. What are Khomeini's thoughts about the West and about those in Iran who hold Western ideas in high esteem?
4. From this speech, what do you see as being Khomeini's appeal? Could it be seen as having global appeal? To what extent is he speaking to a global audience?

28.2 THE COLLAPSE OF COMMUNISM

Dirk Philipsen, *Interviews with Industrial Workers* (1990)

The collapse of communism in eastern Europe was comparatively peaceful for a revolution, a fact often attributed to the new means of communication that can dampen the need for violence. Across the Soviet sphere, activists, working in a long tradition of opposition, protested so forcefully, and the Soviet government under Mikhail Gorbachev reacted so passively, that one regime after another gave way to more democratic forces. Just after the collapse of communism in East Germany, former industrial worker Dirk Philipsen interviewed factory hands there and obtained this testimony about the closing days of communism, its final collapse, and the lives of this group of workers under the communist system.

BERND K.: [born 1935, began work as a factory apprentice in 1950, joined the Communist party in 1975, and became a full-time union official in 1980]: . . . [W]hy did this revolution happen so peacefully? It could only happen so peacefully, not because so many people came together on the streets but because the whole system was so rotten, was so finished at that point, that everybody, even in the party, all the way up to

the central leadership, must have realized that things could not continue like that. . . .

RUDI E.: [born 1938, worked as a boiler and tank worker, then studied engineering; joined the party in 1957]: . . . In August [1989] the big wave of emigrations via Hungary and Czechoslovakia began, and they brought things into the press, such as that people were "abducted by Western agents," and "these are the methods the West is employing." . . .

DORIS C.: [born 1934, apprenticed in 1949 as a lathe operator, later employed as an assistant engineer, active as a party member in the unions, especially in women's issues]: . . . We had a lot of big laughs at the time about all the ludicrous stories they were making up. . . .

RUDI E.: . . . About people who had been drugged and did not wake up until they got to Vienna. You have to imagine that such things were on the front page of the official party newspaper. They were actually trying to convince us that the West was employing such methods in order to worsen the situation in our country. Of course, we usually found out, as most people had already suspected, that there was no truth to such accounts. . . . [T]his was their method of telling us that we should not worry, and that we could easily live without those people. . . .

Michael H. Hunt, *The World Transformed: 1945 to the Present; A Documentary Reader* (Boston: Bedford/St. Martin's, 2004), 310–311.

DORIS C.: The straw that finally broke the camel's back was Honecker's [Eric Honecker, Communist leader of East Germany at the time] statement that "we are not going to shed a tear for these people." We were simply outraged, everywhere, young people and old people alike. This statement was just impertinent. Every evening we saw on Western television thousands of young GDR citizens who had fled to the West German embassies or had made it across the border in some way, and then this comment "we are not going to shed a single tear." . . .

BERND K.: . . . You have to understand how completely we were walled in; very few people had been allowed to travel and to see for themselves what the West was like. And those who were allowed usually did not talk about it because they did not want to risk their chance of getting a [travel] permit again. . . .

DORIS C.: . . . And sometimes people simply did not believe what they told us after they had returned. Or people were accused of just wanting to bitch and complain about the GDR when they told us how things looked in the West, when they conveyed such golden pictures of the West.

How much and how openly could you, and did you, discuss such matters in the workplace?

Leonhard B.: [born 1948, apprenticed as a machinist in 1965, joined the party in 1967, and left it in 1978]: In the shops we discussed these things a lot.

I guess one thing I still don't understand is that there was such a debate about this. After all, you could all receive Western radio and TV, so you should have had a pretty good impression as to how things looked in the West, didn't you?

DORIS C.: Yes, everybody watched Western TV. . . .

BERND K.: . . . But you simply could not imagine the dimensions of it all, the technological level, the availability of consumer goods. . . . But whereas we had to wait for an apartment or a house for more than 15 years and had to pay these incredibly overpriced amounts for certain goods, or

simply could not get certain basic goods or had to wait for them forever, it was just mind-boggling, at least to me, when I went over there for the first time.

. . . Of course we watched Western TV, saw Western advertisements, and such, but the reality of it all just blew me away. When I went to a home appliance store in the West for the first time, I walked through the aisles and just mumbled to myself, like a senile old man, "This can't be true, this is unbelievable, I must be dreaming." They had all the things I had been trying to get at home for years, and not just in one kind, but in hundreds of variations. . . . The same was true with grocery stores. We never had to go hungry in the GDR, never, but we had to stand in line for cheese or meat, and often had no selection, and certain things we just never saw. And if you then went to KaDeWe [a large West Berlin department store with a well-stocked food department], you just thought you were on another planet.

RUDI E.: I think the main thing is that we were never exposed to any of this. We were walled in, things were kept away from us, we were lied to. And then, all of a sudden, we realized things could also be done or organized differently, and that's when it all began, when we began to rethink everything. . . . [After 1987] more people were allowed to travel, from some 400,000 before to some 1.5 or 2 million per year afterward. But that way, people could get their own personal impressions, and that had to have some consequences sooner or later.

Examining the Evidence

1. How do these East German workers feel about their fallen communist government?
2. To what do these workers attribute their change of heart about communism?
3. What are their major grievances concerning how the communist system operated?
4. To what extent did consumer issues shape their frame of mind and arouse a "global consciousness"?

28.3 THE TOLL OF AIDS ON AFRICA

Justice Edwin Cameron, *The Deafening Silence of AIDS* (2000)

The spread of AIDS around the world in the 1980s and 1990s was another consequence of globalization. Activists in many countries led the crusade to slow the progress of the disease and find a cure to help the millions infected with the deadly virus. These activists came from many parts of society, including the gay community, labor unions, public health, and medical research. Although many cultures resisted changing their customs to prevent AIDS from spreading, and although other countries refused even to acknowledge the existence of an epidemic, the disease could not be ignored. South Africa, where the labor unions led in building AIDS awareness, felt the effects of AIDS not only among its own people but among those migrants who sought to benefit from the country's superior health facilities. Edwin Cameron (b. 1953), a justice on South Africa's High Court, described the impact of AIDS in a 2000 lecture, part of which is excerpted here. In this speech, Cameron acknowledges that he, too, is infected.

I t is a great honor to be asked to deliver the first Jonathan Mann Memorial Lecture. It is fitting that this remembrance should have been created to honor Mann's memory and legacy. He more than any other individual must be credited with first conceiving and constructing a global response to the AIDS epidemic. This he did not only as founding director of the World Health Organization's Global Programme on AIDS between 1986 and 1990, but also after he left the WHO, in his theoretical and advocacy work within the discipline of public health. It is particularly fitting that the lecture should be initiated at the start of the first international conference on AIDS to take place on African soil. . . .

Mann's years in Africa yielded insights that later proved critical. His work among Africa's at-risk communities, with Africans living with HIV and with those dying from AIDS, with the health-care personnel, mothers, sex workers and government bureaucrats in Africa formed the basis of an insight he later termed a "very intense, emotional, and personal" discovery. This was his realization during the 1980s that there are empirical and theoretical links between human rights abuses and vulnerability to HIV/AIDS. In each society, Mann later wrote, "those people who were marginalized, stigmatized and discriminated against—before HIV/AIDS arrived—have become over time those at highest risk of HIV infection."

Mann's statement cannot be accepted without nuance, since in some African countries it is precisely mobility and relative affluence that have placed people at risk of exposure to HIV. But Mann's analysis here had led him to a more fundamental and general insight, one that formed the focus of his future work and advocacy: his realization that health and human rights are not opposing, but rather complementary, approaches to what he called "the central problem of defining and advancing human well-being." . . .

Sound reasons rooted not only in respect for human dignity, but in effective public health planning, necessitate a just and nondiscriminatory response to AIDS, and that recognition of and respect for individual human rights does not impede prevention and containment of HIV, but actually enhances it. . . .

Amid the grievous facts of the epidemic, the one gleam of redemption is the fact that nowhere have the doctrines of public health overtly countenanced repression and stigma, discrimination and isolation, as legitimate governmental responses to AIDS. . . .

Justice Edwin Cameron, High Court of South Africa, Johannesburg, Plenary Presentation, First Jonathan Mann Memorial Lecture, XIIIth International AIDS Conference, Durban, July 9–14, 2000. Edited and reprinted in *Health and Human Rights* 5, no. 1 (2000), 7–19.

In the fourteen years since Mann left Zaire for Geneva in 1986, the epidemic has manifested momentous changes. The two most considerable are the demographics of its spread and the medical-scientific resources available to counter it.

In its demographics HIV has altered from an epidemic whose primary toll seemed to be within the gay communities of North America and Western Europe, to one that, overwhelmingly, burdens the heterosexual populations of Africa and the developing world. The data are so dismaying that reciting the statistics of HIV prevalence and of AIDS morbidity and mortality—the infection rates, the anticipated deaths, the numbers of orphans, the health-care costs, the economic impact—threatens to drive off, rather than encourage, sympathetic engagement. Our imagination shrinks from the thought that these figures can represent real lives, real people, and real suffering. . . .

Beneficent social effects have come with the medical breakthrough. The social meaning of the new drugs is that the equation between AIDS and disease and death is no longer inevitable. . . . Among the public at large, fear, prejudice, and stigma associated with AIDS have lessened. And persons living with HIV/AIDS have suffered less within themselves and in their working and social environments. . . .

This near-miracle, however, has not touched the lives of the majority of those who most desperately need it. For Africans and others in resource-poor countries with AIDS and HIV, these drugs are out of reach. For them, the implications of the epidemic remain as fearsome as ever. In their lives, the prospect of debility and death, and the effects of discrimination and societal prejudice, loom as huge as they did for the gay men of North America and Western Europe a decade and a half ago. . . .

I speak of the gap not as an observer or as a commentator, but with intimate personal knowledge. I am an African. I am living with AIDS. I therefore count as one among the forbidding statistics of AIDS in Africa. I form part of nearly five million South Africans who have the virus.

I speak also of the dread effects of AIDS with direct experience. Nearly three years ago, more than twelve years after I became infected, I fell severely ill with the symptomatic effects of HIV. Fortunately for me, I had access to good medical care. . . .

If, without combination therapy, the mean survival time for a healthy male in his mid-forties after onset of full AIDS is 30–36 months, I should be dead by about now. Instead, I am healthier, more vigorous, more energetic, and more full of purposeful joy than at any time in my life.

In this I exist as a living embodiment of the iniquity of drug availability and access in Africa. This is not because, in an epidemic in which the heaviest burdens of infection and disease are borne by women, I am male; nor because, on a continent in which the vectors of infection have overwhelmingly been heterosexual, I am proudly gay; nor even because, in a history fraught with racial injustice, I was born white. My presence here embodies the injustices of AIDS in Africa because, on a continent in which 290 million Africans survive on less than one U.S. dollar a day, I can afford monthly medication costs of about U.S. $400 per month. Amid the poverty of Africa, I stand before you because I am able to purchase health and vigor. I am here because I can afford to pay for life itself. . . .

Instead of continuing to accept what has become a palpable untruth (that AIDS is of necessity a disease of debility and death), our overriding and immediate commitment should be to find ways to make accessible for the poor what is within reach of the affluent. . . .

Instead, from every side, those millions living with AIDS in resource-poor countries have been disappointed. International agencies, national governments, and especially those who have primary power to remedy the iniquity—the international drug companies—have failed us in the quest for accessible treatment.

In my own country, a government that in its commitment to human rights and democracy has been a shining example to Africa and the world has at almost every conceivable turn mismanaged the epidemic. So grievous has governmental ineptitude been that South Africa has since 1998 had the fastest-growing HIV epidemic in the world. It currently has one of the world's highest prevalences. Nor has there been silence about AIDS from our government, as the title of my lecture suggests. Indeed, there has been a cacophony of task groups, workshops, committees, councils, policies, drafts, proposals, statements, and pledges. But all have thus far signified piteously little. . . .

In our national struggle to come to grips with the epidemic, perhaps the most intractably puzzling episode has been President Mbeki's flirtation with those who in the face of all reason and evidence have sought to dispute the etiology of AIDS. . . .

At the international level, too, there have been largely frustration and disappointment. At the launch of the International Partnership Against AIDS in Africa in December 1999, UN Secretary-General Kofi Annan made an important acknowledgment: "[o]ur response so far has failed Africa." The scale of the crisis, he said, required "a comprehensive and coordinated strategy" between governments, intergovernmental bodies, community groups, science, and private corporations. That was seven long months ago. In seven months, there are more than 200 days—days in which people have fallen sick and others have died; days on each of which, in South Africa, approximately 1700 people have become newly infected with HIV.

In that time, the World Bank, to its credit, has made the search for an AIDS vaccine one of its priorities. President Clinton, to his credit, in an effort "to promote access to essential medicines," has issued an executive order that loosens the patent and trade throttles around the necks of African governments. And UNAIDS, to its credit, has begun what it describes as "a new dialogue" with five of the biggest pharmaceutical companies. The purpose is "to find ways to broaden access to care and treatment, while ensuring rational, affordable, safe and effective use of drugs for HIV/AIDS-related illnesses." . . .

In my own country, a small and under-resourced group of activists in the Treatment Action Campaign, under the leadership of Zackie Achmat,

has emerged. In the face of considerable isolation and hostility, they have succeeded in reordering our national debate about AIDS. And they have focused national attention on the imperative issues of poverty, collective action and drug access. In doing so they have . . . renewed . . . the faith that by action we can secure justice. . . .

Ten months before his death, in November 1997, Mann called on an audience to place themselves "squarely on the side of those who intervene in the present, because they believe that the future can be different." . . .

We gather here in Durban as an international grouping of influential and knowledgeable people concerned about alleviating the effects of this epidemic. By our mere presence here, we identify ourselves as the 11,000 best-resourced and most powerful people in the epidemic. By our action and resolutions and collective will, we can make the future different for many millions of people with AIDS and HIV for whom the present offers only illness and death. . . .

The world has become a single sphere, in which communication, finance, trade, and travel occur within a single entity. How we live our lives affects how others live theirs. We cannot wall off the plight of those whose lives are proximate to our own.

Examining the Evidence

1. According to Edwin Cameron, what particular problems does Africa face as a result of the AIDS epidemic?

2. According to Cameron, how do AIDS and human rights relate to each other?

3. What connection does Cameron see between poverty and AIDS?

4. According to Cameron, what actions need to be taken to combat AIDS?

5. How would you characterize the tone of Cameron's speech—partisan, objective, emotional, practical, scientific, or something else?

28.4 SWEATSHOP WARRIORS

Rojana Cheunchujit, *Interview* (1990s)

Migration swelled around the world at the end of the twentieth century and continues today. People moved from the countryside to the city and from nation to nation to find work. Many migrated to escape wars, with the hope of finding peace and a livelihood in another nation. Whereas well-to-do people with technical skills migrated under good conditions, poor migrants were often smuggled into countries illegally and paid huge fees to be transported. After that, they might be exploited in sweatshops because their illegal status left them without protection from authorities. Illegal immigrants might also be constantly on the move to escape detection or to find better conditions. This document offers the experience of Rojana Cheunchujit, a Thai woman who was enticed to come and work in the United States but found a grim reality awaiting her.

I was born January 26, 1970, in Thailand in the village of Petchaboon. My parents worked in the rice fields when I was growing up. I have one brother and two sisters and I am the oldest. . . .

I went to school in Thailand, but only for nine years, and finished middle school. I sewed eight or nine years in Thailand, starting when I was 15 but sometimes would do other things. A village elder introduced me and my husband. I didn't want to get married, [laughs] but I didn't want my parents to worry about me so I got married when I was 19. . . .

I worked in a big factory in Bangkok, and in many sewing factories before coming to the US. . . .

I came to the US in 1994. When I was still in Thailand this person came to the village to recruit people to work at the shop in El Monte. He told me that the pay was very good. He said that if I wanted to come to the US, he would be able to arrange it for me for 125,000 baht [US $5,000] which I paid him.

I came to the US with my friends, not with my family. I thought I would stay and work in the US for three years. What happened to me after I came? [laughs] Well, that's a long story! I was locked up in the sewing shop by the owners. They fed us poorly. . . . As soon as I arrived in this country, they took me directly to El Monte [where] they basically told me I would have to work continually, non-stop and only have a day off from time to time. This was completely the opposite of what I had been told in Thailand before coming here. . . . I realized I had been duped. . . .

There were over 70 Thai workers at the shop. We worked 20 hours a day for the whole one year and four months I was there—until the day I was liberated. I cooked for myself. We ordered food from the owners, but they charged us really high prices, at least twice the amount.

After paying the $5,000 to get here, they told me I had to pay an additional $4,800. They said they would keep me as long as it took to pay off the . . . debt. It didn't matter to them how long they kept you; no specific amount of time was calculated. . . .

The owners threatened to set the homes of our families on fire if we dared to escape because they knew where all of us were from, about our villages back in Thailand. Some people actually got punished. One person tried to escape but was unsuccessful; they beat him up pretty badly. . . . They did this to intimidate us.

The day the government raided the factory, we heard knocking on the door; they went to each unit and banged real hard. The banging woke us up and we were so scared that we didn't know what to do. . . . We didn't know if we were finally going to be set free or if we were going to get in more trouble. So no one dared to open the door. The doors were locked from the outside to keep us in. If there had

Miriam Ching Yoon Louie, ed., *Sweatshop Warriors: Immigrant Women Workers Take on the Global Factory* (Cambridge, MA: South End Press, 2001), 235–242.

ever been a fire there was no way that we could have gotten out; we would have been trapped.

One of the policemen broke down the door and shoved it in. In fact he hit one of the workers on the forehead—my friend Kanit. . . . We were all told to come out, sit down in the driveway, and just wait. Then later they sent the INS bus to take us away to the detention-center.

Oh, my God! We were all so confused. We were interviewed by everyone, by the Department of Labor, by the INS, by lots and lots of people [including the US Attorney's office, State Labor Commissioner's office, and Employment Development Department]. Then about two or three days after we had been in detention, we met the folks from the Thai CDC [Centers for Disease Control] and KIWA. But that was after the Thai Consul General had already come and spoken with us.

When the Consul General came to see us, he told us to go back home to Thailand, that there was no need for us to be here. He said we were here illegally and what we did was wrong. He said it was our fault that we put ourselves in this situation. He said that we were just fighting against a brick wall by staying here, and we were being a burden on the US government!

Everybody was confused. We didn't know what to do. Me too, I was confused. But I got one idea after I met Chancee [Thai CDC Director], Julie [Asian Pacific American Legal Center attorney], and Paul [KIWA organizer]. I thought, "Okay I need these people." So I signed up with them.

The INS agent who was in charge of our case was very confusing. It was hard to know what his real intentions were. Although he was nice and friendly to us, he was not against the idea of deporting us. . . . I began to doubt the INS' intentions toward us and whether they were really trying to help us.

Julie, Paul, and Chancee gave us their phone numbers the first time they came to see us. A lot of us decided to give them our A numbers [alien registration number that INS assigns to every detainee] so that they would be allowed to meet with us. The INS asked each of us who we had called and a lot of people were afraid to say anything so they didn't. When they took us down to the downtown office while Julie, Chancee, and Paul were waiting for us

at the Terminal Island Detention Center, I realized that we were in the wrong place. . . . Then J kept pounding on the door and telling the INS to take us all back to Terminal Island because that was where Chancee, Julie, and Paul were waiting to meet us. I told this all to the Thai interpreter working for the INS and asked them to tell the INS to bring us back.

It turns out that at the same time, Chancee, Julie, and Paul had called the INS. Steve Nutter from the garment workers union also called and threatened to call the press to see how the INS would answer their questions. They finally took us back to Terminal Island. When we saw Chancee, Paul, and Julie waiting for us there, we got so happy. My gosh! They kept us on Terminal Island for nine, almost ten days before they let us out. We kept going back and forth to the downtown center to be processed.

When we finally got out, Oh! Oh! [laughs] It was like being a group of tourists with Chancee as our guide. We could see so many new things. Wow! We got a big smile. They took us to a place to look at the stars, to the park for a barbecue, to the beach, and to Disneyland. We got free tickets to Disneyland. We went there in three buses all given for free. It was a lot of fun. After we got out, Chancee, Julie, and Paul found us three different shelters to live in for over a month and a half. They had asked the Thai temples to take us in, but they had all refused. That's another bad story. The day that we were liberated from the detention center, some people from the Thai community invited us to a reception at a Thai temple to celebrate our freedom, but it turned into a media disaster. They had promised us they would not invite the media to the reception at the temple. But when our bus arrived the whole place was filled with press people from everywhere with their cameras. We couldn't get into the temple to worship and pay respects to Buddha at the shrine; we couldn't eat. The reporters kept pulling us to speak to the TV cameras and pushing their microphones into our faces.

It was really terrible! We asked Thai CDC to take us back to the shelters. Then we could eat and rest. Aiiii! At that time we were afraid the owners would punish us and our families. In fact when my mother saw my face on TV in Thailand, she fainted. She did not come out of it and recover for two days because she was sick and worried.

The Thai press did us an injustice. After the big disaster at the Thai temple, we left on the school bus that took us back and forth from the shelter. Because the Thai press did not know where the bus was taking us, they reported in the Thai papers, which also reached Thailand, that we had disappeared and that no one knew where we went after we boarded the school bus. So they scared everyone [including] all our family members back home.

A little over a week after being liberated from El Monte, the telephone company donated phone-cards to [us] so we could call our families back home; we each got three minutes. After that we made collect calls. My mother was really sick after hearing the news, and she couldn't stop crying. I told her what had happened to me, everything, everything.

Now my mother is watching my children at home in Thailand. How long will I stay here? Wow! I'll stay until I am no longer afraid of being punished when I return home, as long as the safety of my family and me can be assured. . . .

The first [garment] shop I worked for after I got out was a Thai shop close to here. Now I'm working for another Thai shop with Mexican workers. The shops are small. At my first job there were about 12 or 15 people. Now it's almost 20 people where I work. It's a different shop and better than the first place. It's clean. I think the salary is okay, it's much better. . . . Sometimes its half and half Thai and Mexican and sometimes there are more Latino workers than Thais. . . .

Because of the oppression I went through I can now be very direct and assertive. It kind of forced me to express myself more, and be less tolerant of wrongs. [laughs] What I've learned from this whole experience and ordeal is a lesson that will stay with me for the rest of my life. Sometimes it hurts so much that I get numb and lose all feeling. Of course, after meeting so many caring people like the folks involved in this case, like Chancee, Julie, Paul, and the people at Thai CDC and KIWA, it really helped us to overcome the terrible things we went through. We felt like we were part of a larger family of people who really cared for us, people who loved us whom we could trust.

For example, all of them were very sensitive to our needs, fears, and concerns. They would always ask us first and never forced us to do anything. They let us make our own decisions. I believe I got stronger. In the very beginning, throughout the first year and a half every time questions like this came up from reporters or anyone else, talking about what happened always touched us emotionally and made us break down. We were always crying. We've cried so much. The fact that we're able to sit through this and *not* cry and have to break down kind of shows that we have become stronger. Yes, it's very rare to sit through this without crying. [laughs] Chancee would translate for eight or nine of us, like Kanit and all of our friends. First one person would start to cry, then all of us would start to cry and everybody would end up crying! Chancee and Julie would be crying too. We still see each other and some of the people live together. Chancee keeps a list of our addresses and numbers, but everyone is always moving around.

I like the Retailers Accountability Campaign [initiated by KIWA and Sweatshop Watch] because it's like an act of resistance that shows we are not willing to tolerate and accept these poor working conditions. It makes the workers' voices heard and known. It goes beyond laws that might not really have much of an impact, because people can hear directly from the workers. We have picketed, leafleted, and visited different department stores.

We try to go into the department store, meet with the management, and educate the consumers to support the boycott for accountability. We get promises from consumers not to shop at the department store again unless they change their policy. After meeting us some consumers told us they felt bad about what happened to us and promised they wouldn't go back and shop there anymore.

The garment factory owners threaten to go to Mexico to get the work done. But when they do, they have problems. When the clothes are delivered back here, there's repair work that needs to be done. They expect the local factories here to do the repair work because it wastes too much time sending it back down to Mexico. So this is just a threat.

Participating in the campaign was not scary, not after what we'd been through! Maybe others think that I am a troublemaker out to cause problems. But really, all of the workers being part of this campaign makes us feel like we are helping develop a better understanding among the general public about who we are and about working conditions in the garment industry. We are finally letting the people know about what happens to the money they spend on a piece of clothing, where that clothing came from, who made it, and how little they got paid. This campaign might help redistribute the wealth; it might help people understand that workers are not getting their fair share. We want people to know that the clothes they wear are being produced by the same kind of people as us, the workers who were slaves in El Monte.

Examining the Evidence

1. Describe Rojana Cheunchujit's life.
2. What individual challenges did Cheunchujit face in the United States?
3. What kinds of support did Cheunchujit find as an illegal immigrant?
4. What are Cheunchujit's attitudes toward her working life?
5. Describe her national and ethnic identity. Does she really have one?

28.5 WANGARI MAATHAI AND MARY ROBINSON, "WOMEN CAN LEAD THE WAY IN TACKLING DEVELOPMENT AND CLIMATE CHALLENGES TOGETHER" (2010)

Wangari Maathai and Mary Robinson are two notable twenty-first-century activists supporting the protection of both the environment and human rights. Maathai led a movement for reforestation in Kenya, despite the harassment of leading politicians and businesspeople in that country who so threatened her life that she went into exile. Maathai won the Nobel Peace Prize in 2004 for her "contributions to sustainable development." Robinson was the first woman president of Ireland and then became an active High Commissioner for Human Rights at the United Nations. Together they produced the following document concerning women and the environment.

The time has come for women leaders to influence the narrative on climate change and how we address its impacts. . . .

Decades of environmental mismanagement, combined with the increasing impacts of climate change, are putting social and economic development efforts at risk. Changing precipitation patterns are skewing traditional seasons and undermining the agricultural rhythms of farmers. More frequent extreme weather events . . . are damaging lives, livelihoods and infrastructure.

Those studying the phenomena recognize that developing countries, whose economies are already precarious and where so many people, especially women, depend directly on the natural world for food, water and fuel, are being hardest hit. It is poorer households and communities and, in many countries, indigenous groups already pushed to the most marginal lands, who are least able to cope. . . .

Some of the biggest constraints to achieving these global development objectives—the impacts of climate change and other environment-related threats—continue to be routinely sidelined in development policies and practice. Until this changes, there is little hope of permanent gains. . . .

Women leaders must insist we address environmental and development challenges in tandem. . . . A more coherent approach also requires much greater attention and action to address the particular challenges facing women and girls and their role in advancing sustainable development. In sub-Saharan Africa and other regions, drought exacerbated by climate change is contributing to chronic crop failures,

---

Wangari Maathai and Mary Robinson, "Women Can Lead the Way in Tackling Development and Climate Challenges Together," *Huffington Post,* September 20, 2010, http://www.huffingtonpost.com/wangari-maathai/women-can-lead-the-way-in_b_731621.html.

deforestation and water shortages, with devastating impacts for girls and women. The primary food producers and procurers of water and fuel for cooking are women. Environmental changes are resulting in women being forced to travel farther to secure food, water and fuel for their families. This has been shown to have negative impacts on nutritional levels, educational attainment and work opportunities, to say nothing of quality of life issues overall.

But not only are women bearing the brunt of environmental and development setbacks—they are also a powerful source of hope in tackling climate and other environmental threats, and their voices must be heard. As the success of the Greenbelt Movement in planting millions of trees in Kenya has demonstrated, women can be an extraordinary force for positive change. Their knowledge and experience are fundamental to mitigating the effects as well as adapting to the inevitable changes wrought in local communities by shifting climatic patterns.

The absence of women, particularly those from the global South, from national and international discussions and decision making on climate change and development must change. The battle to protect the environment is not solely about technological innovation—it is also about empowering women and their communities to hold their governments accountable for results. . . . To make a real difference, women need greater access to the education, resources and new technologies required to help design adaptation to a rapidly changing environment. Climate mitigation and adaptation strategies must be developed with women, not for them, and women must be involved alongside men in every stage of climate and development policymaking.

Examining the Evidence

1. What arguments do Wangari Maathai and Mary Robinson present on behalf of environmental activism?
2. How do they envision work at the grassroots level?
3. What in the document would make Wangari Maathai and Mary Robinson be seen as dangerous?
4. How important is the debate over the environment and environmental activism and in what ways?

MAKING CONNECTIONS

1. What aspirations and experiences of women are found in this chapter's documents?
2. What global concerns do the speakers and authors of these sources express? What personal concerns are expressed?
3. How have issues facing humankind changed since the nineteenth century?
4. Based on these documents, what factors make it difficult to address global problems with a unified front?

ACKNOWLEDGMENTS

Chapter 14 [14.3] Pg. 218: Republished with permission of Brill Academic. Edward L. Farmer, *Zhu Yuanzhang and Early Ming Legislation: The Reordering of Chinese Society Following the Era of Mongol Rule* (Leiden: Brill, 1995). Permission conveyed through Copyright Clearance Center, Inc. **[14.6]** Pg. 225: From *Corpus of Early Arabic Sources for West African History*. Translated by J. F. P. Hopkins. Edited by J. F. P. Hopkins and N. Levtzion. Copyright © 1981 J. F. P. Hopkins and N. Levtzion. Published by Cambridge University Press. **[14.7]** Pg. 228: Republished with permission of John Wiley and Sons, Inc. *Venice: A Documentary History, 1450–1630*, David Chambers and Brian Pullan, eds., (Oxford, UK: Blackwell, 1992). Permission conveyed through Copyright Clearance Center, Inc.

Art Pg. 222: The Persian Prince Humay Meeting the Chinese Princess Humayun in a Garden, c.1450 (gouache on paper), Islamic School, (15th century)/Musée des Arts Décoratifs, Paris, France/Bridgeman Images.

Chapter 15 [15.1] Pg. 234: Reprinted with permission of the University of Utah Press. **[15.2]** Pg. 236: Republished with permission of University of California Press. *The Essential Codex Mendoza*, Frances F. Berdan and Patricia Reiff Anawalt, eds. (Berkeley: University of California Press, 1992). Permission conveyed through Copyright Clearance Center, Inc. **[15.3]** Pg. 238: Republished with permission of University of Texas Press. Juan de Betanzos, *Narrative of the Incas*, Roland Hamilton and Dana Buchanan, eds. and trans. (Austin: University of Texas Press, 1996). Permission conveyed through Copyright Clearance Center, Inc. **[15.4]** Pg. 241: From *The Huarochirí Manuscript: A Testament of Ancient and Colonial Andean Religion*, translated and edited by Frank Salomon and George L. Urioste. Copyright © 1991. By permission of the University of Texas Press. **[15.5]** Pg. 243: Father Gabriel Sagard, *The Long Journey to the Country of the Hurons*, edited by George M. Wrong, translated by H. H. Langton (The Champlain Society, 1939): 121–125. Reprinted with permission.

Chapter 16 [16.2] Pg. 250: Republished with permission of Brepols Publishers NV. *Italian Reports on America, 1493–1522: Accounts by Contemporary Observers*. Geoffrey Symcox, ed. (Turnhout: Brepols Publishers, 2001). Permission conveyed through Copyright Clearance Center, Inc. **[16.3]** Pg. 252: Matthew Restall, Lisa Sousa, and Kevin Terraciano, eds., *Mesoamerican Voices: Native-Language Writings from Colonial Mexico, Oaxaca, Yucatan, and Guatemala* (New York: Cambridge University Press, 2005). Copyright © 2005 Matthew Restall, Lisa Sousa, Kevin Terraciano. Published by Cambridge University Press, reprinted with permission. **[16.4]** Pg. 254: Excerpt(s) from *Hernán Cortés* by Hernán Cortés, edited by Anthony Pagden, translated by Anthony Pagden. Translation copyright © 1971 by Anthony Pagden. Used by permission of Viking Books, an imprint of Penguin Publishing Group, a division of Penguin Random House LLC. All rights reserved. **[16.6]** Pg. 260: Matthew Restall, Lisa Sousa, and Kevin Terraciano, eds., *Mesoamerican Voices: Native-Language Writings from Colonial Mexico, Oaxaca, Yucatan, and Guatemala* (New York: Cambridge University Press, 2005). Copyright © 2005 Matthew Restall, Lisa Sousa, Kevin Terraciano.

Published by Cambridge University Press, reprinted with permission. **[16.7]** Pg. 261: "The true history and description of a country populated by a wild, naked, and savage man-munching people, situated in the New World, America . . .," in *Hans Staden's True History: An Account of Cannibal Captivity in Brazil*, by Hans Staden. Michael Harbsmeier and Neil L. Whitehead, eds. and trans, pp. 47–49, 54–56, 82–83, 97–99. Copyright 2008, Duke University Press. All rights reserved. Republished by permission of the copyright holder. www.dukeupress.edu.

Chapter 17 [17.1] Pg. 266: Republished with permission of Brill Academic Publishers. *Timbuktu and the Songhay Empire: Al-Sadi's Tarikh al-sudan Down to 1613 and Other Contemporary Documents*, John O. Hunwick, ed., (Leiden: Brill, 1999). Permission conveyed through Copyright Clearance Center, Inc. **[17.2]** Pg. 267: Republished with permission of Brill Academic Publishers. *Timbuktu and the Songhay Empire: Al-Sadi's Tarikh al-sudan Down to 1613 and Other Contemporary Documents*, John O. Hunwick ed., (Leiden: Brill, 1999). Permission conveyed through Copyright Clearance Center, Inc. **[17.3]** Pg. 269: Copyright © British Academy 1987. All rights reserved. **[17.5a]** Pg. 276: J. D. La Fleur, trans. and ed., *Pieter van den Broecke's Journal of Voyages to Cape Verde, Guinea and Angol (1605–1612)* (London: Hakluyt Society, 2000). Reprinted with permission of The Hakluyt Society. **[17.5b]** Pg. 279: Reprinted with permission of Hackett Publishing Company, Inc. All rights reserved.

Chapter 18 [18.1] Pg. 283: Copyright © 1967 by the President and Fellows of Harvard College. All rights reserved. **[18.3]** Pg. 288: Reprinted, with permission, from *The Baburnama: Memoirs of Babur, Prince and Emperor*, trans. Wheeler M. Thackston, pp. 112–13, 269–71. Copyright 1996, Freer Gallery of Art and Arthur M. Sackler Gallery, Smithsonian Institution. **[18.4]** Pg. 291: Reprinted, with permission, from *The Jahangirnama: Memoirs of Jahangir, Emperor of India*, trans. Wheeler M. Thackston, pp. 133–34, 184–85. 368. Copyright 1999, Freer Gallery of Art and Arthur M. Sackler Gallery, Smithsonian Institution. **[18.5]** Pg. 293: William P. Cummings, ed. and trans., *A Chain of Kings: The Makassarese Chronicles of Gowa and Talloq* (Leiden: KITLV Press, 2007), 87–91.

Chapter 19 [19.1] Pg. 300: Konstantin Mihailović, *Memoirs of a Janissary*. Trans. Benjamin Stolz. Ed. Svat Soucek (Ann Arbor: Published under the auspices of the Joint Committee on Eastern Europe, American Council of Learned Societies, by the Dept. of Slavic Languages and Literatures, University of Michigan, 1975). Reprinted with permission of Michigan Slavic Publications. **[19.2]** Pg. 302: *Mamluks and Ottomans: Studies in Honour of Michael Winter*, David J. Wasserstein and Ami Ayalon, eds. (London: Routledge) Copyright © 2006. Reproduced by permission of Taylor & Francis Books UK. **[19.3]** Pg. 305: *Mamluks and Ottomans: Studies in Honour of Michael Winter*, David J. Wasserstein and Ami Ayalon, eds. (London: Routledge) Copyright © 2006. Reproduced by permission of Taylor & Francis Books UK. **[19.4]** Pg. 308: Galileo Galilei, *Sidereus Nuncius, or The Sidereal Messenger*, trans. and ed. Albert van Helden (Chicago: University of Chicago Press, 1989). Copyright © 1989 The University of Chicago. All rights reserved. **[19.5]** Pg. 310:

Reprinted from *The Life of Glückel of Hameln, 1646–1724: A Memoir*, edited by Beth-Zion Abrahams, by permission of the University of Nebraska Press. **[19.6]** Pg. 313: Reprinted from *The Travel Diary of Peter Tolstoi: A Muscovite in Early Modern Europe*, Max J. Okenfuss, trans., with permission from Northern Illinois University Press. Copyright © 1987 Northern Illinois University Press.

Chapter 20 [20.1] Pg. 319: From Heinrich von Staden, *The Land and Government of Muscovy: A Sixteenth-Century Account*, trans. and ed. Thomas Esper. Copyright © 1967 by the Board of Trustees of the Leland Stanford Junior University. All rights reserved. **[20.2]** Pg. 321: Hsü Hsia-k'o, *The Travel Diaries of Hsü Hsia-k'o*, ed. Li Chi (Hong Kong: Chinese University of Hong Kong Press, 1971). Reprinted with permission of the Chinese University of Hong Kong Press. **[20.3]** Pg. 322: *Voices from the Ming-Qing Cataclysm: China in Tigers' Jaws*, Lynn A. Struve, ed. and trans. (New Haven: Yale University Press, 1993). Copyright © 1993 by Yale University Press. Used by permission of the publisher. **[20.4]** Pg. 326: Republished with permission of University of Hawaii Press. Engelbert Kaempfer, *Kaempfer's Japan: Tokugawa Culture Observed*, ed. and trans. Beatrice M. Bodart-Bailey (Honolulu: University of Hawaii Press, 1999). Permission conveyed through Copyright Clearance Center, Inc. **[20.5]** Pg. 328: Lady Hong, *Memoirs of a Korean Queen*, ed. and trans. Yang-hi Choe-Wall (Boston: Routledge, 1985) Copyright © 1985. Reproduced by permission of Taylor & Francis Books UK. **[20.6]** Pg. 330: Antonio de Morga, *Sucesos de las Islas Filipinas, 1609*, trans. and ed. J. S. Cummins (London: Hakluyt Society, 1971). Reprinted with permission of the Hakluyt Society.

Chapter 21 [21.1] Pg. 335: From *Annals of His Time: Don Domingo de San Antón Muñón Chimalpahin Quautlehuanitzin*, ed. and trans. James Lockhart, Susan Schroeder, and Doris Namala. Copyright © 2006 by the Board of Trustees of the Leland Stanford Junior University. All rights reserved. **[21.2]** Pg. 336: James Lockhart and Enrique Otte, trans. and eds., *Letters and People of the Spanish Indies: The Sixteenth Century* (Cambridge: Cambridge University Press, 1976). Copyright © 1976 Cambridge University Press. Published by Cambridge University Press, reprinted with permission. **[21.3]** Pg. 338: Republished with permission of University of New Mexico Press. Ursula de Jesús, *The Souls of Purgatory: The Spiritual Diary of a Seventeenth-Century Afro-Peruvian Mystic*, trans. and ed. Nancy E. van Deusen (Albuquerque: University of New Mexico Press, 2004). Permission conveyed through Copyright Clearance Center, Inc. **[21.4]** Pg. 340: Reprinted with permission of Hackett Publishing Company, Inc. All rights reserved. **[21.5]** Pg. 341: Republished with permission of Pennsylvania University Press. *Defending the Conquest: Bernardo de Vargas Machuca's Defense and Discourse of the Western Conquests*, ed. Kris Lane, trans. Timothy Johnson (University Park: Pennsylvania State University Press, 2010). Permission conveyed through Copyright Clearance Center, Inc.

Chapter 22 [22.1] Pg. 350: Republished with permission of Columbia University Press. Jacques-Louis Ménétra, *Journal of My Life*. Introduction with commentary by Daniel Roche. Translated by Arthur Goldhammer (New York: Columbia University Press, 1986). Permission conveyed through Copyright Clearance Center, Inc. **[22.3]** Pg. 353: Reprinted with permission of Brill Academic Publishers. *Al-Jabarti's Chronicle of the First Seven Months of the French Occupation of Egypt, Muharram-Rajab 1213/15 June–December 1789*, ed. and trans. by S. Moreh (Leiden: Brill, 1975). Permission conveyed through Copyright Clearance Center, Inc. **[22.5]** Pg. 359: Republished with permission of University of Oklahoma

Press. Manuel Belgrano, "The Making of an Insurgent" in *Latin American Revolutions, 1808–1826: Old and New World Origins*, ed. John Lynch (Norman: University of Oklahoma Press, 1994). Permission conveyed through Copyright Clearance Center, Inc.

Chapter 23 [23.1] Pg. 363: Republished with permission of Princeton University Press. E. Patricia Tsurumi, *Factory Girls: Women in the Thread Mills of Meiji Japan* (Princeton, N.J.: Princeton University Press, 1990). Permission conveyed through Copyright Clearance Center, Inc. **[23.7]** Pg. 371: *China's Response to the West: A Documentary Survey, 1839-1923*, by Ssu-yü Têng and John King Fairbank (Cambridge, MA: Harvard University Press). Copyright © 1954, 1979 by the President and Fellows of Harvard College. Copyright © renewed 1982 by Ssu-yü Têng and John King Fairbank.

Chapter 25 [25.1] Pg. 384: Excerpt(s) from *Zapata and the Mexican Revolution* by John Womack, Jr. Copyright © 1968 by John Womack, Jr. Used by permission of Alfred A. Knopf, an imprint of the Knopf Doubleday Publishing Group, a division of Penguin Random House LLC. All rights reserved. **[25.2]** Pg. 386: Excerpts from *Somme Mud: The War Experiences of an Infantryman in France, 1916-1919* by E. P. F. Lynch, edited by Will Davies. Copyright © 2008 by Will Davies. Used by permission of Doubleday Publishing Group, a division of Penguin Random House LLC. All rights reserved.

Chapter 26 [26.1a] Pg. 401: Getulio Vargas, "New Year's Address, 1938," in *The Brazil Reader*, Robert Levine, John Crocitti, eds., pp. 186–189. Copyright, 1999, Duke University Press. All rights reserved. Republished by permission of the copyright holder. www.dukeupress.edu. **[26.1b]** Pg. 403: "Ordinary People: Five Lives Affected by Vargas-Era Reforms," in *The Brazil Reader*, Robert Levine, John Crocitti, eds., pp. 206–221. Copyright 1999, Duke University Press. All rights reserved. Republished by permission of the copyright holder. www.dukeupress.edu. **[26.3]** Pg. 406: Republished with permission of the Navajivan Trust. **[26.4]** Pg. 408: Republished with permission of Taylor and Francis Group LLC Books. *A Revolution of Their Own: Voices of Women in Soviet History*. Barbara Alpern Engel and Anastasia Posadskaya-Vanderbeck, eds., Sona Hoisington, trans. (Boulder, CO: Westview Press, 1998). Permission conveyed through Copyright Clearance Center, Inc.

Chapter 27 [27.2b] Pg. 419: Reprinted by permission of John Hawkins and Associates. Copyright © 1956 Richard Wright. **[27.4]** Pg. 423: Flora Nwapa, *Efuru*. (London, UK: Heinemann Educational Books, 1966), 279-281. Used with permission of Pearson Education Limited.

Art Pg. 421: HIP/Art Resource, NY.

Chapter 28 [28.1] Pg. 430: Republished with permission of Mizan Press. *Islam and Revolution: Writings and Declarations of Imam Khomeini*. Hamid Algar, trans. (Berkeley, CA: Mizan Press, 1981). Permission conveyed through Copyright Clearance Center, Inc. **[28.2]** Pg. 431: "The party, the workers, and opposition intellectuals: East German workers, joint interview," in *We Were the People*, Dirk Philipsen , pp. 97–139. Copyright, 1992, Duke University Press. All rights reserved. Republished by permission of the copyright holder. www.dukeupress.edu. **[28.3]** Pg. 433: Copyright © 2000 by the President and Fellows of Harvard College. All rights reserved. **[28.4]** Pg. 436: Reprinted with permission of Miriam Ching Yoon Louie.